A Shared Heritage

The Growth of Civilizations in India and Iran

A Shared Heritage

The Growth of Civilizations in India and Iran

edited by Irfan Habib

Aligarh Historians Society

Tulika

Published by **Tulika Books**
44 (first floor), Shahpur Jat, New Delhi 110 049, India
www.tulikabooks.in

First published in India 2002
First reprint 2004
Second reprint 2012

Third reprint 2019

ISBN: 987-93-82381-03-7 (Pb)

Designed by Ram Rahman

Contents

Acknowledgements

In the natural process of the development of national histories there is the recurring danger that one's grasp of past could become so insular that many large movements, which could not be restricted to modern territorial boundaries, might escape proper attention. The present volume may be seen as an effort to explore how much the growth of civilizations in India and Iran owes to what each of these countries has received from the other, and to bring out how much of their history we will miss if we overlook the heritage that they share.

The volume originated in papers presented by the contributors (which, as the reader will see, includes several distinguished names) at a panel on the historical relationships between India and Iran, 29–30 December 2001, organized under the auspices of the Aligarh Historians Society, at the 62nd session of the Indian History Congress hosted by the Bhoj Open University, Bhopal. We are most grateful to both the Indian History Congress and the Bhoj Open University for providing us space and other facilities.

The holding of the panel was supported by a grant from the Office of the Cultural Counsellor, Embassy of the Islamic Republic of Iran. I am especially thankful to Mr Issa Rezazadeh, the Cultural Counsellor, and Mr M.H. Mozaffari, Director of the Cultural Counsellor's Office, for taking interest in our endeavour. The only matter of regret is that we could not have with us any Iranian colleagues to provide perspectives from the Iranian side. Unfortunately, some difficulties in the issuance of visas prevented their participation.

All the contributors have placed us in much debt by giving us revised versions of their contributions. Professor Irfan Habib, who has edited the volume, agreed to enlarge his opening address at the panel into a longer Introduction in order especially to take up aspects which could not be covered by the various individual papers, as the papers, being pieces of research, had in each case a necessarily limited scope. He thus takes a wide-ranging view of the two countries' relationship from prehistory down to their common struggle against colonialism.

The text has been processed by Mr Muneeruddin Khan, and the paper work looked after by Mr Arshad Ali. Mr Idris Beg did most of the running about. To all three of them many thanks are due.

And, finally, all expressions of gratitude would be inadequate for what we owe to Mr Rajendra Prasad and Ms Indira Chandrasekhar of Tulika Books. When they agreed to publish this volume, they could scarcely have imagined being pressed to carry out the entire work in so extraordinarily short a time.

Aligarh
December 2002

SHIREEN MOOSVI
Secretary, Aligarh Historians Society

Introduction: A Shared Past

Irfan Habib

The close relationship between the Indian sub-continent and the Iranian world (that is, the zone of Iranic languages) is determined to a great degree by facts of geography. The mountainous barrier that isolates India from the rest of Asia is the most forbidding in the north, where stand the Great Himalayas, the highest mountains in the world. On the west the barrier forms really the eastern edge of an extensive plateau stretching across Afghanistan and Iran to the Mediterranean; and it is here that the moutain-wall has the most numerous and convenient gates leading into and out of India. The dry zone in which it lies excludes the presence of forests, which on the eastern Indian frontier makes passage so difficult.[1] It is on the plateau we have spoken of that the speakers of the Iranian languages, notably, Persian (including Tajik) Pashto, Baluchi, and Kurdish, live. In terms of modern political boundaries, the countries of Iran, Afghanistan and Tajikistan, with parts of Turkey and Pakistan, mainly constitute this Iranic world. While India's western mountain ranges have formed a natural barrier for it (pre-1947 India, that is), the mountains' relatively easy passages have always created conditions for cultural and commercial contacts across them; and the attempt in the following essay is to show that the mutual access provided by these has played an important part in the formation of civilizations on both sides of the barrier.

India and Iran in Prehistory

By the onset of the geological epoch of Pleistocene, nearly two million years ago, the geographical setting we have described was more or less fixed. True, there have been some lifts, much erosion, the advances and retreats of ice sheets and glaciers and shifts of sea-coasts as the Ice Ages came and went; but these for our present purpose are of little moment. The main fact is that from two million years ago onwards the Iranian plateau provided the routes into India by which successive human species, the *Homo habilis*, *Homo erectus* and *Homo sapiens sapiens* (the Anatomically Modern Man) arrived here from Africa. The latter continent seems, on the present evidence, to have been the main powerhouse for the evolution of human species throughout the Pleistocene. With the likelihood that the earliest fossil bones (of 1.7 million years ago) at Dmanisi, Georgia, are those of the *Homo habilis* (and not of *Homo erectus*, as previously thought), the same species must be deemed to be the author of the Oldowan tools found at Riwat, near Islamabad, in Pakistan, dated to about two million years ago. Nearby, the Potwar Plateau has yielded flaked pebble tools, dated 1.6 million years ago. Since these are apparently the earliest flaked pebble tools to date, we can imagine that the technique now diffused in the direction opposite to that of the arriving species. In Iran the earliest flaked pebble tools go back to no more than 800,000 years ago (in Keshef-rud valley, north-eastern Iran).[2] On the other hand, the Acheulian tools (characterized by the hand-axe) are found in the Potwar Plateau no earlier than 700,000 years ago, while at the Omo Sites and Konso in East Africa, these, associated with *Homo erectus*, go back to twice that age. A diffusion from Africa, through West Asia and Iran, to India may be assumed, though it is true that there appear to be no Acheulian sites *en-route* as early in time as the finds in the Potwar Plateau.

The arrival of the Anatomically Modern Man can be dated with slightly greater precision than his precursors. Outside of Africa, his presence is established around 100,000 years ago in Palestine, but within South Asia there is good fossil evidence for him no earlier than 31,000 years ago, in Sri Lanka. Finds of microliths take modern human settlement in Sri Lanka further to 35,000 years ago. One can therefore assume that the modern human arrived in India through Iran during the long period 100,000–35,000 years. For our imagination to play upon it, the story is complicated by the intervention of *Homo sapiens neanderthalensis* (the Neanderthal Man), a human with a heavy jaw, thick forehead ridge and robust body, but with nearly as large a cranium as that of the modern human. Neanderthal skeletal remains are found in Palestine, Syria and Iran about 60,000 years ago. In Western Iran the Neanderthal fossils were recovered from two sites, at Shanidar (60,000 years ago) and Bisitun (in association with the Neanderthaler's characteristic 'Levallois Mousterian' tools). A Neanderthal fossil, with Levallois tools has been found at Teshik Tash in Uzbekistan, and a possible one (again with Levallois tools) at Darra-i Kur in North Afghanistan.[3] The Neanderthal Man had evolved in Western Europe out of *Homo Erectus* some time before 200,000 years ago and survived there until 30,000 years ago. His expansion into West Asia and Iran up to the borders of India took place probably 50,000 years ago, and suggests that there was a Neanderthal wave from Europe *behind* the first wave of modern human expansion out of Africa.[4] In Palestine there is some evidence of even a mixed population of Neanderthalers and modern humans;[5] and one can, perhaps, conjecture that as the Neanderthalers spread eastward through Iran they became increasingly assimilated (or eliminated) by the previously existing modern human populations whom they encountered. Survivals of Levallois techniques, as, for example, at Mula Dam in Maharashtra (dated 31000 years ago), are possibly the result of such assimilation. For the present, however, the speculation about any possible Neanderthal presence in India, cannot be pursued any futher, despite the tantalising evidence from Iran, Transoxania and Afghanistan.

Once our modern human species had established itself in India, the next important shift in techniques was probably the one to microliths, which enabled stone tools to be fixed to wooden or bamboo handles. For this we have to turn southwards, since, as we have noted, it is in Sri Lanka that microliths have been dated to a time as early as 34,000 years ago; and the more developed 'geometric' microliths are also found there as early as 28,000 years ago. These are the earliest dates for microliths in South Asia, and some of the earliest in the world. A case could, perhaps, be cogently made for a northward diffusion, reaching Afghanistan some 16,000 years ago, since microliths have been reported from levels of this date at Aq Kupruk.[6] Similar dates are assigned to the cultures producing microliths (including geometric microliths) in Iran (the Zarzian culture, 15000 to 12,000 years ago) and the Levant (Geometric Kebaran Complex, 14,500 to 12,500 years ago).[7] A westward transmission from South Asia to West Asia *via* Iran is thus not impossible.

Iran and the Origins of the Indus Civilization

A major point in social evolution in the Old World came with what V. Gordon Childe called the Neolithic Revolution, marked by the arrival of agriculture and pastoralism. Where the change occurred earliest was in the arid zone, extending from Egypt to the Indus basin, where steppes and deserts alternate with oases and alluvial river valleys. So far as we can judge, agriculture appeared first of all in the Jordan valley in West Asia, possibly as early as 12,000 years ago (10,000 BC) and almost certainly by 8,000 BC. Wheat (einkorn and emmer) and barley, pulses and flax had by now been domesticated. Pastoralism came soon after: the first domesticated animals were sheep and goats, their domestication beginning in Western Iran, around 7000 BC. The presence of domesticated sheep and goats at Aq Kupruk in Northern Afghanistan, dated 1000–7500 BC, would be still earlier; but some doubts have been raised about the stratification worked out for the site.

In view of this evidence, the dramatic discovery of Mehrgarh as the earliest site of the Neolithic Revolution needs to be set in its proper context. Mehrgarh, administratively within Baluchistan, is situated below the Bolan Pass in the Kachi Plain, an extension of the Indus basin. Around 7000 BC two species of six-row barley, as well as two-row barley, and einkorn and emmer wheat began to be cultivated here. The possibility exists of a local wild two-row barley having been domesticated, but such local innovation is much less likely for wheat. Given the early dates for wheat and barley cultivation in the Levant, a diffusion of cereal agriculture eastwards from that area across Iran is the more probable process, especially in the light of the early cultivation of barley and wheat (before 6000 BC) at Jeitun in Turkmenistan, just north of the Iranian Plateau. Mehrgarh gives evidence of goat domestication at its earliest levels, and by *c.* 5500 BC the indigenous *zebu* (humped cattle: *Bos indicus*) had also been domesticated. This suggests that once the domestication of sheep and goats had been mastered, the technique could be applied at different centres independently to the bovine species as well. (The subsequent domestication of the water buffalo in India offers another such example of technique-extension).[8]

While there is little doubt that it was essentially the diffusion of agriculture across the Iranian plateau that triggered the neolithic revolution in the Indus basin,[9] there were also crops that Iran and West Asia, in turn, received from India at a subsequent stage. The history of cotton has been pushed to a very early date, by the discovery of charred cotton seeds at Mehrgarh, datable to around 5000 BC. But, then, 'cotton fibres adhering to textile impressions in lime plaster', were found at the site of a pastoral camp in eastern Jordan, placed within the rather long time-range of 4450–3000 BC.[10] It is likely, therefore, that cotton cultivation had travelled much westwards, from the Indus basin across Iran in the fourth millennium BC, if not earlier.

At a later stage, the same happened with rice. Rice of the domestic kind (*Oryz sativa*) arrived in India travelling from China (where its cultivation was established by 5000 BC), possibly *via* Thailand and Myanmar. By the third millennium BC it was cultivated in eastern and central India. It is reported from Harappa in the Panjab and Gufkral in Kashmir around 2000 BC.[11] Rice cultivation soon crossed the Indus, and there is good evidence for *Oryz sativa* from the Swat valley in the North West Frontier Province of Pakistan from around 2000 BC onwards.[12] In Swat we are already on the eastern margins of the Iranic world; and it is therefore surprising that rice cultivation should not have spread into Iran for a full two millennia that followed. The question has, indeed, been raised whether Iran proper had at all taken to rice cultivation before the Arab conquest of the seventh century AD.[13]

Iran and the Indus Civilization

In Gordon Childe's scheme the Neolithic Revolution was followed by the Urban Revolution, based on a larger production of agricultural surplus and the development of various craft techniques, such as the use of the potter's wheel, the making of fired bricks, copper and bronze metallurgy, wheeled cart, etc. For a long time, the Indus Civilization (*c.* 2500–2000 BC), obviously sharing many craft techniques with Mesopotamia, had yet seemed to stand alone, so as to suggest that in every major respect it had indigenous origins. The geographical gap has, however, now been very largely filled by further archaeological discoveries. First of all, the eastern line of influence of the Proto-Elamite culture, with its principal seat at Susa (in the Mesopotamian part of southwestern Iran), has been extended much farther towards the Indus basin, with the unearthing of a Proto-Elamite tablet at Shahr-i Sokhta, in Sistan on Iran's border with Afghanistan, and the discovery of Proto-Elamite pottery at Miri Qalat in western Baluchistan. Secondly, there has been the discovery of a whole new civilization in the Helmand basin (southern Afghanistan and Iranian Sistan) with its great urban centre at Shahr-i Sokhta, just mentioned. The civilization also embraced a smaller town, Mundigak, near Kandahar. While the beginning of the Helmand Civilization is placed slightly earlier than that of the Indus Civilization, it was still largely contemporaneous, extending from *c.* 2600 to *c.* 2100 BC.[14] Clearly, all these developments towards urbanism in Mesopotamia, Iran, Afghanistan and the Indus basin, could not but be interlinked, though it is very difficult for us to say which feature of its own social or economic life, a particular culture achieved independently for itself and which it imported from outside. By the much earlier dates for its urbanization as well as for earlier attainment of the art of writing, Mesopotamia must still have precedence over all other parts of the region; and this being the case, the importance of the Iranian Plateau as the intermediate zone between Mesopotamia and the Indus basin must be given due importance when we consider the factors behind the evolution of the Indus Civilization.

The last statement may be deemed to need qualification in that the sea route between Mesopotamia and the Indus basin—the country which to the Mesopotamians was known as 'Meluhha'—also became important with time. Since the monsoons were not yet discovered, the seafaring ships were forced to hug the coasts, but the sea route still bypassed the Iranian coast. The Indus ships, leaving the last Indus port on the Baluchistan coast, namely Sotkakoh (guarded by the Indus fortress of Sutkagen-dor near the Pakistan-Iran border), sailed across the Gulf of Oman, to anchor in havens in Oman, such as Ras al-Junayz. Oman was known in Mesopotamia as the country of 'Magan'. The ships then entered the Persian Gulf and made for the ports of 'Dilmun', the part of Arabian coast and islands extending from Bahrain to the island of Faylakah, off Kuwait. Thereafter they sailed up the Euphrates and Tigris rivers to trade with Mesopotamian cities.[15] Why the southern Arabian coast of the Gulf was preferred by these ships to the northern or Iranian (which was not the case in medieval times, when the Persian ports such as Hormuz and, later, Bandar Abbas, were the ports of call for most Gulf ships) needs to be considered. The reasons might have been navigational, commercial or even political in nature: we just do not know. However, whether Iran was concerned in the seafaring or not, we must remember that the main period of trade between the Indus Civilization and Mesopotamia was between 2350–2000 BC; there is no evidence of the sea trade existing on any scale during the centuries when the Indus Civilization was evolving out of the early (or pre-) Indus cultures, *c.* 3200–2500 BC. Earlier relations between the two regions must, therefore, have been overland; and there Iran could not have been by-passed.

These remarks may be regarded as a rather sketchy prelude to Professor K.M. Dhavalikar's study (in this volume) of India-Iran contacts in prehistory. The reader will see that he comprehensively considers the items traded between Iran and the Gulf countries, on the one hand, and India, on the other, during the period of the Indus civilization. He concludes that while the commerce dwindled after the collapse of the Indus Civilization, it did not entirely disappear. It is significant that he reaffirms Professor H.D. Sankalia's thesis about the channel-spouted cups of the chalcolithic site of Navdatoli (south-western Madhya Pradesh), having earlier analogues in those of Tepe Hissar and Sialk in Iran.

The Indo-Iranians

Towards the end of his essay Professor Dhavalikar raises the problem of fitting the Elamite-Dravidian connection and the spread of Indo-European (especially Indo-Iranian) languages in the history of the region. If there is substance in David McAlpin's thesis of a Proto-Dravidian language, based essentially on links found between Elamite and the Dravidian languages (one of which, Brahui, is now confined to north-eastern Baluchistan), then Iran and the Indus basin must have shared a common language-ancestry at the time of the Indus Civilization, and before the spread of the Indo-European languages.[16] Though many historians tend to accept the existence of Proto-Elamo-Dravidian for a fact,[17] there is still considerable division of opinion about it among linguists.[18] One can at the moment only consider the hypothesis probable but not proved.

The position with regard to the Indo-European languages is on a different plane altogether. The affinities are certain. They are so strong between the Indo-Aryan and Iranian branches of the family, as to lead linguists to propound the earlier existence of a Proto-Indo-Iranian or, for short, a Proto-Aryan language.[19]

There can be no doubt that the problems of language change posed by historical linguistics cannot be brushed under the carpet in the manner Edmund Leach would like us to do.[20] To cite one example of the weakness of his position, we may take his objections to the proximity of the languages of the *Rigveda* and the *Avesta*. The fact that both texts were written down very late and were till then carried in memory,[21] can have a bearing on the question of the proximity of their language only if it can be shown that at the time they were written down it was possible for Brahman and Zoroastrian priests to intermingle and speak to each other. Since such would be an obvious fantasy for any period after 500 BC, one must accept that the two texts were committed to memory at a time much before their transcription, at a period, that is, when the speakers of the languages of the two texts had not long separated. And this is precisely what the basic assumption of historical linguists is when they conceive of an ancestral language like proto-Aryan, out of which the languages of the two texts originated and date it to a time much before 1500 BC.

The whole Indo-European problem has in fact been greatly clarified in the last two decades by a brilliant work by Renfrew and a cautious comprehensive study by Mallory.[22] Despite considerable differences in their conclusions, it is obvious that neither considers race as a determinant of language. It can easily be demonstrated that the ability to speak a particular language has nothing to do with inherited genes. Nor has population displacement been the only way in which one language has displaced another. While the spread of English in the present territory of the United States may be seen as the result of both genocide and displacement of the earlier indigenous inhabitants, such has not been the case with the spread of either Turkic or Arabic languages in medieval times. Renfrew has suggested 'elite dominance' as a major factor behind language change in such cases; and one need not, therefore, set a wholesale biological change in the population as the test of whether the Indo-Iranian or any other languages could have arrived from outside India and Iran.[23] It is most likely that the initial speakers of the intruding languages constituted a small minority in the entire population of the countries concerned, and their arrival might leave no trace in the genetic record.

Archaeology offers admittedly only limited help in reconstructing the history of unwritten languages, since languages can subsist within quite different material cultures. Such a test as the presence of the domesticated horse in the archaeological record has then a significance that must be understood in precise terms. The original Proto-Indo-European word, reconstructed as *(*h*)*ekwos*, meant a horse, whether wild or domesticated.[24] If the horse is absent from archaeological finds at the sites of a culture, it could yet be a culture of

Indo-European speakers, such as did not use the horse. But it could not, in all probability, be one of the Vedic-Aryan speakers, since the *Rigveda* assigns great prominance to the horse and the horse-drawn chariot. It is for this reason that the presence of the horse becomes such a test for the Vedic Indo-Aryans, and, similarly, for the Avestan Iranian, for the *Avesta* too has horses and chariots. So long as archaeology has a consistent story to tell about the absence of the true horse in India, previous to 2000 BC,[25] and of its first appearances, in clay as well as skeletal remains, in the Ghalighai Culture IV of Swat (1800–1400 BC) and Pirak culture Ib (1600–1400 BC) and Pirak III (1300–800 BC), one can only conclude that the *Rigveda* cannot be dated earlier than *c.* 1500 BC, and that those who used horses in Swat and the Kachi plain (where Pirak is situated) probably spoke a language allied to the Vedic. Given such evidence and the geography of the *Rigveda*, with its verses centred on *Sapta-sindhava*, Seven Rivers (the Panjab), an Aryan movement into India proper from the northwest is as near established as any fact can be in prehistory.

Professor R.S. Sharma, who has already considered the whole question of the arrival of Indo-Aryan language-speakers in a separate work,[26] surveys in his contribution to this volume ('Glimpses of Indo-Iranian Connections of Earliest Times') the major interpretations of the linguistic and archaeological evidence about both the Elamite-Dravidian connection and the arrival of the Indo-Iranians on the borderlands of India and Iran by about 2000 BC. From here one can take the trail followed by Gherardo Gnoli in his pursuit of the origins of Iran.[27] Gnoli shows that in interpreting Avestan geography, one must guard against the transposition of territorial, river and mountain names in later Zoroastrian tradition from the eastern Iranic world to the western. Essentially, the early Avestan region comprised the sixteen countries (*dahyu*) (compare the sixteen *mahajanapadas* in India!), which, as far as they can be identified, all lie within a region comprising Afghanistan, eastern Turkmenistan, the North West Frontier Province and the Panjab.[28] The last-named (Panjab) is called Hapta-hendu, the exact equivalent of the Rigvedic Sapta-sindhava.[29] We must, therefore, visualise a time where the Vedic and Avestan worlds shared a large area between themselves—before the former moved more to the east and the latter to the west.

On both the two texts, the *Rigveda* and *Avesta*, and their relationship much has been written.[30] Professor K.M. Shrimali's study of the 'religious trajectories' in this volume is especially important in that it brings out not only the many common features of their beliefs, deities and rituals, in name as well as in essence, but also their original composers' pastoral roots which are essential for understanding the cults and concepts that find expression in them. Seen in this light one may consider the Indo-Iranians as essentially pastoral nomads who also took to seasonal cultivation. Their horse-chariot riding chiefs and warriors thus played a role similar to a host of nomadic successors, moving behind them, like the Iranic Scythians (Sakas), the Kushans, the Huns, the Turks and the Mongols. The Aryans must have established themselves initially as a dominant group within linguistically alien populations, as the Mitanni did among the Hurrians in northern Mesopotamia during *c.* 1500–1300 BC. The fact that the Mitanni, who were masters of the art of chariot-driving and horse-racing, spoke an Indo-Aryan, and not an Iranic, language,[31] is a further proof that the Indo-Aryans and Iranians were considerably mixed as they separated in and around Afghanistan at an earlier period. In both India and Iran the Aryan languages were then gradually imposed over populations that had used other tongues (though the Mitanni language, it is true, was absorbed by the Hurrian). Why the Aryan languages should have thus prevailed is not easy to explain. It may have been due, partly at least, as Professor Kosambi suggested, to their religious success, that is, to the ability of the Vedic religion in India and the Pre-Avestan and Avestan in Iran, to accommodate alien communities and their beliefs and rituals within their fold.[32] In any case, a comparative study of how the language-change occurred in Northern India and in Iran might be of much use in resolving the puzzle.[33]

The Transmission of Early Science and Writing

Gnoli's emphasis on the Avestan region being situated largely to the east of present-day Iran fits in with what we know of the political history of western Iran. Here the kingdom of Elam continued, with its thriving culture and script, down to the time of the Babylonian conqueror Nebuchadnezzar I (1125–04), who won a great victory over the Elamites. After a revival of the Elamite kingdom, *c.* 800 BC, both Elam and Babylon came under the domination of Assyria from 691 onwards. Ultimately, Elam was incorporated in the Iranian Achaemenid empire under Cyrus the Great (559–30 BC).

These particulars are important because Elam could serve as

the transmitting agent for the great advances in the knowledge of mathematics and astronomy that were made in Mesopotamia, but principally in Babylon, during the second millennium BC. The Sumerians had invented the system of positional values in their notation under a sexagesimal system (a forerunner of the later Indian decimal notation), and the Babylonians made calculations of square roots and developed algebra with solutions of linear and quadratic equations. They also anticipated Pythagoras's theorem 1500 years before its articulation by the Greek mathematician. They succeeded in fixing the equinoxes and determined both the lengths of solar and lunar years fairly accurately. The seven-day week was their creation. Under the Kassites (*c.* 1700–1171 BC) they began to use numbered years within each ruler's reign; and in the sixth century BC Babylon gave the first era to the world, the first used year of the era, 3200, corresponding to 553 BC. In astronomy they attained such proficiency in observation as to begin making predictions about the movements of heavenly bodies and so developed an omen astrology during the period 1400–900 BC.[34]

It can be seen that India in course of time received many of these contributions to knowledge (including, alas, astrology) at various times. Numbered years, in the form of regnal years, are first known to have been used by Asoka, *c.* 250 BC, in his inscriptions. The first era is used in Indian inscriptions of the first centuries BC and AD, this being the problematic Old Saka era, with the epoch variously placed from 248 to 83 BC.[35] These dates make it clear that the system of numbered years began to be used at such a late date that it might have been received from Mesopotamia only very indirectly through the agency of the Greeks. Other Mesopotamian contributions might, however, have arrived much earlier directly through Iran. This could, for instance, be the case with the implied statement in the *Vedanga Jyotisha* that the shortest day is 12 *mahurtas* and the longest 18.[36] Such a ratio might be given quite naturally by a Babylonian astrologer on the basis of observations in Northern Iraq, but an Indian astrologer can hardly be imagined as climbing the Karakoram Range to arrive at it. Similarly, the system of *tithis* the 'lunar days', thirty of which made a nominal month of 30 days, goes back in Mesopotamia to about 2000 BC, when merchants at Kanesh (Anatolia) were using 5-day weeks, six of which made a month.[37] If the *Vedanga Jyotisha* was compiled *c.* 500 BC, the debt to Babylon must have been incurred before the establishment of the Achaemenid empire, and we must then suppose a pre-Achaemenid transmission through Iran. This was undoubtedly partial and certainly oral, for the Indians in *c.* 500 BC were still not conversant with writing. This backwardness, perhaps, explains why numbered years and eras and other complex mathematical ideas originating in Babylon had to wait until the Greek intrusion helped introduce to India these Babylonian achievements along with other elements of Greek science.

Another great achievement of other civilizations that India took so much time to adopt was, indeed, writing. The Indus civilization had a script, a logo-syllabic one with over 400 characters. But it vanished with the disappearance of that civilization by 1900 BC. No archaeologist has yet succeeded in unearthing any marks anywhere in India, until after 300 BC, that can be accepted even as a fragmentary piece of writing or true graffiti. The Achaemenids were the first Iranian speakers to adopt writing even before they established their empire in the sixth century BC. The golden tablet of Teispes (675–40 BC), king of Fars, shows that Old Persian (still fairly close to Sanskrit) had begun to be written in cuneiform characters. By this time, however, Aramaic, a semitic language written in an alphabet derived ultimately from Egyptian writing, had spread in western Asia as a kind of *lingua franca.* As the Achaemenids constructed the first real empire in the world, extending from the Indus to the Mediterranean, they naturally found Aramaic to be the most convenient for administrative use. Even Old Persian began to be written in Aramaic, which ultimately led to the creation of the Pahlavi script in Sasanian times.[38] The Indus basin remained under the control of the Achaemenids from the sixth century BC until Alexander destroyed their empire in the latter half of the fourth century BC. Bivar has collected references from Persepolis Fortification tablets to travellers, Persians and Indians, who journeyed from Gandhara, Hindush (Sind) and other eastern territories to Susa and other towns in western Iran.[39] It was inevitable from such contacts that writing should arrive in eastern Iran and India. A cuneiform cylinder seal has been found at Herat and two fragmentary cuneiform inscriptions at Kandahar; and these probably belong to Achaemenid times. No Aramaic inscriptions survive from Achaemenid times, but Asoka's edicts in Aramaic at Taxila, near Kabul as well as at Kandahar leave us in no doubt that Aramaic writing must have become well established in Afghanistan and the Panjab by the previous century (fourth century BC).[40]

The appearance of Aramaic in the Indian dominions of the Achaemenids probably best explains the grammarian Panini's reference fifth–fourth century BC) to writing (*lipi*), the first reliable pre-Mauryan reference to it. Since Panini lived in or near Taxila, the capital of Gandhara, he might well have been referring to Aramaic, or even Kharoshthi, one of the two earliest Indian scripts.[41] The earliest known Kharoshthi inscriptions are those of Asoka. As shown by Buhler it has all the features of a script carved out of Aramaic (like which it runs from right to left) to suit Indo-Aryan pronunciation. Like Aramaic again, it does not distinguish between long and short vowels.[42]

With Brahmi, the script used most for his edicts by Asoka and the ancestor of the alphabets of all Indian languages, except those that use Arabic or Roman scripts, the case is different. Running from left to right and carefully distinguishing between long and short vowels, there is little affinity with Aramaic in it beyond that of being also an alphabet. The discovery of certain potsherds at Anuradhapura, Sri Lanka, containing Brahmi letters, dated to fourth century BC or earlier, has introduced a new dimension in the discussion; but the uncertainties involved, the lack of reliability in carbon-dating for the required precise chronology and the possibility of later intrusions into earlier strata, necessarily undermine the significance of this piece of evidence. Unless the traces of earlier proto-Brahmi writing are discovered, the likelihood remains that Brahmi was a deliberately crafted script, perhaps, under Asoka's own aegis, taking its direction of writing from Greek, but otherwise creating letters and vowel signs partly on principles already established in the formation of Kharoshthi. Here we may bear in mind the fact that Asoka has also left two Greek inscriptions at Kandahar; and so some familiarity with Greek among his officers must be assumed. Even if, then, Brahmi was a deliberately invented script, the concepts on which it was based necessarily came from alphabets such as Aramaic and Greek; and for the Indian knowledge of Aramaic, as the ultimate source of inspiration for the invention, Iran was surely largely responsible.

India and Iran in the Age of Hellenism

Alexander's victorious campaign (327–25 BC) in what is now Pakistan, opened the gates to a whole epoch of cultural exchange, for which his early death (323 BC) had no more significance than an episode. After a long conflict, Greek and Iranian cultures co-existed on the same terrain; and with India as the third side, a fascinating cultural triangle was created. In his paper in this volume Professor U.P. Arora examines a number of facets of this remarkable interchange. While undoubtedly the transmission of Greek learning and ideas played the part of a catalyst in the development of mathematics and science in India, I should like here to comment only on the Indo-Iranian part of the cultural exchange.

One has read from school text books onwards about the Sakas who followed closely upon the Bactrian (or Indo-) Greeks to govern large parts of Pakistan, northern India, Gujarat, western Madhya Pradesh and Maharashtra during the first century BC to fourth cetnury AD. They have been linked to the Scythians described by the Greek authors and the Sakas of Achaemenid documents, and their earlier conditions of life have been portrayed as those of relatively cultured nomads. That they spoke an Iranic language comes through from the terms that appear in their Prakrit inscriptions such as the name of their country 'Sakastan' in the famous Mathura lion capital inscription (first century AD),[43] giving us the first mention of a famous Iranian territorial name (whence Sagistan, Sijistan, to modern Sistan), the tell-tale suffix *-stan* proclaiming the Sakas' affinity to the Iranians. Their fondness for the Iranian word *kshatrapa* or *kshaharata* (ruler) further underlines the affinity. Harmatta has tried heroically to reconstruct their dialects from words and names found in their inscriptions in India, and he points to close links with the Khotanese Saka (known to us from later documents), which too was an Iranic language.[44]

Ignoring the 'Pahlavi' interlude under Gondophares (first century AD), the ethnic name indicating the claimed link with the Parthians of Iran, we have the Kushans. They might have originated as a branch of the Yeuh-chi and emigrated from Western China, but at the time they enter Indian history, their language was an Iranic one, called Bactrian by modern historians. This language used Greek characters for its script. The language came to be known first of all from Kushan coins and inscriptions (the latter confined to Afghanistan, except for one near Termez, north of the Oxus).[45] The Kushan emperors of the first and second centuries AD used the Iranian title *shaonano shao* ('shah of shahs') alongside the Prakrit /Sanskrit *maharaja rajatiraja* and Greek 'Basileus Basileon', which indicates the three major languages in use in their empire, extending from Transoxania to upper Gangetic basin. The cultural pluralism within their empire is shown by the fact that Kanishka, the emperor so much praised in Buddhist tradition, not only patronised Buddhism but also had Zoroastrian divinities on his coins besides deities from the Hellenistic and Brahmanical pantheons.[46]

The Kushan empire with its Bactrian-Iranic language, and the coexistence of Buddhism and Zoroastrianism within it, probably played some role in the entry of Buddhism into Iran. While Buddhist remains of the period are extensive in Afghanistan and Central Asia, they are not visible in Iran proper.[47] But the intrusion of Buddhism into Iran is established by its being one of the recognised sources of Manichaeism. Mani (216–76), the founder of this most interesting faith, expressly claimed as his precursors the Buddha, Zoroaster and Christ. Buddhism certainly influenced the elements of metempsychosis in Manichaean beliefs, and still more the three ethical 'seals' (*muhrs*) prescribed for the elders, namely, vegetarianism, abstenance from causing harm to living beings, and celibacy.[48] Manichaeism was to enjoy for some centuries a large amount of influence in different localities from the Mediterranean to China, and its texts or their fragments are preserved in various languages ranging from Greek to early Turkic. One of the major sources of our knowledge about Manichaeism is the famous Arabic *al-Fihrist* of ibn al-Nadim (987–8 AD); and through accounts like these Mani's ideas found their way also into the spiritual world of Islam. Manichaen influence can be seen, for example, in the Ishraqi or 'illuminationist' thought of Shihabuddin Suhrawardi (1155–91). There can, therefore, hardly be much doubt that some Buddhist notions incorporated in Manichaeism were also taken over by Muslim mysticism (*sufism*), which found its strength chiefly in the Iranic world. Sufic ideas of metempsychosis, the sufi emphasis on avoidance of meat, and even the concept of *fana* (annihilation) could thus go back through a complex genealogy to the elements of Buddhism known in Iran in the time of Mani.

Apart from religious transmissions, there were also exchanges in the mundane world. In this volume Ishrat Alam presents much information on transfers of technology in the ancient and medieval times between India and Iran. I have little to add to what he says, except to touch on two points. The chain of pots ('potgarland') on the vertical wheel appears in India, as he says, in the sixth century AD. But in the Mediterranean world the potgarland was in use much earlier being present in the already developed device, known to historians of technology as *saqiya*, the geared waterwheel. The 'paternoster chain' was used in Pompeii in Italy, *c.* 100 BC, and soon afterwards in Egypt, where it seems to have been used first as an extension of the noria (wheel with pots on circumference) without the gearing mechanism, as must have been the case in India too after the sixth century AD until the full complements of the *saqiya* ('Persian wheel') arrived here sometimes before the sixteenth century.[49] It is thus a fair inference that the use of the potgarland travelled from eastern Mediterranean to India across Iran in the early centuries of the Christian era. This, as may be seen in Ishrat Alam's paper, was also the case with the rotary hand-mill that appears in the Roman world in the third century AD and at Taxila in the sixth century—with Iran as the obvious channel of diffusion.[50]

There is yet another transmission that might have taken place in these centuries, one which was to have great significance for land-transport as well as agriculture. Kohl-Rollefson in a recent study of the one-humped camel ('dromedary'), which unlike the Bactrian camel can work in warmer climes, shows considerable vagueness about the date of its arrival in India.[51] The first representation in sculpture of the animal, it is true, is rather late, in the Mandor frieze (Rajasthan) datable to the twelfth century.[52] But there is a definitive statement in the account of Sind (Sin-tu) by the Chinese pilgrim Xuan Zhuang (Hsuan Tsang), who visited it in *c.* 641: 'The camels', he says, 'are small in size and have only one hump.'[53] This would mean that dromedaries were already to be found in Sind before the Arab conquest (AD 712–14). It is widely held that the dromedary was first domesticated in Arabia, and from there was carried to Iran. Kohler-Rollfeson cites R.W. Bulliet to say that it was only under the Sasanians (208–651 AD) in Iran that 'depictions of one-humped camels start to predominate in seal impressions and on silver plates showing Bahram Gur.'[54] It is, then, very likely that it was during the Sasanian period that the dromedary was brought from Iran to Sind, to be taken from there to other parts of Northwestern India.

There is still more to the contacts between India and Sasanid Iran. In 1318, Amir Khusrau gave as one of the arguments for the superiority of India over other countries that it had given to the world 'the decimal notation (*hindsa*), the didactic fables (*Dimna*) and chess (*shatranj*).'[55] The Sasanian role in the transmission of the first is doubtful. The firm evidence of the Indian use of numerals with positional values seems itself to be no earlier than the sixth century;[56] and there is no reference known to me of the transmission of this knowledge to the Arabs through Sasanian channels. But it is otherwise with the other two achievements claimed by the poet for India.

The *Dimna* here represents the *Panchatantra*, the famous collection of fables in Sanskrit of which the original composition probably belongs to the Gupta period (fourth–fifth centuries AD).[57] The collection was translated into Pahlavi (Middle Persian) by Burzoe, reputedly at the court of the Sasanian emperor, Anushirwan (531–79). Although the Pahlavi version is lost, we know of its original contents from a Syriac translation, of AD 570, which fortunately has survived. From this we learn that Burzoe's version lacked some fables and derived at least three from the *Mahabharata*. In the eighth century ibn al-Muqaffa made an Arabic translation from the Pahlavi version calling it *Kalila wa Dimna*, after the two jackals, Karataka and Damanaka. Finding that the original fables were far too cynical and worldly, he added an account of the trial of Dimna, to underline the doubtful message that justice wins in the end. From this a Hebrew version was made in the twelfth century, whence a Latin followed in the thirteenth; and hardly any significant European language was left by the sixteenth century which did not have a version made from the Latin one. In Persian a twelfth-century rendering of the Arabic *Kalila wa Dimna* was given a refined literary form under the title *Anwar-i Suhaili* in 1504.[58] Thus the Sasanid translator became responsible for the diffusion of the *Panchatantra* throughout the world, in a manner seldom enjoyed by books other than religious texts.

As for chess, the Indians had developed a dice game with a board of 64 squares in the early centuries of the Christian era. It had four players, each with pieces from the King downwards, the pieces moving with throws of dice. The game was called *chatarunga*.[59] That it essentially reached Sasanid Iran in the sixth century in this form is shown by the fact that the Iranian name *shatranj* is a corruption of the Sanskrit *chatarunga*. Whether it was in India or Iran that the game was converted into a two-player game and divested of dice, is not clear. There is, however, a story in the annals of the Arab conquest of Sind, of chess being played between a fugitive Brahman prince of Sind and a neighbouring ruler, *c.* 714 AD, as a two-player game.[60] How far the story can be given weight is a difficult matter, since the present text, a seemingly literal version of the original Arab annals, belongs to the early thirteenth century. Chess in due course made its way from Iran and reached western Europe by the thirteenth century.

Medieval Times

Upon the Arab conquest, 637–51, Iran exprienced a religious and social upheaval of great magnitude. This is not the place to describe the nature of the transformation within Iran, but the points that are of relevance to the relationship with India may be underlined. First of all, since Arabic now became the sole language of the learned and educated, it becomes difficult to separate the Arab from the Iranian elements in the ensuing common civilization. It is practically impossible to define in ethnic terms a man like Alberuni, scientist, polymath, the first of all Indologists: he came from Khwarazm with its own Iranic dialect, spoke Persian, knew Turkic, and wrote exclusively in Arabic. In one sense, his 'Indica' or *Kitab al-Hind* (*c.* 1035) can be treated as the Iranic world's greatest intellectual endeavour towards an understanding of India; but one may, with equal justice, set Alberuni's great work in the line of writings in Greek and Arabic (with no intrusion of Persian), in whose tradition Alberuni plainly saw himself.

But already by Alberuni's time, a distinctly Iranian culture had taken shape. Firdausi's *Shahnama*, completed *c.* 1009–10, often acclaimed as the National Epic of Iran, represented both its revived language (often called by historians 'New Persian') and its old proud spirit.[61] With astonishing rapidity Persian supplanted Arabic in the eleventh century in the entire Iranic world, as the main literary and administrative language. Henceforth Arabic was practically restricted to the domain of theology and the exact sciences.

At this point of triumph, however, the Iranian civilization was faced with a fresh challenge. The nomadic Turk intrusions from Mongolia and Western China had begun in the sixth century when a vast steppe Turk empire had been established in Central Asia whose subject peoples spoke various Iranic dialects.[62] In the succeeding centuries Turkic immigrations and the high value given to Turkic slave-soldiers created large numbers of Turkic communities within Iranian lands. By the eleventh century, the Turks began to provide a large segment of the ruling class, and the Turkic language began to supplant Iranian dialects not only in Xinjiang and Transoxania but also lands much further to the south. In Iranian consciousness the Turk became an ethnic rival, and in the *Shahnama* of Firdausi the conflict was given an ancient complexion: the territorial name of Turan, a region adjoining Sind on the west in Sasanid and early Arab times, was transferred to Transoxania and the ancient Turanians (despite their Iranian or Aryan names) were transformed into Turks.[63] By the thirteenth century among the Turks too a feeling of hostility prevailed against the Taziks or Tajiks, the free-born Iranians.[64] And yet, even though Turkic (and its emerging regional dialects) made great inroads into the domain of Persian as the spoken tongue, Persian still remained the preeminent literary language even in the areas where Turkic now came to be spoken.

We need not, therefore, be surprised that despite the apparent Turkic dominance in the Delhi Sultanate and the constant endeavour to restrain the Tazik elements, during the thirteenth century, it was the latter who seem to have won in the end even in the political arena.[65] The Iranian predominance over the Turkic influence was still greater in the cultural sphere. A Turk by descent ('Hindustani Turk' by self-definition), Amir Khusrau (*d.* 1325) was one of India's greatest poets in Persian. He tells us that with the arrival of 'the Ghorids and Turks', it was the Persian language which the Indian people took to, though in a subsequent verse he tells us of Persian, as well as Turkic and Arabic, being spoken in India.[66] Turkic was not used at all in either the administration or in literature in the Delhi Sultanate, and its words appear only among nobles' titles, such as 'Alp Khan' or 'Qutlugh Khan'. In contrast to the large amount of Persian and Arabic written material from the thirteenth–fifteenth centuries, not a single Turkic document seems to have survived from that time in India.

One may say, therefore, that the Ghorian conquests, which led to the establishment of the Delhi Sultanate (1206), prized open Northern India for a massive infusion of Persian culture at practically all levels. Ishrat Alam in this volume examines the influx of technological devices that followed, thereby giving substance to Kosambi's dictum about 'Islamic raiders . . . breaking hidebound custom in the adoption and transmission of new techniques.'[67] In his paper on Iranian influences on medieval Indian architecture, S.A. Nadeem Rezavi identifies Iranian elements in the architecture of both the Sultanate and Mughal periods. It has always seemed strange to me why the arch, vault and dome so much used in Sasanid architecture, along with lime and gypsum mortar,[68] were not employed in India at all until the thirteenth century. One begins to fear, from such instances, that political upheavals have often been needed to break the inertia of stable civilizations.

There is a concentration, in this volume, justifiable, perhaps, in the light of the importance of the subject, on the period of the Mughals and the Safavids, covering the sixteenth and seventeenth centuries. Both Rezavi and Alam also deal with it in their papers. Professor Iqtidar Alam Khan studies the nature of the Iranian migrations to India after the establishment of the Safavid regime in Iran. Professor Iqbal Husain looks at the way in which ideological influences from Iran shaped the evolution of Akbar's religious thought. Professor S.P. Verma traces the process by which Iranian painting by mingling with Indian traditions and Renaissance art, but shaped also by Akbar's great love for realism and humanism, received reincarnation in Mughal art as one of the great schools of painting of the world. The economic parallels between the Mughal and Safavid empires are studied by Professor Shireen Moosvi: the eternal question nags us, if we are in the Marxist historiographic tradition, as to how far these regimes represented the final expressions of the Asiatic Mode of Production. Najaf Haider examines an important facet of the commercial relationship between Iran and India, looking at it from the point of view of Safavid Iran.

These studies take up crucial issues of cultural and economic relationships, but naturally leave out certain other areas of no little significance. One of these is literature. The Iranian contribution to Persian poetry in India was so considerable, from 'Urfi to Sa'ib, that this is, indeed, a regrettable lacuna.[69] The work of these poets often lay within a tradition in poetry that came to be known in Iran as *sabk-i Hindi*, the Indian Style. This is marked by a tendency towards indirect statements through semantic puzzles and difficult metaphors and analogies. Such a style often suffered deterioration by producing an obscure maze in the name of poetry, but it was also helpful to poets who wished to express the boldest ideas, which, if stated directly, might have cause great scandal. It came to be rejected in Iran during the nineteenth century. Perhaps, one can see the difference when one compares the profound scepticism of Ghalib, so often couched in 'the Indian style', with the declaratory enthusiasm of Iqbal.

Professor Iqbal Husain's essay in this volume suggests the need further to explore the wide area in which the connexions between the developments in religious thought in Iran and India can be traced.

Shah Isma'il's proclamation of the Twelver Shi'ism at Tabriz in 1501 established a regime in Iran in which two elements henceforth co-existed, though not without some discomfort: (a) a glorification of the Shah's own position as a religious guide of the Qizilbash, in whose eyes he came to enjoy the position of God's representative in matters both spiritual and secular; and (b) the imposition of an organised class of Shi'ite orthodox clerics, with a view to eliminating all religious dissent.[70] It can be argued that (a) proved very attractive an idea to the Indian Emperor Akbar (1556–1605) whose ambitions as a sovereign were unlimited, while (b) was utterly to be rejected, not only because a theological class could conceivably limit Akbar's own power, but also because religious tolerance was the cornerstone of his practical policies and the primary requirement of his espousal of the principle of *Sulh-i Kul* (absolute peace).[71] If Akbar's 'circle of disciples' (*iradat-gazinan*)[72] could be regarded as an attempt to create a sect of faithful followers on the lines of Shah Isma'il's fanatical *murids*, his policy of religious tolerance yet stood in absolute contrast to the Safavid persecution of Sunnis and dissident sects.

Yet Safavid Iran was not all narrow-mindedness. It produced two men the influence of whose thought lent support to the cause of tolerance and reason in India. A Parsi priest Azar Kaiwan, born *c.* 1536 was educated in Muslim *madrasas* in Iran and tried to revive the great illuminationist project of Shihabuddin Suhrawardi. After spending twenty-eight years at Khum, apparently dedicated to the laying the foundations of his Sipasi sect, he left Iran and settled in the Indian city of Patna (Bihar), where he died in 1618. His (grand-?)son, Kaikhusrau Asfandyar completed in Orissa, *c.* 1653, his celebrated work on religions, the *Dabistan* (popularly called *Dabistan-i Mazahib*). Though he places his own sect within the Parsi religion, with whose account he begins, it is obvious that the Sipasis believed that truth could be found in all religions, along with much extraneous matter.[73] Its author's anxiety to present all religions as accurately as possible, with all the dissents and differences within each, is patent; and this makes it a practically unique work for its time.

An important intellectual development in seventeenth-century Iran was the formulation of the doctrines of Sadru'ddin Shirazi (Mulla Sadra) (*d.* 1640). Akbar and his circle had rejected theology and attempted a reconciliation between reason and sufism; Mulla Sadra's system sought to combine within one framework all the three elements: theology, sufism and philosophy.[74] Sadra met with considerable clerical hostility because under his system rational ideas could be allowed to flourish. Indeed, he and his sufic friend Mir Abu'l Findiriski (*d.* 1640–41) were well-known teachers of the sciences (*hakimmiyat*);[75] and the latter's pupil and friend Kamran Shirazi (*d.* 1640–41), who came to India to engage in commerce at Agra, was an uncompromising rationalist and sceptic.[76] Kamran Shirazi might be thought to be a radical of a rather extreme stance, but far more sedate elements among Indian theologians and scholars were also converted to Mulla Sadra's doctrines. Mulla Nizamu'ddin (*d.* 1748) the founder of the Farangi Mahal Sunni school of theologians at Lucknow, who obtained a great reputation as a teacher, wrote 'a gloss on a commentary on the *Hikmat* of Hakim Sadra Shirazi.'[77] Mulla Sadra had thus entered the syllabi of Sunni learning by this time. Apparently, the sectarian divide could not prevent the intellectual interchange between the scholars of India and Iran; and for this the generally tolerant policy of the Mughal empire must receive its due share of credit.

Struggle for National Liberation

Both India and Iran entered the modern age, like most Asian countries, under colonial shadows. Professor Mushirul Hasan offers in this volume wide-ranging reflections on the encounter between the West, on the one hand, and Iran and India, on the other. One of India's great poets, Muhammad Iqbal (1877–1938) saw the West as a challenge to Islam, and took to Persian poetry in order to convey his message to the Muslims of both Iran and India. Professor V.N. Datta in his paper on Iqbal's message in his Persian and Urdu poetry underlines the call he gave to Muslims for seeking their salvation not within a theologically constrained Islam, but within an Islam possessed of the original, vibrant essence. There is no doubt that many verses of Iqbal would greatly appeal to the votaries of the Iranian 'Islamic Revolution' of 1979.

Unlike Iqbal, however, we are concerned not with Iran and Islamic India, but with Iran and India. By this very choice of ours, perhaps, the terms are laid by which we cannot agree with Iqbal's basic assumption of Islam as the only uniting force among people struggling against Western oppression. (When Iqbal turns to thinking about India or the ordinary people, he too has to write differently.)[78] The resistance to colonial exploitation and oppression might have been seen by its early participants as a conflict of religions: The Indian rebels of 1857. Hindus and Muslims shouted 'Deen, Deen!' (Faith, faith!) and shed their blood together. But, in reality, colonialism is not a religious crusade: it is a system of political and economic dominance. It too can make use of religion, to win support for itself or divide its opponents. It is instructive to see what happened in Iran when the crucial moment arrived in 1953, and Kermet Roosevelt, the US representative, with $1 million to dispense, overthrew the government of the venerable nationalist Mossadegh by a bloody *coup*. The great Iranian clericals, the Ayatullahs of Qom, and the fiery Ayatullah Abol Qasem Kashani, then, conveniently looked the other way, and the Americans and the British coolly brought back the Shah to retake control of Iranian oil once again.[79] It would surely be a mistake to discount the secular elements within the Iranian national movement, from liberal democrats to Communists, and to only see the Shi`ite theologians as the natural leaders of Iranian resistance to foreign dominance. Similar approaches highlighting the religious element in the Indian National Movement are also coming to the fore in India, with the unprecedented successes of the `Hindutva' forces in the political arena, and their increasing desire to portray themselves as the major force in the country's past fight for freedom.[80]

An Iranian historian has noted: 'Any consensus on the meaning of the Iranian past has been torn up by the deeply felt disagreement among Iranians over the meaning of the Iranian present.'[81] Surely, if there be an Iranian, for whom the pre-Islamic civilization of a whole millennium and a half holds no message, and an Indian, who can feel no pride in Kabir and Akbar, then the fault is not with the past but with the present. Despite post-modernist cliches, we cannot recreate the past to our own liking, so long as there is some room left for rationality and critical appraisal of what E.H. Carr calls 'historical facts.' A part of this past is the proximity of the civilizations of the two countries, India and Iran, from the very days of their origins, as has been the purpose of this introduction to demonstrate. There will hopefully yet come a time when we will realise the full 'meaning' of this past, and discern the ways in which all humanity is interlinked beyond the ties of race and faith.

Notes and References

[1] For the geography of these 'Western Borderlands', see O.H.K. Spate and A.T.A. Learmonth, *India and Pakistan: A General and Regional Geography*, 3rd ed., London, 1967, pp. 480–503. On p. 494 the authors say that 'the importance of this northwestern angle as the great entry into India is a commonplace of historical geography.' It is often overlooked that the 'entry' point is also an 'exit' point, and traffic can move both ways.

[2] For the finds in the Potwar Plateau and its neighbourhood, see R.W. Dennell in *Man and Environment*, Vol. 20(1), 1995, pp. 21–28; S.M. Ashfaque and Saleem ul Haq in *Pakistan Archaeology*. No. 23, 1987–88, pp. 1–42, and B. Allchin and R.W., Dennell in *Man and Environment*, No. 24, 1989, pp. 1–20; and M. Salim, 'The Paleolithic Cultures of Potwar', *Journal of Central Asia*, Vol. 20(2), 1997. On Keshef-rud see V.A. Ranov, *et al.*, in *History of Civilizations of Central Asia*, Vol. 1, (ed.) A.H. Dani and V.M. Masson, Paris, 1992, pp. 55–6.

[3] At Darra-i Kur only a right temporal bone of a hominid was found: 'it could fit into a partly Neanderthal population like that of Skhul (Palestine) just as well as a modern one' (J.L. Angel's analysis quoted by Bridget Allchin, in *History of Civilizations of Central Asia*, I, pp. 81–82. See also Warwick Ball and Jean-Claude Gardin, *Archaeological Gazetteer of Afghanistan*, Vol. I, Paris, 1982).

[4] For a recent survey of our knowledge about the Neanderthals see Peter Bogucki, *The Origins of Human Society*, Oxford, 1999, pp. 54–68.

[5] Arthur J. Jelinik in: *History of Humanity*, I, (ed.) S.J. De Laet, UNESCO, Paris, 1994, p. 158.

[6] Cf. A.P. Derevyanko in *History of Civilizations of Central Asia*, I, pp. 94–5.

[7] Cf. Ofer Bar-Yosef in: *History of Humanity*, I, pp. 248–50.

[8] The preceding two paragraphs rely heavily on the information assembled in David R. Harris (ed.), *The Origins and Spread of Agriculture and Pastoralism in Eurasia*, London, 1996, especially the contribution of A. Gerrard, S. Colledge and L. Martin (pp. 204–26), F. Hole (pp. 263–81), D.R. Harris and C. Gosden (pp. 370–89), and R.H. Meadow (pp. 390–412), and the editor's 'Conclusion' (pp. 252–74).

[9] Much is sometimes made of Gurdip Singh's discovery of burnt levels at around 7500 BC in the course of his palynological research in the Rajasthan lakes, which Singh took to imply a clearing of the ground for purposes of cultivation (cf. Gregory L. Possehl, *Indus Age: The Beginnings*, New Delhi, 1999, p. 259, 443–46). It should, however, be borne in mind that regular burning was also resorted to by hunter-gatherers to improve the growth of edible wild grasses (Gordon Hillman in: D.R. Harris (ed.), *The Origins and Spread of Agriculture and Pastoralism*, pp. 177, 179–80). Gurdip Singh's finding is therefore no proof that agriculture, that is, the sowing and harvesting of domesticated plants, had been achieved in Rajasthan by that early date—though the date itself would be still later than the beginning of agriculture in the Levant.

[10] R.H. Meadow in: D.R. Harris (ed.), *The Origins and Spread of Agriculture and Pastoralism*, pp. 396–7.

[11] H. Fujiwara *et. al.*, 'Rice and Ragi at Harappa', in: Nayanjot Lahiri, *The Decline and Fall of Indus Civilization*, Delhi, 2000, pp. 368–80; G.L. Possehl, *Indus Age: The Beginnings*, pp. 246–49, for evidence of rice in India. On the larger subject of the origins and diffusion of domesticated rice, see Ian C. Glover and F.W. Higham in: D.R. Harris (ed.), *The Origins and Spread of Agriculture and Pastoralism*, pp. 413–41.

[12] Cf. Giorgio Stacul, *Prehistoric and Protohistoric Swat, Pakistan (c. 3000–1400* BC), Rome, 1987, pp. 40, 49, 157, 159, 165.

[13] Glover and Higham, in: D.R. Harris, *The Origins and Spread of Agriculture and Pastoralism*, pp. 417–19, raise the question, and, while confessing to not having examined the archaeological reports from the region, speak of their 'impression—that rice cultivation there did not significantly precede the expansion of Islam.' The editor comments that this is 'essentially correct', though 'historical sources' suggest that 'rice was cultivated in Persia, Mesopotamia and Jordan in pre-Islamic times'.

[14] There is no single full-scale study of this civilization known to me. M. Tosi *et al.*, in *History of Civilizations of Central Asia*, Vol. I, Chapter 9, offer a good survey. See also papers in the journal *East and West*, Rome, Vols. 23, 26 and 28, and in *South Asian Archaeology*, 1977, 1979 and 1981 volumes.

[15] For the Indus-Gulf trade see See Shereen Ratnagar, *Encounters: the Westerly Trade of the Harappan Civilization*, Delhi, 1981; and Dilip K. Chakrabarti, *The External Trade of the Indus Civilization*, New Delhi, 1990.

[16] McAlpin, *Proto-Elamo-Dravidian: The Evidence and its Implications*, Philadelphia, 1981. (I have seen citations and discussions of this important work, but not read it myself.)

[17] Cf. Muhammad A. Dandamaev, *A Political History of the Achaemenid Empire*, Leiden, 1989, p. 1; Colin Renfrew, 'Language Families and the Spread of Farming' in: D.R. Harris, (ed.), *The Origins and Spread of Agriculture and Pastoralism*, p. 81.

[18] Cf. Walter A. Fairservice, *The Harappan Civilization and its Writing*, New Delhi, 1992, p. 17.

[19] Cf. T. Burrow, 'The Proto-Indoaryans', *Journal of Royal Asiatic Society*, NS. 2, 1973, pp. 123–40.

[20] See Leach's 'Aryan Invasions over Four Millennia', originally published in 1990, and conveniently reprinted in Nayanjot Lahiri (ed.), *The Decline and Fall of the Indus Civilization*, pp.117–38. Leach's essay essentially treats a number of doubtful motives, false judgements, overstatements and slips on the part of individual writers, as sufficient reason to dismiss the strongest possible linguistic evidence, which is not directly confronted at all. His admirers amongst India's recent anti-Max Muller brigade need to note that Leach can only establish his position by holding that 'the Vedas add up to a miscellany of undatable texts of unknown origin' and 'are not primary in either a chronological sense or a theological sense' (ibid., pp. 136–7).

[21] Cf. Leach in: N. Lahiri (ed.), *The Decline and Fall of Indus Civilization*, pp. 134–35.

[22] Colin Renfrew, *Archaeology and Language: The Puzzle of Indo-European Origins*, London, 1987; J.P. Mallory, *In Search of the Indo Europeans*, London, 1989.

[23] Cf. Kenneth R.A. Kennedy, 'Have Aryans been identified in prehistoric skeletal record from South Asia', in: George Erdosy (ed.), *The Indo-Aryans of South Asia: Language, Material Culture and Ethnicity*, Berlin, 1995/Indian (ed.), New Delhi, 1997, pp. 32–66.

[24] Mallory, *op.cit.*, pp. 161–63.

[25] See Possehl, *Indus Age: the Beginnings*, pp. 185–9, and Richard H. Meadow in: D.R. Harris, *The Origins and Spread of Agriculture and Pastoralism*, p. 406.

[26] Ram Sharan Sharma, *Advent of the Aryans in India*, New Delhi, 1999. For another well-reasoned work see Rajesh Kochhar, *The Vedic People: Their History and Geography*, Hyderabad, 2000.

[27] Gherardo Gnoli, *The Idea of Iran: An Essay on its Origin*, Rome, 1989.

[28] Ibid., pp. 51–56.

[29] The consonant ṣ in Indo-Aryan was largely converted into *h* in Avestan. Thus *asura=ahura.*

[30] On the Avesta as a historical source there is a useful essay by P. Oktor Skjaervo in George Erdosy (ed.), *The Indo-Aryans*, pp. 155–76.

[31] Cf. O.R. Gurney, *The Hittites*, Harmondsworth, 1952, pp. 123–25, 128–9. A similar inference follows from what we know of a possibly proto-Aryan people called the Kassites, appearing in Western Iran and Mesopotamia after 1800 BC. These people, whose own language remains unknown, worshipped, along with a number of local deities, the gods Shuriash and Maruttash, widely believed to represent the Indo-Aryan gods Surya and Marut. No other remnants of Kassite language, except their Aryan-looking ethnic name, survive. (See J. Harmatta, in: *History of Civilization of Central Asia*, Vol. I, (ed.) A.H. Dani and V.M. Masson, Paris, 1992, pp. 370–72.)

[32] For the assimilative elements in Brahmanism see D.D. Kosambi *An Introduction to the Study of Indian History*, Bombay, 1956, esp. Chapters IV and V.

[33] In India this would involve not only the early history of Dravidian languages, but also the origins of Prakritisms found in both the *Rigveda* and the Mitanni dialect, and such curiosities as the 'L' dialect that underlay Asokan Magadhi in eastern India.

[34] Leonard Woolley, *Beginnings of Civilization* (UNESCO: *History of Mankind*, Vol. I, Part 2), New York, 1965, pp. 406–432, offers an authoritative survey of Mesopotamian contributions to mathematics and astronomy. It is a pity that the UNESCO's second effort, *History of Humanity*, Vol. II, Paris, 1996, has nothing comparable to this account.

[35] Cf. Richard Saloman, *Indian Epigraphy*, New Delhi, 1998, p. 182. It must be understood that the years of the epoch are irrelevant for evidence of first

use. The Kaliyuga era of 3102 BC is first attested only in the Aihole inscription of AD 634–35!

36 G. Thibaut: in Debiprasad Chattopadhyaya (ed.), *Studies in the History of Science in India*, New Delhi, 1982, II, pp. 486–7.

37 Cf. L. Woolley, *Beginnings of Civilization*, p. 417.

38 Cf. R. Ghirshman, *Iran from the Earliest Times to the Islamic Conquest*, Harmondsworth, pp. 163–4.

39 See H.A.R. Bivar's chapter, 'Indus Lands', in: *The Cambridge Ancient History*, 2nd ed., Vol. IV (*c.* 525 to 479 BC), (ed.) J. Boardman *et al.*, Cambridge, 1988, pp. 194–210.

40 On these inscriptions see B.N. Mukherjee, *Studies in Aramaic Edicts of Asoka*, Calcutta, 1984.

41 Richard Saloman, *Indian Epigraphy*, pp. 11–13. The term *lipi* itself is probably derived from Old Persian *dipi.*

42 Cf. ibid., pp. 51–54.

43 Sten Konow, *Kharoshthi Inscriptions* (being *Corpus Inscriptionum Indicarum*, Vol. II), Calcutta, 1929, pp. 46, 48–49.

44 J. Harmatta in: *History of Civilizations of Central Asia*, II, (ed.) J. Harmatta, Paris, 1994, pp. 409–16.

45 Ibid., pp. 422–33.

46 Cf. B.N. Mukherjee, *The Rise and Fall of Kushana Empire*, Calcutta, 1988, pp. 386–89.

47 See R.E. Emmerick, 'Buddhism among Iranian Peoples', in: Ehsan Yarshater (ed.), *Cambridge History of Iran*, Vol. 3(2), Cambridge, 1985, pp. 949–64.

48 See G. Widengren in: E. Yarshetar, *op. cit.*, pp. 960, 983, 985; R. Ghirshman, *Iran*, pp. 315–16.

49 For an interpretation of the Mediterranean evidence, see Thorkild Schioler, *Roman and Islamic Water-lifting Wheels*, Odense, 1973, pp. 168–9.

50 For my own observations, also cited by Ishrat Alam, see *Indian Journal of History of Science*, Vol. 35(3) (2000), pp. 247–9.

51 Ilse Kohler-Rollefson, in: D.R. Harris, *The Origins and Spread of Agriculture and Pastoralism*, p. 288.

52 Cf. J.H. Marshall and Daya Ram Sahani, in: *Archaeological Survey of India: Annual Report, 1909–10*, Calcutta, pp. 97–98, with illustration.

53 Samuel Beal, *Si-Yu-Ki, Buddhist Records of the Western World*, London, 1884, II, p. 272. Cf. Thomas Watters, *On Yuan Chwang's Travels in India, 629–645 AD*, London, 1905, II, p. 252, who, in his abridgement of the narrative, just mentions 'dromedaries'.

54 I. Kohler-Rollfeson, *The Origins and Spread of Agriculture and Pastoralism*, p. 288.

55 Amir Khusrau, *Nuh Sipihr*, (ed.) Mohammad Wahid Mirza, London, 1950, p. 170.

56 My own discussion of the evidence will be found in *Indian Journal of History of Science*, Vol. 35(3) (2000), pp. 271–4.

57 Cf. A. Berriedale Keith, *A History of Sanskrit Literature*, London, 1920, pp. 246–48.

58 See C. Brockelmann's masterly article, reprinted in *Encyclopaedia of Islam*, 2nd ed., Leiden, 1978, Vol. IV, pp. 503–06, from where much of the preceding information is taken.

59 For a description of this game in India see Alberuni's account (*c.* 1035) in his *Kitab al-Hind* (transl. Edward C. Sachau, *Alberuni's India*, London, 1910, I, pp.183–5). Cf. A.L. Basham, *The Wonder that was India*, New York, 1950, p. 208.

60 *Chachnama*, ed. Umar bin Muhammad Daudpota, Delhi, 1939, pp. 232–3. The phrase *shah mat shud* ('checkmate',) was to be uttered by the host ruler as a signal for the fugitive prince's murder; the conspiracy failed, however. The English word 'checkmate' incidentally derives from the Persian words *shah mat*, 'the king is beaten'.

61 For the formation of New Persian and its early literature down to Firdausi, see Jan Rypka, *History of Iranian Literature*, Dordrecht, 1968, pp. 71–171; and, for a shorter account, G. Lazard in: R.N. Frye (ed.), *The Cambridge History of Iran*, Vol. 4, Cambridge, 1975, pp. 595–632.

62 On the Turk empire see D. Sinor and S.G. Klyashtorny in: *History of Civilizations of Central Asia*, III, (ed.) B.A. Litvinsky, Paris, 1996, pp. 327–48.

63 See Ehsan Yarshater (ed.), *The Cambridge History of Iran*, Vol. 3(1), Cambridge, 1983, pp. 409, 613. On the earlier Turan, see Irfan Habib in: *Proceedings of the Indian History Congress*, Aligarh (1994) session, Calcutta, 1995, p. 78. Since Turan was within the Indian borderland, may one imagine that the *Shahnama* or its precursors transferred an ancient tradition of Indo-Iranian hostility to a different ethnic theatre altogether?

64 This too is the case of a curious transfer. 'Tazik' (Persian: *tazi*) was Middle Persian for Arab, seen as a marauder. Perhaps, because of increasing Iranian predominance in Muslim polities, the name was transferred to the Iranians by non-Arab outsiders. See Pushpa Prasad, 'The name "Tajik"', in: Aligarh Volume of Papers for the Indian History Congress, 1995, pp.215-19.

65 Cf. I. Habib, 'Formation of the Sultanate Ruling Class of the Thirteenth Century', in: *Medieval India-1*, (ed.) I. Habib, Delhi, 1992, pp. 1–21.

66 *Nuh Sipihr*, *op.cit.*, pp. 178–79.

67 D.D. Kosambi, *An Introduction to the Study of Indian History*, p. 370.

68 A.U. Pope and P. Ackerman, *A Survey of Persian Art*, reissue, Teheran, 1964, I, p. 428; II, pp. 551–2 and *passim*; III, pp. 908–9.

69 See Jan Marek's study of Indo-Persian literature in the Mughal period, in: J. Rypka, *op. cit.*, pp. 721–34.

70 See the excellent analysis in Said Amir Arjomand, *The Shadow of God and the Hidden Imam*, Chicago, 1984.

71 Cf. Irfan Habib, 'A Political Theory for the Mughal Empire—a Study of the Ideas of Abu'l Fazl', in: *Proceedings of the Indian History Congress*, Patiala (1998) session, Aligarh, 1999, pp. 329–40; Iqtidar A. Khan, 'Akbar's Personality Traits and World Outlook', in: *Akbar and his India*, (ed.) I. Habib, New Delhi, 2000, pp. 79–96; and M. Athar Ali, '*Sulh-i Kul* and the Religious

Ideas of Akbar', in: *Studies in History*, New Delhi, IV(i), 1982, pp. 27–39. The questions raised by the Shi'ite transformation of Islam in Iran for Akbar and his circle have yet to be critically studied.

72 Abu'l Fazl, *A'in-i Akbari*, ed. H. Blochmann, Calcuta, 1867–77, pp. 158–61.

73 The most clearly printed, and the sole annotated edition of the *Dabistan-i Mazahib* is that of Riza Zadeh Malik, Tehran, Solar 1342, 2 vols. It is not, however, a critical edition of the text.

74 Cf. S.H. Nasr in: *Cambridge History of Iran*, Vol. 6, (ed.) P. Jackson and L. Lockhart, Cambridge, 1986, pp. 678–87.

75 The originally Jewish scholar, poet and martyr, Sarmad (*d.* 1660) learnt *hakimmiyat* under both these scholars before coming to India (*Dabistan-i Mazahib*, (ed.) Malik, I, p. 215).

76 Ibid., pp. 337–41.

77 Thus a contemporary testimony: Azad Bilgrami, *Ma'asiru'l Kiram*, ed. Abdu'l Haq, Hyderabad (Dn.), 1910, I, pp. 220–21.

78 To take examples from his Urdu poetry, where these 'lapses' occur more frequently, see such post-1908 verses of his as 'Ram', 'Nanak', 'Panjab ke Dihqan se', 'Iblis ka farman', and 'Dozakhi ki Manajat' (*Kulliyat-i Iqbal: Urdu*, Aligarh, 2001, pp. 177, 239, 444, 608, 666).

79 See Roy Mottahedeh, *The Mantle of the Prophet*, New York, 1985, pp. 126–33, for the story of how Mossadegh's fall was brought about. A cautious Western historian tells us: 'This tenacious rumour [of American purchase of men to overthrow Mossadegh] has been fully confirmed and is now seen as incontrovertible' (Gavin Hambly in *Cambridge History of Iran*, Vol. 7, (ed.) P. Avery and G. Hambly, Cambridge, 1991, p. 263). Hambly's account of the *ulama's* abandonment of the nationalists (ibid., p. 262) is identical with that of Mottahedeh.

80 For such a portrayal, through a series of misstatements and insinuations, see the new official textbook of the Government of India's National Council of Educational Research and Training (NCERT), *Contemporary India*, by Hari Om *et al.*, New Delhi, 2002. This book is now required reading for pupils of Class IX in schools affiliated to the Central Government's board. In its entire narrative of the National Movement, Jawaharlal Nehru has been practically blacked out, with no mention of his socialist views; and the Communists have been blackened. One hopes that the Iranian school pupils are offered a fairer description of the various elements involved in their national struggle.

81 Roy Mottahedeh, *The Mantle of the Prophet*, p. 9.

The Indian emperor Jahangir embraces the Iranian Shah ‘Abbas I above the globe to govern a world in which the lion and the goat can live together in peace. Miniature by Abu’l Hasan, Mughal artist, *c.* 1620.

Iranian gem-cutter in the Deccan. Adilshahi painting, early seventeenth century.

India–Iran Contacts in Prehistory

M.K. Dhavalikar

Contacts between India and Iran were very intimate during the medieval period as also in the early historical period when some of the northwestern regions of the sub-continent—Sindh and Gandhara—formed part of the Achaemenian empire (Wheeler 1947–48). Even earlier, in the fourth millennium BC, Elam in southern Iran extended from Mesopotamia into Baluchistan before its annexation into the Achaemenian empire in the sixth century cent BC.With the discovery of the Indus civilization in the early twenties of the twentieth century, a few artefacts that turned up at Harappan sites, Harappa and Mohenjodaro, indicated that the antiquity of the contacts between the two regions could be stretched back to the third millennium BC. This was quite natural as these countries were neighbours with a common border between Baluchistan and Iran. The nature of this contact, however, could become clear only during recent years when large scale excavations in both countries brought to light fresh evidence demonstrating that the contact was not of the nature of a few knick-knacks of one country finding their way into the other, but that there was regular trade between them. This became evident because of the discovery of hundreds of inscribed clay tablets in the excavations carried out in West Asia recording the lists of traded good (Leemans 1960). There is evidence to show that this trade began as early as the early centuries of third millennium and developed in the middle of the millennium reaching its zenith during the time of Sargon of Akkad (2371–16 BC). But shortly after, it dwindled during 2200–2000 BC and was reduced to a trickle in the early second millennium BC. For a thousand years, from 1600 BC to sixth century cent BC, there does not seem to have been any contact for which the deteriorating environment was to a great extent responsible (Singh 1971). This was a period of stress and strain almost all over the Old World when many of the early civilizations were shattered because of the onslaught of a people who had weapons of iron and the fast moving steed-horse.

The flourishing trading contact with West Asia in the third millennium is evident from references in the cuneiform documents which record that trade goods were imported from three countries in the east namely Dilmun, Makan and Meluhha, in that order. Although these have been respectively identified with Bahrein, Makran Coast and India (the Harappan territory), it has also been argued that they all were three different provinces of the Indus civilization in India (Thapar 1975). This view, however, has not been accepted and it is now generally held that, of the three, Meluhha was Harappan India for the simple reason that raw materials for the trade goods from Meluhha was available only in India. Thus in the pre-Harappan (or the Early Harappan) times the contact with Iran is indicated by the occurrence of shell bangles at Shahr-i-Sokhta (*c.* 2800 BC) in Elam (South Iran) (Durante 1979). They are made of chank shell (*Xancus pyrum*) which is found only at two places in India namely Saurashtra coast from Jamnagar to Veraval and the Gulf of Mannar in the south which, however, was not exploited at such an early date. It has been surmised that the shell bangles were cut at the factory site at Balakot in Sindh (Durante 1979) but it is highly likely that the raw material was obtained from Saurashtra as the particular variety of shell is plentifully available in that region. It may be mentioned in this context that a rich shell cutting centre of the Harappan period has been discovered at Nageshwar near Jamnagar (Hegde *et al.* 1990). It has been observed that the Harappan traders from Sindh were making forays into Kutch and Saurashtra for procuring raw materials which they stored in the small but well-fortified Harappan settlements as at Surkotada and Desalpar in Kutch which were later transported to their industrial centres like Chanhudaro and Balakot in Sindh. When the trade developed, they established manufacturing centres in Saurashtra itself such as those at Nageshwar, Kuntasi and others (Dhavalikar 1994).

All this trade between India and West Asia which has been recorded in the tablet inscriptions was both overland and by sea. The overland trade was carried through Sindh, and Iran being midway, had to pass through it. The sea trade too had to pass through Iranian ports for the simple reason that the marine technology was still in a primitive state and the boats therefore had to keep close to the coast. It is therefore highly likely that Tepe Yahya in south Iran served as a central place in this trade, as argued by Lamberg-Karlovsky (1972).

Trade goods

The numerous tablet inscriptions that have been found in West Asia record lists of articles imported from Meluhha. Many of these have been reported from sites in Iran such as Sialik, Hissar, Tepe Yahya, Shahdad and so on. It is clear that they were exported from India. They are as follows.

Carnelian beads

Carnelian is a semi-precious stone, reddish in colour and extremely fine grained. Although it is found in different regions of the sub-continent, it is abundant in Gujarat. It occurs in the veins of rocks of the Satpuras and was mined from pre-Harappan times. Even today the Cambay bead industry is in a flourishing state (Arkell 1936). Carnelian beads are found in a variety of shapes, but the most common is the long barrel shape, with the length ranging from 5 cm. to 10 cm., and a few specimens are even 12 cm. in length. They were in great demand in Mesopotamia as their occurrence indicates. Another variety was that of etched beads which had white patterns etched on the bead by a chemical process (Beck 1933). Carnelian beads have been reported from several sites in Iran which include Hissar, Shah Tepe, Marlik, Shahdad, Shahr-i-Sokhta, Tepe Yahya and so on. The etched variety too occurred at some of these sites as at Susa and Hissar (Chakrabarti 1990: 98; Chakrabarti and Moghadam 1977). In Gujarat, Lothal was a very important centre for manufacturing beads as is evident from the bead factory discovered at the site (Rao 1982: II, 580ff). Since the colour of the stone is not uniform, the stones—rough-outs—were heated in a kiln which lent them a deep rich hue. Kuntasi (district Rajkot) was also an important centre for beadmaking (Dhavalikar *et al.* 1994).

Gold Beads

A jewellery hoard recovered in the course of excavation at Lothal contained, among other items, a few gold beads with axial tubes that belong to the third phase of Period A. The beads are disc-shaped and have the perforation in the form an axial tube in the middle (Rao 1982: XXIX, B). Identical specimens have also been reported from

Harappa and Mohenjodaro, but their occurrence at Hissar in Iran is significant. The latter, however, are oval and rectangular in shape. They have been assigned to Period III B which is contemporaneous with the Mature phase of the Indus civilization. Similar beads occur at many sites in Iran and even in Greece. It suggests that the technique of making these beads was widespread in many parts of the Old World, and one has therefore to agree with Romila Thapar's observation that this process was 'probably not brought about by invasion or large-scale migration so much as by migration of technologies and ideas, travelling repeatedly across the borders of northwestern India and West Asia over many centuries, and in both directions' (Thapar 1975: 341).

Copper

Among the goods imported from Meluhha into West Asia, the most enigmatic is copper for the simple reason that even at present India is deficient in copper and imports it in large quantities. But the Meluhhans, like their present-day successors—the Gujaratis and the Sindhis—were hardcore merchant-traders and exported whatever was possible, keeping with them the minimum that was needed. The export of copper to West Asia is confirmed without a shadow of doubt on the basis of the copper ingots found at Lothal and at Susa. These are bun-shaped ingots bearing close similarity in size, weight and their composition and are thus identical at both sites. What is more, in the excavation at Lothal, a copper-smelting furnace was found in which was a pottery bowl for melting copper ingots (Rao 1989: II, 520ff). The trace elemental analysis of specimens from both sites would have strengthened Rao's view of export from Lothal but the identical shape of the buns and their uniform weight suggests that they may have originated from Lothal.

It is indeed interesting that the corpus of copper objects form Harappan sites is impressive. The smelting furnace at Lothal was a circular structure of mud bricks (1.80m. in diameter and 67.5 cm. deep) and was located near the coppersmith's workshop. The mud plaster on bricks was completely vitrified because of prolonged use and some molten metal was noticed on the ground (Rao 1985: II, 520ff). The bun-shaped ingot contained 99.81 per cent pure copper. It is noteworthy that the ingots from Susa, like those from Lothal, have a concave undersurface and short projections. A copper-smelting furnace was also uncovered at Kuntasi (Dhavalikar *et al.* 1996: Fig. 6.2a).

The general opinion seems to be that India is deficient in copper, maybe for our present needs, but it must be stated that there are rich deposits of copper in western India which the Harappans must have exploited. There are four known sources of copper today (Raghunandan *et al.* 1981) and the most important among these is the Deri-Ambamata belt (district Banaskantha, Gujarat) which runs to a length of 8–10 km. its maximum width being 100 m. and the depth at places up to 480 m. This belt continues upto Sirohi in Rajasthan and large dumps of slag of about 0.6 million tons are found in the area from Ambaji to Kumbharia. There is evidence of mining the ore from this area from about the first century AD upto fifteenth century (Sharma 1968). In the same Banaskantha district is located the Kui-Chitrasani belt which runs to a length of 45 km. up to Kui in Sirohi district of Rajasthan. The Harappans may have exploited these deposits.

Incidentally, the term Meluhha has been explained as Meluhha>*melakkha* (Prakrit)>*mlechchha* (Sanskrit). Among the many diverse meanings of *mlechaha*, the one that is significant is copper which suggests that because copper was imported into West Asia from western India, it got the name Meluhha in the same way as Cyprus got its because of copper (*cupros*) and Argentina because of silver (*argent*) (Dhavalikar 1997a).

Wood

Varieties of timber were imported from Meluhha in West Asia for building construction and making boats. Teak (*Tectona grandis*) and Deodar (*Cedrus deodara*), which grow abundantly in the Himalayan foothills, was used by the Harappans for boat-building and making agricultural implements and carts and the same may have been imported into West Asia. Texts refer to a throne made of Meluhha wood inlaid with lapis lazuli (Ratnagar 1981: 98). It may be mentioned that *sisum* wood was exported in the early historical times from the port of Broach to Susa (Gershevitch 1957) and it is therefore likely that this also happened in the protohistoic times. The wood is available in the forests of Girnar and the Western Ghats.

Lapis Lazuli

Lapis (*lajavard*, Iranian and Gujarati *rajavaral*) is recorded to have been an item of import from Meluhha, but it is doubtful whether it was imported into Iran for the simple reason that the Badakshan mine in Afghanistan which has the finest lapis in the Old World, was much nearer and seems to have been exploited by the Iranians. Lapis workshops have been encountered at Shahari-i-Sokhta near the Afghan border, and also at Tepe Yahya in south Iran. India does not have much lapis worth the name and whatever little is available is of a coarser variety (Chakraborti 1978). But it is noteworthy that in the early centuries of the Christian era lapis was exported from western India. Romila Thapar (1975: 9–10) has noted the occurrence of the stone in the northern part of Satpuras which is known as Vaidurya-Parvat (Greek *oroudian*) and it is therefore not unlikely that the same may have found way to the Yahya workshops. It may be noted that some of the lapis beads in West Asian museums have been found to be of sodalite that originated in India (Kenoyer.pers.comm.). This is an instance of unfair trade practice of protohistoric times.

Shell

Another important item of trade was shell, particularly the chank shell (*shankh*) (*Xancus pyrum*). It was used for making bangles and inlays. It is abundant on the western coast of Saurashtra and the excavations at Nageshwar have brought to light a flourishing shell-cutting industry at the site, a sort of industrial estate of our own times (Hegde *et al.* 1990). It is also available in Sindh and similar centres were located at Balakot and Allahdino. In Iran, the excavation at Shahr-i-Sokhta have yielded a number of shell objects such as beads, pendants, two small vessels and two stamp seals as also wasters. They also occur at Tepe Hissar, Tepe Yahya and Bampur which is in Iranian Seistan (de Cardi 1970).

Nageshwar, an important shell cutting centre (district Jamnagar) is located 8 km. southeast of Poshitra Bay and 6 km. east of Pindar Bay coasts. The ancient site is littered with thousands of fragments of chank shell (*Turbinella pyrum*) which is the same as *Xancus pyrum* and Gastropod (*Chicoreus ramosus L*) along with shell bangles, inlay pieces and ladles. The geomorphological investigations indicate that the sea level was higher some 4,000 years ago (Gupta 1977) and a creek was formed rendering Okhamandal almost an island when the Harappans lived here.

Ivory

Cuneiform inscriptions record that ivory was imported from Dilmun. But Dilmun has been identified with Bahrein where there were no elephants. However, only once ivory has been mentioned as coming from Meluhha. It is highly likely that ivory trade was probably in the hands of Arab middlemen as was the case later in the early centuries of Christian era. It is therefore evident that ivory was exported from India and in this context it may be noted that Saurashtra was known for elephants as stated by Kautilya (*Arthasastra*: II, 50). Harappan sites have yielded evidence of ivory carving. Ivory beads have been reported from Hissar in Iran.

Seals

Steatite stamp seals constitute a distinctive feature of the Indus civilization. They occur at Lothal, Surkotada, Bagasra, Dholavira and other sites in Kutch and Saurashtra. Harappan-like seals and seal impressions have been found at Iranian sites too (Potts 1999: 120). From Tepe Yahya comes a pottery fragment stamped with an Indus seal and a seal itself from Kalleh Nissar. The typical Harappan bull appears on a cylinder seal from Hissar as also from Susa. Besides, three Harappan seals have been reported from the Luristan region. A terracotta cake from Tepe Yahya bears in the middle a square seal impression depicting a person seated in the typical Indian cross-legged posture and with raised hands whereas the potsherd with the Indus seal impression has also an inscription in the Harappan script. It is radiocarbon-dated to 2320 + 135 BC when the trade between the two countries was at its zenith.

Reserve slip ware

A particular type of ceramics known as reserve slip ware which occurs at many Harappan sites, supposed to be of West Asian origin. It also occurs in Iran in the third millennium BC levels and the technique of making it is said to have come to India from West Asia. The vessels of this ware are treated with two slips of two different colours, one over the other; the upper one is removed at places exposing the lower slip, thus creating a contrasting pattern. Pottery of this variety has been reported from Lothal, Surkotada, Dholavira, Kuntasi and many other sites in Gujarat, and in Iran it is found at Bampur which is in Iranian Seistan (de Cardi 1970: 279, fig. 17.8). Although it has been argued that the technique may have been independently evolved in India (Chakrabarti 1975: 337ff), it is likely that its origin can be traced in Iran considering the fact that it was a specialized technique.

Silver

A number of articles are mentioned in the cuneiform inscriptions as imports from India (Meluhha) but there is hardly any mention of exports from West Asia. What did the Harappans get in exchange? It has been argued that the exports may have been 'invisible', that is, those perishable items such as foodstuffs, cloth, wool, leather, fish, perfumes and even slaves which have not left any trace in the archaeological record (Crawford 1973). Even though there is no archaeological evidence, they would have found mention in the tablet inscriptions. But the documents are silent and we have only to make a guess. It is highly likely that the Iranians paid for their imports from India in the form of silver. India is deficient in silver, but a good quantity of silver has been reported from Harappan sites, especially Mohenjodaro and Harappa and the recent work at Kunal (Haryana) and Mandi (UP) have yielded excellent silver jewellery (Lal 1998: 7–10, 48). It is pertinent to point out in this context the discovery at Mohenjodaro of a few pieces of silver with cuneiform symbols punched on them (Kosambi 1941).

This silver in all likelihood came from Iran as Mesopotamia does not have much of it, but there are large deposits in Iran in the southwest region of Lake Urmia, Damghan area, Fars and southeast Iran. It must be mentioned that silver is always obtained as a by-product of smelting of other metals such as lead, copper, gold, and zinc. (Ratnagar 1981: 140ff). But in India, even today silver has to be imported in large quantities. It is surprising that there is no mention of silver in the *Rgveda*; there is no word for it and in the later Vedic literature it is referred to as 'white gold' (*rajata-hiranya*). The metal was impure to Vedic Aryans to whom it was nothing but tears of god Rudra (Altekar 1953: 17). But in Iran there were silver weapons which figure in Elamite texts, and silver jewellery and even ingots have been found at Susa.

Miscellaneous Articles

There are quite a few articles from Harappan sites which are strikingly similar to those in contemporary Iran. Thus the fish-scale design on Harappan pottery is to be seen on Susa I ceramics, and perforated jars at Yahya. The typical humped bull of India is carved on stone vases at Yahya. (Asthana 1976: 42ff). The leaf-shaped knife from Hissar III is paralleled at Kuntasi and so also the triangular arrowheads. (Dhavalikar *et al.* 1994: 218; fig. 7.18–7.19). Cubical chert weights from Iranian sites can easily be mistaken as Harappans. (Asthana 1976: 54). The obsidian flake from Prabhas Patan (Dhavalikar 1984) possibly came from eastern Iran where it is well documented (Beale 1973: 136). Spiral-headed copper/bronze hairpins were common in both the countries. (Piggott 1947–48)

The trade between India and Iran that began in early third millennium, peaked during *c.* 2500–2200 BC after which it began to dwindle possibly because of, among other factors, the adverse environment. It seems that severe aridity set in from *c.* 2000 BC in India (Singh 1971) while in West Asia there were a series of tectonic movements (Weiss *et al.* 1993). Some exchange may have been there as can be inferred from the obsidian flake from Somnath and stealite stamp seals, one each from Prabhas Patan and Rangpur (Dhavalikar 1997b: 108–09, Fig. 2.12) but it completely stopped by mid-second millennium till the time of Darius in the sixth century BC.

Iranian Contact with Chalcolithic Cultures

The trade between India and Iran dwindled from the beginning of the second millennium BC as is clear from the evidence from excavations. But since they are neighbours some interaction was natural. This was the period that witnessed large-scale migration of peoples and it is precisely this time which, according to some scholars, marked the advent of the Vedic Aryans in India. The close affinity between the Vedic Sanskrit and the language of the *Avesta* is always cited in support of this hypothesis. This, however, is rather hard to accept for the simple reason that the *Rgveda* is much earlier than the *Avesta* in point of time and it is now argued that the Aryans came to India from Bactria-Margiana region (Parpola 1988). Be that as it may, the Aryan problem is beyond the purview of the present paper, but it must be conceded that there must have been some interaction between the two peoples as they were neighbours.

In the middle of the twentieth century, with the discovery of post-Harappan chalcolithic cultures in central India and the Deccan, the problem arose about their authorship. The late Professor H.D. Sankalia then undertook excavation at Navdatoli incentral India with a view to testing the historicity of Puranic legends. Initially, he was of the opinion that probably Bhils, an aboriginal tribe of western India, may have been the succesors of Malwa and other chalcolithic cultures of central and western India. But his large-scale excavation at Navdatoli in 1957–59 yielded evidence of Iranian elements in the material equipment of the Malwa culture people. This led him to review the whole problem afresh. He noticed that there were close similarities in pottery forms and their design ornamentation between the Malwa painted ceramics and those from some Iranian sites. The chalices and pedestalled bowls from Navdatoli have no parallels in the country but have almost exact analogues in Iran. The channel-spouted cups are not different from those at Hissar and Sialk. These are specialized forms and so also is the design element, and as such they cannot be brushed as mere coincidences, but are significant. He states:

> It is not possible to say who these people were. Aryans or pre-Aryan Nagas, for instance, as the Puranic traditions imply. Evidence is, however, accumulating to suggest that the painted pottery people of the Narmada valley . . . had relations with or were influenced by the late Iranian Bronze (and Early Iron) Age cultures knowing the horse, in addition to the channel spouted cups . . . we have another specialized vessel which occurs only in Necropolis B at Sialk. (Sankalia *et al.* 1958: xii–xiii)

His views were further substantiated by his excavations that yielded additional evidence. 'Prolonged study of the pottery of the historic and the protohistoric period in India and outside has led the writer to postulate the view that these exotic forms show Iranian or West Asiatic contacts or influence' (Sankalia *et al.* 1971: 415; 1973).

Sankalia's views were vehemently criticized by D.K. Chakrabarti (1977: 32–34) who argued that the analogies were far too general to be of any use in a valid and meaningful archaeological comparison. According to him, the parallels are mere coincidences and may be of independent evolution. However, it must be conceded that the analogues are highly specialized forms which have no parallels in India either earlier and even later. Vessels with stands, pedestals, handles and lugs have hardly antecedents in India and the chalices and pedestalled bowls from Navdatoli form a class by themselves and are enigmatic. They are later in point of time than their analogues in Iran and need explanation.

Elamite and Dravidian

Elam in southern Iran, as already stated, extended into Baluchistan in the fourth millennium BC. The Elamite is said to belong to the Dravidian language group. Although the Proto-Elamite, which was in use from the fourth millennium BC to 2200 BC, has not been deciphered yet, the script is very similar to the Harappan script. From mid-third millennium, the Elamite adopted the cuneiform script. Since it has been argued that the Harappan civilization was non-Aryan —Dravidian—and that Brahmi, a Dravidian language, is spoken in a few hilly pockets of Baluchistan, it has been hypothesized that the Dravidians, like Aryans, came into India from the west and are not the autochthons of South India. From Elam they migrated to the Indus valley through Baluchistan when the Indus civilization was at its zenith and thence moved to South India (McAlpin 1978). This theory, however, does not credit the Dravidians as the authors of the Indus civilization and some new evidence is becoming available to substantiate it.

Indo-Aryans

The trading contact between India and Iran that existed in the third millennium did not continue in the second millennium which was a period of great upheaval. It marks the arrival of Aryans in India, according to some whereas others hold that it is from India that the Aryans spread into other lands. This has been the knottiest problem in the history of India and in spite of the best efforts of renowned scholars, the solution is nowhere in sight. We need not here enter into a discussion of this problem, but can only state that although there is no evidence from archaeology, the linguistic evidence, which is quite formidable, clearly indicates that the Vedic Aryans and the early Iranians in all likelihood formed one group in the hoary past, but were separated later in the second millennium BC. This is evident from the close similarity between the language of the *Rgveda* and that of the *Avesta* which is later in than the former.

Some evidence has now become available that compels us to review the problem afresh. K.A.R. Kennedy who has examined almost every ancient human skeleton found in South Asia, writes:

> When multi-variate studies are made using data from populations of the Mediterranean Western Asia and the area influenced by the ancient Harappans in South Asia, a biological continuum extending over some five millennia is demonstrable. In short, the ancient Harappans are not markedly different in their skeletal biology from their present day inhabitants of northwestern India and Pakistan which, in turn, share a high frequency of phenotype characters with both and ancient living people of Afghanistan, Iran and the lands bordering the Aegean and the Mediterranean. (Kennedy 1984: 102)

The latest evidence from the excavations at Harappa is also corroborative:

> Together these data suggest that Harappan phase individuals . . . bear closest affinities to populations from the west, i.e. from the Iranian plateau to and the Near East . . . with closest affinities outside the Indus valley to the inhabitants of Tepe Hissar III (3000–2000 BC), these biological data can be interpreted to suggest that peoples to the west interacted with those of the Indus valley during this and the preceding Proto-Elamite period and thus may have influenced the development of the Harappan civilization. (Hemphill, Lukacs and Kennedy 1991: 74)

Further, it has also been noticed that biologically there was no difference in the Harappan population of the Mature phase of Cemetery R37 and the late phase represented by Cemetery H at Harappa, implying thereby that they were one and the same people. This is a very significant conclusion that deserves close attention. It is pregnant with many possibilities which, however, lie beyond the scope of the present paper. But it suggests that there was very intimate interaction between the people of India and those of Iran, even in prehistoric times.

References

Altekar, A.S., 1953, 'Origin and early history of coinage in India', *JNSI*, 15: 1–26.

Arkell, A.J., 1936, 'Cambay and the Bead Trade', *Antiquity*, 10: 292–305.

Asthana, Shashi, 1976, *History and Archaeology of India's Contacts with Other Countries*. Delhi: B.R. Pub. Co.

Beale, G.W., 1973, 'Early Trade in Highland Iran', *World Archaeology*, 5: 133–48.

Beck, Horace, 1933, 'Etched Carnelian Beads', *Antiquaries Jr.*, 13: 384–98.

Chakrabarti, Dilip K., 1974, 'Gujarat Harappan connection with West Asia—A Reconsideration of the evidence', *JESHO*, 18: 337–42.

———, 1977, 'India and West Asia: Alternative Approach', *Man and Environment* 1: 25–38.

———, 1978, 'Lapis lazuli in Early India', *Man and Environment.* 2: 51–58.

———, 1990, *The External Trade of the Indus Civilization*. New Delhi: Munshiram Manoharlal.

Chakrabarti, D.K. and Parveen Moghadam, 1977, 'Some unpublished Indus beads from Iran', *Iran*, 15: 166–68.

Crawford, H.E.W., 1973, 'Mesopotamia's Invisible Exports in the Third Millennium BC', *World Archaeology*, 5: 232–41.

De Cardi, Beatrice, 1970, *Excavation at Bampur*. New York.

Dhavalikar, M.K., 1978, 'An Early Warehouse on the Western Coast', *Puratattva*, 9: 100–03.

———, 1984, 'Sub-Indus Cultures of Central and Western India', in B.B. Lal and S.P. Gupta (eds), *Frontiers of Indus Civilization—Sir Mortimer Wheeler Comm. Vol.* New Delhi: Books & Books.

———, 1994, *Cultural Imperialism: Indus Civilization in Western India*. New Delhi: Books & Books.

———, 1997a, 'Meluhha: The Land of Copper', *South Asian Studies*,13:275–79

———, 1997b, *Indian Protohistory*. New Delhi: Books & Books.

Dhavalikar, M.K. *et al.*, 1996, *Kuntasi: A Harappan Emporium on West Coast*. Pune: Deccan College.

Durante, S., 1979, 'The utilization of *Xancus pyrum* (L) at Shahr-i-Sokhta—Further evidence of cultural contacts between India and Iran in the 4th—3rd millennium BC', *South Asian Archaeology 1975*. 27–42. Leiden: E.J. Brill.

Gershevitch, I., 1957, 'Sisoo at Susa', *BSOAS*, 19: 319.

Gupta, S.K., 1977, 'Quarternary Sea-level changes on the Saurashtra Coast', in D.P. Agrawal and B.M. Pande (eds), *Ecology and Archaeology of Western India*, 181–93. Delhi: Concept Pub. Co.

Singh, Gurdip, 1971, 'The Indus Valley Culture seen in the context of Post-Glacial climatic and ecological changes in NW India', *Archaeology & Physical Anthopology, in Oceania* 6: 177–88.

Hegde, K.T.M., *et al.*, 1990, *Excavations at Nageshwar 1984*. Baroda.

Hemphill, B.E., J.R. Lucaks and K.A.R. Kennedy, 1991, 'Biological adaptations and affinities of Bronze Age Harappans', in R.H. Meadow (ed.), *Harappa Excavations 1986–90: A Multi-disciplinary Approach to Third Millennium Urbanism*, 137–82. Madison: Monographs in World Archaeology.

Kennedy, K.A.R., 1984, 'Trauma and Disease in the Ancient Harappans', in B.B. Lal and S.P. Gupta (eds), *Frontiers of Indus Civilization, Wheeler* Vol. 425–36. New Delhi: Books & Books.

Kosambi, D.D., 1941, 'On the Origin and Development of Silver Coinage in India', *Current Science*, 10: 395–400.

Lal, B.B., 1998, *India 1947–97: New Light on the Indus Civilization.* New Delhi: Aryan Books International.

Lamberg-Karlovsky, C.C., 1971, 'Trade Mechanisms in Indus-Mesopotamian interrelations', *Journal of American Oriental Society*, 92: 145–62.

Leemans, W., 1960, *Foreign Trade in the Old Babylonian Period.* Leiden: E.J. Brill.

McAlpin, D.W., 1978, 'Linguistic Prehistory: The Dravidian Situation', in M.M. Deshpande and P.E. Hook, *Aryan and Non-Aryans in India.* 175–83. Ann Arbor: University of Michigan.

Parpola, Asko, 1988, 'The Coming of the Aryans to Iran and India and the Cultural and Ethnic Identity of the Dasas', *International Jr. of Dravidian Linquistics*, 17: 85–229.

Piggott, Stuart, 1947–48, 'Notes on certain pins and a mace head from Harappa', *Ancient India*, 4: 26–40.

Possehl, Gregory, 1979, *Indus Civilization in Saurashtra.* Delhi: BR Publishing Corpn.

Potts, D.T., 1997, *The Archaeology of Elam.* Cambridge: Cambridge Univ. Press.

Raghunandan, *et al.*, 1980, 'Exploration for copper, lead and zinc in India', *Bulletin of Geological Survey of India*, Series A. Economic Geology No. 47. Calcutta: Government of India.

Rao, S.R., 1965, 'Shipping and Maritime Trade of the Indus People', *Expedition* 7: 30–37.

———, 1979 and 1982, *Lothal: A Harappan Port Town (1955–62).* New Delhi: Archaeological Survey of India.

Ratnagar, Shereen, 1981, *Encounters: The Westerly Trade of the Harappan Civilization.* New Delhi: Oxford University Press.

Sankalia, H.D. *et al.*, 1958, *Excavations at Maheshwar and Navdatoli* (1952–53) Poona: Deccan College.

———, 1971, *Chalcolithic Navdatoli (1957–59).* Poona: Deccan College.

Sharma, N.L., 1968, 'A note on the old copper workings of Amba Mata near Abu Road Station', in *Copper: Progs. of Symposium on Copper.* Geological Survey of India, Misc. Pub. 13. Calcutta: Manager of Publication.

Thapar, Romila, 1975, 'A Possible Identification of Meluhha, Dilmun and Makan', *JESHO*, 18: 1–42.

Weiss, H. *et al.*, 1992, 'The Genesis and Collapse of Third millennium North Mesopotamian Civilization', *Science*, 261: 995–1004.

Wheeler, R.E.M., 1947–48, Iran and India in Pre-Islamic Times, *Ancient India*, 4: 85–103.

Glimpses of Indo-Iranian Connections in Earliest Times

R.S. Sharma

In the pre-Indo-Aryan phase the Indus culture emerged in India. In the same phase the Elamite culture rose in southwestern Iran. In the third millennium BC just as Egypt, Mesopotamia and Indus valley had their own scripts, so also had Elam.

Close contacts between Iran and India appeared in the third millennium BC. We have considerable evidence of trade between the Indus culture and Mesopotamia in that period. Trade played such a crucial role that its decline is considered by some to be a cause of the fall of the Indus civilization (Ratnagar 2000: 84–104). Since Elam, lying east of the Tigris, was the neighbour of Mesopotamia, it may have traded with the Indus Valley: the land route of Indian trade with Mesopotamia passed through Susa, the capital of Elam. Further, Elam lay close to the Persian Gulf through which also India and Mesopotamia traded with each other. Several pieces of evidence are adduced by the archaeologists to pinpoint Elamite influences on Indian tools, seals and ceramics. S.R. Rao states that there is close similarity in the size, weight and composition of the copper ingots from Susa in Elam with those from Lothal; both of them, according to him, had established trade contacts (Rao 1973: 80). However, a comparison between the metal tools of the two countries shows that Elamite axes, spears and daggers were more advanced (Rao 1973: 81).

H.D. Sankalia speaks of Iranian or Western Asiatic contacts or influence in the Deccan chalcolithic pottery and also in the case of pottery from several places in Rajasthan and Sindh. He underlines the similarity in typical forms and designs in pottery from Indian sites on the one hand and ceramics from Susa in Elam, on the other (Sankalia 1974: 458–59).

S.R. Rao states that two crouching antelopes are engraved in the typical Sumerian and Elamite fashion on a seal from Mohenjodaro. He adds that eagle, which was a popular motif in Mesopotamia and Elam, is also found on a seal from Harappa. He adds that several animals engraved on the Indus seals appeared in the same style as they appear in Elam and Mesopotamia (Rao 1973: 93). We therefore cannot ignore the archaeological evidence for contact and similarity between Elam and the Indus culture in the late third and early second millennia BC. We have also some evidence for trade between the two areas during the same period.

Contacts through arts, crafts and trade between the two areas can be linked with the spread of the Proto-Dravidian language in the Harappan area. At present Brahui, a form of Dravidian language, is spoken in Afghanistan and Pakistan. In Pakistan it is spoken in Sindh and Baluchistan (Sharma 1995: 67–70; 1999, 54–56). Around 1980 the total number of Brahui speakers was estimated at 6,00,000 (Andronov 1980: 15). It has now been shown that the Dravidian language was linked with the Elamite language. The Elamites had developed a script closer to the Sumerian by the latter half of the fourth millennium BC. The language found in the Elamite inscriptions of the third millennium BC is connected with the Dravidian language. The linguist, MacAlpin, holds that both the Elamite and the Dravidian languages belong to the same language family and postulates the presence of a Proto-Elamite-Dravidian language. According to him, the Brahui language found in Baluchistan is derived from this language and belongs to the northern Dravidian family. MacAlpin throws light on the pastoral vocabulary of the Proto-Elamite Dravidian language and shows that with the progress of the Dravidians in the Indian subcontinent, this vocabulary underwent modifications (Mallory 1991: 44–45).

It is significant that the Proto-Elamite-Dravidian language has only one type of word for brick. This discovery is of the greatest importance because bricks were used on a large scale in the Harappan culture and the other neighbouring urban civilizations of the Bronze Age. However, in none of contemporary cultures were bricks used on such a large scale as in the Indus culture. It will be worthwhile to investigate whether burnt bricks orginated in Elam and travelled to other areas including the Indus area. After the end of the Harappan culture, burnt bricks are not found in northern India until 300 BC, although mud bricks are probably mentioned in later Vedic literature. According to

MacAlpin, the Proto-Elamite-Dravidian culture disintegrated around 4000 BC. Whatever the exact date of this event might be, historians are gradually accepting the close relationship between the Elamite language and the Dravidian language which includes Brahui (ibid.).

That the Proto-Dravidian language orginated in the Elamite area and spread from there via Pakistan and western India eventually to south India is broadly accepted by scholars from different countries. These scholars include M.S. Andronov (1970 and 1980); M.B. Emeneau (1969); J.P. Mallory (1991); F.C. Southworth (1997); and T.R. Trautman (1979). Dravidian words are found even in *Rgveda* (*RV*), but so far they have not been reported from the *Avesta.* This may be due to the fact that the *Avesta* was not composed in south-western Iran, that is Elam. More importantly, all the fragments of the *Avesta* had not been recovered so far. Only one fifth of the total *Avesta* is available at present.

The spread of Proto-Dravidian language or Brahui from southwestern Iran to the Indian subcontinent presupposes the movement of the Elamite people. These movements were made possible because of the continuous long-distance trade and other contacts between the Harappan people and the Elamite people during the third and second millennia BC. Trade facilitated contacts between the two peoples in arts and crafts. It is therefore possible that the Elamite traders and craftsmen along with pastorialists spread the Proto-Dravidian language in the northwestern part of the Indian subcontinent. Thus it will appear that the archaeological evidence regarding Elamite contact with India coincides with the linguistic evidence regarding the spread of the Proto-Dravidian language in the Indus valley.

The post-Elamite phase of Indo-Iranian relations began around 2000 BC. Close similarities between the Indian and Iranian cultures are shown by the *Rgveda* and the *Avesta.* The *Rgveda* covers the period from 1500 BC to 1000 BC and mainly concerns areas of east Afghanistan, northwestern frontier and Panjab. The *Avesta* concerns Iran and Afghanistan. Earlier this text was placed in the middle of the first millennium BC, but now its earliest portions are placed by Burrow in *c.* 1200 BC; some of its portions are considered more archaic by other scholars. In any case numerous words occurring in the Vedic Sanskrit of the *Rgveda* can be easily converted into the Iranian words of the *Avesta* by pronouncing some consonants differently.

The similarity in the form of the words in the two texts is

reinforced by similarity in their cultural contents. The linguistic evidence pointing to cultural similarity between Iran and northwestern India is supported by archaeological evidence. Recent excavations in Central Asia, Iran and the Indian subcontinent (Pakistan) reveal several features which are shared by the cultures of the three areas.

In the second millennium BC several centres of culture in Central Asia contributed to the formation of the Aryan culture. The Andronovo and BMAC cultures seem to be important in this context. They first developed in the Sintasta river east of the southern Urals. Around seventeenth centrury BC the Sintasta cemetery shows the earliest light horse-drawn chariots in the Central Asian steppes. Five caves contained remains of chariots with those of ten-spoked wheels and their horses. It may be noted that the Mitanni, who spoke an Indo-Aryan language in upper Mesopotamia (*c.* 1400 BC) were the masters in chariotry (Parpola 1988: 145).

The second, that is Bactria–Margiana Archaeological Complex (BMAC), developed in south Central Asia. The BMAC roughly includes south Turkmenistan, northern Afghanistan and part of south Uzbekistan in 1900–1500 BC. It shows the presence of the horse, spoked wheels, soma-drink cult, fire cult and cremation (Parpola 1997: 366–74; R.S. Sharma 1995: 49). It had a proto-urban culture based on the use of bronze which had declined by 2000 BC. Recently Hiebert has discovered an inscribed seal. The symbols found on seal do not resemble any of the inscriptions—Egyptian, Mesopotamian or Harappan. The seal is dated around 2200 BC by Hiebert . Since urban culture in BMAC is seen as a Greater Iran culture under Elamiie influence, seal symbols may also be compared with the Elamite inscriptions.

According to Fairservice, the pastoralists who moved to the Indian borderlands came from Bactria-Margiana Archaeological Complex or the (BMAC) which saw the genesis of the culture of the *Rgveda* (Fairservice Jr. 1997: 206–12). It is suggested by Parpola that the Mitannis and the Proto-Indo-Iranians moved from here. The Mitannis went to Syria and the Proto-Indo-Iranians went to Iran. According to several archaeologists from the BMAC people migrated to southeastern Iran, southern Afghanistan, Gandhara and the Quetta regions. Hiebert, a strong champion of the theroy of local cultural tradition, doubts massive population movements. However, burial assemblages including artefacts and ceramics suggest to him the movement of the people from the oases of both Bactria and Margiana to the periphery of the

Indus valley. He hesitates to associate with the movement the introduction of the Indo-Iranian languages, which seems to imply both Indo-Iranian and Indo-Aryan speeches (Hiebert 1997: 200–02).

Giorgio Stacul suggests earlier cultural waves from Iran and Afghanistan in the Swat valley before 2000 BC (Stacul 1984: 271–75), but the horse depiction on the potsherd (1700–1400 BC) may be connected with the horse-using people in the Andronovo culture in Central Asia. This is supported by Elena Kuzmina who points out that the domestic architecture and burial rites of the Gandhara grave culture look like the regional variants of the Andronovo culture lying in the north (Mallory 1991: 230). She adds that the ceramics of Dashly Tepe (in north Afghanistan) and Sapalli Tepe (in south Uzbekistan) have better analogies for the type of the pottery we find in the Gandhara grave culture (ibid.: 231). This indicates the impact of migration of the BMAC people on the Swat valley.

Climatic change was the main cause of migration. Many paleo-climatists hold that extreme aridity and feezing-point conditions prevailed in Central Asia in the late third and early second millennia BC (Masson 1992: 243–44). According to Khazanov, 'the second millennium BC was at its driest at the turn of the second and the first millennium BC. Archaeological data would confirm this suggestion' (Khazanov 1984: 95, quoted in Dhavalikar 1995: 209). Evidently bitter cold and dry climate turned the agriculturalists mainly into pastoralists and forced them to migrate to warmer and rainy regions. Adequate archaeological evidence has been adduced to demonstrate the movements of the semi-nomadic peoples in Central Asia in the second millennium BC and at the turn of the first millennium BC. (Dani and Masson 1992: chps 14 and 20). The movement of cattle and other pastoralists is also attributed to a social and political schism between the urban elite and cattle pastoralists in the second millennium BC (Fairservice Jr. 1997: 210–11).

It is not easy to locate the routes taken by the speakers of the Proto-Vedic language. The widely prevalent notion that the Vedic Indians and the Avestan Iranians lived together for a long time in Iran before the departure of the Indo-Aryans to India does not have adequate archaeological support for the presence of both Indo-Iranians and Indo-Aryans on the mainland of Iran. Probably the Proto-Indians and Proto-Iranians lived in Turkmenistan for some time.

Discussing the decline of the Bronze Age civilization and the movement of the tribes, Masson states that in, contrast to Turkmenistan and Transoxiana, sedentary farming communities did not bring new areas under cultivation in southern Afghanistan and southeastern Iran (Masson 1992: 352). He adds: 'For northeastern Iran, where the outstanding Hissar-Turang-Tepe culture flourished during the developed bronze period, no data are yet available to show what happened to the society after these large centres were depopulated at the beginning of the second millennium BC' (ibid.: 351–52). The sudden collapse of the urban civilization in eastern Iran and in Afghanistan around 2000 BC is also underlined by Tosi and other archaeologists (Tosi, Shahmirzadi and Joyenda 1992: 215). Further, they notice a radical and rapid decline of the large (urban) centres in all the enclaves of Central Asia after 2200 BC (ibid.: 200). The widespread urban decay may have increased the ranks of pastorals and agriculturists who looked for new lands because of climatic conditions and social conflicts. However, consequences of urban decay will be clear if more archaeological work is done on the second millennium BC (cf. ibid.: 215).

According to Harmatta the Proto-Iranian language was separated from the Proto-Indo-Aryan around 3500 BC. He adds that in the third millennium BC one group of the Proto-Indo-Aryans moved southward along the eastern coast of the Caspian Sea and conquered the Gorgan valley in northeastern Iran where we find a large number of horse skeletons. Harmatta's decipherment of the names of Arisena and Somasena on an Agade inscription of *c.* 2300–2100 BC suggests that the Proto-Indo-Aryans had reached Mesopotamia via Iran. Ultimately they moved further to the west and became a part of the Hurrian society in Mesopotamia. This accounts for the names of important 'Vedic' deities in Kassite inscriptions of *c.* 1600 BC.

Speaking of the movement of the eastern branch of the Indo-Europeans around 1500 BC, Ghirshman (1954) suggests almost the same route of its migration to Mesopotamia as Harmatta (1992). According to him the warrior element in this branch moved eastward round the Caspian Sea, crossed the Caucasus and pushed to the great bend of the Euphrates. They settled among the local Hurrians and eventually founded the kingdom of Mitanni in north Mesopotamia or modern Syria and the valley of the northern Zagros (Ghirshman 1954: 61). In our view these were Proto-Indo-Aryans, whose gods Indra, Varuna, Mitra and Nasatya appear in the Mitanni inscription of the fourteenth century BC.

References

Andronov, M.S., 1970, *Dravidian Languages*, Moscow 'Nauka' Publishing House.
———, 1980, *The Brahui Language*, Moscow 'Nauka' Publishing House.
Benveniste, E., 1973, *Indo-European Language and Society*. London: Faber and Faber.
Burrow, T., 1973, 'The Proto-Indoaryans' in *Journal of the Royal Asiatic Society*.
Dani, A.H., and V.M. Masson, 1992 (eds) *History of Civilizations of Central Asia*, Vol. I, Paris: UNESCO Publishing.
Dhavalikar, M.K., 1995, *Cultural Imperialism (Indus Civilization Western India)*, New Delhi: Books and Books.
Emeneau, M.B., 1969, 'The Non-Literary Dravidian Languages' in Norman H. Zide (ed.), *Current Trends in Linguistics*, Vol. V, *Linguistics in South Asia*, Mouton, The Hague.
Fairservice (Jr.), W.A., 1997, 'Central Asia and the RgVeda: The archaeological evidence', in George Erdosy, (ed.), *The Indo-Aryans of Ancient South Asia*.
Ghirshaman, R., 1954, *Iran From the Earliest Times to the Islamic Conquest*, Harmondsworth: Penguin.
Harmatta, J., 1992, 'The emergence of the Indo-Iranians; the Indo-Iranian languages' in A.H. Dani and V.M. Masson, (eds), *History of Civilizations*.
Hiebert, Fredrik T., 1997, 'South Asia from a Central Asian Perspective' in George Erdosy, (ed.), *The Indo-Aryans of Ancient South Asia*.
Khazanov, A.M., 1984, *Nomadism and the Outside World*, Cambridge University Press.
Mallory, J.P., 1991, *In Search of the Indo-European Language, Archaeology and Myth*, London: Thames and Hudson (paperback edn).
Masson, V.M., 1992, 'The Bronze Age in Khorasan and Transoxania' in Masson (eds), *History of Civilizational of Central Asia*.
———, 1992, 'The decline of the Bronze Age Civilization and movements of the tribes' in A.H. Dani and V.M. Masson (eds), *History of Civilization of Central Asia*.
Parpola, Asko, 1988, 'The Coming of the Aryans to Iran and the Cultural and Ethnic Identity of the Dasas' in *International Journal of Dravidian Linguistics*, Vol. XVII, No. 2, pp. 85–189.
———, Asko, 1997, 'The Problem of the Aryans and the Soma: Textual-linguistic and archaeological evidence', in George Erdosy (ed.), *The Indo-Aryans of Ancient South Asia*, New Delhi: Munshiram Manoharlal.
Rao, S.R., 1973, *Lothal and the Indus Civilization*, Bombay/Madras: Asian Publishing House.
Ratnagar, Shereen, 2000, *The End of the Great Harappan Tradition*, New Delhi: Manohar.
Roux, George, 1966, *Ancient Iraq*, Penguin.
Sankalia, H.D., 1974, *Prehistory and Protohistory of India and Pakistan*, Poona: Deccan College.
Sharma, R.S., 1995, *Looking for the Aryans*, Madras: Orient Longman.
———, 1999, *Advent of the Aryans in India*, New Delhi: Manohar.
Smith, R. Morton, 1984, 'What is in a name (in ancient India)?' in *Journal of Indo-European Studies*, 12.
Southworth, F.C., 1997, 'Reconstructing Social Context from Language; Indo-Aryan

and Dravidian Prehistory; in George Erdosy, (ed.), *The Indo-Aryans of Ancient South Asia.*

Stacul, Giorgio, 1984, 'Harappan Post-urban Evidence in the Swat Valley' in B.B. Lal and S.P. Gupta, (ed.), *Frontiers of the Indus Civilization*, New Delhi: Books.

———, 1987, *Prehistoric and Protohistoric Swat (C. 3000–1400 BC)*, ISMEO, Rome.

The Rgveda Samhita with the commentary of Sayana, 1933–35, 5 Vols, Vaidik Samshodhan Mandal, Poona; tr. by R.T.H. Griffith, 1986, Delhi: Motilal Banarsidass.

The Sacred Book of the East, 1965, Vol. XXXI, *The Zend-Avesta*, Part-III, *The Yasna, Vispard, Afrinagan, Gahs* and Miscellaneous Aspects, tr. L.H. Mills and (ed.) F. Max Muller, Motilal Banarsidass (rpt).

The Sacred Books of the East, 1988, Vol. 23, *The Zend-Avesta*, Part II, *The Sirozahs, Yasts and Nyayis*, tr. James Darmesteter and (ed.) F. Max Muller, Delhi: Motilal Banarsidass.

The Sacred Books of the East, 1992, Vol. 4, *The Zend-Avesta*, Part I, *The Vendidad*, tr. James Darmesteter and (ed.) F.Max Muller, Delhi: Motilal Banarsidass.

Tosi, M., S.Malek Sharmirzadi and M.A. Joyenda, 1992, 'The Bronze Age in Iran and Afghanistan' in A.H. Dani and V.M. Masson, (ed.), *History of Civilizations.*

Trautmann, T.R., 1979, 'The Study of Dravidian Kingship' in Madhav M. Deshpande and Peter Edwin Hooks (eds) *Aryan and Non-Aryan in India*, Ann Arbor: University of Michigan Press.

The *Ṛgveda* and the *Avesta*

A Study of their Religious Trajectories

K.M. Shrimali

A comparative study of religious beliefs, concepts, cults and practices of people of the *Ṛ*gved*ā* (more appropriately *Ṛksaṃhitā*) and the *Avesta* makes it imperative that one focuses on their contexts and milieu, on the one hand, and their bearing on the problem of 'Aryans', on the other.

The search for the 'Aryans' is a quest as old as Indological studies. In the late eighteenth century, William Jones was overawed by the linguistic similarities between Sanskrit and the classical and modern European languages. The establishment of the Asiatic Society in Calcutta in 1784 and the publication of the *Asiatik Researches* gave a tremendous spurt to the quest for commonality between India and Europe. For more than a century the field was almost a monopoly of linguists, with occasional contributions by some scientists interested in floral and faunal studies. However, with the publication of *The Aryans* by the renowned Marxist archaeologist V. Gordon Childe in 1926, the enquiry was greatly diversified and an archaeological approach to the Aryan problem came to be recognized as a valuable methodological aid. Nevertheless, the picture resulting from the analyses undertaken in the last two centuries is far from conclusive. No wonder, we are still getting studies under such titles as J.P. Mallory's *In Search of the Indo-Europeans* (1989) and R.S. Sharma's *Looking for the Aryans* (1995).

The family of the Indo-European languages, to which languages of the *Ṛksaṃhitā* and the *Avesta* belong, constitutes perhaps the biggest linguistic group of the world. Inevitably, therefore, the problem of 'Aryans' needs to be looked at not with reference to any specific modern-day geographical frontier—say, India or Iran specific. Its horizon is perhaps more global. Mallory has remarked:

> Three-quarters of the member states of the United Nations recognize an Indo-European language as an official language of state . . . Indo-European homelands have been found everywhere between the Atlantic and Pacific Oceans and at both the North and South Poles! Temporally, the Proto-Indo-Europeans have been assigned to anywhere between the Neanderthals *circa* 80,000 years ago to as recently as *circa* 1600 BC.[1]

The Texts and Their Transmission

The *Avesta* and the *Ṛksaṃhitā* are considered the most archaic and oldest of texts of the Iranians and the Indo-Aryans respectively. There are similarities galore in the structures of the two texts and mechanisms of their transmission. Both have their 'early' and 'younger' layers. Thus, in the *Avesta*, the Gathas and the Vendidad would respectively correspond to these layers. In the *Ṛksaṃhitā*, on the other hand, of the ten *maṇḍalas* (books), the first and the tenth are recognized as relatively later compositions—most of the remaining books (specially II–VII) bear the halo of being the so-called 'family-books', and, therefore, considerably 'older'.[2]

At a general level, it is often argued that the language of Gathas is comparable in antiquity to that of the *Ṛgvedā* and that the Indo-European elements in Gathas have stylistic and doctrinal parallels in the Vedas.[3] In more specific contexts, namely, processes of textual transmissions, our texts share many analogous features. Building on the oft-cited 'defective nature of the archetype of all the manuscripts', Kuiper once pointed out:

> at the time when the older text (written in Pahlavi characters) was transcribed in the newly created Avestan script, the exact form and the meaning of the text was, in some Gathic passages at least, no longer precisely known. This means that the authentic text of the prophet's own words had not been *entirely* preserved by an uninterrupted oral tradition, and that, in some doubtful passages at least, the only thing the transcribers could do was to transcribe as accurately as possible the word forms they found in the older manuscript. In these cases there was *only a graphical transmission of the sacred text*.[4]

In the case of the *Ṛksaṃhitā*, too, it needs to be underlined that the potentialities of being misunderstood were infinitely greater.

After all, it is anything but a text emanating from the words of a prophet. Though the problem of authors of this *saṃhitā* is insufficiently investigated,[5] it is seldom disputed that more than 1,000 hymns of the extant text were compositions of several *ṛṣis* (seers). While the existence of a written text of the *Avesta* during the reign of the last Arsacid is now an established fact, such certainty eludes us in case of the *Ṛksaṃhitā*, whose oral transmission was an extremely long-drawn exercise. In this process, therefore, even the most learned ones in the society seem to have forgotten the real meanings of the compositions. That Yāska had to compose *Nirukta* within about half—a millennium (perhaps in *circa* 500 BC) to explain the etymology of countless obsolete words of this *saṃhitā* shows that the transmission of the text must have been flawed. The *Ṛksaṃhitā*, as it stands today, does not represent the contemporaneous Rgvedic tradition in its entirety. Rather, it represents only those portions which a particular school (the Sākala recension) decided to preserve. The Rgvedic language is much older than Sanskrit (*saṃskṛta* literally meaning 'put together') which was the name given to language on its regulation by the grammarians.[6]

Stipulating 'two distinct layers in the evolution of the *Ṛgveda*', Dandekar worked out a process *(saṃhitākaraṇa)* through which stray *mantras* were made into a *saṃhitā*. 'The Vedic *mantras* must have been originally composed in a living dialect, which we may call proto-Rgvedic. These *mantras* were, later on, worked upon by the hymn-makers who purposely used an archaic-looking, priestly, artificial dialect, not their own vernacular.'[7]

The geographical horizon of the *Avesta* is almost exclusively eastern Iran but it does have some references which indicate the presence of Proto-Indo-Aryans in northern central Iran bringing them within striking distance of Near East (invasions of Hurrian country). These are the references which occur from time to time in the *Avesta* to the Māzanian (Mazana = territory between the southern shore of the Caspian sea and the Alburz mountain range) *daevas*. Juxtaposition of the Mazanian *daevas* and the Varaenian *druj*-adherents signifies the geographical spread of the *Avesta* in western Iran as well.[8]

Where do we situate the *Ṛksaṃhitā*? With the two-stage evolution of the text in mind, it seems more than likely that the composers/redactors must have had a shifting locale. More so, when the overall nomadic pastoralism, as would be shown below, constituted the most arresting milieu of the people of the text. In view of the process of the transmission of the text outlined above, it was suggested long ago:

> 'A major portion of the Vedic *mantras*, in their *primary* form, was produced in the region around Balkh; only their revision, priestly obscuration, artificial archaization and *samhitakarana* were accomplished in the land of the seven rivers (Saptasindhu).'[9]

It is generally understood that notwithstanding very infrequent occurrence specifically of '*Saptasindhu*', the 'seven rivers' covered an area that extended from the modern Afghanistan in the northwest to western Uttar Pradesh in the east—the river Ganga which is also mentioned rather rarely, perhaps constituted the easternmost frontier of the Rgvedic locale. Present-day regions of Jammu and Kashmir, Panjab (pre-1947), and Rajasthan formed part of the geographical horizon of the Rgvedic people, who do not seem to be too much familiar with Gujarat. The trek from Balkh to the land of the 'seven rivers' has received some support from archaeological finds.[10]

A comparative study of the *Avesta* and the *Ṛksaṃhitā* derives further strength from chronological complementarity of the two texts, in addition to stylistic overlaps pointed out above. Chronological assessments of the *Avesta* have often been based on that of Zoroaster. There is a growing realization that the traditional date of this Prophet, namely, *circa* 600 BC needs considerable upward revision and that there is a case for placing him between 1200 and 1100 BC.[11] Similarly, barring some ultra-nationalist historians in India who tend to push back the antiquity of the *Ṛksaṃhitā* to the fourth millennium BC, a fairly large number of historians, linguists, archaeologists, both in India and abroad, are inclined to accept a span of about 500 years (*circa* 1500–1000 BC) for the evolution of the earliest Vedic text. The same chronology is suggested for the extant *Avesta* as well.

The Milieu

Who constituted the Avestan people? Of course the people of Zoroaster's own tribe. But not just that. Given the geographical horizon of the *Avesta*, much wider social base seems to be the ground reality. Many people living in different parts of ancient Iran were not necessarily 'Avestan'-speaking and yet they formed the people 'of the Avesta'. They shared in transmitting, and in part composing, the holy texts.

Since the late 1880s several studies have focused on the social milieu of the extant *Avesta*. Amongst very early reconstructions is W.Geiger's, which describes it as being simple and archaic one, divided essentially between priests and other men.[12] Invoking Zoroastrian terms such as *vāstrya, vāstar, vāstrya fšuyant,* subsequent linguistic studies identified 'other men' as cattle-tending pastorals. On the other hand, referring to *āthravan, rathēštar, vāstryo fšuyant,* in 1930 Dumezil put forward the theory that the tripartite divisions of the Younger Avestan and Vedic society (brahman, kshatriya, vaishya) shared a proto-Indo-Iranian origin.

Assessing Zoroaster's milieu Zaehner wrote in 1961:

> On the one side he found a settled pastoral and agricultural community devoted to the tilling of the soil and the raising of cattle, on the other he found a predatory, marauding tribal society which destroyed both cattle and men, and which was a menace to any settled way of life. Their gods were like unto them: never were they good rulers, delivering over, as they did, the ox to Fury (*aēshma*) instead of providing it with good pasture.[13]

More recently, however, Polomé has come out rather strongly against Dumézil's overarching theory of tripartite class divisions amongst Indo-Europeans. Maintaining that a classless society would have been characteristic of Indo-European peoples in their pastoral period, Polomé contends:

> The trifunctional hierarchization of society . . . [has] to be viewed diachronically as part of a dynamic process of development. . . . In the older pastoral society, we rather expect *unranked* descent groups. As the community grows and *diversifies*, the extended family 'swarms' for economic reasons; moving to establish new settlements leads to profound social changes with *ranked* descent groups and *full-time craft specialization.*[14]

Underlining that most of the earlier scholars have been oblivious of the need to distinguish between the older 'Gathic society' and that of the 'Younger' *Avesta*, and accepting Polomé's characterization, Boyce argues that 'the Gathas appear indeed to mirror ancient Iranian society still at this pastoral stage, the community of 'cattle and men' (*pasu vira, Y.*31.15; 45.9), experiencing violent changes but not yet driven to the 'swarming' represented by the great migrations from the steppes southward into Iran, which led, it seems, to evolution of social classes (with a parallel but independent development in Vedic India)'.[15]

In the Gathas women figure as dependent socially on men (father and husband) whom they look after (*Y*.53.4), but as spiritually their equals (*Y*.46.10). The Avestan people attached immense importance to lineage, and venerated the souls of their ancestors (*fravashis*).

Boyce is inclined to accept Dumézil's when she argues that the 'Younger' Avestan society saw the firm establishment of the three classes. Although *vastryo fšuyant* is used for the third class, its dominant representative is now the farmer. The merit of irrigating, drainage, tilling the soil, sowing corn, and cultivating fruits is stressed (*Vd*. 3.4, 23–31), since all these activities reduced barrenness. 'Corn (*yava-*) shall man eat' Ahura Mazda is made to declare (*Vd*.5.20), which indicates the change from meat to bread as the basic diet. There is still no mention of town-life, but in a late passage a fourth class is recognized, that of the *hūiti*, the craftsman or artisan (*Y*.19.17). The use of metals was increasing—beside the traditional stone pestle and mortar (*hāvana-*) others of metal (*āyah-*) are mentioned (*Y*.22.2); but the payments were still reckoned in traditional manner in units of livestock (*Vd*. 9.37-38). In *Vd*. 7.41–7.42 a donkey (*kathwa-*) appears, a southern animal unknown of old on the steppes. The dog was highly esteemed (*Vd*. 13.39–13.40, 44–49) probably since the Old Avestan pastoralists had relied on herd-dogs.[16]

The milieu of the *Ṛksaṃhitā* has many parallels with that of the *Avesta*. It would be futile and perhaps somewhat anachronistic to call it merely a 'Sanskrit' text and a text of the 'Aryans'. That there are numerous people who were not 'Sanskrit'-speaking is evident even to a casual reader. How else does one explain the presence of *mṛdhravāchās* (supposedly speakers of 'false speech'), who are often despised, perhaps because of their non-Sanskritic dialect? Suniti Kumar Chatterjee, one of India's greatest linguists, traced extensive elements of Austric and Dravidian languages in 'Indo-Aryan speech', and suggested: 'It is likely that racial and cultural fusion (including linguistic) had commenced between Aryan and the Dāsa/Dasyu people outside the soil of India itself—in Iran, in all likelihood.' He was exceptionally emphatic in pointing out that the non-Aryan, non-Vedic, pre-Vedic, non-Sanskrit in Indian culture constitute 12 *annas* in a rupee, that is, three fourth of Indian culture.[17] More recent studies, too, have exploded the myth of monolithic linguistic complexion of the *Ṛksaṃhitā* and have identified several Dravidian, Prakritic and Mundari influences therein.[18]

Further, the overall material milieu of the people of the text has also become considerably clear. Two inter-related conspicuous features of this milieu are, (a) tribes were essentially pastoral, and (b) class divisions are not identifiable in these tribes.[19] A perusal of the *Ṛksaṃhitā* leaves us in little doubt that as far as the earlier 'family books' are concerned, pastoral economy was the main basis of tribal communities.[20] Cattle constituted the chief form of wealth in the psyche of contemporary tribal society and the inter-tribal as well as intra-tribal tensions were invariably occasioned largely by the keenness to acquire cattle wealth.[21]

Communities based on pastoral activities are able to collect resources for their bare subsistence. There does not seems to be any distinction between the producer and the consumer. Any postulation of a class society (bipartite or tripartite as in the case of the *Avesta*) in the *Ṛksaṃhitā* is not sustainable. It is well known that the *Puruṣa Sūkta* (*RV.* X.90) referring to the fourfold social order (comprising brahman, rājanya, vaishya and shūdra) is an interpolation. It is not improbable that some tribal chiefs may have been duly respected for their physical strength and possibly also for their leadership qualities. But references to such people acquiring leadership on account of their heredity are difficult to come across in the *Ṛksaṃhitā*. More significantly, notwithstanding their high ranks, these leaders distributed their subsistence resources within their tribes. Even if this social configuration was not completely egalitarian, it could not be designated as a class or caste society either. After all, we do not see in the *Ṛksaṃhitā* any reference to such people who may have lived their lives by simply lording over and exploiting the actual producers of wealth. All members of the tribe were both producers as well as consumers of their wealth.[22]

The 'family books' of the *Ṛksaṃhitā* present a society which is analogous to Polomé's characterization of Indo-European people and like the Gathic society, communities of 'cattle and men' dominated its landscape. It is largely in the interpolated layers that one starts witnessing a gradual transition to agriculture.[23] The overall milieu of both the *Avesta* and the *Ṛksaṃhitā* is noticeable for plurality of heterogeneous elements that were gradually absorbed and modified by one another.

The Method

'The historian will devise a theory to explain how 'Indians', or Proto-Indians', or 'Para-Indians', or 'Proto-Aryans' could come into western Asia and exercise the influence inferable from these linguistic traces.[24] The linguist is entitled to be more modest. Strictly speaking, he is not dealing with 'Indians' or 'Proto-Aryans', but with 'Indo-Aryan' or 'Proto-Aryan' terms and names. We cannot reconstruct Proto-Aryan religious terms—and much less Proto-Aryan religious ideas—by simply and naively projecting Rgvedic data into Proto-Aryan times. A reconstruction can be attempted only by a careful confrontation of Vedic and *Avestan* terminology.'[25]

The divide between the historian and the linguist, as proposed by Thieme, is uncalled for. Nor do we share the skepticism displayed by scholars *vis-à-vis* literary and archaeological sources.[26] An example of multi-pronged thrust can be seen in Gnoli's cautionary proposition about Iranian religions. He suggested that one must try to ascertain, with the help of archaeological findings, what part was played by the Anarian substratum, from the Elam civilization to the so-called Helmand civilization which came to light in the 1960s during the excavations at Shahr-i Sokhta, in Iranian Seistan. A thorough investigations into more recent times is also necessary in order to see whether there are to be found, among religions of the Hindukush, between Nuristan and Dardistan, any fossilized remains of ancient proto-Indo-Aryan religions.[27]

The perils of overlooking different strata of the *Avesta* have been mentioned above. That archaeological cultures can be correlated with the problem of textual stratification is shown by the diggings in the steppes and in the regions suggested by Gnoli. Thus the Early (Gathic) *Avesta* is placed in the Late Neolithic and the Later *Avesta* (Vendidad) as being the product of Iranian Bronze Age. Before the Bronze Age reached the Asian steppes (from *circa* 1700 BC), the weapons of the young warrior-herdsmen (Gathic *mārya/mairya),* comprised clubs, sling-stones, bows, and arrows. Deities in the Vendidad, however, are provided with more effective, and costly bronze weapons, and also the costly horse-drawn chariot (giving mobility). The earliest known chariots, from 'not later than 1500 BC' were found in Sintashta graves (a group of pit-burials by a settlement in a bend of the Sintashta river) in the south Cheliabinsk region on the eastern flank of the central Urals. Excavators identified Sintashta community (which supported itself by pastoralism, with a little farming) as Iranian, with differing beliefs about after life, thus providing seedbed for Zoroaster's new teachings. Wikander and Bruce Lincoln stand accused for overlooking this archeological transition from the Gathic to the 'younger' Avestan society.[28]

In the context of the Indian subcontinent, H.D. Sankalia, the doyen of Indian archaeologists, has been a vocal exponent of correlating Vedic-Epic and Puranic texts with archaeological cultures. Though his numerous assertions, particularly those that are related to equations of archaeological cultures with 'Aryans', have not found universal acceptance, yet his hypothesis of Iranian elements in Chalcolithic cultures in central India and the Deccan[29] has been recently endorsed by Dhavalikar. Steering clear of the 'Aryan problem', Dhavalikar has categorically brushed aside critics of Sankalia's hypothesis and stressed:

> it must be conceded that the analogues are highly specialized forms which have no parallels in India either earlier and even later. Vessels with stands, pedestals, handles and lugs have hardly antecedents in India and the chalices and pedestalled bowls from Navdatoli form a class by themselves and are enigmatic. They are later in point of time than their analogues in Iran and need explanation.[30]

Notwithstanding Dhavalikar's equivocation on the 'Aryan problem', several recent studies have invoked combined evidence from the *Avesta*, the *Ṛksaṃhitā* and archaeological cultures of the Zhob, Gomal and Swat valleys.[31] Since the problem cannot remain India-centred and has to be linked with the Indo-Europeans, the archaeological cultures of the Eurasian steppes spanning over three millennia (*circa* 4500–1500 BC) such as the Sredni Stog, Pit Grave of Yamna and Andronovo cultures need to figure prominently. Some of the major conclusions based on such a multi-pronged analysis are:

(a) the archaeological remains of the *puras* of the *dāsas* mentioned in the *Ṛksaṃhitā* may be seen in the circular structures at Dashli-3 in the Amu Plains rather than in the Harappan settlements as Wheeler once thought in his famous view of Indra, the Rgvedic hero, as the destroyer of these 'forts'.
(b) The *Soma* cult of the *Ṛksaṃhitā*, comparable with the *Haoma* cult of the *Avesta*, is as central to the problem of the Indo-

Aryans as the horse.[32] The archaeological traces of this ritual drink are seen in the remains at Togolok-21 in Margiana (southeastern Turkmenistan).

(c) In the Indian subcontinent, the archaeological counterparts of the Rgvedic cultures appear not in the mature Harappan culture but in the borderland cultures of the Swat and Gomal valleys, the Pirak complex in Baluchistan and perhaps also in Periano Ghundai. It emerges clearly in south central Asia in the Bactria Margiana Archaeological Complex and in the cultures of south Tajikstan. Crucial evidences in these contexts comprise horse-centred remains/antiquities, as indeed has been the evidence at Sintashta graves as well.[33]

On Religious Beliefs, Cults and Practices

There are several difficulties in working out pre-Zoroastrian religions of Iran as the data is somewhat fragmented. 'We can postulate the existence of other religions only through a careful analysis of those elements contained within Zoroastrianism that can be linked to a pre-Zoroastrian paganism and through an Indo-Iranian comparison. That is to say that we have no sources other than Zoroastrian, for any Iranian religion.'[34]

This situation is very similar to what obtains in the reconstruction of many of the so-called lesser/'heterodox' religious systems in India. To illustrate, we have no text *of* the Ājīvikas or *by* the Ājīvikas. What compounds our difficulties is that we do not have any text *for* the Ājīvikas. Whatever we know about them is worked out on the basis of allusions to them in brahmanical and non-brahmanical-works, which are invariably not very sympathetic even if they are not entirely hostile towards them.[35]

Given such a nature of textual evidence, the invocation of methodology worked out above becomes an imperative. The homogeneity of the two 'Aryan' peoples (Indo-Aryans and Iranians) is seen most clearly in matters of religion, mythology, and cults and is still reflected in their oldest and most archaic texts, though religious reforms, mainly that of Zarathustra, have caused significant changes. As a matter of fact, both the Veda and the *Avesta* themselves contain allusions to earlier hymns and singers, such as references to the pride of singer to have made a song 'as never before', Vedic *apūrvyam*, Avestic *apaourvīm* 'without a previous one, that is, without precedent'.

However, to what extent mythological themes and motives originate from that period, remains an open question.[36]

This common heritage is reflected, among other things, in the names of abstract concepts, such as the leading religio-philosophical concept of Indo-Iranian **ṛta-*, Vedic *ṛta,* Avestan *aša-*, Old Persian *ṛta-* 'truth, rightness, divine order based on truth'; or cult terms, such as Vedic *yajña-*, Avestan *yasna-*, Indo-Iranian *yazna-*'sacrifice' with an accent on animal sacrifice and such libations as *Āb-zōhr* (to Āpas—water) and *Atakshzohr* (to Atar—fire—Agni); Vedic *mantra-*, Avestan *mathra-* 'priestly utterance' (literally: instrument of thought, that is, formulated meditation, Indo–Iranian *mantra-)*; or the priestly titles Vedic *hotar-*, Avestan *zaotar-*(Indo-Iranian *zhautar-*) and Vedic *atharvan-*, Avestan *āthrauan-/athaurun-*; ritual objects: *kuśa/barhis* = *barsom* (cf. Herodotus referring to strewing grass for animal sacrifice). Despite a veil of Zoroastrianization, *Avesta* provides a large number of pre-Zoroaster deities of Iran, both those celebrated in the *Yashts* and those otherwise referred to, giving us a fair idea of a reasonably comprehensive inventory of the original Iranian pantheon.[37]

The same holds true of the *Ṛksaṃhitā* as well. We have a mélange of deities of different character. A comparison of the two helps in building some kind of a proto-Indo-Aryan pantheon. Worthy of mention, in addition to the cult of gods Āpas, Ātar, Gaeus Urvan, and Haoma are the nature gods such as Āsman ('heaven'), Zam ('earth'), Hvar ('Sun'), Māh ('moon' and the two winds Vāta and Vāyu. To this pantheon also belonged gods who symbolized / personified or deified abstract ideas (like Vedic *Mitra-*, Avestan *Mithra-*, Indo-Iranian **Mitra-* 'god Treaty,' derived from the Indo-Iranian appellative **mitra-* 'pact, treaty'). Cultic gods are, for example, the Fire (Vedic *Agni-*, but Avestan *Ātar-*) and the Indo-Iranian **Sauma-*, Vedic *Soma-*, Avestan *Haoma-*, originally a plant from which an intoxicating drink was pressed. Both Fire and Soma etc., play important parts in the sacrifice and symbolize aspects of the sacrifice itself. Yet another common inheritance seems to the mythological First Man, Yama, son of Vivasvant (Vedic *Yama-*, son of *Vivasvant-*; Avestan *Yima-*, son of *Viuanhant-*), who reigns in the realm of the dead.

Goddesses

The only significant female deity in traditional Iranian religion was Ārdvi Sura Anāhitā, the strong undefiled waters, source of all waters on earth, and of the cosmic ocean. She has variously been identified as the Cannanite Anat, the Anatolian Anaitis, and the Mesopotamian Ishtar. Ahura Mazda, the creator of all, has entrusted her with watching over his work. From her comes all fertility, for, she 'purifies the seed of males and the womb and milk of females' and 'extends her powers of life to all living creatures' (*Yasht* V.5). Described as radiant, beautiful, and nobly born, full of strength and courageous nobility, Anāhitā 'advances on a four-horsed chariot and crushes the demons, the tyrants, all hurtful beings.' Portrayed wearing golden mantle and necklace and a golden crown decorated with rays of the sun and a hundred stars, she is 'a slender maiden with noble bearing . . . who has a very trim waist, ample breasts, and white arms adored with bracelets.' Often, Anāhitā is considered an Anarian substratum of Iranian world.

According to the Greek historian Strabo (1st century BCE), the daughters of noble families were compelled to serve as prostitutes in her temples in Anatolia before they might marry, although this story is historically dubious since it is a practice ascribed earlier by Herodotus to the Babylonian worship of Ishtar.

Out of the seven Amaesha Spentas[38] three are conceived as feminine: Armaiti (Devotion)), Haurvatat (Integrity) and Ameretat (Immortality). Armaiti, described as presiding over the earth and as the giver of pasture and cattle, embodies the ethical principles of faithful obedience, religious harmony, and worship. Haurvatat and Ameretat represent the ideals of vigour and are the sources of life and growth.

Much has been written about goddesses in the *Ṛksaṃhitā* and the paradigm has generally been to ascribe their obvious subordinate status[39] to the patriarchal/patrilineal influences. It is also argued that the trend in the Rgvedic theology was towards 'dethronement or devaluation of the mother goddesses.'[40] It is a well-known fact that the number of hymns that are exclusively addressed to goddesses are very few. Goddess Uṣas is perhaps an exception—twenty-one complete hymns are addressed to her. In most cases, however, female divinities largely figure as sub-texts of male deities such as Agni, Indra, Varuna, Maruts and the Viśvedevas. *Prima facie*, the range of goddesses seems to be quite extensive—from the relatively better-known Pṛthivī, Uṣas, Aditi, Indrānī to malevolent Sasarparī, Nirṛti, Kṛtyā, Dhīṣaṇā and such decrepit entities as Sinivālī, Rākā and Guṅgu. Then there are Naktā,

Bhāratī, Ilā, Varūtrī, Roḍasī. Many of these female deities figure in multiple roles of sister, mother, wife or lover.

A recent study based on the 'family books' of the *Ṛksaṃhitā* brings into focus a gendered construction of goddesses therein.[41] Essentially, it seeks to situate these divinities in the context of Agni, Indra and the Viśvedevas. The starting point of this analysis is the well-known structure of the Rgvedic hymns, namely, hymns addressed to Agni occupy the first place, followed by those to Indra, and then those to other deities, including the Viśvedevas. Some of the major conclusions are:

(a) While the masculine identity of Agni is not in doubt, he is occasionally conceived in feminine terms, Sarasvatī, Āpah, Aditi, Uṣas, Pṛthivī figure in association with him. Representations of these goddesses and their relations with Agni are marked by a degree of flexibility and fluidity. These are relations of mutual support between son and parents/mothers and husband/wife/lover. Relations are not envisaged in hierarchical terms.

(b) Goddesses *vis-à-vis* Indra present a different narrative. The overarching presence of Indra accounts for his overall hostile relations with female divinities. While Agni was an offspring of Waters (Apāṁ Napāt, *RV.* V.41.10), Indra was Apāṁ netā (leader of the Waters). Indra revels in putting goddesses in their places. The classic example, of course, is his fight with and rape and defeat of Uṣas (*RV.*II.15.6 and IV.30.8-11).[42] In contrast, Uṣas was Agni's *patnī* as well as *jāra, i.e.*, wife and lover (*RV.* VII.6.5 and VII.9.1 respectively).

(c) Numerous goddesses figure in relation with the Viśvedevas and a host of other 'smaller' male gods. Roḍasī stands in relationship with the Maruts in the same vein as Uṣas stood *vis-à-vis* Agni, namely, as mother/wife/lover. Roḍasī is also characterized as being full of nourishment, cattle and pasture. Guṅgu, Sinivālī, Rākā are invoked for childbirth.

(d) While male deities are endowed with attributes of power, valour,[43] immortality, omniscience, youthfulness, goddesses are generally kept away from such traits.

Highlighting such gendered nuances in the Rgvedic pantheon is welcome. However, in her enthusiasm to relate goddesses of this pantheon with specific social contexts, Roy has indulged in an over simplification. She is inclined to consider the specificities of Agni, Indra and the Viśvedevas hymns in terms of priesthood, chiefly power and ordinary men / women respectively. This is essentially subscribing (without saying so) to Dumézil's concept of tripartite class divisions as a trait of Indo-Europeans. As already mentioned, this is questionable and perhaps also untenable, not only as a general hypothesis for the Indo-Europeans but also in the specific context of the 'family books' of the *Ṛksaṃhitā*, which have provided the core source of Roy's thesis.[44]

Further, Roy speculates that Agni's flexible and fluid relations with goddesses 'may be connected with the very functions of a priesthood . . . to gain social acceptance'. This reminds us of the contention of Max Weber, who had sought to explain the emergence of Tantricism (with its accent on the *pañcha-mākaras* involving supposedly degenerate orgiastic sexual practices) in terms of brahmins' greed to expand their clientele. The untenability of Weberian contention has already been exposed.[45]

In so far as some of the relatively well-known goddesses such as Uṣas, Aditi, Pṛthivī, etc. cut across the threefold divide amongst male deities, the need to look for alternative social bases becomes imperative. May we see such a scenario in the context of the pre-class and largely pastoral milieu of the 'people of the *Ṛgveda*'? Does the relative unimportance of agriculture, specially in the 'family books' of the text, account for goddesses being 'secondary citizens within the pantheon'? From a more positive standpoint, the association of goddesses with cattle/cow and their relative inactivity in agricultural sphere need to be probed more extensively. In the *Avesta*, Armaiti (one of the three feminine Amaesha Spentas) is described as the giver of pasture and cattle. In the case of the *Ṛksaṃhitā*, such associations are relatively more frequent. In *RV*, V.41.8, the deified cow (*go*) is requested to come rapidly with gifts. The term *dhenu* (milch cow) is transported to feminized elements. A prayer (*RV*, V.43.1) is also addressed to *sapta dhenu* (seven cows) for wealth. Roḍasī is characterized as being full of nourishment, cattle and pasture (*RV*, VII.99.3). Pṛthivī is associated with prosperity, typified by the imagery of being full of ghee and milk (*RV*, VI.70.1–2). The rivers Vipas and Sutudri (identified with the modern day Beas and Sutlej respectively), conceived as deities representing waters are compared with swift mares and cattle (*RV*,

III.33). A hymn to Rātri (the personified night, *RV*, X.127) ends thus: 'I have offered my hymn as a cow is offered.' Arañyāni, the elusive spirit of the forest is described thus: 'Sometimes you catch a glimpse of her, and think it is cattle grazing ...Now I have praised the Lady of the Forest . . . although she tills not, the mother of all things of the wild' (*RV*, X.146).[46]

Animal/Cattle Sacrifice

Given their enormous importance as means of production, means of exchange, measures of wealth, and signs of prestige, there exists a constant demand for cattle within pastoral societies. Amongst the earliest religious beliefs of humankind is : what man himself eats, that he should offer to gods—his Divine Guest; and what is offered should be partaken of in communion by worshippers. So long as the cattle rearers do not use dairy products and employ animals in agriculture and transport, they continue to eat meat of their domesticates. Cattle rearers offered meat to their gods and in return asked for cattle wealth so that their practice of sacrificing cattle and eating meat might continue. Is it any wonder then that cattle sacrifice was an important part of proto-Indo-Aryan religions, reflecting the prominent position of cattle within the society and economy of India and Iran alike. There is no ambivalence in the prime position of cattle in the early *Ṛksaṃhitā* and the Gathas of the *Avesta*, although some scholars have maintained that most references to cattle should be taken metaphorically or allegorically, while granting that the stimulus for bovine imagery would still come from the real possession of cattle.[47]

Zoroaster declared in *Yasna* 31.9–10 : 'the man who is not a herdsman, despite his striving, may have no share in the good news,' that is, he may not share in Zoroaster's own message. And in *Yasna* 46.19: 'Men of Faith will secure a cow and an ox and all that they desire through Good Mind *(vohu manah)*.'[48] In addition to *vohu manah*, Gaeus Tashan 'Creator of the Bull' and Gaeus Urvan 'Soul of the Bull' are also invoked in the Gathas.

Herodotus' account of animal sacrifice amongst Persians is:

> And this is the sacrifice of these Persians with regard to the aforesaid gods. . . . And whichever one of them wishes to sacrifice leads the beast [an ox or sheep] to an open place clear of dirt, and he calls the god, being wreathed with a tiara chiefly of myrtle. Now in truth,

> they do not pray for blessings for the sacrificer himself but pray for good to come to all Persians and to the King, for he [the sacrificer] thinks himself to be among all the Persians. Then, having cut the victim into pieces limb from limb, boiled the flesh, and strewn the softest grass, particularly clover, he then places all flesh on top of this. When this is arranged, a man—Magus—standing beside him sings a theogony, as it is not their custom to perform sacrifices without a Magus. Having waited a little, the sacrificier carries away the flesh, and uses it as he pleases. (I.132).[49]

While discussing animal sacrifice one needs to remember that 'ritual slaying' involving blood offerings probably made its appearance independently amongst nomadic herders and cultivators. Amongst hunting cultures, small but symbolically important part of animal slain during hunt is offered. Slaying is not part of sacrificial action but precedes. 'Ritual slaying' has the twin objective of not only maintaining the cosmic order, but also furthering the cause of material sustenance—blood becomes the symbol *par excellence* of fertility, be it of the animals or of the crops.

That animals were sacrificed in large numbers in the Gathic society is indisputable. The sacrifice was accompanied by prayers that made it sacred and justified it as a religious act through which the spirits of the household animals being sacrificed became absorbed into a divine entity called Gaeus Urvan (the 'Soul of the Bull').

Animal sacrifice to Anāhitā (goddess of waters and fertility), of '100 horses, 1000 cows, 10,000 sheep' is repeatedly attested in the Zoroastrian hymn to this deity. This is a general formula; but a passage in Plutarch *(Lucullus,* 24) suggests that cows were, in fact, particularly sacrificed to Anāhitā, since it is said that in Armenia, where her worship was strong, great herds of cows were kept which were dedicated to the goddess. In the late Avestan text, the *Nirangistan,* a cow is sacrificed beside (and presumably to) the waters.

Carrying out substantive field work in the Yazd plains in 1963–64, Boyce looked at the cult of shrines (of Bībī Shahrbānū, Bānū-Pārs, etc.) and pilgrimage that developed after the downfall of the Sassanians at the hands of the Arabs.[50] The pilgrimage to these shrines is a very important element in the lives of Persian Zoroastrians. It has been argued that these shrines were originally dedicated to Anāhitā. Shahrbānū meaning 'Lady of the Land' comes very close to Anāhitā, who was also designated as 'the Lady'—in the Paikuli inscription Narsch invokes 'Ohrmazd and all the gods, and Anāhitā who is called the Lady.' Both the shrines of the Yazd plains are marked by their close proximity to water resources. Furthermore, sacrifice of both male and female animals, including *gāv* ('cow' including 'bull') was performed at all these shrines. It was only after the visit of Maneji Limji Hataria,[51] the first emissary of the Parsis who came to Persia in 1854, that the practice of sacrifice of cows at Bānū-Pārs was stopped. The lesser sacrifice of sheep and goats is still offered annually at Bānū-Pārs; and similar sacrifices are made also at Bībī Shahrbānū. Even Hataria made no attempt to end these—apparently, only the sacrifice of cows shocked him.

The problem of Zoroaster's view on sacrifice is an extremely thorny one. It is clear from a very few texts, most notably *Y.*32.12 and 14 that he condemned cattle sacrifice,[52] but this is not expressly extended to sacrifice of any other animals. Moreover, such sacrifices are recommended in the Younger *Avesta* (e.g. *Vd.* 18.70, *Yt.*8.58) and continue to the present day while cattle sacrifice has virtually disappeared. The Prophet's prohibition probably applied only to the bovine species.[53]

Assuming that Zoroaster's condemnation of cattle sacrifice was extremely limited, yet not all men approved his exhortations. Some gave active opposition to him personally; others, by cunning and violence, sought to hinder the spread of his message, perhaps because it threatened their vested interests. For such evil men we read in *Yasna,* 32.10–12: *'The wise Lord has condemned those who take the life of the 'ox' with ecstatic cries!'* Such men, in the Prophet's view were leaders of the older cult, the *karapans,* who (he claimed) preferred money or possessions to righteousness or the ministry of men. In *Yasna* 44: 20 he says: 'Have false gods ever been good masters ? This I ask of those who . . . in their cult, take part with *karapans* and *usigs* to give the 'ox' over to violence!'[54]

As far as the animal sacrifices in the *Ṛksaṃhitā* are concerned, that of horse is obviously very conspicuous (*RV,* I.112–113). It became a very major sacrifice *(aśvamedha)* in subsequent times. The Sintashta graves' evidence, mentioned above, is a pronounced indicator of its prevalence. The horse was sacrificed either independently or together with other animals in areas between the Black and Caspian Seas from about the mid-fifth millennium BC.[55]

Cows, bullocks and 'kine in calf' were sacrificed to Agni (*RV*, II, 7.5.). There are several other allusions, both in the 'family books' and in the interpolated tenth *maṇḍala* of the *Ṛksaṃhitā*, where we get to read about the cooking of the meat of the bull or the wild mighty buffalo or ox for Agni and Indra. *Rgveda*, V.29.8 mentions the celebration after Indra's victory that entailed a sacrifice of 300 buffaloes which were consumed by Agni, who had also drunk, as Maghavan (Indra), three lakes of *Soma*. In *RV*, VIII.43.11 Agni is called *uksannaya* and *vasannaya*, that is, 'eater of ox' and 'eater of marrow' respectively. Indra cooked the 'wild mighty buffalo' for his parents (*RV*, VIII.58.15). In two hymns addressed to Indra and *ṛṣi* Vasukra (*RV*, X.27–X.28) Indra's successful battles against enemies are followed by *vṛṣabha pachanā* ('cooking of bull'): 'Bulls they dress for thee (Indra) and of these thou eatest when, Maghavan, with food thou are invited.' In *RV*, X.91.14, many animals such as horses, bulls, oxen, barren cows, rams are 'set apart' and 'offered up' for Agni.[56]

Ritual drinking (the symbol of strength-giving) undertaken at the time of animal sacrifices was common to both the *Avestan* people as well as those of the *Ṛksaṃhitā*. For the former, it comprised *Haoma* and for the latter it was *Soma*. Was it a plant or its sap, or even a hallucinogenic mushroom such as *Amanita muscaria* is not certain.[57] Over the years, the identification with ephedra is gaining ground, as already pointed out. The complex of rites, myths and legends connected with *haoma* belongs to the pre-Zoroastrian proto-Indo-Aryan tradition and is at the centre of a scenario dominated by the warlike god Indra in the *Ṛksaṃhitā*. The Hom Yasht (*Yasna* 9–11) is dedicated to *haoma*.

Soma is also the name of a god, a plant and the hallucinogenic juice squeezed from that plant. Wondrous praises of Soma infuse the verses of the *Ṛksaṃhitā* with lively depictions of kinetic ecstasy. Inspired by Soma, for example, the 'blind person sees [and] the crippled person walks forth' (*RV*, VIII. 79.2). One seer exclaims, 'I in my grandeur have surpassed the sky and this vast earth. . . . I am great! Great ! Flying to the skies! Have I not drunk the *soma*? (*RV*, X.119.8, 12). Another poet priest exults in ecstasy: 'We have drunk the *soma* [and] have become immortal! We have gone to the lights [and] have found the gods! What can hatred and the malice of a mortal do to us now. The splendid drops I have sipped have set me free' (*RV*, VIII. 48.3–5). Like many ancient peoples, people of the *Ṛksaṃhitā* connected the growth of plants with the moon, with which Soma, the king of plants, was later identified. A whole *maṇḍala* (ninth) of this text deals exclusively with Soma.[58]

Aša and Ṛta

An integral concept of the sacred domain of Zoroastrianism is the Avestan passage: *aesham vohu vahishtaem asti, viz.,* 'Truth is the Highest God or the Richest Wealth'. *Arta, Aša or ṛta* = Truth, is amongst important moral and spiritual ideals of Iranianism. Compare this with injunction of Indian epics: *nāsau dharmo yatra na satyamasti*—that indeed cannot be dharma or Righteousness, where there is no Truth.[59]

The Indo-Iranian concept of *ashavān* was transformed by Zoroastrian tradition into Amaesha Spentas which contained various positive meanings, from that of truth to that of a cosmic, ritual and moral order. The Iranian *ashavān* and Rgvedic *ṛtavan* stood, although with different shades of meaning, for 'the initiate'. The blessed state of *aša* manifests itself through light (*Y.*30.1) and *aša* is to be found in 'solar dwellings' (*Y.*53.4; 32.2; 43.16). The 'Initiate' is, then, first of all a 'seer', one who has access to mysteries of the other world and who can contemplate a luminous epiphany (*khvarenah*—'Splendour'—mystical light—Cf. *Yt.*19). Kuiper calls all this as 'Aryan Mysticism' and compares it with the *aphitaṃ ṛtam* of the *Ṛgveda.* The ancient 'Aryan' belief that *ṛta* resides in the realm of the dead still survives in the doctrine of the Younger *Avesta* (*Y.*16.7) that the souls of the deceased dwell in the 'sun-possessing' abode of *asa.* The luminosity of both *aša* and *ṛta* is frequently underlined in our texts.[60]

There is growing realization that both *aša* of the *Avesta* and *ṛta* of the *Ṛksaṃhitā*, which have hitherto been understood in the sense of 'moral' or 'cosmic' orders, actually served a much bigger role. That both were identified with the contemporary material order is now considered to be a greater reality. One of the main purposes of *Yasna* is to strengthen, through consecration, the material world in which constant supply of cattle is the prime requisite. Apart from *vohu manah* guarding and protecting cattle, *Yasna* 29.6–7 also mentions: '*the Wise Lord in agreement with Righteousness (aša) created for the ox the sacred formula of the oblation of fat.*' In the *Ṛksaṃhitā*, too, there are several verses which allude to *ṛta* assuring the people their cows, their water, their food, their material wealth and means of susbsistence.[61]

In the relatively egalitarian society of the *Ṛksaṃhitā*, equitable distribution of these means of subsistence was equated with the maintenance of the material order. Though many gods such as Brahmaṇaspati (*RV*, II. 23.15), Agni (*RV*, V.3.9), the Maruts (*RV*, V.57.8) Indra (*RV*, VII. 20.6) are occasionally associated with *ṛta* and on one occasion (*RV*, V.43.6) even the goddess Earth is called *ṛtajña* (the 'knower' of *ṛta*),[62] maintenance of *ṛta* was characteristically held to be the major responsibility of Varuṇa. He was *ṛtasya gopā* or *ṛtavān* (Lord of *ṛta) par excellence.* It is perhaps not a mere coincidence that with the break up of tribal bonds and the emergence of class distinctions leading to baser instincts of greed, malevolence, and acquisitiveness, people start lamenting the loss of *ṛta* and one sees a corresponding decline of the acceptability and influence of Varuṇa as well.

Of 'Gods' and 'Demons'

An important aspect of comparative study of the religious trajectories is the question of allusions to *daevas, devas,* and *ahuras, asuras* in the *Avesta* and the *Ṛksaṃhitā. Baga* ('one who distributes'), and *yazata* ('one who is worthy of worship') were some other terms used in the *Avesta* to refer to divine beings. Are these allusions to mutually antagonistic 'gods' and 'demons'? Also relevant in this context are the Mitanni treaties referring to Mitra, Varuṇa, Indra and Nāsatya who figure severally or collectively in the two texts. Thus, while Varuṇa is mentioned exclusively in the *Ṛksaṃhitā*, Mitra figures in both in the sense of 'gods'. Though Indra-Nāsatyas are mentioned in both the texts, they are treated as *devas* ('gods') in the *Ṛksaṃhitā* but as '*daevas*' ('demons') in the *Avesta.*

The malefic or demonic connotaion of *daevas* is often attributed to Zoroaster coming to terms with old polytheistic Iranian religion. In this later form of religion Indra, Saurva and Nāṇahaithya—who had prominent positions in the Indian pantheon as Indra, Śarva and Nāsatyas—became arch demons. They were opposed respectively by the Amaesha Spentas Aša, Kshathra Vairya, and Armaiti.[63]

The problem of differing connotations is not confined to '*devas*' and '*daevas*'. It holds true of '*ahura*' and '*asura*' as well. While there is little dispute about 'divinity' of '*ahura*' in the *Avesta,* the same is not the case with the '*asura*' *par excellence* in the *Ṛksaṃhitā, i.e.*, Varuna. His juxtaposition with Indra is often seen in terms of the juxtaposition between 'god' and 'demon'.

'*Daevas*' and '*Asuras*', when seen in 'malefic/demonic' sense, are sometimes considered to be representing a process, *viz.*, 'gods' *becoming* 'demons' or the process of 'demonisation' of deities.[64] Alternatively, however, and perhaps more plausibly, the issue of 'gods' and 'demons' in the *Avesta* and the *Ṛksaṃhitā*, could be understood in terms of patterns of movements of Indo-Europeans. Several paradigms explaining factors, timing and sequence of these movements are in the field.

In the early twentieth century Gray had put forward his hypothesis thus:

> From Central Asia, through the open reaches east of the Caspian which have given access to the Iranian plateau to conqueror after conqueror, there came at an undatable period an invasion (or a series of invasions) of people who spoke an Indo-Iranian dialect which represented the Indo-European hard sibilant by *s*, and who termed their deities **deivos*. In their turn these invaders were gradually driven south by another invasion (or series of invasions) by a kindred people (or peoples) who had changed the hard sibilant *s* to *h*, who called their divinities *ahuros*, and who had, as kindred people often have, somewhat different vocabularies. These *h*-peoples (the later Iranians) gradually expelled the *s*-peoples until the latter finally made their way to India.
>
> In their contacts the *h*-peoples adopted some of the words of their *s*-enemies, but since they already had corresponding terms of their own . . . they had no need to add them to their vocabulary except as referring to their foes. Hence, these terms of the *s*-peoples, expelled or conquered, formed no real part of the vocabulary of the *h*-peoples, as they did of the word-stock of the *s*-peoples, and the former employed them only in a derogatory sense, applying them solely to beings, human or superhuman, whom they hated and despised as hostile and malign.[65]

Commenting on 'Iranians and their close brother the Indian Aryans', the renowned linguist Suniti Kumar Chatterji considers them as branches of 'primitive' Indo-Europeans—Aryans or Indo-Iranians emerged in the mid-third millennium BC. About the so-called 'Aryan' names in Mesopotamian and Asian documents, Chatterji calls them 'Pre-Vedic' and 'Pre-Avestan', for, he dates the 'Indian Vedas going back to the twelfth–tenth centuries'.[66]

More recently, the accent has been on somewhat different lines. It is argued, for instance, that climatic changes such as prolonged aridity in the second millennium BC propelled the steppes people to undertake a southward march. The quest for water became a catalyst in this movement. Walter A. Fairservis Jr. arguing for the Rgvedic people as forming part of a Central Asian Bronze Age civilization, has attributed this movement of cattle and other pastorals to a social and political schism between the urban elite and cattle pastorals. Burrow, on the other hand, postulates a movement of surplus population and locates it in the age when prospecting for metals (precious/or otherwise) was being actively pursued. He draws on the linguistic analysis of Waššukhani ('Mine of precious metals'), the capital of the Mitannis —Indo-Aryan *vasu* stands for 'wealth' and not adjective *vasu* (meaning 'good') as in Iranian; and *khani*, of course, is 'mine'.[67]

If one is not obsessed with India-centric view of the problem of 'Aryans', it appears fairly probable that the aforesaid movements may have taken place between *circa* 2000 and 1500 BC. From archaeological point of view, the area of the Andronovo culture (between 35° and 55° northern latitudes and 55° and 78° eastern longitudes) is fast emerging as the most likely epicentre, from where separate branches went to Iran and northwest India. Burrow had proposed the split between Indo-Aryans and Iranians in *circa* 2000 BC *before* their languages established themselves in their eventual homes. Dandekar's view about the chronological evolution of the *Ṛksaṃhitā* has been pointed out above. He is also known for maintaining a distinction between the so-called 'Aryan period' and 'Vedic Indians'. For him, the former represents times when 'ancestors of Vedic Aryans and the Iranian Aryans were living together, presumably in the region round about Balkh.' The 'Vedic Indians' marked a subsequent phase and represented 'Vedic Aryans who were advancing towards Saptasindhu.'[68]

The confrontationist argument in the relationship between 'gods' and 'demons' appears less convincing as compared to alternative hypotheses. It is a well-known axiom of linguistics that words keep on changing their meanings either because of natural process of evolution or due to exigencies of a changed milieu of people. In this sense, treating '*asura*' in the *Ṛksaṃhitā* as 'demon' requires a fresh scrutiny.

Long ago, Dandekar pointed out that the Vedic word *asura* was much older than the classical Sanskrit word *sura* (god) and that the former did not represent the opposite of the latter. Originally, the word *asura* stood for a being, who possessed the largest amount of magical potency. It was only later when it acquired the connotation of 'demon' that the word *sura* was artificially coined. *Asu* was sought to be compared with the magical potency of *mana*. On account of his enormous 'magic power' he creates the universe, regulates it into an orderly whole, and wields the most supreme sovereignty over it: his unique power is called *māyā*. In *RV*, VII.88.6, Varuṇa is called *yakṣin*, a magician.[69] Further, as an *asura*, Varuṇa is also closely associated with Mitra, Ādityas, Aditi, and *ṛta*, all having connotations of 'binder'.[70] It may be recalled that in the Boghazköy inscription of the fourteenth century BC, Varuṇa and Mitra are invoked not singly like Indra, but 'together with their group.' This affinity and its associated trait of being 'binder' explains their invocation as witnesses to the treaty. Dandekar is an exponent of the Varuṇa-*ṛta* religion going back to the 'Aryan period', which was superseded by the Indra religion, and in the final stage a compromise between the two was brought about by the Vāsiṣṭhas. *RV*, VII.83.9 reflects this compromise whereby Indra 'conquers', but it is Varuṇa who 'rules'.

A detailed study of *asura* Varuṇa, proceeding on the basis of the late nineteenth century suggestion of J. Darmesteter and P. von Bradke, who had proposed that the epithet *asura* simply meant 'Lord, overlord, sovereign', suggests that it could be both human and divine. These lords commanded some force of fighting men and this 'rank' was not an inherent quality but was bestowed or assigned. The usage was not restricted to friendly leaders and gods—an enemy leader, too, was called an *asura*.[71]

Who were the *daeva*-worshippers? Their condemnation is often taken as an important characteristic of Zoroastrianism. In addition to the *daevas* recounted above, *daeva*-worshippers were the people who worshipped the *daevas* as well as the gods, or some of the gods, worshipped by Mazdayasnians. In a late Avestan passage (*Yasht* 5.94f), the *daeva*-worshippers offer libations to Anāhitā, although she evidently was not a *daevī*; the Zoroastrian author portrays Anāhitā as rejecting these libations. The same holds true of Mithra. Aṇgra Maiṇyu is comparative late-comer among the *daevas*. Essentially, then, the *daevas* in the Avesta were not necessarily antagonistic to *ahuras*. These were deities of an early phase of tribal movements, with whom the later day Zoroastrianism was trying to come to terms in varied ways.

Finally, did 'gods' and 'demons' have their domains ? The

Avesta has no words for a consecrated building or temple fire. The Younger *Avesta* alludes to *gāhambār,* which were seasonal festivals marked by communal worship and merry-making—celebrations that were scattered irregularly through the year. Significantly, originally, these were associated with events in the pastoral and farming year. The tradition that 'spring butter' *(zaramaya-raogna)* was the best of all foods clearly goes back to the Old Avestan times, and the joy of a pastoral people in fresh products from their cows after winter's deprivation.

A hymn about Avestic Mithra reads : 'His place is of the width of the earth' (*Yt.*10.44), which is compared with one on the Rgvedic Mitra (*RV,* III.59.7): 'the wide one, who holds embraced heaven with his greatness, [holds] embraced the earth with his glory.' Such descriptions are taken as portrayals of the geographically limitless power of the Vedic gods. Each deity has a special task and character but no geographical limits and has no relation to the importance of a place of worship. This lack of territoriality of Vedic polytheism is contrasted with later Hinduism, wherein each city, each town, each village has its temples and each house its images, its *kula-devatās.* Paul Thieme's contention that the later day Hinduism is, in type, much more similar to Anatolian religion than Vedic religion deserves special attention, specially when the self-appointed custodians of Hinduism are homogenizing and Semitizing it.

Notes and References

1 Cf. 'The Indo-European Phenomenon: Linguistics and Archaeology' in A.H. Dani and J.P. Mohen (eds), *History of Humanity: Scientific and Cultural Development,* Vol. II, UNESCO and Routledge, 1996, pp. 80–81. For a recent discussion of the idea of the Aryan and of the origin of 'Aryan' race theory, see T.R. Trautman, *Aryans and British India,* Vistaar Publications, New Delhi, 1997. However, for its critique and underlying neo-colonialist predilections, see D.N. Jha's review in *Indian Anthropologist,* Vol. 27, No. 2, December, 1997, pp. 91–95.

2 V.G. Rahurkar, *The Seers of the Ṛgveda,* Poona, 1964, p. ix calls books II–VII as the 'nucleus of the *saṃhitā* ... to which *maṇḍala* one was prefixed and *mandalas* eight, nine and ten were affixed'. More specifically, however, Rahurkar counts even Book VIII amongst 'family-books'.

3 T. Burrow, 'The Proto-Indo-Aryans', *The Journal of the Royal Asiatic Society of Great Britain and Ireland* (NS), (hereafter *JRAS)* II, 1973, p. 137; Mary Boyce: 'Zoroaster the Priest', *Bulletin of the School of Oriental and African Studies* (hereafter, *BSOAS*), Vol. 33, 1970, pp. 25–26.

4 F.B.J. Kuiper, 'The Bliss of Aša', *Indo-Iranian Journal*, (hereafter, *IIJ*), Vol. VIII, 1964–65, pp. 101–02.

5 A landmark study of this problem is V.G. Rahurkar's work cited above.

6 Cf. Rajesh Kochhar, *The Vedic People: Their History and Geography*, Orient Longman, Hyderabad, 2000, pp. 16–22; K.M. Shrimali, 'Are We Aryans?', *Biblio*, May–June 2000, pp. 7–8.

7 R.N. Dandekar, 'The Antecedents and the Early Beginnings of the Vedic period', Presidential Address, Section I (Ancient Period), *The Proceedings of the Indian History Congress* (hereafter, *PIHC*), Tenth Session held at Bombay, 1947, pp. 49–55.

8 T. Burrow, 'The Proto-Indo-Aryans', pp. 134–135.

9 R.N. Dandekar, op.cit., p. 52

10 '*Saptasindhavaḥ*' is used at one place in *Rgveda*, VIII.24.27. References to the so-called 'seven rivers' lie scattered and their identifications with present-day rivers are fraught with conflicting interpretations. Sometimes, even the much eulogized Sarasvatī is also included amongst these 'seven' and located somewhere in Afghanistan.

11 T. Burrow, 'The Pro-Indo-Aryans', pp. 137–39. See also F.B.J. Kuiper, 'Remarks on the Avestan Hymn to Mithra', *IIJ*, Vol. V, 1961–62, p. 43, where he questions Ilya Gershevitch's (*The Avestan Hymn to Mithra*, Cambridge University Press, Cambridge, 1959) chronology of the Gathas and suggests a date not later than 1000 BCE for the *Avesta*.

12 W. Geiger, *Civilization of the Eastern Iranians in Ancient Times*, tr. D.P. Sanjana, London, 1886, p. 64.

13 R.C. Zaehner, *The Dawn and Twilight of Zoroastrianism*, London, 1961, p. 40.

14 E.C. Polomé, 'Indo-European Culture with Special Attention to Religion' in E.C. Polomé (ed.) *The Indo-Europeans in the Fourth and Third Millennia*, Michigan, 1982, p. 170. R.N. Dandekar, 'Indo-Europeanism and Vedic Mythology: Some Notes' in his *Select Writings*, Vol. I, *Vedic Mythological Tracts*, Ajanta Publications (India), Delhi, 1979, pp. 358–61 questions Dumézil's hypothesis, specifically its exclusivity in terms of the Indo-Europeans, not only from the sociological and anthropological points of view but also for its bearings on comparative mythology. John Brough has also been a strong critic of Dumézil, specially his notion of trifunctional hierarchization of society, in his two contributions: 'Usas and Mater Matuta', *BSOAS*, Vol. 21, 1958, pp. 395–199, and 'The Tripartite Ideology of the Indo-Europeans: An Experiment in Method', *BSOAS*, Vol. 22, 1959, pp. 69–85. In the latter contribution, Brough also shows the presence of trifunctionalism amongst ancient Hebrews as well. See also discussion on goddesses below.

15 Mary Boyce, 'Avestan People' in Ehsan Yarshater (ed.), *Encyclopaedia Iranica*, Vol. III, 1989, p. 63. Elsewhere, Boyce has unleashed an extremely scathing criticism of those who have messed up the 'older' and the 'younger' Avestan societies. These include S. Wikander's study of the so-called 'War-bands' (*Der arische Mannerbund*, Lund, 1938), Bruce Lincoln's analysis

(*Priest, Warriors and Cattle*, California, 1981) of the comparative study of the *Avestan* and the Rgvedic data on proto-Indo-Iranian religion and culture with the help of anthropological insights from East African Nilotic tribes; and G. Gnoli (*Zoroaster's Time and Homeland*, Naples, 1980), who also, following Wikander, made no distinction between Old and Younger Avestan society. Cf. Mary Boyce, 'Priests, Cattle and Men', *BSOAS*, Vol. L, 1987, pp. 508–26.

[16] Mary Boyce, 'Avestan People', pp. 62–66.

[17] S.K. Chatterji, 'Race Movements and Prehistoric Culture' in R.C. Majumdar, *et al.*, (eds), *The History and Culture of the Indian People*, Vol. I, *The Vedic Age*, Bharatiya Vidya Bhavan, Bombay, 1951, specially pp. 156–65.

[18] A.L. Basham, *The Wonder That Was India*, First Indian Edition, Orient Longman, Madras, 1963, p. 387; Madhav M. Deshpande and Peter Edwin Hook (eds), *Aryan and Non-Aryan in India*, Michigan University, Ann Arbor, 1979, pp. 235–315; Madhav M. Deshpande, 'Vedic Aryans, Non-Vedic Aryans and Non-Aryans' in G. Erdosy (ed.), *The Indo-Aryans of South Asia: Language, Material Culture and Ethnicity*, 1995, Indian (rpt), Munshiram Manoharlal Publishers, New Delhi,1997, pp. 67–84; G.V. Devasthali, 'Prakritism in the *Ṛgveda*' in R.N. Dandekar and A.M. Ghatge, (eds), *Proceedings of the Seminar in Prakrit Studies*, Pune University, 1970, pp. 199–205; J. Przyluski in P.C. Bagchi, (ed.), *Pre-Aryan and Pre-Dravidian in India*, p. 8f; Ram Sharan Sharma, *Advent of the Aryans in India*, Manohar, 1999, pp. 51–57. See also, K.M.Shrimali, 'Are We Aryans?', op.cit., p. 8.

[19] Romila Thapar (*From Lineage to State*, Oxford University Press, Delhi, 1984) has identified Vedic society as a 'lineage society' instead of 'tribal society'. Sociologists and anthropologists have underlined the centrality of the concept of *kin* in tribe, clan and lineage. In this context, Ram Sharan Sharma ('From Kin to Class', *Economic and Political Weekly*, Vol. 20, No. 22, 1 June 1985, pp. 960–61) has rightly invoked such Vedic terms as *gotra*, *vra* and *vrāta* to emphasize that blood relationship was not the only basis of kinship. Instead, originally the kin-based groups were formed to collect war booty in the form of cattle and to arrange for sources of subsistence. The term *vaṃśa*, from which the concept of 'lineage' seems to derive its *raison d'etre*, does not even figure in the *Ṛksaṃhitā*. The term 'tribe' not only encompasses kinship, but is also more comprehensive than 'lineage'. Of the three terms, viz. 'tribe', 'clan' and 'lineage', the last one constitutes the smallest whereas the first one is considered to be the largest kin group. 'Clan' represents the intervening stage. For a long drawn debate on the issue see also A.M. Shah, 'Towards a Sociological Understanding of Ancient India', *Contributions to Indian Sociology*, Vol. 20, No. 1, January–June 1986, pp. 117–33, and Romila Thapar's response thereto in *ibid.*, No. 2, July–December 1986, pp. 289–95; R.N. Nandi, 'Anthroplogy and the Study of the *Ṛgveda*', *The Indian Historical Review* (hereafter *IHR)*, Vol. 13, Nos 1–2, July 1986 and January 1987, pp. 153–65; Nandi, *Aryans Revisited*, Munshiram Manoharlal Publishers Pvt. Ltd., New Delhi, 2001; Suvira

Jaiswal, 'Stratification in Rgvedic Society : Evidence and Paradigms', *IHR*, Vol. 16, Nos 1–2, July 1989 and January 1990, pp. 1–34; Jaiswal, 'Mystifying the Aryans', *IHR*, Vol. 20, Nos. 1–2, July 1993 and January 1994, pp. 219–28; Romila Thapar, 'The Aryans Ride Again', *IHR*, Vol. 18, Nos. 1–2, July 1991 and January 1992, pp. 178–79.

[20] For a detailed discussion, see Krishna Mohan Shrimali, *History of Pañchāla*, Vol. I, Munshiram Manoharlal Publishers, New Delhi,1983, pp. 166–68; Ram Sharan Sharma, *Material Culture and Social Formations in Ancient India*, Macmillan, Delhi, 1983, pp. 22–25. Romila Thapar (*From Lineage to State*, pp. 23–26), too, concedes that the Rgvedic society was essentially dependent on pastoral activities.

[21] Romila Thapar's contention (*From Lineage to State*, p. 27) that most of the celebrated battles (including the famous *dāśarājña*) were among the major clans and these conflicts involved 'claims to territorial control and rights of succession to these territories' does not seem to be very plausible. Tribes based on pastoralism, were often on the move and do not yet appear to have been guided by 'territorial' instincts. Further, the vocabulary of wars, too, was cattle-centered.

[22] Romila Thapar, ibid., pp. 29–32 refers to bifurcation of *jana* (tribe) into 'senior lineages of the *rājanyas* and the lesser, junior or cadet lineages (*viś*)' in the Saptasindhu region. Nevertheless, she continues to recognize, 'as long as the wealth came from pastoralism in the main, it had a relatively more equitable distribution'.

[23] This development may have been the outcome of the culture-contact situation wherein the non-Sanskrit speakers seem to have called the shots. A number of key words relating to agricultural activities in the Vedic Sanskrit literature appear to be of non-Sanskritic origin (largely Dravidian and some Mundari), e.g., *lāṅgala, hala* (plough), and such other words as *kuddāla* (hoe), *khala* (threshing floor), *śūrpa* (winnowing basket), *ulūkhala* (mortar and pestle). Notwithstanding the so-called 'linguistic imperialism of the speakers of the Indo-Aryan languages', it is hard to think of 'complete extinction of Dravidian, Munda and whatever other languages were previously spoken by the inhabitants of the Indo-Gangetic plains, and beyond' as Raymond Allchin and Bridget Allchin contend. They, however, concede that the 'Rigveda shows several influences of a non-Indo-Aryan, Dravidian element in the form of phonetic changes, introduction of loan words and names, etc. This presupposes the co-existence of Vedic and Dravidian speaking people in a culture contact situation for a period, perhaps of centuries, before the compilation of the *Rigveda* . . . between 1500 and 1300 BC' (*The Rise of Civilization in India and Pakistan*, Cambridge University Press, hereafter CUP, Cambridge, 1982, pp. 354–56).

24 This has reference to the discovery of 'Aryan' looking names of [Mitanni-] princes on cuneiform documents in Akkadian from the second half of the second millennium BC (chiefly tablets from El-Amarna and Boghazköy, discovered in 1887 and 1906 respectively); several doubtlessly Aryan words in Kikkuli's treatise in Hittite on horse training (brought to light in

archaeological expeditions at Boghazköy between 1906 and 1912); Indian divine names on Cassite documents (Friedrich Delitzsch's discovery in 1884); and a series of names of Aryan divinities on a Mitanni-Hatti and a Hatti-Mitanni treaty (fourteenth century BC). To these may also be added R.N. Dandekar's reference to the discovery of Nuzi (southeastern end of Mitanni kingdom) documents between 1925 and 1931. In sum, as pointed out by Dandekar, this 'Aryan' linguistic material has [a] names of four Vedic gods, [b] 13 appellatives that include four substantives, three adjectives, five numerals and one verb, [c] a number of personal names—some of which seems to be local variations of original Aryan forms. For Dandekar's exposition, see his R.G. Bhandarkar Anniversary Address (1969) entitled 'Some Aspects of the Indo-Mediterranean Contacts', *Annals of the Bhandarkar Oriental Research Institute*, Vol. 50,1969, pp. 57–74.

[25] Paul Thieme, 'The "Aryan" Gods of the Mitanni Treaties', *The Journal of the American Oriental Society* (hereafter, *JAOS)*, Vol. 80, 1960, pp. 301 and 315. For a critique of Thieme's postulates see T. Burrow, 'The Proto-Indo-Aryans'.

[26] Some Indian archaeologists (for example, Dilip K. Chakrabarti, *Colonial Indology: Socio-politics of the Ancient Indian Past,* Munshiram Manoharlal Publishers Pvt. Ltd., New Delhi, 1997), in their zeal for pretentious iconoclasm, have been debunking India's rich literary heritage (Vedic literature in particular). Similarly, Bruce Lincoln in an appendix 'On the use of archaeology in the reconstruction of Indo-Iranian religion' (*Priest, Warriors and Cattle,* pp. 179–84) has been quite dismissive of archaeological evidence and maintains that the study of proto-Indo-Iranian religion rests mainly on 'linguistics, mythic reconstruction and so on'. Such compartmentalized reconstructions are often too blinkered. Castigating 'archaeological purists', Raymond Allchin and Bridget Allchin (*The Rise of Civilization in India and Pakistan,* Cambridge University Press, Cambridge, 1982, p. 354) emphatically asserted: 'To admit such a restriction would, in our view, make a nonsense of our aim of reconstructing the rise of Indian civilization, since it would rule out a large and most interesting part of the evidence.' Historical processes need to be studied through multifarious angles and with data from diversified sources. The relevance of Kosambi's 'Combined Methods in Indology', in this context, is too obvious to be stressed. Cf. D.D. Kosambi, *Combined Methods in Indology and Other Writings,* compiled, edited and introduced by Brajadulal Chattopadhyaya, Oxford University Press, New Delhi, 2002; K.M. Shrimali, 'The Making of an Indologist' (being a review of the aforesaid anthology of Kosambi's writings), *Frontline,* 13 September, 2002, pp. 72–74; Romila Thapar, *Cultural Pasts—Essays in Early Indian History,* Oxford University Press, New Delhi, 2000, Section III: Archaeology and History; R.N.Nandi, *Aryans Revisited* (for fuller details, see n.19). On the correlation of the archaeological and linguistic models of Indian pre- and protohistory, see also Asko Parpola, *Deciphering the Indus Script,* Cambridge University Press, Cambridge, 1994, pp. 125–75. In a devastating critique of

Chakrabarti's notion of history and methods of history writing reflected in his *Colonial Indology*, B.D. Chattopadhyaya ('Confronting Fundamentalisms: The Possibilities of Early Indian History', *Studies in History*, Vol. XVIII, No. 1, January–June 2002, pp. 106–12) identifies them as 'archaeological fundamentalism' which suggests 'a dangerous, uni-dimensional nationalist agenda of writing about the past.'

[27] G. Gnoli: 'Iranian Religions', in Mircea Eliade (ed.), *The Encyclopaedia of Religion*, Vol. 7, 1987, pp. 277–80 citing Karl Jettmar's *Die Religionen des Hindukush*, Stuttgart, 1975 and Giuseppe Tucci, 'On Swat: The Dards and Connected Problems', *East and West* (NS), 27, 1977, 9–103. See also seven contributions (Nos 10–16) on Shahr-i-Sokhta in Bridget Allchin (ed.), *South Asian Archaeology 1981*, Oxford University Press, Cambridge, 1984, pp. 69–128.

[28] Cf. Mary Boyce, 'Priests, Cattle and Men', pp. 508–12, where several comparisons between Sintashta and Rgvedic evidences have also been invoked.

[29] H.D. Sankalia, B. Subbarao and S.B. Deo, *The Excavations at Maheshwar and Navdatoli, 1952–53*, Poona and Baroda, 1958, p. 252; H.D. Sankalia, *Prehistory and Protohistory in India and Pakistan*, University of Bombay, 1962, pp. 271–74; Sankalia, 'Iranian Influence on Early Indo-Pakistani Cultures', in Amalendu Guha (ed.), Central *Asia: Movement of Peoples and Ideas from Times Prehistoric to Modern*, Barnes & Noble, New York, 1971, pp. 53–74

[30] M.K. Dhavalikar, 'India-Iran Contacts in Prehistory', paper presented at the Seminar on Relations between India and Iran' held at Bhopal in December, 2001, *cyclostyled copy*. Not committing himself to any position on the archaeology of 'Aryan problem', the author does recognize: 'the linguistic evidence, which is quite formidable, clearly indicates that the Vedic Aryans and the early Iranians in all likelihood formed one group in the hoary past, but were separated later in the second millennium BC.'

[31] Asko Parpola, *Deciphering the Indus Script*, pp. 142–59; Ram Sharan Sharma, *Advent of the Aryans in India*, Manohar, New Delhi, 1999, pp. 52–97; Rajesh Kochhar, chapters 8 and 9.

[32] Kochhar (op.cit., pp. 108–12) even calls it 'the mascot of Aryans'. Following the reports of British botanist James Edward Tierney Aitchison on the flora and fauna of Afghanistan prepared in the 1880s, Kochhar accepts the identification of the *soma* plant with the species *Ephedra distachya*. Sharma (*Advent of the Aryans*...p. 26) cautions: 'Although this identification is accepted, search for conclusive evidence is continuing.'

[33] On the issue of the correlation between the *Ṛksṃhitā* and Harappan culture, we need recall the following observations of the late B.K. Thapar (former Director-General of the Archaeological Survey of India) and Professor Abdul Rahman of Pakistan (excavator of many arcaheological sites in the Swat, Dir and Peshawar valleys): 'Practically nothing can be gleaned from the *Rigveda* about the appearance or layout of an Aryan settlement.... It is unfortunate that no written records have come to light from excavations to

supply names of different cultural materials. Nor is there anything in the Vedic literature to show that the Indo-Aryan people possessed a specific material culture, such as pottery or particular figurines or objects, which being discovered in the field would enable us to establish kind of identification marks for their migration... And yet there is enough in the *Rigveda* to show that no relationship existed between the mature Harappan cultural milieu and the habitation pattern of the Aryans as described in it' (in A.H.Dani and J.-P. Mohen, (eds), *History of Humanity: Scientific and Cultural Development*, Vol. II, UNESCO and Routledge, 1996, pp. 277–78. It may also be noted that some elements of the material culture of Pirak, specially the cereal remains, stand in the way of their correlation with the *Ṛksaṃhitā* data. While Pirak has yielded wheat, barley, rice, millet and oates, the *Ṛksaṃhitā* is familiar with only *yava* (possibly barley).

34 G.Gnoli: 'Iranian Religions', p. 277.

35 This would include, for example, the *Sāmaññaphala Sutta* in the Buddhist text *Dīgha Nikāya*; Jain *Bhagavatī Sūtra* and a Vedantic text, viz. Madhvāchārya's *Sarvadarśanasaṃgraha.* Chronologically, these allusions span over more than 1500 years, *circa* 3rd century BC to AD 14th century.

For a modern day reconstruction , see A.L.Basham, *History and Doctrines of the Ājīvikas*, London, 1951, Delhi reprint 1981, which is the only full-length authoritative monograph in English. Amongst earlier competent studies is included Beni Madhab Barua's 'The Ājīvikas', *Journal of the Department of Letters* (University of Calcutta), Vol. 2, 1920, pp. 1–80.

36 R. Schmitt, 'Aryans' in Ehsan Yarshater (ed.) *Encyclopaedia Iranica,* Vol. II, 1987, pp. 684–87, points out that such correspondence in idiomatic phrases bear testimony to not only linguistic affinity, but also spiritual and cultural community. Further he draws our attention to B. Schlerath's *Awesta-Worterbuch, Vorabeiten I: Konkordanz,* Wiesbaden, 1968, pp. 148–64, for the most systematic collection of the common elements of the Vedic and Avestic poetic phraseology inherited from 'Proto-Aryans'.

37 'It was in solemnization of pre-Zoroastrian rituals that Zoroaster was trained as priest', argues Mary Boyce in 'Zoroaster the Priest', *BSOAS,* Vol. 33, 1970, p. 25.

38 'Bountiful Immortal Ones'—constitute seven aspects of Ahura Mazda's character—Mazda is the leader of all forces of 'Good'. As a distinguishing trait of Zoroastrian dualism, Amaesha Spentas are in conflict with Ahriman with seven Aešma ('Evils' such as Wrath, Discord, Apostasy, Anarchy, Presumption, Hunger, Thirst)—a conflict in which the 'Evil' is not merely absence of the 'Good' but it is real and substantial force.

39 A recent study describes Rgvedic goddesses as 'secondary citizens within the pantheon', cf. Kumkum Roy, 'Goddesses in the *Ṛgveda*', in Nilima Chitgopekar (ed.), *Invoking Goddesses: Gender Politics in Indian Religion,* Har-Anand Publications, New Delhi, 2002, p. 60.

40 Shalini Shah, 'Sexual Politics and the Cult of the Mother Goddesses in the Mahābhārata', in Nilima Chitgopekar, *Invoking Goddesses,* pp. 67–68 where attention has also been drawn to a passage from the *Śatapatha Brāhmaṇa*

(IX.4.1.6) representing valorization of the male as opposed to the female principle.

[41] Kumkum Roy, *Invoking Goddesses*, pp. 43–61.

[42] Roy somehow seems to be underplaying ramming/rape of Uṣas (*ne yat sīṃ śiśnathad vrsa*, 'when the Bull (Indra) had rammed her', RV IV.30.10). D.D. Kosambi (*Myth and Reality*, Popular Prakashan, Bombay, 1962, p. 61f) sees this as a 'clash of cults of the old mother-goddess being crushed by the new war-god (Indra) of the patriarchal invaders.' Incidentally, Indra's sexuality reflected in various hymns of the *Ṛgveda*, has also not received enough attention from Roy.

[43] Contrast this with Haurvatat and Ameretat (two of the seven feminine Amaesa Spentas), who in the *Avsta*, represent the ideals of vigour.

[44] For a strong rebuttal of Dumézil's notions on Indo-European society and their relevance for comparative Indo-European mythology in general and Rgvedic mythology in particular, see R.N. Dandekar, 'Indo-Europeanism and Vedic Mythology: Some Notes' in his *Select Writings*, Vol. I, *Vedic Mythological Tracts*, Ajanta Publications (India), Delhi, 1979, pp. 358–61. In short, he underlines: 'Dumezil seems to regard mythology as being static. It is, indeed, difficult to believe that any mythological pattern could survive the various inevitable changes in social life . . . the Dumezilian pattern of functional tripartition provides too narrow a frame to contain all the variety and complexity of Vedic mythology.' Ilya Gershevitch, *The Avestan Hymn to Mithra*, Cambridge University Press, Cambridge, 1959, Introduction and John Brough, *BSOAS*, Vol. XXI, 1958, p. 395f, ibid., Vol. XXII, 1959, p. 69f (for fuller details of Brough's contributions, see n.14) are also quite dismissive of Dumezil's theories on Vedic religion.

[45] R.S. Sharma, 'Material Milieu of Tantricism', in R.S. Sharma and Vivekanand Jha (eds), *Indian Society: Historical Probings (in Memory of D.D. Kosambi)*, People's Publishing House, New Delhi 1974, pp. 175–89, reprinted in D.N. Jha (ed.), *The Feudal Order: State, Society and Ideology in Early Medieval India*, Manohar, New Delhi, 2000, pp. 441–54.

[46] For these references to Rātri and Araṇyāni, see A.L.Basham, *The Wonder That was India*, pp. 402–03.

[47] For example George G. Cameron, 'Zoroaster the Herdsman', *IIJ*, Vol. X, 1967–68, pp. 261–81. Arguing that conceptions of wealth and those of holiness are wholly separate, Cameron underplays pastoralism : 'It is my belief that the respect approaching sanctification which the prophet appears to have for cattle can by no means be explained on the basis of the social and economic practice of his audience. . . . It is overlooked that the Iranian plateau, could now or ever have accommodated a peasant economy founded exclusively or even primarily on cattle culture.' References to cattle, pasturage, shepherds and nourishment in the *Avesta* are only metaphors. Further, despite recognizing that the 'Rgvedic Indians were a nation of beef-eaters,' Cameron adds 'it is even possible that the sanctity of the ox and cow in India originated, not with the Indo-European Aryans, but with the indigenous inhabitants among whom they penetrated'.

Cameron gives chronologically (1882–1961) the views on Avestic evidence on the understanding that 'the care and preservation of cattle is a central feature of the Zoroastrian doctrine'. However, he shares Walter Hinz's (*Zarathustra*, 1961, p. 69f) view which identifies three distinct 'Layers' of meanings of Zoroaster's concept of 'the Cow':

[a] mundane or earthy animal;
[b] all living species ('creatures') of animal world, and
[c] flock of 'believing or wishing to-believe humanity, to whom Zoroaster was sent as 'shepherd'.'

Earlier Wolfgang P.Schmid (in *Indogermanische Forschungen*, Vol. 16,1958–59, pp. 1–12) had also suggested that Rgvedic and Gathic utterances to 'cow', 'ox' and 'pasture' were metaphorical (cited by Cameron).

See also Von A. Venkatasubbiah, 'On Indra's Winning Cows and Waters', *Zietschrift der Deutschen Morgenlandischen Gesellschaft (ZDMG)*, Band 115, 1965, pp.120–33 where the mention of Indra's release of waters and cows when he overthrew Vṛtra, Vala, Pipru, Arbuda and Śuṣna is described as 'in all probability conventional.'

Bruce Lincoln ('Cattle' in Mircea Eliade, (ed.) *Encyclopedia of Religion*, Vol. 3, 1987, pp. 123–27) sees 'cosmogonic significance' in the myths of Indra-Vṛtra/Vala encounters.

[48] As the guardian of cattle, *vohu manah* has precedence over other six Amesha Spentas, viz. Truth, Desired Kingdom, Devotion, Integrity, Obedience and Immortality.

[49] Bruce Lincoln: *Priests, Warriors, and Cattle,* p. 66, n.103 cautions: One must be very careful in using foreign evidence of this sort. Surely, one must be careful in reading late and foreign data back into early sources. In case of Herodotus, however, we are dealing with material that can be independently verified by the correspondences in Indian sources. The strength of these correspondences must have been quite strong enabling such a normally skeptical scholar as A.B. Keith (*The Religion and Philosophy of the Veda and Upanishads,* 1925, Indian reprint, Motilal Banarsidass, Delhi, 1970, Vol. II, p. 360) to accept the authenticity of Herodotus' testimony.

[50] Mary Boyce,'Bībī Shahrbānū and the Lady of Pārs', *BSOAS*, Vol. 30, 1967, pp. 30–44. For an extensive discussion of Anāhitā in the *Avesta*, see Max Muller (ed.), *The Sacred Books of the East,* Vol. XXII, Indian (rpt), Motilal Banarsidass, 1996, pp. 52–84.

[51] As a Parsi, he had abhorrence, learnt from the Hindus, of killing cows. His reports of visit to Persia were published as *Ezhāre Syāte Iran* in 1865. Incidentally, even Parsis in India carried out cattle sacrifice till the tenth century AD.

[52] Cf. H.S. Nyberg (*Religionen,* 1938, p. 200): 'Zarathustra battles *for* a normal reception of the divine power of the cow through the drinking of milk and *against* a ritualistic, ecstatic appropriation of that power through wild, sacrificial orgies; *for* the claim of the earth to possess the heavenly power of the cow's urine and *against* the wasting of this heavenly gift through the

slaughter of bulls; *for* the inviolability of the soul of the beast and *against* murderous attacks on its divine life.'

53 Cf. Mary Boyce , 'Ātaš-zōhr and Āb-zōhr', *JRAS,* 1966, pp. 105–07. Two decades later, Boyce made similar assertions in her strong critique ('Priests, Cattle and Men', *BSOAS,* 50, 1987, pp. 508–26) of Bruce Lincoln's *Priests, Warriors and Cattle (1981),* which, she thinks, presented a weakly argued case for Zoroaster having condemned the sacrifice of cattle.

Since the performance/rejection of cattle sacrifice needs to be situated in specific social and material contexts, it deserves attention that in cases where a previously pastoral population has abandoned its earlier mode of production and consequent way of life, the rejection of such sacrifices becomes reasonably pronounced. Thus, for instance, within the Athenian *polis,* details of the foremost cattle sacrifice—the Bouphonia ('Ox-slaying')—reveal a profound uneasiness over the violence and bloodshed inherent in the rite. Towards the end of each Bouphonia, a trial was thus held to assess the guilt of those responsible for the victim's death, such guilt ultimately being assigned to the sacrificial knife with which it was killed, the knife then being punished (and purified) by being thrown into the sea. In India, too, when agriculture harnessed with animal husbandry was replacing pastoralism, religions of the post-Vedic period were consistently and consciously pleading for the cessation of cattle sacrifice.

54 There are as many as thirty references to *uśij* in the *Ṛksaṃhitā*. These were specialists in cattle raids and went out with tribal chiefs to win war-booty, specially cattle.

55 R.S. Sharma, *Looking for the Aryans,* Orient Longman, Hyderabad, 1995, pp. 43–44; J.P. Mallory, *In Search of the Indo-Europeans Language, Archaeology and Myth,* Thames and Hudson, London, 1991, pp. 220–21. R.N. Dandekar suggests in his 'Indo-Europeanism and Vedic Mythology : Some Notes', p. 363: 'One can speak of an Indo-European proto-type of horse-sacrifice; but the Vedic Asvamedha in its totality has to be viewed as an Indian development on account of the inclusion in it of the elements of the pre-Aryan human sacrifice.'

56 I owe these references to Ms Smita Sahgal who is working for her Doctoral thesis on 'Cults of the Bull: A Socio-religious Study of North India' under my supervision. See also K.R. Potdar, *Sacrifice in the Ṛgveda.* That the ritual slaying of buffaloes continued till at least the beginning of the twentieth century in the Tamil, Telugu and Kannada speaking areas of India is known through extensive documentation done by Whitehead in his *The Village Gods of South India* (second edition published in 1921 under the auspices of The Young Men's Christian Association (YMCA) in the series 'The Religious Life of India' edited by J.N. Farquhar and Nicol Macnicol). These sacrifices were offered to village mother goddesses.

57 R. Gordon Wasson, *Soma: Divine Mushroom of Immortality,* New York, 1968; Mary Boyce, 'Haoma, Priest of the Sacrifice', in Mary Boyce and Ilya Gershevitch, (eds), *W.B. Henning Memorial Volume,* London, 1970, pp. 62–80.

[58] For the place of *soma* in Vedic hymns, see S.S. Bhawe, *The Soma Hymns of the Ṛgveda,* Baroda, 1957–62. See also Harri Nyberg, 'The Problem of the Aryans and the Soma: The Botanical Evidence', in George Erdosy, (ed.), *The Indo-Aryans of South Asia*, pp. 382–406. In India, the *soma*-ceremony with animal sacrifice is still solemnized in Kerala, the Godavari region in Andhra Pradesh, and the Thanjavur district of Tamilnadu. At this great ceremony Brahmans of all the four Vedas lay aside ordinary restrictions and revert to the custom of their forefathers by eating meat. The persistence of this observance in India, despite the doctrine of *ahimsa*, proves how strongly it is rooted in the Brahman tradition.

[59] Suniti Kumar Chatterji, *Iranianism—Iranian Culture and its Impact on the World from Achaemenian Times,* The Asiatic Society, Calcutta, 1972, p. 12. Referring to Luders' posthumous publication on Varuna (Vol. I, Introduction, p. 27), Ilya Gershevitch (*W.B. Henning Memorial Volume*, 1959, pp. 6–7) underlines that no true understanding of Indo-Iranian religious thought is possible unless it is realized that its key conception, expressed by *ṛta/aša*, means 'Truth.' This view of Gershevitch has been questioned by Kuiper (*IIJ*, Vol. V, 1961–62, pp. 36–60), who thinks that *aša* could also mean 'cosmic order'.

[60] F.B.J. Kuiper, 'The Bliss of Aša', *IIJ*, Vol. VIII, 1964–65, pp. 96–129.The article also deals with Indo-Iranian cosmology. On *khvarenah*, see G. Gnoli: 'Iranian Religions', in Mircea Eliade, (ed.), *The Encyclopaedia of Religion,* 1987, Vol. 7, pp. 277–80

[61] Cf. N.N. Bhattacharyya, *Ancient Indian Rituals and their Social Contents*, 2nd edition, Manohar, 1996, pp. 82–92; Debiprasad Chattopadhyaya, *Lokāyata—A Study in Ancient Indian Materialism*, 2nd edition, People's Publishing House, New Delhi, 1968, pp. 622–665.

[62] Kuiper in his above cited article (n. 60) draws our attention to the distinction between 'seeing' and 'knowing'. While *aša* is 'seen', *ṛta* is 'known'. Significantly, in this passage of the *Ṛksaṃhitā* (V.43.6), the great goddess is specifically called Aramati, whom Ralph T.H. Griffith (*The Hymns of the Ṛgveda*, revised Delhi edition, Motilal Banarsidass, 1973, p. 258, n. 6) identified with 'Spenta-Armaiti . . . of the Zoroastrians.' In *RV*, V.43.6, Aramati is called a virgin who comes with butter offerings in the morning and evening to Agni, a Celestial Lady who is brought up by Agni. Though rare, some other allusions to Aramati in the *Ṛgveda* are VII. 1.6; VII.34.21 and X.92.4–5, where her traits also include devotion and obedience.

[63] Among important Zoroastrian *daivas* are Aešma ('wrath fury'), known throughout the Zoroastrian tradition; Apaosha ('death') fought by Tištrya, the *yazata* of the star Sirius; Ašto-vīdhātu ('dismembering of skeleton'); Būshyasta ('sloth'); and Nasu ('corpse'), the demon of decay.

[64] A typical example of this tendency is Paul Thieme, 'The "Aryan" Gods' Earlier, in the late 1930s, H.S. Nyberg had made similar contention in his exposition of the religion of Iran.

[65] L.H. Gray, 'The "Ahurian" and 'Daevian' Vocabularies in the Avesta', *JRAS*,

1927, p. 439. For a corrective of this view, specially on the question of migration of Indo-Aryans to India on account of being driven out by the Iranians, see T. Burrow, 'The Proto-Indoaryans', op.cit., pp. 133–34.

[66] Suniti Kumar Chatterji, *Iranianism—Iranian Culture and its Impact on the World from Achaemenian Times,* The Asiatic Society, Calcutta, 1972, pp. 2–6.

[67] Walter A. Fairservis Jr., 'Central Asia and the Rgveda: The Archaeological Evidence', in George Erdosy, (ed.), *The Indo-Aryans of South Asia,* pp. 206–12; T. Burrow, 'The Pro-Indo-Aryans', pp. 124–26.

[68] R.N. Dandekar, 'Asura Varuṇa' in his *Select Writings,* Vol. I, p. 64, n.79. Broadly, Burrow's 'Proto-Indo-Aryans' represent those who belonged to Dandekar's 'Aryan period'.

[69] R.N. Dandekar, *Select Writings,* Vol. I, pp. 53–61. Dandekar clarifies that 'magic' is not to be understood in its vulgar, popular sense. Rather, it should be taken as one of the three stages (other two being 'religion' and 'science') in the evolution of human thought particularly in respect of man's relationship with the world. On Varuṇa's *māyā,* see also Debiprasad Chattopadhyaya, *Lokāyata,* pp. 622–65.

[70] The *Avesta* refers to a compound *mithra-ahura,* which in the later liturgical texts of the *Avesta* commonly occurs as *ahura-mithra.* There is general agreement that the former compound, which is considered to be earlier, cannot be separated from the Vedic compound *mitrāvaruṇā.* Often scholars quoted these two *dvandvas* as proof that the Iranian Ahura Mazdah is no other than Vedic Varuna. Though such an identification is rejected, commonalities between the two, specially their guardianship of 'Truth', are not ignored. Cf. Ilya Gershevitch, *W.B. Henning Memorial Volume,* pp. 44–58.

[71] Wash Edward Hale, *Āsura in Early Vedic Religion,* Motilal Banarsidass, New Delhi, 1986. The combined occurrence of *āsura-adevāh* probably means that these were the so-called 'non-Aryan' enemy leaders who did not worship gods of 'Aryans', especially perhaps Indra. Similarly, *adevic asuras,* the human enemies of the 'Aryan' people, who were described by texts as enemies of Indra, became mythologized into a class of beings who opposed the class of beings called gods. Such contentions imply that Hale subscribes to 'confrontationist' hypothesis, which is probably the result of his being oblivious of the changing meaning of the epithet *asura.* In this context, Burrow's argument ('The Proto-Indo-Aryans', p. 129) deserves recalling : 'It is absurd to assume that a class of gods called Asuras were relegated to the status of demons while every individual member of that class (Varuṇa, Mitra, Āditya) remained a god.' Only the meaning of the word *asura* changed because it fell into disuse.

India, Greece and Iran

A Cultural Triangle

U.P. Arora

The interior of the great Plateau is a waste of salty lakes and marbles with wide tracts of desert. Despite this impoverished appearance. Persia has always held importance as the hub on the great lines of communication, which link east and west. The Medes and the Persians were the two most powerful tribes of Indo-Europeans who came into southwestern Asia. In the ninth century BC they began taking part in campaigns against the Assyrians. In 702 BC Sennacherib was hard pressed by the united forces of the Medes and the Persians and, in 680 BC, they invaded the Assyrian Empire. The Persian ruler, Cyrus, conquered the greater part of the Near East and the Ionian coast-towns and established a great Achaemenian Empire. The empire created by Cyrus, and completed by Dareios (521 to 486 BC) was one of the greatest political organizations of antiquity. These monarchs incorporated in their empire, the most extensive in the history of the world, synthesis of ancient civilizations, for they included under their rule Mesopotamia, Syria, Egypt, Asia Minor, the Greek cities and Islands, and region around the Indus in northwestern India.

Achaemeniad Era: Intermixture of Cultures

The emergence of Achaemenian Empire saw that in Asia Minor and on the shores of the Aegean, the Persians had come face to face with a civilization possessing different types of political and economic organizations. The Achaemenian monarchy was stood opposed to Greek Civilization, with its concept of the liberty of the citizen and the city-state 'polis'. In the Greek world, the citizens, magistrates and priests worshipped their gods; in Persia no gods were visible, the king alone was the emanation of God on earth and towards him millions of human beings were directing their efforts. But Persia and Greece, although different, were nevertheless complementary. Achaemenians were well aware of the superiority of the ancient civilizations included in their empire. Hence large amount of autonomy was granted to them by Cyrus and an astute policy was followed by Dareios, as a result of which these ancient cultures were preserved and favoured at the expense, perhaps, of the stability of the state. With a new spirit of tolerance and justice the empire had removed the barriers and encouraged the intermixture between these ancient cultures.

The empire provided an opportunity of interaction between Indian and Greek civilizations. In the Achaemenian empire, of which the Greeks living in Ionia and the Indians of northwest were integral parts, we have the first definite proof of Indo-Greek connections.

According to Herodotos, India, the twentieth and the last in the list of satrapies distributed by Dareios in his empire, paid the highest tribute to the emperor, which was 360 talents of gold-dust. The statement of Herodotos is corroborated by the inscriptions of Dareios.[1] To both Indian and Greeks who had come close to each other by serving together in the Achaemenian court and army and through various other means, the empire provided the condition more favourable for the interchange of ideas. The Greek cities of Ionia were in close touch with advanced civilizations of the east including India through Achaemenid Persia. It widened their horizon and Ionians became pioneers in the intellectual development of Greece. Some significance may lie in the fact that Greek philosophy and science originated not in Athens, the intellectual capital of classical Greece, but in Ionia on the coast of Asia Minor. The first Greek philosophers were all from Ionia. As the Greeks, whom Indians came to know for the first time, were from Ionia, the name *Yavana* originated. The word *Yavana* is a back formation from the Prakrit term *Yona* which is in turn derived from the old Persian form *Yauna* denoting the Ionian Greeks who were conquered by Cyrus in 545 BC. It first occurs in the Behistun inscription (519 BC) of Dareios I. Used initially for the Ionian Greeks, the term was gradually extended to refer to the Greeks in general and also other foreigners. In medieval India the word *Yavana* was used as a synonym of *Mleccha* and indicated any foreigner.[2]

The Greeks owe their first knowledge of India to their historians and geographers living in the colonized cities of Ionia, for like the Greek knowledge of philosophy and science, history and geography too were also born in Ionia. Of the four Ionian Greek authors, who are known to have discussed India in the period before Alexander, two (Skylax and Ktesias) were in the service of Achaemenian Court, and Herodotos, although not in the service of the Achaemenians, had evidently relied on Persian sources. The Persian nomenclature of some Indian articles in Ktesias' work (for example, *Martichora*) reveals that information on Indian things were conveyed to Ktesias by Persians.[3]

The first Greek who is said to have made a voyage to India and written about his experiences, was Skylax of Caryanda. Dareios was said to have commissioned him with others to explore the Indus to its mouth. Unfortunately the works attributed to Skylax are lost and the surviving fragments are so few that we do not know the contents of his knowledge. According to Herodotos, the result of Skylax's voyage was that Dareios subdued the Indians and made use of this sea.[4] The immediate result of Skylax's discovery of a sea route was that the trade by sea was opened up and there is evidence of Indian wares and perhaps ships making their way to Babylonia in the same century.[5] The significance of Skylax's expedition is shown by the fact that after him both Hekataios and Herodotos used him for their information and wrote accurately of the country through which Skylax had travelled.

From the Indus to the Greek cities on the coast of Asia Minor, the communications between the extremities of the huge Persian polity were now unimpeded by political frontiers. There were well maintained 'royal high roads' linking the empire for swift movements of troops; these provided an opportunity to both Indians and Greeks, who as subjects of the Persian Emperor, came into contact with one another through trade and commerce as well as military and administrative services. There was a great demand for Indian soldiers in the Persian army. Fighting against the Greeks on the Athenian soil, cotton-clad Indian warriors armed with bows of reed and iron-tipped arrows, were the pride of Xerxes' troops.[6] The fighting skill of the Indians was held in great repute, as may be seen from the fact that their contingent was recruited *en masse* by the Achaemenian General Mardarios, whereas only selected one were recruited from other nationalities.[7] There were permanent military colonies in the empire and we have an evidence of Indian colony in Mesopotamia.[8] Even after the end of Achaemenian rule, sometime during the reign of Artaxerxes II (404–395 BC), the Indian soldiers were recruited to serve as mercenaries in Persian army. For example, in the battle of Gaugemala (331 BC) and Arabela (330 BC), the Indians in Persian army had fought against

Alexander.[9] The region of Northwest India and Punjab was an important source of recruiting soldiers for the Persian chiefs. The evidence of Panini bears testimony to the fact that Vahikas were divided into different war-like clans and as mercenaries they lent their services to any one who paid for them.[10]

As the Indian soldiers had visited Greece in the Persian army, so the Greek mercenaries too had reached India in Dareios's army. Fatigued from continuous battles and away from home, many of them appear to have chosen to settle in India. We come to know about one such settlement at Nysa in the Swat Valley, where Alexander had found them, still following the Greek customs and language and claiming descent from Dionysos, the divine conqueror of India.[11] That Greeks had become well known in northwestern region, is attested by the grammarian Panini,[12] a native of Salatura near Taxsila.

There were not only soldiers, traders, sailors and persons in administrative services, who came into contact with one another through the Persian Empire, but also philosophers and ascetic wanderers. Aristoxenos, the musician, a disciple of Aristotles reports a widely believed anecdote of his days, which tells about the visit of a group of Indian philosophers to Greece during the fourth century BC. In Athens they met Socrates and asked him the object of his philosophy. 'An enquiry into the human affairs', he told them. The Indian burst into laughter. 'How' asked the leading Indian sage, 'Can a man understand human affairs if he is ignorant of divine affairs.'[13]

Thus from sixth century BC to fourth century BC, the Persian empire made possible the exchange of ideas between diverse types of people. The results of these exchanges must have been spectacular in the intellectual development. Ionia, Northwest India and other regions of the Persian Empire became the centres of intellectual activities. It is during this period that we notice striking parallels between Indian and Greek civilizations particularly in the domain of philosophy, natural science, medicine and fable literature. Although there is no direct evidence, the possibility of seeing mutual contacts as a causative factor for these similarities, cannot be ruled out.

Parallelism: Philosophy, Fable Literature and Medicine

In the domain of philosophy, the Ionian philosophers, like the sages of the Upanisads, had concluded that a single substance (*Arche*' Brahaman) lies at the basis of all existence. Furthermore, the identification of the element fire with changeability occurs both in Herakleitos and Buddhism. Again like Vaisesikas and some other Indian philosophical schools, the Greek philosophers, Leukippos and Demokritos had also developed atomism. Prior to Demokritos, Indian atomism at first, was taught by some Pakudha Katyayana, an older contemporary of Buddha.[14] The Pythagorean doctrine of metempsychosis unquestionably provides more specific analogies causing scholars to speculate that the idea, as it occured in Greece, was ultimately derived from India. The causal link between a person's current social status and his good or evil deeds in previous birth is found only in India and Greece. Such doctrine was not widely held there, whereas it was undoubtedly a prominent concept in Indian thought. The ancient Greeks were agreed upon the fact that the Pythagorism was an idea alien to their land. But from where it had come, they were not sure. After Alexander's invasion, India came to be known as the land of philosophers, and it was also recognized as the source of Pythagorism. Pythagoras,[15] Demokritos,[16] Plato,[17] Apollonios of Tyana,[18] Lycurgos,[19] and Demetrios of Sourion[20] and many others were reported to have derived their knowledge from India. The German scholar Schroeder making an in-depth study of Pythagorism showed the Indian origin of all the doctrines ascribed to Pythagoras. These include the theory of the transmigration of the soul, the doctrine of the five elements, the character of his religio-philosophical fraternity, his mystical speculation, the prohibition of eating beans, the Pythagorean theorem and the irrational number root '2'.[21] If we recognize the Indian influence on Pythagorism, it was possible only through the Persian empire.

Based on the belief of metempsychosis, the Indian fables also seem to have reached Greece through Persia. The more well known of the Greek animal fables are attributed to the Ionian slave Aesop. Like their Indian counterpart Aesop's fables are also short narratives in which birds or beasts rather than human beings serve as protagonists. In Aesop's fable, 'The Ass in a Lion's Skin' the skin in which the ass is disguised is blown off by the winds. In the *Jataka* version, the ass disguised in a lion skin is betrayed by his own cry. The *Jataka* story of 'The Swan who Dropped the Tortoise', appears in Aesop as 'The Eagle who dropped the Tortoise'. Like these there are numerous fable of Greek and the Indian tradition showing similarities.[22]

Regarding the relationship between the two it may be said that the Indian fables on record, date back to the Upanisadic period. They occur in the *Chhandogya Upanisad* and the tradition may have been even older. When one notices in these fables the cycle of rebirth, their didactic nature, the animals (lions, tiger, monkey, peacock) native to India, and the frequency with which the same fables occur in Indian sources as compared to only once or twice in Greek texts, the theory of Indian origin of Greek fables is strengthened. The westward migration of Indian fables is further corroborated by the evidence of the thirty fables in the Talmud and in Midrashic literature. Except in three or four cases, all these can be paralled either in India or in Greece or in both. In the last instance the Talmudic form invariably follows the Indian, whenever it differs from the Greek.[23] In fact on account of the presence of parallels with European tales in most parts of India and of still other parallels in the old literary collections, a whole generation of scholars was led to regard India as the great home land of most of the European folk-tales.[24]

The exchange in the field of medicine may also have become possible as a result of the communication between the Indian and Greek doctors of the Persian Empire. Hippokrates' (460–433 BC) manual *Gynaiketa* mentioned the Indian formula for dentifrice,[25] which had the characteristic of having been offered along with a precept of general alimentary hygiene, to eat little and to partake of only substantial things. This is in accordance with the Indian Ayurvedic tradition which has always emphasized the curing of diseases by regulating the diet as much as the use of drugs. Likewise Hippokrates' concept on pneumatic is much the same as in the Indian concept of *Vayu* or *Prana.* Attention has also been drawn towards Platos *Timaios* in which there occurs a theory similar to *Tridosa* of the Ayurveda. As in Greece this theory was an isolated one with no indication of its origin and development; the possibility of Indian influence cannot be ruled out.[26]

Greeks on India: Achaemeniad Era

While the civilizations included in the Persian Empire, may be interacting with each other and Skylax and many others may have made voyages to Indian part of the Empire, the misconceptions and vague notions on the geography of India continued to prevail. India of the Persian Empire was considered to be the eastern end of the world. Beyond the Indian Satrapy was thought to be a continuous desert or ocean.[27] Furthermore there existed a view that India was joined with

Ethiopia.[28] In fact Greeks were in the habit of romanticizing and imagining extraordinary creatures in far-off lands like imaginary Hyperboreans in the far North and Ethiopians in the far South. In the geographical conception that prevailed, India was the eastern end of the earth and it was described as abounding in marvels and its people living in a state of idyllic bliss.

Interest in marvels (fabulous races and animals, miraculous objects) idealization of the land (fertility of the soil, abundance of gold, favourite climate, excellent products, largest in size and population) and idealization of the people (most just, long lived, free from diseases, truth loving) alongwith the geographical misconceptions mentioned above, are the dominant trends, which we notice in the Greek writings produced during the Persian hegemony. Skylax, the very first author on India, who was in the service of Dareios, had established this tradition. Ktesias of Knidos, the protege of the Persian King Artaxerxes Mnemon, had left everyone behind him in the narration of such spicy material. In fact, despite having accurate knowledge of India in the later period, these trends continued to exist during the entire period of Graeco-Roman history and also during the middle ages of Europe.

But amidst marvels and exaggeration there are also reports in these accounts which have unveiled some unknown chapters of Indian history. Herodotos' report of the inclusion of Indus region in the Achaemenian Empire, payment of highest tribute in the form of gold-dust, a description of northwestern horses and cotton, Indian soldiers with iron-tipped arrows and mercenaries in Mardonios army, reveal valuable historical information. The description of gold-digging ant has a genuine Indian tradition. Ktesias' report of the Indian articles like steel sword, ivory, cotton, purple dye, pepper, wine, perfumes, gold, silver, precious stone, etc., throws valuable light on northwestern urbanism. Furthermore his report of the Indian war elephant demolishing walls, falconry, talking parrots and monkeys were based on actual facts.[29] The part included in the Persian Empire, covering Pakistan and part of Afghanistan, had contributed significantly in the formation of Indian society and culture. Located at the international trade route, the region witnessed the convergence of several cultural elements—Indian, Chinese, Persian, Central Asian and West Asian. The Indian sources do not speak much on this relay centre between India and the outside world. Fortunately, the early Greek authors of the Persian empire fill up this vaccuum. As in the period before

Alexander the Greek geographical knowledge was confined to north-west, the value of Greek writings belonging to this period of Persian domination is greatly increased for the study of society and culture, developed in the northwest.

Perso-Hellenic Elements and Mauryan Art

Depending on Greeks the Achaemenian Empire decayed, more as the result of the Persian mistakes than of Greek strength. Under the aegis of Macedonia the awakening of Hellenic sentiments delivered Iran into the hands of Alexander the Great. His conquests inaugurated a new era and carried Hellenism throughout western Asia and advanced to the frontiers to the Indus and Central Asia. Iran was now a part of international trade area and was consumer of foreign products as well as an exporting and transit country. The *polis* declined and influenced by Iran, monarchy by divine right became the part of Hellenism under Alexander. Declaring himself as an heir to Dareios, the conqueror had planned to re-establish the empire of Achaemenians. In order to realize his dream of fusing the two great peoples and civilizations, he had arranged a ceremony in Susa to celebrate the inter-communal marriages between Greeks and Iranians, marrying a Persian Princess himself.[30]

The disintegration of the Achaemenian empire on one side and the rise of the Mauryan empire on the other in the aftermath of Alexander's invasion, circumstantially favoured the inauguration of an imperial art of Pataliputra marked by the use of stone, which was an experience hitherto unknown. The absence of monumental stone art in India till the Mauryan period is thought to be on account of the absence of adequate technical knowledge. Marshall,[31] Wheeler,[32] Percy Brown,[33] Nihar Ranjan Ray[34] and many others argue that this technical know-how was introduced to the Indian craftsman by the Persian or Perso-Hellenistic master craftsmen, who had been uprooted upon the defeat of the Achaemenians by Alexander. They sought refuge in the Mauryan empire, where they were provided adequate shelter and appropriate jobs. The chronological priority of Persian art, geographical proximity of Persia with India and political and cultural contacts between Persia and India since the time of Dareios the Great, if not Cyrus, have been further emphasized to support the theory of the Persian origin of the Mauryan Art. Marshall had even thought that the Asokan pillars were carved by the Perso-Hellenistic sculptors who were driven out from Persepolis by Alexander. They had originally gone to Bactria, where they settled down for sometime and at a later date, invited by the Mauryan Kings they reached India.

The view of Coomaraswamy[35], Agrawala[36] and Irwin[37], which supports the indigenous origin theory of Mauryan art does not necessarily negate the Persian element. They believe that during the Asokan and Pre-Asokan periods, India formed part of a very large territory of Asia including the Mediterranean region. Therefore, what is sometimes called 'borrowing' is in fact to be viewed as legacy from a common heritage. Thus, although there are some Persian and Assyrian elements in Mauryan art, they are not due to any 'borrowing' as such. It may be noted that it was the Achaemenian Empire, which for the first time, had provided an opportunity of binding together a large territory of Asia, as a result of which the nations included in the empire developed a common heritage.

Persian influence is visible in nearly every aspect of Mauryan art and architecture. The pillared hall at Kumrahar; the use of stone for pillars and columns; some human figures on grounds of facial features, head dress, etc., and the various art motifs (palmete, the knop or the bud of 'kop and flower', the 'bead-and-reel', rope moulding pattern' on ring-stone and the lion) have been traced to West-Asia, Graeco-Persian or Persian sources. The discovery of a pillar capital of Persian Apadana at the palace of Pataliputra indicates absorptions.[38]

Paul Le Valley[39] has recently drawn our attention towards some Mauryan male nude figures in which he finds as many as five Greek sculptural techniques to depict the subject. These are (1) proportions of the torso; (2) the four-square method of carving; (3) chest musculature; (4) abdominal musculature; (5) treatment of the back. These are too many to be merely circumstantial. Measurement reveals that the pre-Mauryan dancing Harappa torso falls short of the Greek ideal in both the chest and abdominal measurements, with an overall variation of 64 per cent; post-Mauryan Bharhut Yaksi, 47.5 per cent; the Mauryan figure of Lohanipur, on the other hand, falls short only in the abdominal measurement, and then with an overall variation from the Greek of only 1.5 per cent. Likewise the Mauryan Didarganj Yaksi falls short of the ideal by only 2 per cent. The Greek influence on the pre-Kushan nude can be explained according to Valley by (1) oral transmission of theory at the time of Alexander's invasion, and (2) visual examples on the coins of Alexander's successors in Bactria.

The discovery of Kharosthi-label Mauryan inscriptions from Karnataka and Baragaon in Ganga Valley are proof of a definite presence of northwestern craftsmen in the South and mid-India. The inscriptions at Baragaon in Kharosthi refer to Perso-Greek names. It establishes the fact that there were Greek or Iranian artists under the Mauryans and the presence of Iranian or Greek elements in the Mauryan art becomes certain. 'This evidence also reinforces mould of Mauryan art asserting its privileged resources whether in men or money, across the vast expense of the empire and beyond'.[40]

Infact, it was the combined Graeco-Persian art which had influenced the Mauryans. Daniel Schlumberger, an expert on the question of Bactrian art, is convinced that the reason why historians find it difficult to separate the Greek from the Persian elements in Mauryan sculpture, is that those two elements had already merged in Bactria. It was the combined Graeco-Persian art of Bactria which influenced the Mauryans. Bactrian kings in and out of India had issued some of the most magnificently detailed coins ever minted. Most of those coins showed the bust of the ruler on the front, and a Greek god on the back, often nude. Schlumberger argues persuasively that it is only a matter of time before a hoard of Bactrian sculptures is found, which will parallel the coins.[41] On the development of Greek states in Bactria and India, Tarn had emphasized the Hellanistic elements and Narain, the Indian elements. Both failed to see the importance of Iranian elements. In addition to the texts they used on evidence coming from the east of Hindukush. With greater archaeological and numismatic evidence available now, a more balanced approach is possible. The position of Bactria as the '*kernland*' is now established by archaeology.[42]

We also take into account the role of Asoka in interaction with the outside world through his 'Dhamma-Mahamatras'. According to one of his inscription (Rock-Edict XII)[43] the 'Dhamma-Mahamatras' were sent, besides Sri Lanka to Egypt, Syria, Macedonia and Cyre in North Africa. The classical sources also refer to the Greek ambassadors Megasthenes,[44] Daimachos,[45] and Patrokles,[46] who were deputed to Indian kings from the Hellenistic kingdom of Syria. During the reign of Amitrochates (Bindusara)[47] and of some later Maurya king Sophagasenos[48] also there were diplomatic relations between Mauryans and the Seleucids. The Ptolemies of Egypt also had maintained intense relations with India.[49] The discovery of Asokan inscriptions near Kandahar in Southern Afghanistan in Greek as well as in Aramaic[50] clearly shows that Asoka wanted his Dhamma to be spread among the masses, including the Greeks and Persians present on the borderlands as well as northwestern frontier provinces of his empire.

It is reasonable to conclude that the 'Dhamma-Mahamatras' who returned from the Hellenistic lands helped to familiarize the king and his court with the cultural heritage of the countries, including the actual drawings of art and architecture, of past and present, which may have won admiration from Asoka and kindled his imagination. Thus the emergence of monumental art and the changes we see in the formative period of Indian art have to be attributed first to Graeco-Persian connections through the Persian empire and then Bactria after Alexander's return. Asokan policy had further accelerated the process of these interactions.

The Parthian Interlude

When in AD 44, Apollonios of Tyana had visited Taxila, that region was occupied by Phraotes, no doubt a Parthian.[51] The name Phraotes appears to be the distorted form of 'apratihata' which was one of the attributes of the Parthian king Gondophares in found in the Kharosthi legend of his coins.[52] Philostratos' Phraotes has been identified with Gondophernes (Persian Vindapharna, Winner of Colony) who seems to have been originally the Parthian Viceroy of Arachosia under the 'Great king of Kings' Orthagnes (Persian Verethregna, the 'Victorious'). He gradually extended his power in different directions including East Iran and certain other districts of the Parthian empire. The *Periplus* (AD 70–80) refers to the Parthian occupation of Min-negara, the capital of Indo-Scythia.[53]

The success of Gondophernes in upper Kabul valley was short lived. But his success against Sakas in India was more conspicuous. The discovery of a record of his reign at Takht-i-bahi[54] in the Peshawar district corroborates the reference to the Parthian occupation of Gandhara under Phraotes in Philostratos's *Travels of Apollonios of Tyana.* Philostratos writes that the Indian King Phraotes spoke to Apollonios in Greek and informed him that he had read Euripides' *Herakleidai.*[55] The Parthian king, governors, their officials and Secretaries all knew Greek. The work of art and imperial coinage prove that they had patronized Greek artists and writers and brought them to their court. Iran, which the Parthians had liberated from the Greek chiefs had an organized administration in existence bequeathed by the Greeks, cities inhabited by strong Greek colonies and the new-Hellenized Iranian bourgeoisie. The latter class acted as a kind of intermediary between the Parthians and the Hellenes. It collaborated with both sides, guaranteed the administration, undertook the collection of taxes, which came mainly from the wealthy trading cities, and under the control and supervision of royal representatives, was responsible for local government. Parthian Phillo-Hellenism was not merely an indication of the admiration for Greek culture but was rather a political measure required by the situation they found in Iran. Ghirshmann writes,

> the benevolent attitude of the Parthians towards the Hellenistic heritage in Iran was of the highest importance for the future development of Iranian Civilization. It saved the country from disturbing changes, and by making possible a gradual and progressive absorption of the foreign element, led to the formation of a national culture that found its highest expression in Sassanion Civilization.[56]

It was during the reign of Parthian ruler Gondophernes that St Thomas is said to have visited India. In the *Acta Thomae*, the oldest text dealing with St Thomas' mission, the field of the Apostle's work was reported to be Indo-Iranian frontier or northwestern India. There the Apostle was reported to have converted an Indian king named Gudnaphar and later becoming a martyr in the kingdom of Mazda—the northern neighbour of the King Gudnaphar, who may be well identified with the Parthian chief Gondophernes.[57] The other name 'Mazda' in the *Acta* seems to be Iranian origin. The South Indian tradition of associating the Church of Malabar with the coming of St Thomas[58] is a late one and appears to have been derived by the local Christian Communities from some other tradition.

In his work *Travels of Apollonios of Tyana*, Philostratos reports the description of Sun temple at Taxila by Apollonios.[59] The emergence of the Sun cult in the North West appears to be due to the influence of the Iranians.[60] The earliest Sun Temple in India may be that of Jandial in Taxila. Its plan is like a Persian Fire Temple. Its *Pradaksina Patha*, or the passage which forms an ambulatory around the cella, is a feature which we find already at the *Ayadana* (place of adoration) at Susa of Artaxerxes II (405–358 BC). Judging from Iranian analogies the possibility of the Jandial Temple being intended for a fire cult also may be supported by the deep foundation for a tower with steps at the back of the sanctuary. The fire must have burnt on the summit of the tower. The period of this temple has been assigned closer to the date of the Parthian supremacy at Taxila (50 BC–65 AD).[61] There can at any rate be no doubt that Persian customs prevailed at Taxila. Aristoboulos[62] saw here and nowhere else in India corpses exposed to the vultures. This practice of exposing the corpses of the dead on the hills must be among the people close to frontier where Iranian influence was dominant. The Parthian interlude in India must have been of short duration. From the evidence of inscription it appears to have come to an end by 65 AD, when the Kushanas occupied the Gandhar region.

Perso-Hellenic Elements: Kushana's Patronage

Under the Kushanas the Iranian influence continued. Kanishka was attracted not only towards native but also Greek and Iranian gods. Of the Greek gods on their coins there are Helios, Selene and Herakles and of the Persian, Mitro (Mithra-Sun), Mao (Mah-Moon) Athsho (Atash-Fire) Oado (Vat-Wind), Orthagno (Verethraghna), Pharro (Hvarena-glory) and Nana (Anahita). We notice that the Sun and the Moon occur in both their Greek and Persian forms. Sun god is also found on Kanishka's relic casket, which shows that the king must have patronized Sun worship. The Indian Surya acquires a foreign dress under the Kushana, and it is notable that the artistic representation of Surya in India does not tally with the seven horsed chariot described in Indian texts, but it does with the Greek Helios as depicted in Greek texts and art.[63]

From *Brhatsamhita* we come to know that the priests of the Sun-god were Magas, who were Iranian in origin.[64] The *Bhavisya Purana* (Chap. 139) says that when a temple of the Sun was constructed on the banks of the Chandrabhaga (modern Chenab) and no local Brahmana was ready to accept the office of regular priest of the temple. Therefore Magas were called for, from Sakadvipa, who were well known as special sun worshippers. It also informs us that the Magas were sprung from Jarasasta (Zarathustra).[65]

Sassanian Exchange with India

The Sassanian civilization was the culmination of the history of the Iranian nation, as it represented its highest achievement. Except for the Far East, the world, after the disappearance of the Kushan empire, was divided between Rome and Iran. The latter was no longer, as under the Parthians, a partner standing on the defensive but an adversary of equal, if not superior. Although now nationalism was now although dominant, they were fully receptive to foreign influences also. But they had adopted them to the tradition of its native land.

The Sassanians were great patrons of arts, letters and sciences. Possessed of wide interest and an enquiring mind, Shapur I (241–72 AD) had commissioned the translation of numerous Greek and Indian works dealing with medicine, astronomy and philosophy. Hindu books on grammar and horoscopy together with the *Almagest* of Ptolemy were included among the holy books during his reign.[66] The Sassanians chief Khusru I Anoshirvan (531–79 AD) also like Shapur I had patronized the scholars. One of the 120 Greek, Persian and Indian physicians of Anoshirvan was Barzoe. He was reported to have read in some book that in India are high mountains on which certain trees and plants grow out of which an elxir can be made for raising the dead. He was impressed and set about translating their books of wisdom and instruction, one of which was the *Panchantra* under the title *Kalila* and *Dimna*.[67]

There are numerous references to trade with India under the Sassanians. Ammianos Marcellinos, a Greek author from Antioch, who had accompanied the Emperor Julian in his campaign against the Persians in 363 AD writes (XIV, 13, 3) that in the city of Batre, situated not for from the east bank of the Euphrates, a great fair was held in September to which flowed merchandise from India and from China. Among the Indian articles, Masudi refers to Indian gifts to Chosroes consisting of camphor, aloes, a ruby cup filled with pearls, a slave seven cubits tall and a carpet of snake skin.[68]

Kosanas Indikopleutis, a Greek monk from Alexandria, and author of the *Christian Topography* informs us about the Christian church of Persian connections, well established on the Malabar Coast and in Sri Lanka by the early sixth century. He reports that the Christians of Sri Lanka had a presbyter appointed from Persia. Like-wise the bishop residing at Kalliana in Malabar was also of Persian stock. The Indians were 'Persians' that is, Nestorian Christians, who had declared their independence of the Greek hierarchy, and in 489, officially adopted the Nestorian interpretation of Christian doctrine. In consequence, the Indian church likewise became Nestorian.[69]

It was through Iranian empire under the Sassanian that

Indian ascetic ideals travelled Westward and influenced Christian monasticism. Clearly, the two most powerful elements in the shaping of classical Christian thought, were Christian monasticism and the early (fourth century) Christian fathers. The popularity of monasticism bears testimony to greatly intensified other worldliness in the fourth century. In view of the increasing number of people adopting asceticism, the organization of monks into communities and the evolution of an ascetic order having acceptable code or behaviour had become inevitable. The Indian models of asceticism must have attracted piously inclined persons exposed to Indian practice, either in India itself or in Hellenic territory where the presence of Buddhist monks led to the recognition of India as a source of philosophical wisdom so much so that many eminent Greek philosophers were reported by the classical authors to have derived their knowledge from India.[70] It is at this time that Mani (AD 216–217), the founder of Manichaeism, was also said to have visited India, where he had come into contact with Buddhism and other mystic religions. After visiting India he returned to the Sassanid empire where he propagated his teachings and enjoyed friendly relations with Sapor I, but Mazdean opposition under Bahram I led to his death.

Mani was thought to be of noble birth and like Zoroaster, the Buddha and Jesus claimed to have been sent by God to fulfil what had been previously revealed. His doctrine was a religion of redemption in which the dualistic myth provided a rationale for an ascetic ethic. The Elect, to whom all wordly occupations and possessions were forbidden, participated in redemption and were destined for deliverance from transmigration. It is believed that the Manichaeans were the first to imitate Indian ascetic practices. They in turn transmitted the techniques westward to influence Christianity. Thus through the intermediacy of Manichaeism, India exerted a profound influence upon this central aspect of late Hellenistic and medieval Christian life.

It was through the economic and cultural exchanges between India and Iran that India was introduced to western medicine, astronomy, geometry and logic. Indians of the time were certainly familiar with the Iranians, and we see them represented in a fresco in Cave I at Ajanta. The scene is of Persian with sugar-loaf hats, close-fitting tunics and flying scarves, seated cross-legged on sofas, drinking from bowls.[72]

The splendid and gigantic edifice of Sassanian Iran, which had functioned with such magnificence and precision, crumbled to pieces in the space of a few years. But the Arabs did not owe their success to their political superiority or to the genius of their military leaders, it was the ancient world, the world of Asia, Europe, and Africa, that gave them their victory, a world exhausted by war, undermine by social and religious struggle and powerless to resist a united, inspired and resolute enemy.[73]

Notes and References

F. No., and T. refer to the fragments, the author's serial number and the *testimonia* respectively in F. Jacoby's *Fragmente der griechischer Historiker* volumes, Berlin 1923–30; Leiden 1954–58.

1 Whether Cyrus, the founder of Achaemenian empire had included Indian part in his empire remains unsettled. But during Dareios' reign India was certainly included for it is attested both by Herodotos' statement (III, 97) and Dareios' inscriptions. See U.P. Arora, *Greeks on India,* Indian Society for Greek and Roman Studies, Bareilly, 1996, pp. 35ff.

2 For a discussion on the word *Yavana* see A.K. Narain, *The Indo-Greeks,* rpt, Oxford University Press, New Delhi, 1980, pp. 165–69; S.D. Dogra, 'Greek or Yavana Donors in Ancient India', *Puratattva,* No. 8 (1975–76), p. 185, note 1; Samuel Clark Laeuchli, 'Yavana Inscriptions of Western India', *Journal of the Asiatic Society of Bombay,* Dr Bhagavanlal Indrajeet Memorial Volume, 1886, Vols 56–59.

3 U.P. Arora, Greeks on India, p. 7.

4 See F. Jacoby, *Fragmente Griechischer Historiker, hrsg.,* I–IId, Berlin, 1923–30; IIIA–IIIC, Leiden, 1954–58, Skylax, No. 709, F.I., Herod, IV, 44.

5 J.O. Thompson, *History of Ancient Geography,* New York, 1965, p. 81, n. 2.

6 Herod, VII, 65 (Loeb edition).

7 Herod, VIII, 113.

8 K. Karttunen, *India in Early Greek Literature,* Helsinki 1989, p. 49.

9 Arr, *Anabasis,* III, 8, 3–6 (Loeb).

10 *Astadhyayi* V, 3, 114 (Loeb).

11 Arr, *Indika,* 1, 4–5 (Loeb); A.K. Narain, *The Indo-Greeks,* p. 2.

12 IV, 1, 49.

13 Aristoxenos in C. Mueller, *Fragmeta Historicorum Graecorum* in 5 Vols, Vol. II, Paris, 1841, Frag. 31, p. 81 (Euseb, Pr. Ev XI, 3).

14 See A.L. Basham, *The Wonder that was India* (Paperback edn, 1981), p. 499. Basham finds the atom of Buddhists, in some measure resembling the quantum of Planck. The 'atomic theories of ancient India', according to Basham, 'are brilliant imaginative explanations of the physical structure of the world; though it is probably mere coincidence that they agree in part with the discoveries of modern physics, they are nevertheless much to the credit of the intellect and imagination of early Indian thinkers.

15 See Philostratos, *Travels of Apollonios of Tyana,* VIII, 7 (Loeb).

16 Aelian, Varia Historia, IV, 20; Diog. Laert. IX, 34 (Loeb).

17 Pausanias, *Description of Greece*, IV, 32, 4 (Loeb).

18 Philostratos, *Travels of Apollonios*, I, 18.

19 Aristocrates (Plut, *Lycurgus*, C.4) in C. Mueller, *Fragmeta Historicorum Graecorum*, Vol. IV, p. 332.

20 Lucian, *Toxaris*, 34 (Loeb).

21 Schroeder, *Phythagores und die Inder* (Leipsic, 1884). For the influence of Indian thought on Phythagoras, see Winternitz, *Visvabharati* Quarterly, February 1937, p. 8; William Jones, *Works*, III, 236; H.L. Colebrooke, *Miscellaneous Essays*, London, 1873, Vol. I, 436ff.; Richard Garbe, *Philosophy of Ancient India*, Chicago, 1897, 39ff.; F.W. Hopkins, *Religions of India*, New Delhi, 1972 (rpt), pp. 559–60; Macdonell, *History of Sanskrit Literature*, London, 1928, p. 422; Arnold Toyanbee, *Hellenism*, London, 1959, p. 54; H.G. Rawlinson 'India in European Literature and Thought' in G.T. Garratt (ed.), *The Legacy of India*, Oxford, 1939, p. 5; S. Radhakrishnan, *Eastern Religion and Western Thought*, New York, 1953, Vol. I, p. 127.

22 J.W. Sedlar, *India and the Greek World*, Totowa, 1980, p. 101.

23 G.N. Banerjee, *Hellenism in Ancient India*, London, 1920, p. 289.

24 As early as 1838 Loiselcur Deslongchamps (*Essai Sur les Fables Indiennes*, Paris, 1838) had suggested that the origin of many European folk-tales may probably be found in India. But it was Benfey who had put forward this idea with especial clearness and authority in the introduction to his edition of *Pancatantra* (*Pantschatantra. Funf Bucher Indischer Fablen Marchen und Erzahlungen* Leipzig, 1859) 2 Vols. See also U.P. Arora, 'The Folklore in Ancient Indian and Greek Literature', in *Essays on Indology, Polity and Administration—in Honour of Padmabhusan Shri R.K. Trivedi*, edited by S.D. Trivedi in 2 Vols, Delhi, 1989, pp. 341–49.

25 J. Filliozat, *The Classical Doctrine of Indian Medicine*, tr. by D.R. Channa from the French, originally published in 1949, Delhi, 1964 (rpt) pp. 254–55, 263.

26 For the Indian impact on Greek medicine see Royle, *An Essay on the Antiquity of Hindu Medicine*, London, 1837; R.T. Gunthr, *The Greek Herbal of Dioscoridies*, New York, 1959; J. Flliozat. *The Classical Doctine of Indian Medicine*; Schoff, *Journal of American Oriental Society*, Vol. XLII, p. 359; Nikolaos Yalouris, *Alexander the Great*, Thessaloniki, 1980, p. 22; U.P. Arora, *Greeks on India*, pp. 85–87.

27 U.P. Arora, *Greeks on India*, 18ff.

28 U.P. Arora, 'India Vis-a-vis Egypt Thiopia in Classical Accounts', *Graeco-Arabica*, Athens, 1982, Vol. I, pp. 131–40.

29 U.P. Arora, 'Greek Attitude towards the Indians', *Journal of Ganganatha Jha Kendriya Sanskrita Vidyapeetha*, Allahabad, 1983, Baladeva Upadhyaya Felicitation Volume, XXVII Part 1–4, pp. 97–109. Also see U.P. Arora, 'Classical Accounts on India—Some Observations' in *Graeco-Indica, India's Cultural Contacts with the Greek World*, Delhi, 1991, edited by U.P. Arora, pp. 86–108 and *Greeks on India* (Bareilly, 1996), pp. 88–109.

[30] On Susa marriages see Chares, Jac. No. 125, Athen., XII, 538b–539a; Phylarchos, Jac. No. 81, F. 41, Athen. XII, 539B–540a; Arrian, *Anab.* VII, 4, 4–8 and John Maxwell Obrien, *Alexander the Great: The Invisible Enemy, A Biography,* London, 1997 (rpt), pp. 197–201.

[31] J. Marshall, 'The Monuments of India', in *Cambridge History of India,* 1922, Vol. I, pp. 562–63.

[32] R.E.M. Wheeler, 'Iran and India in Pre-Islamic Times' in *Ancient India,* No. 4, pp. 85–101; *Flames over Persepolis,* Chap.VI, London, 1968.

[33] Percy Brown, *Indian Architecture: Buddhist and Hindu Periods,* Bombay, 1942, pp. 10–11.

[34] Nihar Raryan Ray in *The History and Culture of the Indian People,* Vol. : *The Age of Imperial Unity,* edited by R.C. Majumdar and others, Bombay, 1951, pp. 508–09.

[35] A.K. Coomaraswamy, 'Origin of the Lotus (so-called Bell) Capital', *Indian Historical Quarterly,* Vol. 6, pp. 372–75; *History of Indian and Indonesian Art* (Dover Edition), 1965.

[36] V.S. Agrawala, *Indian Art,* Varanasi, 1965, 98–100.

[37] John Irwin, 'Asokan Pillars: A Reassessment of Evidence', *Burlington Magazine,* Vol. CXV–CXVIII; pt I General, 1973, pp. 706–28; pt II, Structure, 1974, pp. 712–27; pt III, Capital, 1975, pp. 631–43; pt IV, Symbolism, 1976, pp. 734–53.

[38] R.N. Misra, 'Mauryan Art: A Re-Appraisal', *Pragdhara,* No. 11, Lucknow, 2000–01, pp. 185–192; S.P. Gupta, *Roots of Indian Art,* New Delhi, 1980 disagrees with the above view and pleades 'for the socio-economic model which stands for the framework in which it is the complexity of the historical situation of the third century BC, which is directly responsible for the kind of art we get. It emphasizes the role of social mobility, partly caused by the *Dhammavijaya* policy of Asoka and partly caused by the growing wealth in the hands of the Middle Class' (p. 340).

[39] Paul Le Valley, 'Greek Influence on Indian Sculptures as early as Alexander's Campaign', *Yavanika,* Bareilly, 2000, No. 6, 1996, pp. 3–27.

[40] R.N. Misra, 'Mauryan Art', pp. 187–189. The inscriptions were discovered by Pant and Jayaswal (P.C. Pant and Vidula Jayaswal, 'Ancient Stone Querries of Chunar: An Appraisal' *Pragdhara,* No. 1, 1990–91, pp. 49–52) and deciphered by Mukherji, 'Some Recently Noticed Kharosthi Epigraphs in U.P.', *Pragdhara,* No. 1, pp. 53–58) and T.P. Verma (his personal communication to discoverers). Mukherji dates them to the first century AD but Verma, supported by Pant and Jayaswal, takes them as Mauryan.

[41] Daniel Schlumberger, 'The Excavations at Surkh Kotal and the Problem of Hellenism in Bactria and India', *Proceedings of the British Academy,* 47, 1961, pp. 77–95.

[42] See Frank L. Holt, *Alexander the Great and Bactria,* Brill Leiden, 1993, 2ff.

[43] *Epig. Ind.,* Vol. II, p. 463.

[44] Strabo, *Geog.,* XV, I, 53–56 (Loeb); Arrian, *Indika,* V, 62 (Loeb).

[45] See Daimachos in F. Jacoby, *Fragmente,* No. 716, T.I. (Strabo, II, 1, 9).

[46] Patrokles in F. Jacoby, *Fragmente,* No. 712, F.3a (Strabo, II, 1, 7); F. 3b

(Strabo, XII, I, 11).

[47] Hegasandros in C. Mueller, *Fragmeta Historicorum Graecorum*, Vol.IV, Frag. 43, p. 421 (Athenaeus, XIV 652F).

[48] Polybios, XI, 34, 11 (Loeb Series).

[49] Ptolemy II Philadelphus (285–246 BC) had sent an ambassador to the court of Bindusara or of Ashoka, whose name was Dionysios. Like Megasthenes and Daimachos, he had also written a book on India, but this work was also lost. See 'Dionysios' in F. Jacoby, *Fragmente*, No. 717, T.I. (Strabo, II, I, 9).

[50] *Epig. Ind.* Vol. 33, p. 333; Vol. 34, pp.1ff and *Journal Asiatique*, Vol. CCLII, pp. 137–57.

[51] Philostratos, *Travels of Apollonios of Tyana* (Loeb Series edn.) II, 36.

[52] W.W. Tarn, *Greeks in Bactria and India*, Cambridge, 1951, p. 341 (quoting from Herzfeld, *Sakastan*, p. 113).

[53] *Perip.*, 38: 13, 3 (Lionel Casson's edition), Princeton, 1989.

[54] D.C. Sircar, *Select Inscriptions*, IInd Edition, 1965, p. 126.

[55] Philostratos, *Travels of Apollonios*, II, 27.

[56] R. Ghirshmann, *Iran*, Pelican, 1954, p. 268.

[57] W.R. Philipps, 'The Connection of St Thomas the Apostle with India', *Indian Antiquary*, 1903, 32, 1ff.; J.F. Fleet, 'St Thomas and Gondophernes', *Journal of Royal Asiatic Society, 1905*, 225.

[58] P.J. Thomas, 'The South Indian Tradition of the Apostle Thomas', *Journal of the Royal Asiatic Society (1924)*, centenary supplement, pp. 203–23.

[60] U.P. Arora, *Greeks on India*, pp. 80–81.

[61] R.A. Jairazbhoy, *Foreign Influence in Ancient India*, Bombay, 1963, pp. 153–55.

[62] Aristob in F. Jacob, *Fragmente*, No. 139, F.42 (Strabo, XV, 1, 62).

[63] R.A. Jairazbhoy, *Foreign Influence in Ancient India*, pp. 151–52.

[64] *Brhatsamhita ch.* 60, 19. Al Beruni Confirms (tr. Edward C. Sachau, *Alberunis India*, Chap. I, p. 21, Delhi, 1989 rpt) that the Magian priests of Persia were called Magas.

[65] Quoted by R.A. Jairazbhoy, *Foreign Influence in Ancient India*, pp. 153–54.

[66] Ibid., p. 155.

[67] Ibid., p. 160.

[68] Ibid., p. 161.

[69] Cosmas Indikopleustes, *The Christian Topography of Cosmas, an Egyptian Monk*, tr. and ed. J.W. McCrindle, New York, 1897, III, 178–79, and XI 337, pp. 118–19 and 365. Jean W. Sedlar, *India and the Greek World,* Totowa, 1980, p. 183.

[70] See above fn. 15 to 20. Also see U.P. Arora, 'Greek Attitude towards the Indians', *Journal of Ganga natha Jha Kendriya Sanskrit Vidyapeetha, Baldev Upadhyaya Felicitation Volume*, XXVII, pt.1–4 (Allahabad, 1983), pp. 97–109.

[71] Jean W. Sedler, op.cit., 208 ff, 299 ff.

[72] R.C. Majumdar, *The Classical Age* (ed. R.C. Majumdar and others, Bombay, 1988, 41th Edition), pp. 638–39.

[73] R. Ghirshmann, *Iran*, p. 349.

Technological Exchanges between India and Iran in Ancient and Medieval Times

Ishrat Alam

India and Iran have had very close relations for the last 3,000 years of their history (ignoring prehistory). Both had a reciprocal flow of scientific and cultural exchanges.[1] Iran was strategically placed in such a way that all caravans starting from Central Asia or India to the Mediterranean had to pass through the Iranian high plateau. On the other hand, India was geographically placed at the centre of a network of linkages, which joined such distant places such as the the Red Sea, Arabian Sea, South East Asia, Central Asia and China. These territories had seen diffusion of various elements of technology through political, commercial or cultural exchanges. In the present paper our aim is to examine the diffusion of different technological devices in which Iran and India served both as transmitter and recipient.

Agricultural Technology

Noria

The 'noria' (derived from the Arabic *naura,* 'the snorter') is an interesting water-lifting device. In it, the buckets or pots are attached to the circumference of a wheel, collecting water at the bottom and discharging it at the top. Needham has traced back its origin provisionally to India in the fourth century BC[2] Irfan Habib has convincingly argued that *chakkavattaka* (turning wheel) referred to in *Chulavagga Nikaya* (AD 350) could be identified with *arahatta-ghati-yantra* (machine attached with water pots).[3] He has argued that it was originally without a pot-chain, which was only added at a later stage. In the Indian context, the term *arahattaghatiyantra* has been referred to in *Amarakosa,* an early Sanskrit lexicon of possibly fourth–eighth century AD, as *'uddhatanam-ghati-yantram salilodvahanam prahe'*.[4] This can be rendered as 'by moving the *ghatiyantra,* water flows from the well'.

The use of the chain of pots or 'potgarland' is implied in it. The presence of the potgarland is attested by the textual and pictographic descriptions or illustrations.[5] Yasodharman's Mandasor inscription (AD 532) also refers to this.[6] Interestingly enough the author of *Abhidhana-chintamani* (twelfth century AD) refers to two categories of water-lifting devices, namely: (i) *Udhaghatakam* and its synonym *ghatiyantra*, and (ii) *Padavartah* and *araghattaka*.[7] Presumably this classification was designed to make a distinction between noria and the ungeared *saqiya*.[8] So far as Iran is concerned al-Muqaddasi (d. 390 A.H./AD 1000) is the first to report the presence of more norias on the river at Ahwaz.[9] This apparently late reference to the noria in Iran should not be considered as indicating its late arrival there. It had already reached the Hellenistic world by first century BC[10] Vitruvius (30 BC) had already described the noria.[11] Laufer found it in Sogdiana (Trans-oxiana) though it has not been dated.[12] It seems very unlikely that the noria could have reached the Roman world from India without passing through Iran. It would seem that Gandhara played an important role in the diffusion of noria from India to Iran. Marshall has reported about large numbers of 'small pear shaped earthen vessels' at the Bhir mound and some at Sirkap.[13] The small vessels were presumably used in the *noria* in the early Christian era.[14] They continued to be in use in Iran. Wulff reports from the files of the ancient irrigation office at Merv that mule or camel-drawn pot wheels (*Saqiyah, Naura*) and also river-driven mills with water lifting buckets attached to them, continued to be in use.[15]

The Persian Wheel

The noria did not involve any gearing mechanism. Gearing mechanism remained confined to the Persian wheel (*Saqiya*). Babur was the first to notice it functioning in India.[16] It has been rightly pointed out that he considered it curious to find water being lifted with the help of wheels (*saqiya*). He obviously did not see any such water-raising device in Central Asia and Afghanistan. This device was actually first used in Roman Egypt in the first century BC.[17] The machine was a comparatively late introduction to the Islamic world, sometime in AD 1000.[18] China received it only around AD 1313.[19] Iran might have received it from Iraq where it was depicted in a painting of twelfth century.[20] India perhaps received the *saqiya*, with right angled gearing, from either Iran or Iraq later than thirteenth century.

The Rotary Grain Mill

The pestle and mortar are the simplest means of comminution since antiquity and are still used for the daily decortication of cereals. After many improvements (mortar and pestle-grain rubber-saddle quern), the transition took place from these oscillatory forms to the true rotary mill and hand quern where the upper discoidal millstone revolved upon a lower stationary stone. The lower stone is always slightly convex, while the upper one is concave with a hole through which grain could be put on the grinding surfaces. Across the whole a bar was placed which moved the upper stone fixed upon a pin rising from the centre of the lower stone. Most handquerns were equipped with a handle serving as crank. The Mediterranean world had developed a manually operated mill by the second century BC[21] In this mill two horizontal handles on each side of the upper stone were fixed. The millers used a back and forth swinging motion. In such mills complete rotation was not possible. Gradually the stone of querns became thinner, flatter and lighter. And with the vertical peg handle the time of full rotary motion arrived. The earliest dateable rotary mill is reported from the Roman world (AD 256).[22] J. Marshall has reported a grinding mill with a peg hole from Kunala monastery, Taxila (fifth century AD).[23] Thus within comparatively short time the rotary grain mill travelled from the Hellenistic world possibly via Iran to India.

The improvements in the milling devices in the Mediterranean world eventually led to the evolution of the drawbar or 'the circular track' by second century BC.[24] In China it is reported in the fourth century AD.[25] In Indian context the earliest possibility of the use of drawbar has been traced at Baijnath in Himachal Pradesh by ninth century AD.[26] We are not very sure about the application of the draw bar in yoking the oxen for threshing. Cattle could be (and even today is) moved in a circular manner without being yoked to a draw bar; Lallanji Gopal's inference from a reference to threshing with oxen in an early medieval requires further consideration.[27] As late as AD 1600, a peasant is shown in a painting from *Razmnama* threshing by rotating an ox without any drawbar.[28] The earliest depiction of a drawbar in India is in fact available only in the depiction of a sugar mill in a manuscript *Mahapurana,* (c. 1540).[29] Besides, the sugar mill drawbar proved immensely useful in water lifts. Was there any relationship between arrival of the drawbar and diffusion of geared *saqiya*? Iran possibly was the route through which drawbar came to India. Here it may be pointed out that India did not receive the complex Iranian oilpress which was analogous to the Chinese one.[30] Iran had possibly received it from China.[31]

Military Technology

Stirrup

The invention of the stirrup immensely improved the striking capability of the horse rider. It added the combined weight of the rider and the horse to, give a greater momentum both to the stirrup and the arrow. The rider's hands, moreover, became free to attack the enemy. Lynn White's classic account of stirrups remain the most definitive till date. He has pointed out that some rudimentary idea of the stirrup had developed in India by the second century BC.[32] He examined the sculptures at Sanchi, Pathaora, Bhaja and Mathura.[33] He identified the Indian stirrup as a loose surcingle.[34] By second century AD big-toe stirrup was also in use.[35] It provided some foot-rest and helped in balancing of the rider.[36] But did not enable the rider to stand up on the horse while charging[37] Even the big-toe stirrup was not widespread in India; for example, horse riders carved in Sanchi stupa (2nd century AD) do not show the big-toe stirrup. Around the same time, in a copper vase from Kulu (first–second century AD), the rider's feet are placed in a stirrup made perhaps of thick rope.[38] Subsequently, it disappears.[39] The proper iron stirrup was invented in China in the sixth century AD, and from there it diffused to Persia and the Islamic world.[40] The final iron-stirrup arrived in India probably in the eleventh century from Khurasan.[41]

Craft Technology

Sericulture

Among the industrial crafts sericulture was one of the most important. While the use of wild and semi-domesticated silks is very ancient in India, the antiquity of sericulture is a subject of debate.[42] So far as Iran is concerned, there is almost a unanimity of opinion among scholars that the domesticated rearing of silkworm had spread to Iran only just before the Byzantium period, that is, possibly by the sixth century AD.[43] It is to be remembered that the Chinese technical skill and artisans tended to travel far and wide. Chinese metallurgists and well-drillers were found in the second century BC in Parthia and Ferghana and textile technologists, paper makers, goldsmiths and painters at Samarqand and Kufah in the eighth century AD.[44] Chinese artisans were demanded by the besieging Chin Tartars from Khaifeng in the twelfth century.[45] Similarly, in the thirteenth century the Chinese traveller Chhiu Chhang Chhun reported the presence of Chinese workmen in large numbers from Shantung to Samarqand.[46] He also reported a large number of settlements of Chinese artisans and Craftsmen between Samarqand and the valley of the Upper Yenisei in the north.[47] Such settlements of Chinese in Central Asian territories and their proximity with Iran must have facilitated the diffusion of certain techniques, and the culture of mulberry silk was presumably one of them. But in India, despite its familiarity with a wide variety of the sturnidae group of silks, the earliest firm evidence for sericulture in Kashmir comes from Mirza Haider Dughlat's *Tarikh-i Rashidi.* (AD 1547).[48] The eggs of the silkworms were imported from Gilgit and Little Tibet (Baltistan).[49] The immediately preceding centuries had witnessed the second impetus to development of sericulture in Persia under Mongol rule (thirteenth-fourteenth centuries).[50] That silk was an item of commerce between India from Iran and western Afghanistan in the thirteenth century is attested by Minhaj Siraj Juzjani.[51] This might also have encouraged the Kashmiri silk weavers to produce their own mulberry silk. Sericulture even spread to Sind in the seventeenth century.[52] So far as Bengal sericulture is concerned (introduced in fifteenth century), the worm is a multivoltine strand which has had a comparatively late history. It was known in China only by eighth century AD.[53] Ma Huan's reference to Bengal silk was perhaps a reference to sericulture derived from China, and not Iran.[54]

Spinning Wheel

A Chinese invention, this was first diffused in Central Asia and Iran. Iran had become familiar with the spinning wheel as early as the twelfth century.[55] In India, the first reference to it dates back to the Sultanate period.[56] The spinning wheel's arrival in India must have increased the productivity of the spinner almost six-fold.[57] Thus Iran contributed greatly to the future expansion of textile production by providing the spinning wheel to Indian textile technology.

Treadles in the Loom

The history of one of the important components of the loom, the treadles where with the shed, controlling sets of warp and weft threads are lifted or depressed, is a little obscure. The Chinese loom was equipped with treadles as early as the second century AD.[58] Ancient India was not in possession of this device. There is a passage in *Diyyaavadana* (first century AD) which Moti Chandra has translated, 'The weaver (*kuvinda*), while engaged in weaving cloth, picked and gathered the cloth and yarn (*avicira-vicirakam*) and with raised head (*abhinirmay dudhasiraskha*) and with the clapping movements of hands and feet (*sphatitam pani pado*) began the weaving operation'.[59] The 'clapping movements of hands and feet' could easily lead one to assume the use of looms fitted with treadles. However, Moti Chandra's rendering of the passage is doubtful. The term *sphatitam* means 'torn', 'lacerated', 'cracked' etc.[60]

Ancient Egypt and classical antiquity were also not familiar with treadles.[61] Europe possibly received the treadles along with the horizontal loom only in the twelfth century AD.[62] In Europe, the arrival of treadles coincided with the advent of the horizontal loom.[63] The period of the Islamic world's acquaintance with treadles is not certain.[64] In India the earliest evidence possibly comes from Maulana Daud's reference to the skill of a weaver. He writes, 'Look at the profession (capability) of the weaver, [when] his hands lift up, [his] feet do not touch the ground'.[65] It was possibly because his feet were on the treadles under them. Thus it is quite possible that it came into use in India during the thirteenth–fourteenth centuries. Shadiabadi (1468–69) defined it as *lauh-pay* (lit. foot-board) as 'wooden strip which the weaver keeps under his feet while weaving cloth'.[66] The treadles are also depicted in an illustration on the same folio.[67] Thus, this change tremendously improved the weaver's capacity to produce more and with little effort. The treadles are also depicted in a late sixteenth-century miniature, 'Idris giving instructions to the mankind in the art of weaving'.[68] They are attested by the subsequent seventeenth-century depiction of the weaver saint Kabir in a Mughal miniature.[69] It seems that loom-treadles were generalized in India before its earliest description in the fifteenth century. It is possible that the treadles of the loom reached India from China through the Islamic world.[70] It is possible that their arrival in India coincided with the spinning wheel, also datable to the thirteenth–fourteenth centuries; but in the absence of precise evidence this remains a matter for speculation. Whenever, this improvement might have occurred, it added greatly to the three motions of the loom-shedding, shuttle manipulation and beating up, which would in turn have increased productivity considerably and also improved the quality of woven cloth.

Draw-Loom

There is a view that India was familiar with the draw-loom or pattern loom as early as the eleventh century.[71] But this evidence seems inadequate in tracing the draw-loom. The use of the compound word *achchutari* induces Vijaya Ramaswamy to suggest that it refers to the draw-loom. This could possibly refer to a loom where more harnesses are attached for a closer control of the warps.[72] Fancy weaves could be achieved by adding more harnesses to the loom.[73] Besides nothing is said of figured patterns. Had India of the eleventh century been familiar with draw-loom, the weavers' guild would not have imposed the caveat in 1538 that 'this mode of weaving should be done only by the Muslims'.[74] In lieu of which they were authorized 'to collect the income from the gifted lands for their weaving'.[75] This regulation not only forbade its practice but also prescribed fines and punishment for any violation of it by the native weavers in the whole of South India.[76] The Chinese were far ahead of the others in loom construction, especially in the evolution of draw-loom. They already had the essentials of draw-loom developed as early as the first century if not the fourth.[77] But to India it possibly came from Iran where the term for drawloom is *destgah-i naqshbandi, dastgha-i naqshbandi and dastgha-i zaribafi.*[78] If the term *maqshband* exclusively means drawloom weaver, then the draw-loom arrived in India in the thirteenth–fourteenth centuries probably from Iran. Muhammad Tughlaq was reported to have employed 500 manufacturers of golden tissues, who wove gold brocades.[79] This was perhaps a new and expensive loom because the two references we have relate to two kings. The next reference to drawloom is implied in Abul Fazl's reference to a certain weaver named Ghiyas Naqshband. The reference to a weaver in the main text of the *Ain* reflects not only Akbar's interest in the craft but also the esteem in which it was held. Was it put to limited use in medieval times because it was more expensive in comparison to ordinary looms?[80] The use of the draw-loom survived into modern times for we have a clear description of the draw-loom in the last decade of the nineteenth century at Murshidabad.[81] The Murshidabad loom had a draw harness which operated on the figure warp only. It consisted of a large number of vertical draw strings. Each draw string was connected to a horizontal gut string in a cross harness. With the lifting of one draw string, the cross harness gut string was lifted and with it mails attached to warp threads were raised, the resulting pattern could be repeated. Besides, the reference to the drawboy sitting on an elevated platfrom manipulating the draw strings makes the identification with the draw-loom beyond dispute. Therefore, if the *naqshband* distinctly means a weaver working with drawloom, it could have been introduced in India as early as the thirteenth–fourteenth century possibly from Iran. Another reason behind our acceptance of Iran as the source of dissemination of draw-loom technology is the structural similarity between the two devices whereas the alternate Chinese model was quite complicated, with fifty to sixty heddles and identical number of treadles as early as the third century AD.[82] In the third century the multiplicity of heddles and treadles were reduced to the manageable number of twelve in a draw-loom by an ingenious engineer Ma Chun (fl.260 AD).[83] On the basis of available evidence, Iran seems to have been the only source of dispersal of drawloom to India.

Carpet-weaving

This was another important textile craft, which was introduced in the Sultanate period from Iran.[84] It received great state patronage during Akbar's reign. Akbar took care to appoint experienced workmen to weave carpets of different varieties in imperial workshops.[85] The chief centres were located in Agra.[86] Fatehpur,[87] Jaunpur,[88] Zafarabad,[89] Alvar,[90] and Lahore.[91] This suggests a somewhat recent import of the technique and its rapid extension. In 1679 Streynsham Master observed at Ellur, Andhra Pradesh, the manufacture of carpets on vertical looms (pile carpet weaving) with coloured woollen wefts woven in accordance with pattern set on paper.[92] He says that the fact that this industry was established a century earlier by Persian immigrants further strengthens the contention that the technique referred to earlier (1558) was a recent importation, and possibly refered to pile carpet-weaving on a vertical loom.[93] His observation 'And every thread being wrought, they share it with a pair of sizers, and then proceed to the next', makes the identification more certain. This technique of cutting the thread end of tightened knot is very similar to the Persian one.[94] Persian weaving technique and tools were thus possibly imported during the sixteenth century.

In another region where the Persian technique could have

come during fifteenth–sixteenth century was Kashmir. During Zainul Abidin's reign (1459–70), a large number of artisans adept in original designs had arrived in Kashmir.[95] We learn from Moti Chandra: 'The Kashmiris mastered the intricacies of shuttle (*turi*) and looms (*vema*), started weaving beautiful and costly silks.'[96] 'The special woollen textiles of foreign origin were woven by the Kashmiris'.[97] 'The painters seeing the patterns (*citra*) and creeper designs (*latakritih*) obtained by intricate weaving process (*vicitrayayan*) are reduced to silence as the figures in a painting'.[98] But the loom is not described. This could be a reference to the loom described in the classic account of Moorcroft and Trebeck,1822.[99]

It may appear that the flow of technological exchange was mainly from Iran to India. Nevertheless India too contributed some very significant tools and techniques to Iran in exchange for what it received.

The Worm-Press

The worm-press or worm-roller (Hindi *charkhi*) is mechanically an advanced device. It consists of two cylindrical rollers joined by a pair of helical gears so as to move in opposite directions, when one of them is turned by hand or crank-handle. Both rollers are horizontally placed and supported by two uprights. After the addition of crank-handle, the lower roller is twined by it on the one end,[100] which communicates motion to the rollers.[101] Once the cotton is fed into the revolving rollers, the fibre is drawn through, and the seeds are expelled and drop to one side.

The prevalence of this device in ancient India is best proved by its widespread presence in India,[102] Cambodia and Xinjiang (Sinkiang).[103] India exercised very powerful influence on Cambodia's culture during the first millennium of the Christian era, since the Indo-Cambodian cultural relationship belongs to the period fifth to tenth century AD,[104] it is likely that the transmission of the device took place at that time. China received cotton-gin with cotton itself from India between sixth to thirteenth century through two routes: through Burma (sixth century) and through Sinkiang (thirteenth century).[105] But the more substantial evidence for its presence in ancient India comes from the Ajanta frescoes where what Schlingloff recognises to be a bowstring device to separate cotton fibres seems really to be a *charkhi.* It is depicted with its characteristic rectangular frame, which has no place in the bow-string device.[106] Both the upper rollers are visible, though they are slender (perhaps of iron). Quite reasonably a crank-handle is not shown (since the crank is relatively a latecomer in technology). A woman is shown moving the upper roller with the left hand and inserting the cotton by the right-hand. This evidence makes it almost certain that the device was known to Indians by the middle of the sixth century AD.[107] This evidence can easily be reconciled with the view that *charkhi* reached China (sixth to thirteenth century) and Cambodia sometime during this period from India. As far as the history of this device in Islamic world is concerned, Irfan Habib could not find any evidence to attest its earlier presence there. It seems that different forms of the Indian cotton-gin were received by the Islamic world which had double-rollers and worm-gearing was lost in the transition.[108] Similar was the case with China.[109]

The Indian origin of this device has no other documentary evidence, but the use of the same mechanical principle in the Indian sugarcane rollers is significant. While there is no early evidence for parallel worm roller in any other civilization, both cotton and sugarcane were indigenous to India. The main difference between the two kinds of rollers is that in the cotton-gin is always mounted so as to rotate horizontally, whereas the sugarcane rollers move vertically owing to the use of cattle-power.

The Ajanta evidence is very significant particularly because the worm-gears are alien to Indian technology.[110] But even if the Ajanta miniatures are overlooked, it has to be established where it was actually invented. China has been thought of as a possible source. But China received cotton-gin with cotton itself.[111] China did not know of worm-gearing since it employed double powered rollers since the Han period. Therefore, it adapted the Indian cotton-gin to its indigenous practices and instead of worm-gearing, the earliest Chinese depiction of cotton-gin of fourteenth century have a separate crank-handle for each roller.[112] The earliest available depiction of the *charkhi* in a miniature Kangra painting of the mid-eighteenth century shows a spiral turn at the end of the rollers.[113] The worm was known to Europe since classical times, but this particular form of worm-gearing is traced back only to the early nineteenth century.[114] There is no evidence for the Islamic world's familiarity with it either.[115] The hardness of Indian cotton also makes it, technically speaking, difficult to gin it on a cotton-gin without worm-gearing.[116] Therefore, the chances of worm-gearing in the

Indian cotton-gin are greater in absence of crank-handle. In view of this it may be concluded that Indian cotton-gin presumably had worm-gearing since its inception and it remained in use till the late nineteenth century.[117]

The dating of another important part of the *charkhi*, the crank-handle is not certain.[118] References such as in the *Bahar-i Ajam* (1740) are not helpful.[119] But the depiction of cotton-gin in a Kangra-painting of the mid-eighteenth century shows the crank-handle along with the spinning-wheel in the seventeenth century.[120] By the eighteenth century, one more improvement could be seen in the cotton-gin depicted in the Kangra painting.[121] It shows parallel grooves in both the rollers which presumably enchanced the grip of rollers. The cotton-gin with worm-gearing and crank-handle increased the efficiency of the cotton gin more rapidly. No further mechanical change can be traced,[122] but at some stage water-power was used to drive the *charkhi* in Pakhli in the Hazara district now in the Punjab.[123] The use of the *charkhi* increased average ginning capacity to clean cotton between six to eight pounds per day by a man/woman.[124]

The Bow-String Device

There is some dispute about the origin of the bow-string device for scutching cotton.[125] Schlingloff has traced the first textual reference to it in one of the *Jatakas* where one reads '*ilthinam kappasa-pothanadhanukam*' (`a woman's bow for carding cotton').[126] Vijaya Ramaswamy has also discovered references to 'bowing' in Tamil texts dating from second century to sixth century AD.[127] *Trikandsesa*, a work of the ninth century refers to its use.[128]

As we have seen, Schlingloff identified a rectangular frame in the Ajanta fresco of the sixth century with the bow-string device. But a rectangular frame cannot perform the function of bow, since it cannot produce the required vibration. This is only possible when the frame is bow-shaped for then it can act as a spring vibrating the wire joining its two ends.[129]

Moti Chandra cites two dictionaries. *Vijayanti* (eleventh century) and *Abhidhanacintamani* (twelfth century) for references to the bow-string device.[130] *The Miftah-ul Fuzala* (fifteenth century) provides the earliest description and depictions of it.[131] Therefore, it could be safely assumed that the bow-string device radiated from India among other cultures. Irfab Habib finds the earliest evidence for familiarity with it in Persian literature only in the eleventh century AD.[132] China received it in the thirteenth century.[133] Europe knew of it only in the fifteenth century.[134]

The bow string device still survives in India practically as it was in medieval time.[135] It is called *dhanuki* in Hindi from Sanskrit/ Pali *dhanukam* or *dhunna* from a different Sanskrit root *dhu*, which means to beat, pummel.[136]

An important part of the bow-string device is the mallet. It is described and illustrated in the *Miftah-ul Fazala* (fifteenth century) along with the bow-string device.[137]

It is therefore very likely that India provided Iran with two very important inventions for processing cotton, viz., the cotton gin and the scutching bow.

Cloth-Printing

After the cloth is washed and bleached, colours can be applied to cloth in various ways, including cloth-printing. Archaeologists have tended to assume a very early date for cloth-printing in India, from the discovery of clay stamps. A.K. Coomaraswamy found an earthenware block anterior to fifth century AD.[138] John Marshall found one 'earthenware stamp' thought to be used for stamping textiles in the second third strata of Sirkap (90 BC–AD 25).[139] R.C. Gaur took a terracotta mould of Atranjikhera for a printing block; this was found in N.B.P. levels, datable to fifth–fourth century BC.[140]

The identification of certain clay moulds as printing blocks, however, remain doubtful. First of all there seems to be an apparent lack of consideration of the force which pressing on a firm surface would impose on 'baked clay'. No earthenware stamps are otherwise known to have been in use for cloth-printing. Roques in his detailed account of seventeenth-century cloth-printing in India refers only to wooden blocks.[141] The individual specimens also make indentification impossible. Thus, the Atranjikhera 'printing block' is not a stamp, but a mould, that is, it has a patern inside of it which can only be impressed on plastic material. Indeed, Gaur admits the possibility of the specimen being intended to impress 'decorations over . . . mud plaster of house walls'[142] though surprisingly he does not take the reader into confidence about the internal mould-like cavities of the stamp. Similarly, the Taxila 'blocks' need to be examined before one can pronounce on the possibility of their use in printing.

Forbes considers block-printing to be of ancient origin in India.[143] But his supposition lacks factual evidence. There is a controversial sentence in Banabhatta's *Harshacarita* (seventh century AD) which reads '*kutila krama rupa-kriyamana pallava prabhagir*'.[144] P.V. Kane expains it as follows.

> On the dyed and dried cloth, some paintings of the various trees were being drawn. The paintings had very great beauty (*Prabhag*). The paintings were being drawn on the inside of the cloth and hence they were done in the reverse order of nature (*kutila krama*), so that the outside (that would be visible to others), would show the beautiful 'pallava' in their natural form.[145]

So explained the text does not justify an assumption of block- printing, for any drawing or painting on the inside of the cloth. Nevertheless, Kane himself had reservation about his translation of the passage[146] V.S. Agrawala interprets it differently and says that the first two words (*kutila krama*) signify an undulating pattern. 'They could also refer to a diagnonal arrangement, with ornamental rows extending from one corner to the opposite, such as we find depicted on a costume in one of the Ajanta murals.'[147] The next word, *rupa* has had from the time of Panini the technical meaning of 'symbol', 'design', 'figure'; and Agrawala considers it to be the same here. He refers to Panini's words '*Rupad ahataprasamsayor-jap*', where the word *rupa* is clearly used for stamping symbols on metallic pieces.[148] On the strength of this allusion to stamping, Agrawala, therefore, considers that block-printing was known during Harsha's time.[149] Whatever the interpretation of Bana's text, it seems firmly established that block-printing began to be employed in India by the tenth–eleventh century.[150] The results of radiocarban tests on two of the sixteenth Ashmolean specimens have conclusively proved that block printed textile were manufactured in India and exported to Egypt by tenth–eleventh century.[151] The reference to an 'instrument' in Manasollasa (twelfth century) has been discussed elsewhere.[152] But the term refers simply to an artisan. Moti Chandra finds the word *uncho* for the profession of calico-printer (*chimpakakaruviesesah*) in *Paiyalacchi* of Dhanapala, a twelfth-century lexicon of indigenous words.[153] In the same work Moti Chandra finds the words *chimpao* or *chimpa* for calico-printer, from which the modern *chip* and *chipi* have originated.[154] In Hemchandra's *Desinamamala*, the word *chappanti* is described as a process by which lotus patterns were drawn (*niyamavisesah yatra padman likhayate*).[155] Some words were in use in fourteenth–fifteenth centuries, *chimpaka* for a female calico-printer and *chipa* for calico-printer.[156] The use of these words with reference to textile industry suggests calico-printing being done in India as early as tenth–eleventh century. Irfan Habib has suggested India's acquaintance with cloth-printing by the fourteenth century.[157] It is to be noted here that fourteen of the sixteen samples of the New berry collection at the Ashmolean Museum range between thirteenth to fifteenth century.[158] It is constantly referred to in medieval period. *Bahar-i Ajam* refers to the use of word *chap* in the eighteenth century.[159]

The indian block print was distinct from Chinese inked stamps (fourteenth century) and Europe, fixation of clours with blocks in the fifteenth century.[160] Iran possibly received it in the thirteenth–fourteenth century when it migrated to Egypt and to the Red Sea port of Quseir al-Qadim.[161] The medieval practice seems to have survived in its original form till recent times.[162] Thus it seems that cloth printing originated in India before the tenth–eleventh century and took a long time to migrate to Iran where it possibly reached sometime in sixteenth–seventeenth century.

Notes and References

1 Gherardo Gnoli, 'Introduction', *History of Humanity, Scientific and Cultural Development*, Vol. III (From the Seventh Century BC to Seventh Century AD), (eds) J. Herrmann and Erik Zurcher, UNESCO, London/Paris, 1996, pp. 115–16.

2 J. Needham, *Science and Civilization in China*, Vol. 4 (II), Cambridge, Ist pub. 1965, rpt 1975, pp. 361–62.

3 Irfan Habib, 'Joseph Needham and the History of Indian Technology', *Indian Journal of History of Science*, 35.3 (2000), pp. 252–53.

4 Amar Singh, *Amarkosa*, ed. Shivdutta Dadhipnatha, Delhi, rpt 1997, pp. 346, No. 27. Amar Singh's period is not firmly established. Some consider him to be of fourth century AD because he was one of the nobles of Vikramaditya. Some consider him a Buddhist, others as a Jain. Max Muller placed him in sixth century AD. Dr Harnley found him belonging to 625–940 AD. Since he was familiar with the Mahayana sect, so he perhaps wrote after seventh century AD. See Nemchandra Sastri (ed.), *Abhidhana Chintamani of Sri Hemachandra*, Varanasi, 1996, p. 9.

5 See especially Irfan Habib, 'Pursuing the History of Indian Technology, Pre-Modern Modes of Transmission of Power', *Social Scientist*, Vol. 20, Nos 3–4, March –April 1992, pp. 8–11, and Irfan Habib, 'Joseph Needham and the History of Indian Technology', pp. 252–57.

[6] Irfan Habib, 'Joseph Needham and History of Indian Technology', pp. 253–54.

[7] *Abhidhanachintamani*, pp. 268, 4, 159.

[8] Irfan Habib, 'Joseph Needham and the History of Indian Technology', p. 257.

[9] Ahmad Y. al-Hassan and Donald R. Hill, *Islamic Technology An Illustrated History*, Cambridge, 1986, p. 41.

[10] Needham, p. 360.

[11] Ibid.

[12] Ibid.

[13] J. Marshall, *Taxila: An Illustrated Account of Archaeological Excavation*; Cambridge, 1951, Vol. II, p. 410.

[14] Irfan Habib, 'Pursuing the History of Indian Technology, Pre-modern Modes of Transmission of Power', *Social Scientist*, Vol. 20, Nos 3–4, March–April 1992, p. 9.

[15] Hans E. Wulff, *The Traditional Crafts of Persia*, Cambridge, 1966, pp. 259–60.

[16] A.S. Beveridge, tr. and ed., *Baburnama*, Vol. II, rpt 1989, Delhi, pp. 486–87, 532. But for a better translation of the passage see Irfan Habib, 'Medieval Technology: Exchanges between India and the Islamic World', *Aligarh Journal of Oriental Studies, Prof. Ram Suresh Tripathi Commemoration Volume*, Vol. II, Nos 1–2, 1985, pp. 200–01.

[17] Needham, p. 352.

[18] Irfan Habib, 'Medieval Technology', p. 202.

[19] Needham, p. 354.

[20] Irfan Habib, 'Medieval Technology', p. 202.

[21] Lynn White Jr, *Medieval Technology and Social Change*, Oxford, 1964, pp. 107–08.

[22] Lynn White, p. 109.

[23] Marshall, II, pp. 485–87.

[24] Irfan Habib, 'Pursuing the History of Indian Technology', p. 5.

[25] Ibid.

[26] Irfan Habib, 'Joseph Needham and the History of Indian Technology', pp. 248–52.

[27] Cited by Irfan Habib, 'Pursuing the History of Indian Technology', p. 5.

[28] I have consulted the painting reproduced in S.P. Verma, *India at Work in Sculpture and Painting*, Aligarh, 1994, Plate No. XI.

[29] Ibid., p. 4.

[30] Hans E. Wulff, pp. 296–97.

[31] Ibid., p. 296.

[32] Lynn White Jr, pp. 14–15.

[33] Ibid.

[34] Ibid.

[35] Ibid.

[36] Ibid., p. 15.

[37] Irfan Habib, 'Technological Changes and Society, 13th and 14th Centuries',

Presidential Address, Medieval India Section, Indian History Congress, Varanasi, 1969, p. 23.

[38] A.L. Basham, *The Wonder that was India*, London, 1982, pp. 134, 189, 374.

[39] Irfan Habib, 'Technological Changes and Society', p. 23.

[40] Lynn White, pp. 17–19.

[41] Ibid., see also Irfan Habib, 'Technological Changes and Society', pp. 22–23.

[42] See Xinru Liu, *Ancient India and Ancient China, Trade and Religious Exchanges* AD *1–600*, Delhi, 1988; Brajadulal Chattopadhyaya, 'South Asia from 200 BC to AD 300' in *History of Humanity*', Vol. III, pp. 373–375. Irfan Habib, *The Economic History of Medieval India A Survey*, Delhi, 2001, p. 4; see also Ishrat Alam, 'History of Sericulture in India to the 17th Century', *Proceedings of Indian History Congress*, Aligarh, 2000, pp. 339–52.

[43] 'Western Asia between 250 BC and 224 AD.' in *History of Humanity*, Vol. III, p. 136; Claude Cahen, 'Tribes, Cities and Social Organization', R.N. Frye (ed.), *The Cambridge History of Iran*, Vol. 4, Cambridge, 1975, pp. 310–11; D. Thompson, *Encyclopaedia Iranica*, London, 1985, p. 229. s.v. *Abrisam*; H.J. Schmidt, *The Encyclopaedia of Islam*, Leiden, 1979, pp. 209–221, s.v. *Harir*.

[44] Needham, Vol. IV (2), p. 20.

[45] Ibid.

[46] Ibid.

[47] Ibid.

[48] Mirza Muhammad Haidar, *Tarikh-i Rashidi*, tr. E. Denison Ross, Patna, 1973, p. 425; observes, 'Among the wonders of Kashmir are the quantities of mulberry trees, (cultivated) for their leaves, from which) is obtained [silk].' See also Walter R. Lawrence, *The Valley of Kashmir*, London, 1895, pp. 366–67; C.E. Bates, *A Gazeteer of Kashmir* refers to another tradition where it is said that the silkworm into Kashmir was introduced shortly before the reign of Akbar by Mirza Haidar of Kashgar who had imported eggs from Bokhara. It seems that this tradition arose out of the first literary reference to silk we find in Mirza Haider Dughlat's account.

[49] Abul Fazl, *Ain-i Akbari*, (ed.) Blochmann, *Bib. Ind.*, Calcutta, 1866–67, Vol. I, pp. 562–63.

[50] Irfan Habib, 'Agrarian Economy' in Tapan Raychaudhuri and Irfan Habib (eds), *The Cambridge Economic History of India*, Vol. I, *c. 1200–c. 1750*, Delhi, 1984, p. 53.

[51] Minhaj Siraj Juzjani, *Tabaqat–i Nasiri*, (ed.) Abdul Hai Habibi, Vol. II, Kabul, 1964, p. 184.

[52] Irfan Habib, 'Indian Textile Industry in the 17th Century', in *Essays in Honour of Prof. S.C. Sarkar*, Delhi, 1976, p. 186.

[53] Dieter Kuhn (ed.), Joseph Needham, *Science and Civilization in China*, Vol. 5 (IX), Cambridge, p. 309.

[54] Ma Huan, *Yeng-yai Sheng-lan, The Overall Survey of the Ocean Shores*, tr. G.V.G. Mills, Cambridge, 1970, p. 163.

[55] Irfan Habib, 'Medieval Technology: Exchange between India and the Islamic World', pp. 203–04.

[56] Ibid., pp. 203–05.

[57] Ibid., p. 205.

[58] Lynn White, pp. 117, 173.

[59] Moti Chandra, *Costumes, Textiles, Cosmetics and Coiffure in Ancient and Medieval India*, Delhi, 1973, p. 29.

[60] See Franklin Edgerton, *Buddhist Hybrid Sanskrit Grammar and Dictionary*, Vol. II, London, 1953, p. 612, s.v. *sphatita.* He has referred to other references from *Divyaavdana*, pp. 83.22, 463.8, 304.7.

[61] R.J. Forbes, *Studies in Ancient Technology*, Vol. IV, Leiden, 1964, pp. 218–19.

[62] Eleanora Carus-Wilson, 'Haberget: A Medieval Textile Connundrum', *Medieval Archaeology*, 13, (1969[1971]), p. 165, has found the earliest European evidence of the horizontal loom in the Talmudic commentary of Rabbi Rashi (d. 1105), written in Northern France, cited in Lynn White, 'Technology Assessment from the stance of a Medieval Historian', *Medieval Religion and Technology Collected Essays*, Los Angeles, 1978, pp. 274–75. Earlier it was believed that it arrived in Europe only in the thirteenth century; see C. Singer (ed.), *History of Technology*, Oxford, 1956, rep. 1957, Vol. II, p. 212. See also, Ahmad J. al-Hassan and Donald R. Hill, *Islamic Technology*, p. 187.

[63] Lynn White, p. 117.

[64] Ahmad J. al Hassan and Donald R. Hill, *Islamic Technology*, p. 187.

[65] Maulana Daud, *Chandayan*, (ed.) Mataprasad Gupta, Agra, 1967, p. 169.

[66] Muhammad ibn Daud ibn Mahmud Shadiyabadi, *Miftah ul Fuzula*, (873 AH/1469 AD), British Library. Or 3299, s.v. *lauhpay.*

[67] Ibid., f. 262a.

[68] Tobby Falk and Mildred Archer, *Indian Miniatures in the India Office Library*, London, 1981. Pl. 3. Cat. 4, p. 47. See also S.P. Verma, 'Sixteenth Century Mughal Miniatures at the Royal Library (Windsor) and India Office Library (London)—A Survey of Hitherto unnoticed Paintings', *Proceedings of Indian History Congress*, 42nd session, Bodhgaya, 1981, pp. 258–67.

[69] See A.A. Ivanova, T.B. Grek, O.P. Akimushkina, *Album of Indian and Persian Miniatures, XVI–XVIII Centuries*, Akademi of Sciences, U.S.S.R., Institute of the People of Asia, Moscow, 1962, Pl. 66.

[70] Irfan Habib, 'Medieval Technoloyg: Exchanges between India and the Islamic World', p. 220.

[71] Vijaya Ramaswamy, 'Notes on the Textile Technology in Medieval India with special reference to the South', *Indian Economic and Social History Review*, Vol. XVII (2), Delhi, 1980, p. 232.

[72] Ibid., p. 232. Ramaswamy thinks that *achchutari* refers 'to the process by which certain cords are attached to the wooden frame on top of the loom, and patterns are produced by pulling the cords in correct sequence (by an assistant) while the weaver threw the shuttle through the resultant sheds'.

There is no evidence, however, to sustain this explanation (ibid., p. 232).

73 Forbes, Vol. IV, p. 218.

74 Cited by Ramaswamy, *I.E.S.H.R.*, Vol. XVII, No. 2, p. 233, while arguing in favour of presence of draw loom in the eleventh century.

75 Ibid.

76 Ibid.

77 Needham, IV(2), p. 69.

78 Hans E. Wulff, p. 206.

79 Shahabuddin Abul Abbas Ahmad, *Masalikul Absar fi Mamalikul Amsar*, in H.M. Elliot, *The History of India*, Vol. III, n.d., Allahabad, p. 578.

80 *Ain-i Akbari*, p. 82.

81 Nitya Gopal Mookerji, 'The Silk Industries of Moorshedabad', *Journal of Indian Art*, Vol. V, London, January, 1984, pp. 7–8.

82 Needham, IV(2), p. 39.

83 Ibid.

84 Irfan Habib, *The Economic History of Medieval India*, p. 4.

85 *Ain-i Akbari*, Vol. I, pp. 50–51.

86 *Ain-i Akbari*, Vol. I, pp. 50–51; Foster (ed.), *English Factories in India* (1618–21), Vol. I, Oxford, 1906, pp. 168, 188; Pelsaert, *'Remonstrantie'* tr. under the title *Jahangir's India*, by W.H. Moreland and P. Geyl, Cambridge, 1925, p. 9.

87 *Ain-i Akbari*, Vol. I, pp. 50–51; Pelsaert, p. 9, Tavernier, *Travels in India*, Vol. II, tr. V. Ball, rev. W. Crooke, Indian edn, 1977, p. 2.

88 W. Finch, *Early Travels in India (1583–1619)*, (ed.) Foster, London, 1921, p. 177; Pelsaert, p. 7.

89 *Ain-i Akbari*, Vol. II, p. 423.

90 Ibid, II, p. 442.

91 Ibid., Vol. I, p. 57; *E.F.I. 1618–21*, p. 51; Pelsaert, p. 31; Manucci, *Storio do Mogor*, Vol. II, tr. W. Irvine, London, 1907–08, p. 424.

92 Streynsham Master, *Diaries of Streynsham Master 1675–80*, Vol. II, (ed.) R.C. Temple, London, 1911, p. 171.

93 Ibid.

94 Hans E. Wulff, pp. 214–16, describes this *'Traditional Craft'* in greater detail.

95 *Rajatarangini*, Vol. VI, Bombay, 1892, p. 137 cited by Moti Chandra, pp. 170, 237.

96 Moti Chandra, pp. 170, 237.

97 *Rajatarangini*, Vol. VI, p. 29, cited by Moti Chandra, p. 170, 237.

98 Ibid, Vol. VI, p. 30. Moti Chandra admits that artisans from Turkestan are not specifically mentioned. Shrivara, the author of *Zaina Rajatarangini* (fifteenth century AD) simply refers to *analpa shilpin*, 'hosts of craftsmen from afar' which might include such artisans from Iran who were presumably familiar with such a weaving process, see also *Srivara's Zaina Rajatarangini*, tr. with text, Kashi Nath Dhar, Delhi, 1994, pp. 236–38.

99 Cf. W. Moorcroft and G. Trebeck, *Travels in the Himalayan Provinces of Hindustan and the Punjab, in Ladakh and Kashmir, in Peshawar, Kabul,*

Kunduz and Bokhara from 1810–1825, Vol. II, (ed.) H.H. Wilson, London, 1837, rpt Delhi, 1971, pp. 179–181.

100 Cf. G.A. Grierson, *Bihar Peasant Life*, Ist Pub. 1855, 2nd Pub., Delhi, 1975, pp. 62–63 (illustration on p. 47); G. Watt, *Dictionary of Economic Products of India (DEPI)*, Vol. IV, London, 1892, pp. 105–06, 115, 123, 147–48, 152–53.

101 By the mid-nineteenth century, the *charkhi* has started having even a wheel at one or ends, Watt, *DEPI*, Vol. IV, pp. 152–53.

102 For its widespread use in India in various province see Watt, *DEPI*, Vol. IV, pp. 105–06, 115, 123, 147–48, 152–53.

103 J. Needham, *Science and Civilization in China*, Vol. IV, pt (2) pp. 122–124.

104 For Indo-Cambodian contacts see R.C. Majumdar, *Inscriptions of Kambuja*, Calcutta, 1953. See also, Himanshu P. Ray, *The Winds of Change: Buddhism and the Maritime Links of Early South Asia*, Delhi, 1994, pp. 87–120.

105 Needham, Vol. IV (2), pp. 122–24, 204.

106 Schlingloff gives a reproduction, op.cit., opp. p. 88. This fresco is reproduced in G. Yazdani, *Ajanta, The Colour and Monochrome Reproduction of the Ajanta Frescoes Based on Photography*, Pt. I, Pl. XII, text, p. 17. The two rollers though not visible in Schlingloff's reproduction are clearly enough visible in Yazdani's. See also Ishrat Alam, 'Textile Tools as depicted in Ajanta and Mughal Paintings', in *Technology in Ancient and Medieval India*, (eds.) Aniruddha Ray and S.K. Bagchi, Delhi, 1986, pp. 129–30.

107 This fresco is in Cave No. I, which dates back to the middle of the sixth century AD. See M.K. Dhavalikar, *Ajanta—A Cultural Study*, Poona, 1973, p. 2.

108 Irfan, Habib, 'Medieval Technology Exchanges between India and the Islamic World', pp. 213–15.

109 Ibid.

110 Harbans Mukhia in his review of *Madhyakaleen Bharat* (ed.), Irfan Habib, No. 1, Delhi, 1981, in *The Indian Historical Review*, Vol. VII, July 1980–January 1981, November 1–2, Delhi, 1981, pp. 272.

111 Needham, Vol. IV(2), p. 127.

112 Needham, Vol. IV(2), pp. 122–124.

113 M.S. Randhawa, *Kangra Paintings of the Bhagvata Purana*, New Delhi, 1960, p. 56, Plate V.

114 Needham, Vol. IV(2), pp. 122–24.

115 Irfan Habib, 'Medieval Technology Exchanges between India and the Islamic World' pp. 213–15.

116 Watt, *D.E.P.I.*, Vol. IV, pp. 152–53.

117 Ibid., Vol. IV, pp. 105–6, 115, 123, 147–48, 152–53.

118 Irfan Habib, 'Needham and the History of Indian Technology', pp. 260–61.

119 Tek Chand Bahar, *Bahar-i Ajam*, s.v. *charkh*. The *Bahar-i Ajam* seems to give the earliest textual evidence for *charkhi* when it refers to the cotton dresser's wheel i.e. cotton-gin (*charkh-i naddafi*).

120 M.S. Randhawa, p. 56. The cotton-gin is prominently shown in Pl.V which illustrates 'Migration from Gokula to Vrindavana'.

[121] Irfan Habib, 'The Technology an Economy of Mughal Empire', *The Indian Economic and Social History Review*, Vol. XVVI, No. I, Delhi, 1980, p. 7, has traced the addition of crank-handle to the spinning wheel during the seventeenth century.

[122] Randhawa, p. 50, Pl.V.

[123] Unlike India, the *charkhi* witnessed improvements in China, in the form of addition of treadle motion to the upper roller besides the crank-handle. This motion was assisted by a radial bob-flywheel. In Japan, the flywheel tended to take the form of single club-shaped weight attached to the shaft by the early seventeenth century (Cf. Needham, Vol. IV(2), p. 123). The Persian gin also had three rollers that were made to press against each other by the manipulation of wedges between their bearings. The rear roller kept off the fibre from the main roller, but its first date of use is not certain (see Hans E. Wulff, pp. 179–80).

[124] Watt, *D.E.P.I.*, Vol. IV, p. 123.

[125] R.J. Forbes, *Studies in Ancient Technology*, Vol. IV, Leiden, 1964, pp. 11–12, admits its prehistoric origin in Europe, but supposes a fresh arrival in Europe in the fifteenth century (ibid., IV, p. 21; R. Patterson in C. Singer (ed.), *History of Technology*, Vol. II, Oxford 1967, p. 115).

[126] Schlingloff, op.cit., pp. 86–89. His identification of the words *pinjanikaya, pinjitam* etc., meaning the scutch bow from the dictionaries of eleventh–twelfthcenturies does not appear very convincing. They could probably mean beating cotton with stick also (as discussed earlier).

[127] Vijaya Ramaswamy, 'A Note on the Textile Technology in Medieval South India', *Proceedings of Indian History Congress*, 40th Session, Waltair, 1979, p. 451. She has expressed same views in 'Notes on the Textile Technology in Medieval India with special reference to the South', *I.E.S.H.R.*, Vol. XVI, No. 2, Delhi, 1980, p. 227.

[128] Purushottamadeva, *Trikandsesa*, Bombay 1937, p. 78.
The shloka reads, '*Kapallasika tarkustarkushanastu Jhamaka Varatani tarkupithi syatpinyanam twlakarmukam*'. I owe this information to Prof. S.R. Sarma, Department of Sanskrit, A.M.U., Aligarh. K.N. Mahapatra, 'Purushottama Deva, The Lexicographer', *The Orissa Historical Research Journal*, Vol. II, Orissa, 1953, p. 71, traces *Trikandsesa* to be a work of 9th century AD.

[129] Needham, Vol. IV (2), p. 127.

[130] Moti Chandra, *Costumes, Textiles, Cosmetics and Coiffure in Ancient and Medieval India*, p. 126.

[131] *Miftah-ul Fuzala*, f.126b and f.259a; Ishrat Alam, 'Textile Tools', pp. 132–33.

[132] Cf. Irfan Habib, 'The Technology and Economy of Mughal India', *I.E.S.H.R.*, Vol. XVII, No. 1, Delhi, 1980, p. 6; Irfan Habib, 'Changes in Technology in Medieval India', *Studies in History*, Vol. II, No. I, Delhi, 1980, p. 17; Irfan Habib, 'Medieval Technology: Exchanges between India and the Islamic World', p. 216.

[133] Needham, Vol. IV (2), p. 127.

[134] Forbes, Vol. IV, p. 21; see also R. Patterson In C. Singer (ed.), *History of Technology*, Vol. II, p. 195.

[135] Cf. Maulavi Zafrur Rehman Dehlavi, *Farhang Istilahat-i Peshawaran*, Vol. II, Delhi, 1940, pp. 5–6. It is called *dhunki* apparently a variant of Sanskrit *dhanukam.*

[136] Cf. J.T. Platts, *A Dictionary of Urdu, Classical Hindi and English*, Oxford, 1960, pp. 548–49, s.v. *dhuniya, dhunna.*

[137] *Miftah ul Fuzala*, f.126b and f.259a, s.v. *Shafshahang.*

[138] A.K. Coomaraswamy, *The Arts and Crafts of India and Ceylon*, (originally published, 1913), New York, 1964, p. 201.

[139] John Marshall, *Taxila*, Vol. II, p. 437.

[140] R.C. Gaur, 'An Early Terracotta Printing Block', in *Bias in Indian Historiography*, (ed.) Devahuti, Delhi, 1980, pp. 276–77; also R.C. Gaur, *Excavations at Atranjikhera Early Civilization of the Upper Ganga Basin*, Delhi 1983, pp. 244, 380, Pl.CI, and 'Early Evidences of Ancient Technology', V.K. Thakur and K.K. Mandal (eds), *Science Technology and Medicine in Indian History, Essays in Honour of Dr D.K. Singh*, Patna, 2000, pp. 1–2.

[141] Roques, in P.R. Schwartz, *Printing on Cotton at Ahmedabad in India in 1678*, Ahmedabad, 19, p. 8.

[142] Gaur, 'An Early Terracotta Printing Block', p. 277.

[143] Forbes, Vol. IV, pp. 138–9; Hans E. Wulff, p. 224, following Forbes commits similar error.

[144] Banabhatta, *Harshacarita*, (ed.) P.V. Kane, 2nd edn, Delhi, 1965, *ucchvasa* IV, p. 14.

[145] Ibid, pp. 54–55 (Notes on *Ucchvasa* IV).

[146] *Harshacarita*, Notes pp. 54–55.

[147] V.S. Agrawala, 'References to Textiles in Bana's Harshacharita', *Journal of Indian Textile History*, Vol. IV, Ahmedabad, 1959, p. 67.

[148] V.S. Agrawala, *India As Known to Panini*, p. 272.

[149] V.S. Agarwala, *Harshacharita ek Samskritik Adhyayana*, Patna, 1953, p. 67.

[150] Ruth Barnes, *Indian Block printed Textiles in Egypt: The Newberry Collection in the Ashmolean Museum*, Oxford, reviewed by Steven Cohen, *Bulletin of the School of Oriental and African Studies*, Vol. 61(3), 1998, pp. 573–74.

[151] Ibid., see also Jenny Balfour-Paul, *Indigo and the Arab World*, Survey, 1997, pp. 125, 228n. 74. Balfour-Paul suggests that some of these fragments including indigo-dyed ones could have been of local origin since techniques of printing on cotton, including discharge printing using wooden blocks, existed in Egypt and Syria at the time. But resist-printed indigo-dyed fragments, mostly of Indian origin, have also been excavated at other sites in Egypt and the Red Sea port of Quseir al Qadim, which date back to the thirteenth and the end of fourteenth centuries.

[152] See Ishrat Alam, 'Textile Tools', p. 136.

[153] Moti Chandra, p. 125.

[154] Ibid.

[155] Ibid.

[156] Ibid., pp. 147, 168.

[157] Irfan Habib, 'Medieval Technology: Exchanges between India and the Islamic World', p. 219.

[158] See Ishrat Alam, 'Textile Tools', pp. 136–137.

[159] *Bahar-i Ajam*, s.v. *chapa, qalib.*

[160] For a detailed discussion see, Irfan Habib, 'Changes in Technology in Medieval India', *Studies in History*, 1980, Vol. II (1), p. 31; see also Irfan Habib, 'Medieval Technology: Exchanges between India and the Islamic World', p. 219.

[161] Jenny Balfour Paul, p. 125.

[162] Hans E. Wulff, pp. 224–27.

The Mughal Empire and the Iranian Diaspora of the Sixteenth Century

Iqtidar Alam Khan

The empire established by the Timurid prince Zahir al-Din Babur in India (1526) was often identified by Indians of the time with the Mongols who had been invading north-western parts of the subcontinent intermittently during the thirteenth and fourteenth centuries.[1] This identification is reflected in it being popularly designated as Mughal Empire (*Saltanat-i Mughalia*).[2] In Central Asia, the same empire was remembered down to the end of the seventeenth century by the familial ties of its rulers with the remnants of Chaghtai *ulus* of the Mongols then controlling parts of Xinjiang (Mughulistan). To demarcate them from the Uzbek chiefs who are also identified as the descendants of Chingiz,[3] the Indian Timurids were generally referred to in Central Asian histories as Chaghtais.[4] The overall cultural profile of the Mughal Empire during its formative years was also influenced by features like Turko-Mongol theory of kingship, the Turani complexion of the nobility,[5] the influence of the Naqshbandi order,[6] and Eastern or Chaghtai Turkish being the lingua franca of the ruling elite,[7] all of which speak of its Central Asian ambience.

All this should clearly set apart the nascent Mughal Empire from the Safavid Empire as it emerged under Shah Ismail (1501–24) and his successor Shah Tahmasp (1524–76), in the first half of the sixteenth century, where it was Western Turkish that was accommodated within Persian culture. The rise of the Safavids can be traced back to the Islamic revival of post Il-Khanid Iran, that was particularly oriented towards eradicating the remnants of Mongol paganism.[8] In the beginning of the sixteenth century, this revival led to an alliance between Turkman nomads and Iranian landed gentry (including 'clerical notables') both of whom were bound together by allegiance to the spirit of Safavid Sufic order. Around the same time the Safavid order assumed a strong Shi`ite orientation and the Twelver Shi'ite doctrines came to acquire the status of state religion and the rulers in effect claimed for themselves the role of *imams*, becoming thereby the temporal and religious heads of the Islamic Community.[9] The Safavid aspiration of being acknowledged by the Timurids as their preceptors and spiritual guides is borne out by their offer of military assistance to Babur and Humayun, in 1512 and 1545, contingent on the latter's agreeing to formally enter the circle of *qizilbashes.*[10] That such an attitude on the part of the Safavids was resented by the Timurids may be gauged by the manner in which they turned their backs on the Safavid allies at Ghajdavan (13 November 1512) and Qandahar (1545).[11]

It is therefore important to discern as to how, with the passage of time, the Mughal Empire, shed many of its Central Asian features and developed a new court culture in which the wider use of Persian, not only as the universal language of imperial administration as part of the unprecedented systematization that the Mughals attempted, but also as the main vehicle of cultural and literary discourse among the ruling elites, was an important manifestation.[12] This court culture was also infused with new artistic tastes and refinements carrying, in part, an unmistakable stamp of Persian influence.[13] Again, in this changed cultural milieu heterodox views and practices came to be tolerated to the point that the large number of Muslims, many of them Persian immigrants subscribing to *asna 'ashari* beliefs were no longer obliged to observe pious subterfuge (*taqiyya*) to avoid persecution at the hands of orthodox Sunnis. So much so that, by the beginning of seventeenth century, the fact of Shi'ites and Sunnis offering prayers in the same mosque was cited as a distinctive hall-mark of peaceable inter-sect relations in the Mughal Empire.[14] This, in a way, was the beginning of the process of creation of sizeable pockets of Shi'ite population in many of the urban centres in North India by the latter half of the eighteenth century.[15]

Another noteworthy manifestation of this court culture was the special respect and courtesy observed by the Mughals in their relations and diplomatic exchanges with the Safavid rulers which was in sharp contrast to the hostility and disdain generally manifested by them in their attitude toward the Shaibanids and Janids of Central Asia.[16] The element of special warmth generally discernible in the Mughal-Safavid relations may, perhaps, also be ascribed to the close personal equations that sometimes existed between individuals belonging to the two ruling families.[17]

Lastly, the inclusion of a large number of men of Iranian origin in the Mughal nobility and also the induction by marriage of women like Nur Jahan and Mumtaz Mahal, from important Iranian families into the Mughal family, tended to create an intellectual climate at the Mughal court where the King's being a Turani, perhaps, no longer remained of crucial significance.[18]

This transformation in the Mughal court culture may be attributed to a variety of factors. Akbar's policy measures curbing the authority of orthodox *ulama* and generally encouraging the spirit of comparative religion were no doubt important factors favouring this development. But undoubtedly the most significant circumstance contributing to this new court culture was the coming to India of a large number of Iranian immigrants to seek employment and patronage in the Mughal Empire.[19] We hope to focus in this paper on this transformation in the Mughal court culture during the sixteenth century by highlighting the contribution of Iranian immigrants in different fields.

I

Both Babur and Humayun, as well as a majority of their nobles down to 1540 were more at home in Turkish than Persian. But with the possible exception of some of the chiefs who were recent immigrants from Mughulistan, and a small number of Uzbek nobles, most of them could speak Persian as well.[20] As a matter of fact, till this time, all over Central Asia, Persian was not only the language of polite discourse, but also the lingua franca.[21] This status of Persian language in Timurid Central Asia was not disturbed by the literary florescence of Chaghtai Turkish towards the end of the fifteenth century. The foremost promoter of this literary upsurge in Eastern Turkish, Mir Ali Sher Navai, was also famous for starting a new trend in Persian literary writing.[22] Many of the Persian poets, scholars and theologians present at the Mughal court during the reigns of Babur and Humayun belonged to the circle of literati patronized in the Timurid principality of Khurasan. These literary figures included Shaikh Zain Khwafi (Babur's *sadr* and author of the *Fathnama* of the Battle of Kanwa 1527)[23] Khwand Amir (author of *Habib us-Siyar* and *Qanun-i Humayuni*)[24] and Mir Abdul Haiy (*sadr* around 1556).[25] Baha al-Din Hasan Nisari has noticed many other Persian literary men of Khurasan who eventually moved to the Mughal court in search of patronage. Among them is included the poet Qasim *Kahi.* Being a native of Kabul, to begin with, he looked down upon those who were going to Hindustan in search of patronage. But, eventually, he came to be attached to Humayun's court at Delhi: Kahi is reported to have composed the chronogram (*Humayun az bam uftad*) yielding the year of Humayun's death. He is known to have became quite influential later under Akbar.[26]

This early influx of Persian literary men into the Mughal court evidently began after the fall of the Timurid principality of Khurasan in 1507 and continued down to the early years of Humayun's reign. The early arrivals were the persons identified with Sultan Husain Baiqara's enlightened rule who were obliged to leave Khurasan after it was occupied by Shaibani Khan in 1507. The persecution of the Sunnis in Khurasan after its annexation to the Safavid Empire 1510[27] seems to have led to the migration by many more educated Khurasanis to the Mughal court where they were apparently employed in various capacities. Several Nishapuris, Hirawis (from Herat), Turbatis (for example, Shihabuddin Khan Nishapuri and Muzaffar Khan Turbati) were possibly Sunnis. They served under Akbar in important positions during the early part of his reign.

By the time Babur came to Hindustan, the day-to-day working of the Lodi administration was carried on through the medium of Persian. This appears to have created an ever increasing demand for personnel possessing proficiency in Persian for manning minor positions in the administration. Sikandar Lodi (1491–1518) is reported to have tried to tackle this situation by promoting proficiency in Persian among non-Muslims.[28] The coming of a large number of Persian literati to the Mughal Empire from Khurasan at an early stage may, therefore, be viewed as a factor enhancing the role of the Persian language in its formation. These Khurasani men of letters also appear to have brought with them novel notions of kingship and state organisation. Some of these notions were sought to be adopted in the emerging Mughal polity in India, a process which, incidentally, also highlights the diminishing impact of the Mongol *tura* (customary law) on the system.[29]

One such set of notions informed the planned reorganization of administration after Humayun's accession (1530) is described by

Khwand-Amir in his *Qanun-i Humayuni.* The central idea of this scheme was to bifurcate the administration at the plane of the central government into two compartments: (a) *sih qism* and (b) *chahar sarkar.* The first, concerned with the management of revenue and organization of production at different levels was entrusted to a team of professional persons not necessarily enjoying high positions in military hierarchy; and the second regulated the orderly distribution of available assets among personnel serving the state in different capacities and was looked after by high military officers. The working of these two compartments of administration were to be coordinated by a senior military officer (*amir*) in his capacity as the agent (*wakil*) of the King.[30] On the face of it, this arrangement appears to be an attempt to revive, in an idealized form the bifurcation of administrative functions into civil and military compartments that some times obtained in the Ghaznavide Empire. There is some basis for imagining that Khwand-Amir himself was the prime mover of this scheme which did not survive his death in 1534. Similarly, the idea of the 'carpet of joy' (*bisat-i nishat*) carrying a zodiacal pattern, where, in relation to high nobles and other rulers of the world, Humayun was assigned a position akin to that of the sun in the solar system[31] or that of the 'divine-splendour (*jalwa-i quds*)' suggesting a halo of divinity round Humayun's person,[32] point to the influence of *Ishraqi* doctrine brought to the Mughal court around this time by the Khurasani immigrants.[33]

II

The next large influx of the Iranians of different ranks and backgrounds into the Mughal service came at the time of Humayun's return to Kabul from Shah Tahmasp's court in 1545. Some of the Iranian notables who came with Humayun on this occasion already had the status of military officers under Shah Tahmasp. They were in fact deputed by the Shah to assist Humayun in his efforts to recover his lost empire. Among them one may find mention of Husain Quli Sultan (brother of Ahmad Sultan Shamlu, the governor of Sistan), Mirza Ya'qub (a maternal uncle of the prince Khuda Banda who was nominated by the Shah to act *muhrdar* of Humayun), Khwaja Rushdi (deputed to act as *diwan*). The Shah also permitted the Uzbek chief, Haidar Sultan Shaibani, and his sons, Ali Quli and Bahadur, known for their bravery and distinguished ancestry, to accompany Humayun to Kabul.[34] Along with these notables, there had followed Humayun, at this time, many other men of lesser ranks, such as Bayazid Bayat himself in the hope of finding employment as functionaries in one of the royal establishments or in the *sarkars* of high nobles. Names of some of these men are incidentally recorded by Bayazid in three separate lists of persons who came to India in 1555 in the retinues of Humayun, Akbar and Bairam Khan.[35] In these lists, one comes across the names of several persons who rose to the rank of nobles during the early years of Akbar's reign. The influx of Iranians to the Mughal court in search of patronage and employment continued throughout the period of Humayun's later stay at Kabul (1545–55) and in the period of Bairam Khan's regency (1556–60) in India. It was during this time that Mir Abdul Latif Qazvini and his relations, as well as the well-known painters, Khwaja 'Abd al-Samad, Maulana Dost and Maulana Saiyid Ali, came to the Mughal court.

The arrival of these men, some of whom had already earned distinction in their special fields appears to have given the initial push to the intellectual and artistic trends that matured in the latter part of Akbar's reign. For example, from Abu'l Fazl's much quoted passage noticing 'Abdu'l Latif Qazwini's arrival in 1556, one may infer that, by then, he had already earned for himself a reputation of being above sectarian differences. Abu'l Fazl also hints that he was in the process of arriving at a world-view imbued with the spirit of 'universal reconciliation (*sulh-i kul*)'.[36]

Similarly, the painters, Mir Saiyid Ali, 'Abd al-Samad, Dost Muhammad and Mir Musavvir, as well as Sayyid Muhammad Mirak (the Khurasanian architect) may be credited for laying the foundation of subsequent achievements in the fields of painting and architecture.

The early illustrations prepared by 'Abd al-Samad and other Iranian painters at Humayun's court preserved in Fitzwilliam Album Cambridge, are indicative of an attempt to introduce 'a fully imperial Persian style into the Mughal atelier.' In the early illustrations of Akbar's reign, namely those of *Tuti-nama*, *Hamza-nama* (1570) and *Anwar-i Suhaili*, a synthesis of Persian style brought by the immigrants and the local artists with whom they collaborated can be seen to be in gestation.[37] In this new style, a quality of decorative perfection of the Persian paintings was sought to be combined with the art tradition of local origin.[38] The synthesis of these two styles in Mughal paintings, according to Beach, 'is among the most fascinating episodes of Indian or Islamic art'.[39]

The inclination to erect buildings resembling those of Timurid Khurasan was quite manifest among the Indian Mughals from the very beginning. The Chahar bagh-i padshahi of Babur at Agra, according to Ebba Koch, was the first attempt at introducing the Khurasani scheme of a walled garden in India. Sabz Burj raised at Delhi in the early part of Humayun's reign (1530–40) carries features like portico (*peshtaq*) modelled after post-Timurid forms, present in the shrine of Momo Sharifan at Ghaznin (*c.* 1500) with its octangular complex of chambers (*hasht-bahisht*). Combined with its 'Mughalized elevation', Sabz-burj served as a standard model for small mausoleums and garden pavilions of Mughal India during the sixteenth century.[40] Humayun's tomb designed by Saiyid Muhammad Mirak with its 'high dome, great arched alcove that gives character to its facade' and 'complex of rooms and corridors forming the interior arrangements', according to Percy Brown, 'characterises it as an example of synthesis of two traditions of building art: the Persian and the Indian'; an 'Indian interpretation' of 'Persian conception'. Such a synthesis in its varying manifestations remained a distinctive feature of Mughal architecture as it flowered under Akbar and his successors.[41]

The most significant impact of the Iranian influx, however, was the perceptible change in the composition of the Mughal nobility which surfaced dramatically in the first twenty yeas of Akbar's reign. Among fifty-one nobles who came with Humayun to India in 1555, sixteen (31.37 per cent) were Iranis or Khurasanis. While the number of Turani nobles was twenty-seven (52.9 per cent). During the first twenty years of Akbar's reign, i.e. 1556–75, among the high nobles enjoying the *mansabs* of 500 and above, the Iranis and Khurasanis, many of whom were known Shi'ites or Tafzilis, represented 38.58 per cent of the total strength. This placed them almost at par with the Turanis representing 39.58 per cent of the total in the same set of ranks.[42]

The Iranis seem to have improved their positions in the nobility during 1562–67 mainly by earning promotious in the course of military operations against rebellious Turani nobles. Many of the Turanis on Akbar's side were rather lukewarm, while the Iranis were usually steadfast and unsparing in their support of the royal cause.[43] This should partly also explain why some tension developed between the two groups during 1564–67 and many of the Turanis came to distrust their Irani colleagues.[44]

The contrary pulls of this situation within the nobility combined with the orthodox intolerance of *Sadr-us-Sadur*. Shaikh 'Abd al-Nabi, seem to have goaded Akbar into adopting a paradoxial policy with regard to Shi'ites down to 1575. On the one hand, he is reported to have extended patronage and favours to many Irani nobles as well as theologians known for their Shi'ite leanings. On the other hand, there are on record two instances of his inflicting in early seventies, capital punishments on highly placed persons charged with Shi'ite 'heresy'.[45] Exhumation of the dead body of the universally respected Shi'ite divine Murtaza Sharifi Shirazi from the proximity of Amir Khusrau's tomb in 1566 was, perhaps, the most blatant of Akbar's actions of this nature.[46]

This paradox became still more manifest in Akbar's attempt to win recognition, through the famous *mahzar* of 1579, as *Padshah-i Islam* and *Sultan-i 'adil* having the authority to arbitrate between different schools of *sunni* jurisprudence. It virtually amounted to the theologians assigning to him the role of the head of Orthodox Sunni Muslims in India at a time when the nobility created by him was already a group in which Iranis (many of them Shiites) and Rajputs and other Hindus put together represented 33.1 per cent (Iranis, 17.27 per cent and Rajputs plus other Hindus, 15.83 per cent) of the total strength.[47] In the immediate context, the *mahzar* was possibly aimed at mobilizing support for Akbar among the ruling elite for overcoming the rising discontent among the nobles over the introduction of branding regulations. This regulation was sought to be enforced rigorously by Akbar from 1574 onwards with the help of a team of able and energetic officers, amongst whom men of Khurasani and Irani origins (for example, Muzaffar Khan Turbati, Khwaja Shah Mansur Shirazi)[48] were conspicuous for their extra zeal. The branding regulation which adversely affected the autonomy and benefits of the nobles particularly alienated a large number of Turanis who till this time represented the largest racial grouping in the nobility. Many of the Iranis, whose strength in the higher ranks of the nobility had become sizeable by 1575, were possibly, also alarmed by this measure.

Both these powerful groups appear to have reacted to *mahzar* adversely. The Sunnis as well as Shi'ites amongst them would have been put off by the suggestion of assigning the role of supreme arbiter in the interpretation of sources of Islamic law (*ijtihad*) to Akbar, as it smacked of an attempt to attribute to him the status of a true guide (*Mahdi*). In so far as the *mahzar* implicitly restricted the scope of study and interpretation of the Islamic law (*ijtihad*) to orthodox schools, the *asna 'asharis* were bound to perceive it as a move towards further restricting the space for the practice of their faith in the Mughal Empire. It is significant that subsequent to the *mahzar*, the *fatwa* of *kufr* against Akbar was issued by a Shi'ite divine, Mulla Muhammad Yazdi, who, according to Badauni, was earlier allowed by Akbar to make statements in his presence that were hurtful for the *Sunnis*[49] The text of Yazdi's *fatwa* is nowhere reproduced. But the circumstances suggest that its main point of reference was the *mahzar* signed exclusively by six leading *Sunni* divines of the realm, though five of them did so reluctantly.[50] One cannot but connect Mulla Muhammad Yazdi's response to the *mahzar* with the fact that in the rebellion of nobles during 1580–81, unlike the revolts of 1564–67, an appreciable number of Iranis were also involved.[51] In short, the *mahzar* not only failed to strengthen Akbar's hands but also tended to open up the sensitive issue of *ijtihad* that had the potential of alienating from him a very large section of the Irani nobles as well.[52]

It is, therefore, understandable that soon after its issuance, the *mahzar* was consigned to cold storage to the extent that in 1594, Abu'l Fazl found it embarrassing to reproduce the text of this document drafted by his own father Shaikh Mubarak.

III

Akbar's turning away from the *mahzar* of 1579, and his recourse to a policy of total tolerance under the principle of *Sulh-i Kul* (Absolute Peace), appears to have paved the way for a fresh influx of Irani notables into the Mughal Empire. Shah Abbas I's harsh treatment of some of the local dignitaries and members of heterodox sects, appear to have contributed to this influx significantly. As Arjomand puts it 'many Nuqtawis, including a truly impressive number of poets, fled to India, Emperor Akbar's land of religious freedom.'[53] A letter written by Abu'l Fazl on Akbar's behalf to Mir Saiyid Ahmad Kashi, a Nuqtawi leader of Iran as well as a revealing passage about him given in the *Alam Ara-i Abbasi*, indicates that Akbar kept himself informed about the Nuqtawis and was also eager to win them over to his doctrine of *sulh-i kul*.[54]

In this background, Akbar's advice to Shah Abbas in 1994 to follow his own example of making no distinction among his subjects on the basis of 'cult or creed' assumes special significance.[55] Shah Abbas, obviously, was not amused by this preaching of *sulh-i kul* by Akbar not only because it militated against the *asna 'ashari* doctrine, but also because it amounted to interfering in affairs of his empire. This is reflected in one of Shah Abbas' letters to Akbar sent in 1599. While being respectful to the extent of comparing their mutual relations with those between a father and son, Shah Abbas expresses his disagreement with Akbar's doctrine of *sulh-i kul* and points out that all prophets have condemned lawless people (*ashqiya*).[56]

The Irani notables who came to the Mughal court during this time included distinguished men of letters like Nurullah Shustri, Shah Fath ul-lah Shirazi, Hakim Lutf ul-lah, Mulla Huzuni, Mulla Mirza Jan, Muzaffar Husain Sabzwari and Jamal al-Din Anju. Some others who had arrived in India before 1580 but became famous at Akbar's court now included Hakim Abul Fath, his brothers Hakim Hamam and Hakim Nur al-Din, and also Saiyid Muhammad Jamal al-Din 'Urfi Shirazi and Sharif Amuli. Among them, perhaps, the most distinguished was 'Urfi who, in his short stay at the court, earned enduring literary fame.[57] This accretion in the strength of the Iranis occupying high positions in the nobility and Akbar's close personal association with many of them[58] appears to have created a general impression that they were gaining an upper hand in the administration after sidelining the Turani and Rajput nobles.[59] It was, perhaps, this situation that is characterized by Badauni as the time when Iraqis (i.e. Shi'ite Iranis) were in great favour. At another place in the same context, he speaks of Shi'ites having become predominant (*ghalib*) and Sunnis the conquered people (*maghlub*).[60]

IV

The increasing impact of Akbar's world-view, informed by his commitment to *sulh-i kul*, from early 1580s onwards freed him entirely from the constraints of the orthodoxy.[61] In this new situation, the Shi'ites among the Iranian nobles and state officials for the first time came to enjoy the freedom of practising their religious rites openly. According to Badauni, Shah Fath ul-lah Shirazi used to perform with great composure his Shi'ite prayers (*namaz*) inside the state hall (*diwan-kana-i khas*),[62] notwithstanding Akbar's disapproval of *namaz* of any kind.[63] It was from the early eighties that Akbar began giving ecclesiastical Islamic offices of *qazis* and *sadrs* of *subas* as well as of the

Central government to known Shi'ites. Important appointments were those of Shah Fath Ullah Shirazi as the *sadr us Sudur*,[64] Nur ul-lah Shustari (known for his strong views on the question of *imamat* and commitment to *fiqh-i Ja'fria*) as the qazi of Lahore[65] and of Hakim Hammam as the *sadr* of the region 'to the east of Ganges'.[66]

This was obviously a new situation where even the ordinary persons subscribing to *asna-i 'ashari* doctrines would no longer be obliged to practice pious subterfuge (*taqiyya*). The example of some of the nobles and highly placed officials of Iranian origin observing *asna-i 'ashari* rites publicly and with great ceremony could also draw to them many Indian Muslims having a *tafzili* bent of mind. The *tafzili* trend was strong among Indian Muslims from quite an early date. It was, for example, inherent in the teaching and rites of the Chishti *sufis*, the most influencial mystic order in India.[67] Several other popular cults centering round semi-mythical figures of *darweshes* and *qalandars* in different parts of the subcontinent also popularized the idea of Ali being the first (*Ali ka pahla number* in a modern popular formula) after the Prophet in the Islamic spiritual hierarchy.[68] A near *tafzili* attitude rooted in Islamic mysticism is also discernible in the beliefs of some of the Turani nobles influenced by the confluence of orthodox and *imamia* doctrines in Timurid Khurasan under Sultan Husain Baiqara.[69] The surviving relatives of Babur's nobles like Muhammad Qasim Khan Shaibani and others who had been with Sultan Husain Baiqara before joining Babur in 1506, as well as the grandchildren of Sultan Husain Baiqara some whom were still with Akbar in 1580s may be counted in this category of the Turanis. The Mughal ruling family were also not immune to the attraction of *tafzili* ideas. Among Babur's sons, for example, Mirza Kamran was a staunch *sunni*. Such an assertion cannot, however, be made with any measure of certainty about Humayun, 'Askari and Hindal. Humayun's commitment to Sunnism was tempered by his scholarly inquiries into its precepts as well as by his interest in Greek philosophy and *Ishraqi* doctrines to the point of his some times claiming *tafzili* beliefs and outlook. Kamran's real brother 'Askari also had a mystic bent of mind; for him 'the source of inspiration (*mushrab*)' was more important than 'the religious order (*mazhab*)'.[70] Another close relation of the ruling family Mirza Sulaiman of Badakhshan is known to have been greatly devoted to the Shaikhs of the Chishti order.[71]

In short, the wide prevalence of *tafzili* sentiment combined with the presence of a large number of Shi'ite Iranis and freedom enjoyed by them to observe their rites openly in the latter half of Akbar's reign appear to have favoured the emergence of a community of Shi'ite Muslims in Mughal India in the sixteenth century. That already by early 1580s urban pockets of Shi'ite Muslim population existed in the Mughal Empire is borne out by Monserrate's description of the 'Musalmans' observing Muharram with 'lamentation and tears' and by walking over fire, all the time shrieking, '"Asson Hossen" (Hasan-Husain).' This description conforms to the mourning over the martyrdom of Imam Husain as practised by Shi'ites. But it also, very significantly, indicates that all the Muslims of a town would participate in the gathering of the tenth of Muharram and no one there would object to the Shi'ite form of mourning.[72] Ordinary Muslims apparently accepted a co-existence which theologians found unacceptable.

Notes

1 For the earliest reference to Babur and his troops as 'Mughals' in a Persian text see Rukn al-Din, *Lataif-i Quddusi* (completed in 1538), Delhi, 1311 H., pp. 8, 33. Compare my comment on this evidence in 'State in the Mughal India: Re-examining the Myths of a Counter-vision', *Social Scientist* (New Delhi) Vol. 30, Nos. 1–2, January–February, 2001, pp. 26–27.

2 For example Bernier's *Travels* published from Paris in 1670 refers to this empire as 'the Empire of the Great Mogul (Des Etats Du Grand Mogol).' This may indicate its being referred to as such by the people during the time Bernier was travelling in India. Cf. *Travels in the Mogul Empire: AD 1656–1668*, tr. Archibald Constable, second edition revised by Vincent A. Smith, London, 1916, p. xxv.

3 The Uzbek chiefs who defeated Amir Najam at Ghajadwan (3 Ramazan 918H/13 November 1512) are referred to by Khwand-Amir (*Tarikh-i Shah Ismail Wa Tahmasp Safavi*, (ed.) Ali Jarrah, Tahran, 1370 Shamsi, p. 80) as *Salatin-i Chingizi*.

4 See for example Khwaja Baha al-Din Hasan Nisari, *Muzakkar-i ahbab* (completed in 1566), (ed.) S.M. Fazlullah, Hyderabad, 1969, p. 93. Babur and his sons are mentioned in the category of Chaghtai rulers (*zikr-i salatin-i Chaghtai*).

5 See R.P. Tripathi's pioneer study of Timurid theory of kingship in his *Some Aspects of Muslim Administration*, second edition, Allahabad, 1959 and also Iqtidar Alam Khan, 'The Turko-Mongol Theory of Kingship', *Medieval India: A Miscellany*, Vol. II, pp. 8–18.

6 Cf. A.A. Rizvi, *Religious and Intellectual History of Muslims in Akbar's Reign*, New Delhi, 1975, p. 429. It is held that down to Akbar's time most of the Turani nobles ('Turks and Mughals') were strongly devoted to Khwaja 'Ubaidullah Ahrar's descendants. See also Baha al-Din Hasan Nisari,

Muzakkar-i Ahbab, pp. 107–8, where Babur's second son, Mirza Kamran, is mentioned as being greatly attached to the Naqshbandi order.

7 That Chaghtai Turkish was the spoken language at the Mughal court down to Humayun's time is borne out by many passages in the sources. From Bayazid Bayat's account (*Tazkira-i Humayun wa Akbar*, (ed.) Hidayat Husain, Calcutta, 1941, p. 101) one comes to know that at an assembly of Humayun's nobles in 1547 most of the princes were again and again reverting to Turkish which forced Husain Quli Sultan, an Iranian, to complain that he was not following the conversation. Recording his meeting with the Afghan chief Daulat Khan Lodi on 5 June 1525 Babur (A.S. Beveridge, *Baburnama in English*, reprint, London, 1969, p. 459) mention his talking to him through an interpreter. It suggests that Babur himself spoke in Turkish which Daulat Khan found difficult to follow. Muzaffar Alam ('The Pursuit of Persian: Language in Mughal Politics', *Modern Asian Studies*, Vol. 32, No. 2, 1998, pp. 318–19) interprets this passage differently: He thinks Babur was speaking in Persian. It is, however, difficult to imagine that Daulat Khan would have needed an interpreter's help in understanding anything spoken in Persian. Besides the fact that in its structure and vocabulary Pashto is very close to Eastern Persian, one may also remember, in this regard, Muhammad Qasim Firishta's testimony (*Ta'rikh-i Firishta* (1607), Vol. I, Nawal Kishore, p. 187) that, under the Lodis, the circle of persons having proficiency in Persian had expanded considerably. Cf. Z. Safa in *The Cambridge History of Iran*, Vol. 6, (ed.) Peter Jackson and Laurence Lockhart, Cambridge, 1986, p. 913–14, for the fact that in the beginning of the sixteenth century 'the language used at the Safavid court' was Turkish, not Persian.

8 B.S. Amorett, 'Religion in the Timurid and Safavid Periods', *The Cambridge History of Iran*, Vol. 6, (ed.) Peter Jackson and Laurence Lockhart, pp. 610–14, 629–34.

9 Cf. Said Amir Arjomand, *The Shadow of God and the Hidden Imam*, Chicago, 1984, pp. 122–24 and B.S. Amorett in *The Cambridge History of Iran*, Vol. 6, pp. 224–40.

10 Cf. S.A.A. Rizvi, *Religious and Intellectual History of Muslims in Akbar's Reign*, p. 51 and Sukumar Ray, *Bairam Khan*, Karachi, 1992, p. 77. Both have noted that the donning of the Persian or Shi'ite cap (*taj*) by Babur and Humayun amounted to their accepting the Safavid ruler as their preceptor.

11 See A.S. Beveridge's note in *Babur-nama in English*, p. 361 and Bayazid Bayat, *Tazkira-i Humayun wa Akbar*, (ed.) M. Hidayat Hosain, Calcutta, 1941, p. 50. Bayazid writes that after having wrested Qandahar from Safavid officers, Humayun wrote to the Shah to lend (*batariq-i 'aryat*) him Qandahar 'for a few days.' This was the starting point of long Mughal-Safavid tussle over Qandahar.

12 See Muzaffar Alam, 'The Pursuit of Persian Language in Mughal Polities', *Modern Asian Studies*, Vol. 32, No. 2, 1998, pp. 325–35.

13 Percy Brown (*Indian Architecture*, Calcutta, 1942, p. 89) emphasises Persian Cultural inspiration as an important factor shaping the Mughal

architecture. While, according to Milo Cleveland Beach (*Mughal and Rajput Painting, The New Cambridge History of India*, I, 32, Cambridge, 1992, p. 10), Mughal court painting was dominated by 'the accepted artistic standards of the Iranian court.'

[14] See Jahangir's well known remark in *Tuzuk-i Jahangiri*, (ed.) Saiyid Ahmad, Ghazipur and Aligarh, 1863–64, p. 16.

[15] Cf. *Malfuzat-i Shah Abdul Aziz Dehlvi*, cited by Muhammad 'Umar, *Islam in North India: During the Eighteenth Century*, New Delhi, pp. 176–77.

[16] This is illustrated by Akbar's response to 'Abdullah Khan Uzbek's proposal in 1577, for an anti-Safavid alliance. Despite his nursing a grievance over the occupation of Qandahar by Shah Tahmasp in 1559, Akbar not only spurned the idea of a Mughal-Uzbek alliance against the Safavids, but also rebuked Abdullah Khan for using disrespectful language about them. Akbar knew that, following Shah Tahmasp's death (1576), the affairs of the Safavid Empire were in great confusion; yet he chose to be protective about them. This desire to appear polite survived even the outbreak of hostilities over Qandahar during, 1649–53. This is borne out by the letters exchanged between the two courts after Aurangzeb's gaining the throne in 1658. Cf. Riazul Islam, *Indo-Persian Relations*, Lahore, 1970, pp. 39–40, 52–53, 102, 108–09, 113, 124–25.

[17] See for example Shah Tahmasp's letter to Akbar sent by the hand of Saiyid Beg Safavi in 1562. (Abu'l Fazl *Akbarnama*, ed. Agha Ahmad Ali and Abdur Rahim, Vol. II, Calcutta, 1873–87, p. 171–72). There is a statement hinting that the Shah contemplated 'a familial connection (*nisbat*)' with Humayun which his untimely death caused to 'remain hidden behind the veil of invisible (*dar parda-i ghaib manad*)'. This speaks of close personal equation that appears to have developed between Tahmasp and Humayun since latter's visit to Iran (1543–45). It was, apparently, not much affected by Humayun's going back on his promise to hand over Qandahar to the Safavid officers accompanying him in 1545.

In this context, it is appropriate also to take into consideration Shah Tahmasp's supposed letter to Hamida Bano Begam purportedly sent around the same time as the above letter. The text of this letter is included in Abu'l Qasim Namakin's *Munshaat-i Namakin* (MS University Collection No. 26 f. 242 a and b). I.A. Zilli ('Early Correspondence between Shah Tahmasp and Akbar' in *Islamic Heritage in South Asian Subcontinent*, ed. Nazir Ahmad and I.H. Siddiqui, Jaipur, 2000, pp. 230–31, 232–34) treats it as a genuine letter written with the aim of inducing Hamida Bano Begam to support the restoration of friendly ties between 'the two courts'. In his view, Hamida Bano's accompanying Humayun to Iran, 'presumably led the Shah claim a special relationship with her.' But on a closer examination, this letter appears to be a draft prepared by the way of literary exercise in which there is an attempt to paraphrase Shah Tahmasp's letter to Akbar. In this paraphrasing the statement: 'Regarding the late asylum of brotherhood (i.e. Humayun), we have entertained in our heart (ideas) of familial connections (*nisbat ba akhwat panah marhume nisbatha ba khatir manzur dashta*)' is changed to 'regarding that repository of Chastity (i.e. Hamida Bano Begam), we had other ideas in the dignified mind (*nisbat badan 'asmat panah digar andeshaha ba-khatiri khatir khutur dasht*).' It is, perhaps, this awkwardly worded praphrasing that has led I.A. Zilli to imagine the Shah's claim to a 'special relationship' with Humayun's widow. I have a hunch that Riazul Islam did not include this letter in his excellent *Calendar* of documents on Indo-Persian relations because of its spurious nature. That he 'missed' this document in the *Munshaat-i Namakin*, as imagined by I.A. Zilli (f.n.1), is perhaps too hasty a judgement.

[18] Cf. Athar Ali, *The Mughal Nobility under Aurangzeb*, Bombay, 1966, p. 18. Commenting on the position of Turanis at the court, Athar Ali cites an interesting anecdote recorded by M'amuri: 'An officer of Aurangzeb's court who went so far as to say in imperial presence that the word of a Turani could not be trusted, only earned a mild reproof asking him to remember that his Emperor was also a Turani.'

[19] S.A.A. Rizvi, (*Religious and Intellectual History of Muslims in Akbar's Reign*, p. 262) refers to the view in *Tarikh-i Alfi's* that the immigrants were attracted by the wealth of India and also by the situation in the Mughal Empire where it was possible for immigrants to rise to the status of nobles in a short time. S. Amir Arjomand (*The Shadow of God and Hidden Imam*, p. 198, on the other hand, attributes it to religious persecution in Iran.

[20] See f.n. 7 where it is argued that Chagtai Turkish was the spoken language at the Mughal court during the reigns of Babur and Humayun. But from a passage of Bayazid one may infer that by 1570 apart from an old Uzbek noble (Sikandar Khan), most of the persons present at a reception given by Mun'im Khan at Jaunpur were, able to understand a Persian *ghazal* recited there (*Tazkira-i Humayun wa Akbar*, p. 306).

[21] *Babur-nama in English*, p. 7. In Ferghana the entire population of the *vilayat* of Asfara located in the hill country, 65 miles south-west of Marghinan, was Persian speaking.

[22] Compare Z. Safa, in *Cambridge History of Iran*, Vol. 6, p. 914.

[23] Cf. Nahal al-Din Nisari, *Muzakkar-i Ahbab*, p. 245. He was a descendant of some one distantly related to the famous sufi of fifteenth century Khurasan, Shaikh Zain al-Din Khwafi, and is reported to have held the office of *sadr* under Babur as well as Humayun. The *Fath-nama* by him in Persian after the battle of Kanwa (1527) is reproduced in *Babur-nama*. He later expanded this document in his *Tabaqat-i Baburi*, which was also the first attempt to prepare a Persian version of Babur's memoirs.

[24] C.A. Storey, *Persian Literature: A Bio-Bibliographical Survey*, Vol. I, London, 1970, pp. 101–09. Hidayat Hosain's Preface, *Qanun-i Humayuni*, Calcutta, 1940, pp. I–XXXVI. These scholarly notices of Ghiyas al-Din surnamed Khwand-Amir and his works are quite exhaustive. According to Babur (*Babur-nama in English*, pp. 605), finding life at Herat difficult, Khwand-Amir came to Hindustan in 1528 and took up service under him. His last work, *Qanun-i Humayuni*, was compiled, *c.*1535, at Gwalior. Khwand-Amir died during Humayun's march to Gujarat (1535–37).

[25] Cf. Abdul Qadir Badauni, *Muntakhab ut-tawarikh*, (ed.) Ahmad Ali *et al.*, Vol. II, p. 65; Vol. III, p. 65.

[26] *Muzakkar-i Ahbab*, p. 470; also Hadi Hasan, 'Qasim Kahi (868–988 A.H.); His Life, Times and Work', *Islamic Culture*, Hyderabad, July 1953.

[27] Cf. Zain al-Din Wasafi, *Bada'i ul-Waqa'i Wasafi*, (ed.) Alexander Baldin, Moscow, 1961, pp. 2–4. There is an exaggerated notice of 'persecution' of Sunnis in Khurasan following its occupation by Shah Ismail in 1510. He cites the following couplet as a commentry on the situation: 'All the lands siezed by Qizilbash, were found by the World [turned] into a garden of tulips [i.e. soaked in blood].'

[28] *Ta'rikh-i Firishta*, Vol. I, p. 187 see also f.n. 7.

[29] Iqtidar Alam Khan, 'State in the Mughal India: Re-examining the Myths of a Counter vision', *Social Scientist*, Vol. 30, Nos. 1–2, January–February 2001, pp. 19–20.

[30] *Qanun-i Humayuni*, (ed.) M. Hidayat Husain, Calcutta, 1940, pp. 34–43, 48–50.

[31] *Qanun-i Humayuni*, pp. 110–12, Cf. Riazul Islam, *Indo-Persian Relations*, p. 36. In a letter sent by Shah Tahmasp to Sultan Sulaiman of the Ottoman Empire some time before 1543, he complains that the rulers of Iran, Turkey and Central Asia were assigned places in this arrangement in a manner as if they were Humayun's subordinates.

[32] Rafi' al-Din Ibrahim Shirazi, *Tazkirat ul-muluk*, MS., Br. Library, Add. 23,883, f.158a and b; also see Shah Tahmasp's letter to the Ottoman Sultan cited in f.n. 31, where this practice is denounced as amounting to claiming divine powers.

[33] See Irfan Habib, 'A Political Theory for the Mughal Empire—a Study of the Ideas of Abu'l Fazl', *Proceedings of the Indian History Congress*, 59th (Patiala) session (1998), pp. 332–34, where the influence of ishraqi theory on Abu'l Fazl's doctrine of *farr-i izidi* is discussed.

[34] Bayazid Bayat, *Tazkira-i Humayun wa Akbar*, pp. 35–36.

[35] Bayat, pp. 176–87.

[36] *Akbarnama*, Vol. II, p. 18.

[37] Milco Cleveland Beach, *Mughal and Rajput Painting*, (*The New Cambridge History of India*, I:3), Cambridge, 1992, pp. 16, 20–21, 25, 28–29.

[38] S.P. Verma, 'Akbar's School of Painting' in *Akbar and His Age*, (ed.) Iqtidar Alam, New Delhi, 1999, p. 273–74.

[39] Beach, *Mughal and Rajput Painting*, p. 31.

[40] Ebba Koch, *Mughal Architecture: An Outline of Its History and Development*, Munich, 1991, pp. 33–34, 37.

[41] Percy Brown, *Indian Architecture*, Calcutta, 1942, pp. 89–90. For a notice of Saiyid Muhamad Mirak, under whose supervision Humayun's tomb was built on the model of Nawsherwan's burial palce, see *Muzakkar-i Ahbab*, p. 103.

[42] Cf. Iqtidar Alam Khan, 'The Nobility under Akbar and the Development of his Religious Policy, 1560–80', *Journal of Royal Asiatic Society*, London, Nos. 1 and 2, 1968, pp. 30, 35, Appendix I.

43 Khan, 'The Nobility under Akbar', pp. 30–31.

44 *Akbarnama*, Vol. III, pp. 162, 178. The Turani's were unhappy over Khan-i Jahan's appointment as the commander of the army in Bengal in 1576. They did not cooperate with him because he was perceived as an Irani and Shi'ite.

45 The examples of theologians with Shi'ite leanings patronized by Akbar during this early period are those of Mir Ala al-Din Lari and Mir Murtaza Sharifi Shirazi. See 'Abdul Qadir Badauni, *Muntakhab-ut tawarikh*, II, pp. 55, 84, 198, 255; Vol. III, pp. 67, 84. See also Rafi al-Din Shirazi, *Tazkirat ul Muluk*, f. 177 b.

46 'Abdul Qadir Badauni, *Muntakhab-ut tawarikh*, Vol. II, p. 99; Vol. III, p. 442.

47 Iqtidar Alam Khan, *'The Nobility under Akbar'*, pp. 34–35.

48 Both were Iranis who met violent deaths in 1580. Muzaffar Khan died fighting the rebels in Bengal and Shah Mansur was excuted by Akbar on the charge of conspiring with Mirza Hakim. This charge was based on a forged letter planted by Shah Mansur's enemies at the court. See *Akbar-nama*, Vol. III, pp. 116–18, 227, 290–94, 304, 501.

49 *Akbarnama*, Vol. III, p. 309; *Muntakhab-ut tawarikh*, Vol. II, 211, 276. Cf. S.A.A. Rizvi, *Religious and Intellectual History of Muslims in Akbar's Reign*, pp. 158, 161, 211.

50 Cf. *Muntakhab-ut tawarikh*, Vol. II, p. 270. The signatories were; (1) Abdullah Sultanpuri (Makhdum ul-Mulk); (2) Shaikh 'Abdu'l Nabi; (3) Qazi Jalal al-Din of Multan; (4) Sadr-i Jahan, the *Mufti*; (5) Shaikh Mubarak; (6) Ghazi Khan Badakhsh.

51 For the racial break-up of the total number of nobles participating in the revolt of 1580–81, see *Journal of the Royal Asiatic Society*, (London), 1968, No. 1 & 2, p. 36 (Appendix 4).

52 For a contrary argument see S.A.A. Rizvi, *Religious and Intellectual history of Muslims in Akbar's Reigns*, p. 158.

53 Said A. Arjomand, *The Shadow of God and the Hidden Imam*, p. 198.

54 Cf. Riazul Islam, *The Calendar of Documents on Indo-Persian Relations, 1500–1750*, Vol. I, pp. 101–04.

55 See ibid., Vol. I, pp.123–24. [Calendar No. A36].

56 Ibid., Vol. I, pp. 128–29 [Calendar No. A39].

57 Cf. *Ruqa'at-i Hakim Abu'l Fath*, pp. 5, 19–20, 33, 'Abd al-Qadir Badauni, Vol. II, pp. 246–48, 315–16; Vol. III, 137–38, 167–68, 285–88. See also S.A.A. Rizvi, *Religious and Intellectual History of Muslims in Akbar's Reign*, pp. 123–24, 191.

58 Akbar's personal proximity to Shah Fath Ullah Shirazi is borne by the following couplet composed by Faizi on his death. 'The Emperor of the world had his eyes full of tears at his death, Alexander wept tears of regret because Plato left the World.'

59 See Aziz Koka's letter to Jahangir in an untitled collection of documents in Br. Library, MS., Add. 16,859.

60 Abu'l Fazl (*Akbarnama*, Vol. III, p. 273) admits that some 'wicked people'

had come to allege around this time that Akbar had become a Shi`ite. According to him, this misunderstanding was created by Akbar's policy of allowing the Shi`ites to present their point of view frankly in the discussions of *Ibadatkhana*. For Badauni's comment on their situation see *Muntakhab-ut tawarikh*, Vol. II, p. 308. My attention to this evidence was directed by its citation in Nawab Muhammad Abbas Talib Safavi's scholarly Urdu work *Din-i Ilahi ke anasir-i arb`a*, p. 83.

61 See I.A. Khan paper in *Journal of Royal Asiatic Society*, London, Nos. 1&2, 1968, where I have studied the development of Akbar's religious policy of the earlier phase ending in the 'debacle' of the *Mahzar* (1579). It is suggested that, subsequent to 1580–81, Akbar's enlightened religious policy based on his philosophy of *sulh-i kul* unfolded, more or less, smoothly.

62 'Abdul Qadir Badauni, *Muntakhab-ut tawarikh*, Vol. II, p. 316.

63 See *Akbar-nama*, MS. Br. Library, Add. 27,247, f. 404a, for a memorandum recorded by Akbar on requests and queries by his son Murad deputed to Malwa some time in 1591. To a query whether performing *namaz* inside the army was to be 'forbidden', Akbar replied that a person performing *namaz* deserved 'admonition (*nasihat*)' so as to help him see 'the path of reason (*rah-i 'aql*)'. But, if he persisted in his ways such a person was not to be forced to abandon his rites of worship, as this would amount to violation of *sulh-i kul*. See also Iqtidar Alam Khan, 'Akbar's Personality Traits and World outlook—A Critical Reappraisal', *Akbar and His India*, (ed.) Irfan Habib, Delhi, 1997, p. 95.

64 Abdul Qadir Badauni, *Muntakhab-ut tawarikh*, Vol. II, p. 343.

65 Ibid., Vol. III, pp. 138.

66 Ibid., Vol. II, pp. 296.

67 For Shaikh Nizam al-Din's sayings emphasising the *fazilat* of Ali see *Fawaid ul Fawad*, reprint with Urdu translation by Hasan Sani Nizami, New Delhi, 1999, pp. 329–30, 422–23.

68 For example the cult of Shahbaz Qalandar in Sind. The Urdu line (*Ali ka pahla number*) is from a devotional song of the cult. Cf. *Dabistan-i Mazahib*, Nawal Kishore, Lucknow, 1904, pp. 215–16, for the notice on the cult of Saiyid Jalal Bukhari: the practitioners justified their practices with reference to Safavid customs.

69 On the trend towards Shi'ism in Khurasan under Sultan Husain Baiqara, see S.A.A. Rizvi, *Religious and Intellectual History of Muslims in Akbar's Reign*, p. 48; B.S. Amoretti in *Cambridge History of Iran*, Vol. 6, (ed.) Peter Jackson, p. 612.

70 *Muzakkar-i Ahbab*, pp. 107–7, 216, Muhammad Qasim Firishta (*Tarikh-i Firishta*, Vol. I, p. 237) quotes Humayun as saying to Shah Tahmasp that, unlike his brother Mirza Kamran, he always had 'love for the family of the Prophet (*muhabbat-i khandan-i risalat*)'.

71 *Muzakkar-i Ahbab*, p. 124.

72 Monserrate, *The Commentary of Father Monserrate*, tr. J.S. Hoyland and S.N. Banerji, Oxford, 1922, pp. 21–22. [I owe this reference to Mr. S. Ali Nadeem Rezavi].

Iranian Ideological Influences at Akbar's Court

Iqbal Husain

Humayun's short stay in exile in 1545 in Iran and his return to India to regain his lost kingdom resulted in an influx of a number of Iranian scholars, nobles and soldiers along with him. From now on the gates for social and intellectual exchange seemed to open still more widely between the two countries. On Akbar's accession to the throne (1556), this contact grew further owing partly to the religious policy of the Safavid regime in Iran, which made continued residence in Iran awkward for several people who held beliefs different from those of the ruling house. On the other hand, Akbar's policy of religious tolerance and the favour he showed especially to Iranian emigrés, made India a major attraction for Iranians of all persuasions. Iran itself was in an ideological ferment, and the emigrés belonged to the most varied schools of thought. This paper aims at examining the ideas the emigrés brought to Akbar's Court and the extent to which these influenced Akbar's mind.

We must begin by considering the extent of Iranian influence at the court itself. Iranian immigration in the second short phase of Humayun's reign (1555–56) was considerable. A number of Iranians were awarded important positions in the State.[1] Prominent among them were Bairam Khan, Wali Beg Zu'lqadr (including his two sons, Ali Quli and Bahadur Khan), Afzal Khan, Ashraf Khan, Khwaja Abdul Majid, Khwaja Ataullah, Mir Shahabuddin, Khwaja Abul Qasim and others.[2] The trend continued under Akbar. Professor Athar Ali's study shows that out of eighteen central ministers in Akbar's reign (1574–1605), as many as eleven were of Iranian origin, three were Turanis and four Indians (two Hindus and two Muslims).[3] This shows the extent to which the Iranians were placed in the higher levels of the bureaucratic structure and the degree of their proximity to the Emperor.

Akbar grew up under the guardianship of Bairam Khan (a Shi'ite) and Mir Abdul Latif: the latter had been persecuted in Iran allegedly for holding Sunnite beliefs but was thought to be a Shi'ite in India.[4] Such antecedants made Akbar open to views that came from sources outside the orthodox Sunni tradition to which his family subscribed.

It has been argued that, 'Akbar came increasingly under the influence of the pantheisitic *sufi* doctrine, roughly from 1571'.[5] In this connection the presence of a leading Indian scholar Shaikh Mubarak in Agra should be kept in mind. The Shaikh had acquired considerable knowledge of various religious sects and was greatly inclined to the Ishraqi creed of Shihabuddin Suhrawardi Maqtul, the great Iranian *sufi*, as well as the ideas of Ibn Arabi. Mubarak obtained his early traditional education at Nagaur and Ahmedabad. At the latter place he studied the various schools of law, the Malikite, Shafite, Hanafite and Hanbalite as well as Shiite. He studied Ibn Sina and Ibn Arabi, besides the Ishraqi philosophy of Shihabuddin Suhrawardi Maqtul.[6]

The founder of the Ishraqi philosophy Shihabuddin Suhrawardi (d. 1191), expressed his mystical notions and teachings in his *Kitab hikmat-al Ishraq* (the philosophy of illumination) and other works[7]. His works appear to have been widely read in the Islamic world though the orthodox theologians had strong objections to some of the statements he made. Yet Shihabuddin Suhrawardi is regarded, besides Ibn Arabi, as one of the most significant exponents of the movement which attempted to explain the Quran and the doctrine of Islam largely in an esoteric and allegorical way.[8] Shihabuddin's philosophy of Ishraq is traced to Plato's *Republic*, where God is presented under the symbol of the Sun without which nothing would exist.[9] He held that 'the source of all being and thought is . . . beyond the essence, beyond the ideas themselves. To it, man should turn . . . with his entire soul'.[10] Suhrawardi saw himself as an heir to Empedocles, Pythagoras and Plato, the Iranian Prophet Zoroaster and many others, mentioned in the pre-Islamic traditions, as representatives of the 'eternal heaven' that animated all true sages. He saw some of the eminent *sufis* as men within whom this leaven was at work.[11] Thus to the Ishraqis the Sun is the symbol of God-derived spiritual light or the Light of Lights, from which, by irradiation emanate the *Anwar-i Qahira,* the Great Lights.

By the epiphany, the whole hierarchy of the *Anwar-i Qahira,* from degree to degree, illuminates the presence of each lower degree.[12] Shihabuddin's concluding words in the *Partau Nama* were to create a great impression at Akbar's court, as we shall see: 'Whoever knows wisdom and is assiduous in praising and revering the "Light of Lights" (*Nuru'l Anwar),* they give him the "Kingly Light" (*Khurra-i Kiyani*) and bestow upon him the "luminous ray" (*farr-i nurani*) and "the lightening-flashing (cloud) of God" (*barq-i Ilahi*), clothing him in the robe of authority and status'.[13] Suhrawardi disagrees with Avicenna's notion that the soul could ascend from darkness to the light by knowledge and holds that his allegory ignores the illumination of understanding concerning the 'supreme experience'. Suhrawardi also differs with many fundamental points propounded by Plato and also criticises Aristotle,'whose philosophy he looks upon as a mere preparation for his own system of thought'.[14] Iqbal states that Shihabuddin claimed that the 'ultimate principle of all existence is the *Nur-i Qahira,* the Primal Absolute Light, whose essential nature consists in perpetual illumniation: 'Nothing is more visible than light, and visibility does not stand in need of any definition'. Shihabuddin Suhrawardi lays emphasis on comprehending the purely intellectual side of Transcendental Philosophy so that any student of his thought must thoroughly acquaint himself with Aristotelian philosophy, logic, mathematics and Sufism. He advises them that their mind should be completely freed from any taint of prejudice and sin, so that they may gradually develop the inner sense, which verifies and corrects what the intellect understands only as theory.[15]

Such was the thought that Shaikh Mubarak imbibed from his early studies, and which he transmitted to his sons Faizi and Abul Fazl, who were trained under his close care. Shaikh Mubarak's stay in Agra and discourses on religious matters from 1543 onward appear to have aroused the jealousy of the orthodox section of the *ulema.* He was accused of spreading heresy and innovation, and was forced to leave Agra in 1569–70.[16] Faizi who had been admitted to the Court in 1567[17] urged Akbar to intervene. The Shaikh with his family could return to Agra only upon Akbar's intervention.[18]

The period from 1571 to 1580 is quite important for the development of Akbar's religious ideas. During this period, he went through several experiments (or experiences) so as to satisfy his own search for spiritual truth and understanding. This period also coincides with large-scale immigiration from Iran. Hakim Abul Fat'h of Gilan and Hakim Nuruddin, two sons of Maulana Abdul Riza Gilani, came to India and found patronage under Akbar. Their father had been tortured to death by Shah Tahmasp who (apparently falsely) suspected them to be Sunnis.[19] By his intelligence and good manners Abu'l Fat'h soon became a close companion of Akbar and exercised considerable influence at the court[20]. By 1575 Shaikh Mubarak's son, Abul Fazl was also admitted to the Court. Hakim Abu'l Fath Gilani, and Abul Fazl soon became friends. Badauni who was also then admitted to the Court tells us about what Akbar's mental state was at the time:

> Questions regarding *sufism*, learned discussions, enquiries into subtleties of philosophy and *fiqh* increasingly attracted His Majesty's attention. He spent whole nights repeating the name of Almighty God; he continually occupied himself, pronouncing 'Ya Huwa' (O God) and '*Ya Hadi*' (O Guide) which he had learnt through the Divine inspirations. His heart was full of reverence for him, who is the True Giver. Moved by a feeling of gratitude for his past successes, he would sit many a morning alone in prayer and meditation on a large flat stone from an old ruined building, which lay near the palace in a lonely spot, savouring the bliss of the early hours of dawn.'[21]

When such were Akbar's feelings, as described by an orthodox critic, we can imagine how disappointed he was in encountering the solidly technical and factious response of the theologians. Another theologian reported his appeal to the *ulema* in the following terms: 'My sole object', Akbar is reported to have told them,

> O wise men and Mullas, is to ascertain the truth, to find out and discover the reality. Take care, therefore, that you are not induced to conceal the truth, or to say anything contrary to the truth because of your human passion. If you do, you are responsible before God for the consequences of your impiety.[22]

While Akbar was searching for truth, Shah Abbas's harsh measures made a number of persons of Ishraqi and Nuqtawi persuasions to flee to India. Prominent among them were Wuqu'i Neshapuri, Hayat Kashani, Mulla Safi Mazandrani, Hakim Ibadullah Kashani, Abdul Ghani Yezdi, Mir Sharif Amuli, Mulla Muhammad Yezdi and others. Some of them were of the Nuqtavi persuasion, being followers of Mahmud Pasikhwani.[23] Mahmud had taught that the particles of the body do not disintegrate on earth but are absorbed as a single mass into the soil and then re-emerge in vegetation or solid form possibly to be consumed by living beings. Mahmud Pasikhwani also claimed to be the re-incarnation on a higher plane both of Prophet Muhammad and Ali. The Nuqtavi doctrine also recommended celibacy as the celibate could reach the rank of *Wahid* (Unique) and were capable of advancing to the rank of Allah. The Nuqtavi doctrine had also the cyclic concept of time, divided into epochs, each epoch being of 8000 years. To them, the Arab epoch was entrusted to a *mursal-i kamil* (a perfect messenger) and the Persian epoch was to be presided over by a Persian expositor.[24] Clearly, the ideologies of the Ishraqis and Nuqtavis were in direct clash with the traditional orthodox Islamic thought specially with those which did not allow any *ijtihad* (innovation) and stuck to *taqlid* (tradition).

The arrival of the Ishraqis and Nuqtavis appears to have caused some resentment among the orthodox section at Akbar's Court. Badauni, himself a representative of the orthodox section, alleges that Abul Fazl and Hakim Abu'l Fath turned Akbar away from Islam. Elsewhere he complains that Ali Akbar Herati (*alias* Sani Khan), a Nuqtavi, impressed upon the Emperor that he, and he alone, was 'the promised man' who was to appear, in accordance with a numerical values of the letters comprising the word '*shakhs*', in the year 990 A.H./ 1582, quoting for this the words of Mahmud Pasikhwani.[25] Interestingly at another place he says that Haji Ibrahim Sirhindi on the basis of a spurious manuscript, attributed to Ibn 'Arabi, declared that 'the *Khalifa* of the age would have many wives and would shave his beard'.[26]

These new influences began to modify Akbar's policy that until early 1570's had followed conventional lines. As late as 1572 a *farman* of his addressed to the *Muhtasib* (Censor of Morals) of Bilgiram directed the addressee to eradicate Shi'ite heresy from there.[27]

Akbar's interest in Ibn 'Arabi went on increasing as the time passed. He began to listen attentively Ibn Arabi's writing on *Wahdat al-Wajud* (Unity of Existence). The doctrine of *Wahdat al-Wajud*, writes Irfan Habib, though it did not claim a rational basis, was still a strong ideological challenge to orthodox thought in the post-Ghazali period; and Iqtidar Alam Khan adds that it is the acceptance by Akbar of Ibn Arabi's ideas that is characterized by Abul Fazl as the elevation of his intellect (*Khirad*) to a high pedestal (*buland paigi*).[28] Ibn 'Arabi's idea that all that is not part of divine reality is an illusion, in turn, led Akbar to the notion that all religions are equally illusory, but must be tolerated in the state of *sulh-i kul*, (Absolute Peace). Akbar's letter to Shah Abbas, urging him to treat all people kindly, suggests that he was here asking him to stop persecuting those who held Ishraqi and Nuqtavi ideas. The famous *Mahzar* of 1579 shows some elements of Ishraqi and Nuqtavi influences in that it holds Akbar as a specially chosen individual, being *Imam-i Adil*, *mujtahid* and *Padshah-i Islam*. Shaikh Mubarak's own remark appended to his signature on this document was that 'this is something I desired with all my heart and have for years waited for'.[29]

The *Mahzar*, however, did not fully satisfy Akbar. In the *Akbar Nama*, Abul Fazl states that the power and function of interpretation of law (*ijtihad*) authorized by the *Mahzar* were inferior to the position of His Majesty.[30] Akbar was now in search of an ideology that could raise him to a much higher position,[31] and so he looked more deeply into Ibn 'Arabi's teachings.

Shaikh Tajuddin was a *sufi* and was regarded as 'pantheist among *sufis*, second only to Ibn 'Arabi.' Akbar used to meet him regularly, and listened whole night to his *sufi* trifles and to his explanations of some verses of the Quran or the traditions of the Prophet. The phrase '*Insan-i Kamil*' (Perfect Man) was supposed to refer to the ruler of the age, since

> the nature of a king was holy. . . . Even the *sijda* (prostration) which people mildly call *zaminbos* (kissing the ground) he allowed as the due of the *Insan-i Kamil*; he looked upon the respect due to the king as a religious command, and called the face of the king *ka'ba-i muradat* (the sanctum of desires) and *qibla-i hajat* (the cynosure of necessities).[32]

Henry Corbin points out that Ibn 'Arabi's theory does not amount to simple monoism, or pantheism.[33] Yet Abul Fazl considered that Ibn Arabi's thought could be used to justify the tolerance of reason as of other dissentient and contradictory elements.[34] The adoption of *sulh-i kul*, directly invoked Ibn 'Arabi's philosophy. Its higher form was *muhabbat-i kul* (absolute love). For the ruler, *sulh-i kul* meant a policy of tolerating all religious differences. Pursuing the principle of *sulh-i kul*, Akbar began to hold discussions with leading men of all religions.[35] Abu'l Fazl says: 'Broad indeed is the carpet (world) which God has spread, and beautiful the colours which he has given it' and he refers to the couplet that the lover and the beloved are in reality one. Only idle talkers speak of the brahmin as distinct from his idol.[36] By 1580 Akbar appears to be well set in persuing a policy in which not only were all religions tolerated, but all kinds of religious views had equal access to him. How little his position conformed to what was the norm in Europe and much of Asia is shown by the Jesuit missionary Monserrate's remark that 'he (Akbar) cared little that in allowing everyone to follow his own religion he was in reality violating all relgions'.[37] The change in Akbar, Monserrate saw, was the result of his continuous pondering about what could be a true religion of God; and to this question he constantly gave the most earnest thought.[38]

If Ibn 'Arabi provided the space for Akbar's concepts of *sulh-i kul* and *insan-i kamil*, it was perhaps the Ishraqi philosophy, with its impeccable Iranian antecedants, that provided the essential principles with which the space was to be filled. We have seen that Shihabuddin Suhrawardi in the concluding position of his *Partau-nama* had spoken of 'the Light of lights,' and asserted that whoever is assiduous in revering 'It', is clothed in 'kingly light' (*Khurra-i Kayani*) and has the 'luminous ray' (*farr-i nurani*) bestowed on him. Abu'l Fazl obviously invokes this assertion to make the point that since 'kingly light' and 'the luminous ray' are the same, a just king obtains thereby the spiritual light as well. Adroitly rephrasing Shihabuddin Suhrawardi, Abu'l Fazl says: 'Royalty is a light emanating from God, and a ray from the sun, the illuminator of the universe, the argument of the book of perfection, the receptacle of all virtues. Modern language calls this light *farr-i izidi* (divine light); and the tongue of antiquity called it *Kaihan-khurira* (world-illuminating light).'[39]

The sun and light thus played a prominent part in the fairly short list of beliefs that Akbar inculcated among his small sect of disciples. When his subjects brought water for him to breathe on, to fulfil their desires, he placed it 'in the rays of the world-illuminating Sun'; and when a candidate for discipleship was accepted, this was done on a Sunday, 'when the world-illuminating Sun is in its highest splendour'.[40] His son Jahangir, after his accession (1605), recalling his father's beliefs, and proposing to instruct his own circle in them, he enjoined upon the initiates: 'Honour the luminaries (the Sun, Moon, etc.), while are mainfesters of God's light, according to the degree of each'.[41]

This is a simplified statement of the Ishraqi doctrine, through and through. It is absurd to say, on the basis of these statements, that 'Akbar worshipped the sun as the visible representative of God'.[42] It is unfortunate that, for such a long time, in the studies on Akbar, his roots in the earlier Irano-Islamic thought were so largely ignored.[43]

On the other hand, there is little that is specifically 'Nuqtavi' in Akbar's beliefs. Any emphasis on numbers or incarnation in any form is totally absent. This is despite the fact that a known Nuqtavi adherant, Sharif Amuli,[44] not only retained a high position under Akbar, but also received promotion under Jahangir, with some favourable observation recorded by that king about his knowledge of sufism.[45] It seems, therefore, that though Akbar freely borrowed from Iran, he did so with a spirit of discrimination.

Notes and References

1 Iqtidar Alam Khan, *The Political Biography of a Mughal Noble: Mun'im Khan Khan-i Khanan*, 1497–1575, New Delhi, pp. xvi–xvii; Afzal Husain, 'Growth of Irani Elements in Akbar's Nobility', *Proceedings of the Indian History Congress*, 1975, pp. 166–79.

2 Bayazid Bayat, *Tazkirah Humayun wa Akbar* (ed.), Hidayat Husain, pp. 36, 87. Abul Fazl, *Akbar Nama*, I, pp. 218–342.

3 *The Apparatus of the Mughal Empire*, New Delhi, 1985, Table I, pp. xxvii–xxviii.

4 *Akbar Nama*, Vol. II, p. 20 see-Iqtidar Alam Khan, 'The Mughal Court Politics during Bairam Khan's Regency', *Medieval India-A Miscellany*, I. Aligarh, 1969.

5 Iqtidar A. Khan, *Akbar and his India* (ed.), Irfan Habib, New Delhi, 1997, p. 86.

6 S.A.A. Rizvi, *Religious and Intellectual History of the Muslims in Akbar's Reign*, New Delhi, 1975, p. 80.

7 For the essential facts of Shihabuddin Suhrawardi's life see *Encyclopaedia of Islam* (henceforth *EI*), IV, pp 119–20. For an insightful short interpretation, see Roy Mottahedeh, *The Mantle of the Prophet: Religion and Politics in Iran*, New York, 1985, p. 149.

8 Otto Spies and S.K. Khatak (tr. and ed.), *Three Treatises on Mysticism*, 1935, p. 14.

9 Dr Muhammad Iqbal is of the view that the application of Greek dialectic to Islamic theology aroused the spirit of critical examination which began with Al Ash 'ari and found its complete expression in the scepticism of Al Ghazali. Even among the patronalists there were some more critical minds, such as Nazzam whose attitude towards Greek philosophy was not one of servile submission but of independent criticism. Al Ghazali, Al Razi, Abul Barkat and Al-Amidi, the defenders of dogma, carried on a persistent attack

on the whole fabric of Greek Philosophy. So did Ibn Taimiyya and others. Shihabuddin Suhrawardi himself endeavoured to substantiate the helplessness of pure reason by his refutation of Greek thought in a work entitled. 'The Unveiling of the Greek Absurdities' (See, *The Development of Metaphysics in Persia*, Lahore (n.d.) pp. 94–95. Hereafter cited as *Metaphysics*).

10 *EI*, IV, pp. 119–20.

11 *The Mantle of the Prophet*, p. 150.

12 *EI*, Vol. IV, pp. 119–20.

13 *Partau Nama* (ed. and tr.) Hussein Ziai, cited in Irfan Habib, 'A Political Theory of Mughal, Empire', *Proceedings of Indian History* Congress, 1998, p. 339 and n 35.

14 *Metaphysics*, p. 97.

15 *Sharah i Anwariyya, Al Harwai's* Commentary on Al Ishraqis, *Hikmat Ishraq*, cited in *Metaphysics*, pp. 98–99. The author of *Dabistan i Mazahib*, Vol. I, Tehran Solar 1362 (ed.) Rahim Zada Malik, p. 315 says that the wise men of Greece up to Plato were Ishraqis, and so Aristotle followed their philosophy.

16 Abul Fazl, *A'in-i Akbari*, (hereafter *A'in*), *Bibliotheca Indica*, Vol. II, pp. 548–49.

17 *Ain*, Vol. II, pp. 208–9; Abdu'l Qadir Badauni, *Muntakhab-ut Tawarikh*, II, pp. 198–99.

18 Rizvi', *Religious and Intellectual History*, pp. 123–24.

19 Badauni, II, p. 211.

20 Badauni, II, p. 198.

21 Badauni, II, pp. 200–201.

22 Nural Haq, *Zabdat-ut Tawarikh*, 157bf., *vide* Rizvi's *Religious and Intellectual History*, p. 114.

23 Mahmud Pasikhwani followed Fazllullah Astrabadi's *hurufism*. Durwesh Khusrau a man from Qazwin became the leader of the Nuqtavis in the latter half of the sixteenth century. He questioned the dogmas of Islam and the pure faith of the Imam. See *Cambridge History of Iran*, vol. 6, 1986, pp. 623–24, 645; Nazir Ahmad, *'Firqa-i Nuqtavi par ek tairana nazar'*, *Fikro Nazar*, Aligarh, July 1960, pp. 32–58.

24 *EI*, VIII, 1995, pp. 115–16.

25 Badauni, III, pp. 286–87.

26 Ibid.

27 *Sharaif-i Usmani*, Ms. Research Library, Department of History, 26a–32aff.

28 Cited by I.A. Khan in, *Akbar and his India*, p. 87.

29 Badauni, II, p. 272.

30 *Akbar Nama*, I, p. 269.

31 Badauni, II, p. 256.

32 Ibid.

33 *Creative Imagination in the Sufism of Ibn 'Arabi*, London, 1970, pp. 97 et passim.

[34] For a detailed study see Athar Ali, 'Sulh-i Kul and the Religious Ideas of Akbar', *Studies in History*, New Delhi, IV (i), 1982, pp. 27–39.

[35] *Akbar Nama*, III, pp. 271–73.

[36] *Ain*, I, p. 171.

[37] Monserrate, *Commentary on his Journey to the Court of Akbar* (tr. and ed.) John S. Hoyland and S.N. Banerjee, Nagpur, 1922, p. 142.

[38] Monserrate, p. 180.

[39] *A'in* I, p. 2 H. Blochmann's translation, rev. D.C. Phillott, I, Calcutta, 1927, p. 3, has been followed with slight modifications. Compare the term *Khurra-i Kayani* with *Kaihan-khoura.*

[40] *A'in*, I, pp. 159–60; Blochmann's translation., I, pp. 173–4.

[41] *Tuzuk-i Jahangiri*, tr. A.Rogers and H. Beveridge, London, 1909, I, p. 61.

[42] Blochmann in his translation of the *A'in*, op.cit., I, p. 3 n. Elsewhere too Blochmann forces his own views on his text when, for example, he renders *A'in-i Iradat-gazinan* (regulations for disciples) as 'Ordinances of the Divine Faith' (translation, I, p. 175).

[43] Aziz Ahmad, *Studies in Islamic Culture in the Indian Enviroment*, Oxford, 1964, p. 179, was, perhaps, the first to note that Akbar borrowed his ideas from earlier Islamic thinkers.

[44] Badauni, II, pp. 258–9.

[45] *Tuzuk-i Jahangiri*, tr. by Rogers and Beveridge, I, pp. 47–48. The emperor found Sharif Amuli to be 'a pure-hearted, lively-spirited man'.

Iranian Influence on Medieval Indian Architecture

Syed Ali Nadeem Rezavi

Indo-Muslim architecture, as it developed in medieval India, heavily borrowed stylistic, idiomatic (characteristic forms, architectonic and decorative), axiomorphic (forms appropriate to the purpose of the structure) and aesthetic traditions from Iranian, Trans-Oxanian and regional Indian styles. This borrowing was much heavier after the establishment of the Mughal dynasty. Mughal architecture borrowed extensively from the Delhi Sultanate, Sharqi, Gujarat, Malwa, Bengal and Rajasthani styles, as well as from styles abroad, so much so that it has itself been defined as a synthesis of these foreign and indigenous styles.[1]

Historically speaking, there are two *genera* of arcuate styles, the Roman and the Parthian, which heavily influenced the emergence of 'Islamic' architecture. A sub-*genera* (or 'complex') of the Parthian genus, the Iranian style of architecture, which includes the Ilkhanid (Mongol), Timurid and post-Timurid traditions, became a matrix for the Turkish and Indian regional styles, of which the Mughal or 'pan Indo-Islamic' variant was the most developed.[2] The Timurid tradition includes elements of architecture which Timur and his successors, the Muzaffarids of Fars, Kirman and Isfahan, and Timur's grandson Shahrukh, imbibed from Persia and applied in Samarqand, Bukhara and Herat. The post-Timurid variant of the Iranian style developed under the patronage of the Shaibanids and Astrakhanids. The Safavid variant was the culmination of the Iranian style of architecture.[3]

A large number of Iranian architectural features are perceptible in Indian architecture since the establishment of the Delhi Sultanate in the twelfth century. The first monumental Sultanate structure, the Qutb complex, comprising the *Quwwatul Islam* Mosque, the *Qutb*

Minar and the *Alai Darwaza*, reflect Iranian concepts and origins. Modelled after the Ghurid period mosques, the *Quwwatul Islam* follows the Seljuqid Iranian plan of the four-*aiwan* courtyard mosque, with certain modifications.[4] The four-*aiwan* courtyard mosque plan was one in which an integrated enclosed space was created by the symmetrical repetition of *aiwans* (portals) and arcades on the main and transverse axes, thus creating a structure with a centralized courtyard flanked by cloisters and portals on three sides and a prayer chamber and a portal on the side facing the *qibla*.

At the *Quwwatul Islam* Mosque (*c*. AD 1197), however, the Iranian *aiwan* is replaced by a central ogee-shaped arch flanked by two lower arches. At the *Arhai din ka Jhonpra* Mosque at Ajmer, constructed two years later (i.e. in AD 1199), we get three engrailed ogee-shaped arches instead of *aiwans*. Over a century later, in the more authentic Iranian fashion, an *aiwan* replaced the central arch. The first example of such a construction is the *Jahanpanah* Mosque at Delhi (*c*. AD 1343). In the Delhi Sultanate version, the atrophied four-*aiwan* mosque appears to have been preferred, since the tendency was to retain only one of the four *aiwans*, that of the western *liwan* (ante-chamber). This modified four-*aiwan* Iranian mosque plan appears to have been followed throughout the Sultanate period in India.

In elevation, the medieval Indian mosques were more templar in form, however, deriving from the well-established temple architectural traditions of the country where they were being constructed. The four-centred Iranian arch, nevertheless, found ready acceptance among the early medieval architects of India from the Khalji period onwards. Similarly, the arabesque patterns were also readily imbibed by Indian masons. The medieval Indian arabesque carvings, first exemplified on the *maqsura* (screen) of Qutbuddin Aibak at the *Quwwatul Islam*, are much more naturalistic than what is found in their Ghurid Iranian homeland, where they were flatter and abstract. The *Shah-i Mashhad Madrasa* in Gharjistan (Afghanistan) appears to have inspired the Indian masons who carved the *maqsura* of the *Quwwatul Islam* Mosque added by Sultan Iltutmish. The carvings and arabesque patterns on the Tomb of Sultan Iltutmish too appear to have been inspired by the *Shah-i Mashhad Madrasa*. The Tughluq period saw the profuse use of rubble stone as the basic medium of construction, and thus stone carvings and arabesque patterns were not generally resorted to. However, the Mughal period marked their reappearance. The Delhi Sultanate tomb plans too appear to have followed the Seljuqid and Iranian traditions. The domed square-chamber Tomb of Sultan Iltutmish, which was one of the first extant tomb structures to be constructed under the Delhi Sultans (AD 1236), appears to have followed the traditions which were finally established at the Tomb of Shad-i Mulk at Samarqand (AD 1371–83). The Iranian paradisical imagery in funerary architecture, which became so forceful later, was also introduced from Iranian traditions into India during the reign of Iltutmish. Subsequently, the Tughluq tombs of Muhammad bin Tughluq and Firuz Tughluq were also in the same tradition.

The Iranian impact on medieval Indian architecture was much more forceful after the establishment of the Mughal empire. A study of the Mughal architecture reveals that the Mughals, who considered themselves to be the heirs of the Timurid tradition, borrowed heavily from the Iranian style which had developed under the Ilkhanids, Timurids and Muzaffarids. When Babur marched into India, he brought along with him two Iranian architects, Ustad Mir Mirak Ghiyas of Herat and Ustad Shah Muhammad of Khurasan.[5] According to Lisa Golombek, the Shaibanids of Bukhara were a conduit for the transmission of Timurid architectural forms to the Mughals.[6] It should be borne in mind that much of the synthesis of the Iranian style with the Indo-Muslim style of architecture in India took place only till the reign of Akbar. The reign of Shahjahan is marked by the heavy influence of indigenous styles on Mughal architecture.

Idiomatically and axiomorphically, one of the most important marks of Iranian influence on the Mughal architectural tradition was the *chaharbagh*, the four-quartered paradisical garden with its intersecting water channels lined with walkways (*khiyabans*), platforms, water chutes, tanks and fountains, flower-beds, fruit-bearing trees and foliage, all surrounded by screen walls and gateways.[7] These *chaharbagh* gardens were to become the standard setting for Mughal tombs. In these gardens, the focus was the centre, marked by the construction of a large platform. Typical examples of funerary gardens from the Mughal period are Humayun's Tomb at Delhi, the Tombs of Akbar and 'Mariam' at Sikandara (Agra), the Tomb of I'timadud Daulah at Agra, and the Tomb of Jahangir at Shahdara, Lahore. In the Taj, the focus was shifted from the centre to the periphery, namely, the riverfront, where the mausoleum was constructed. Further enhancement of the riverfront was provided by constructing octagonal bastions flanked by a mosque (west) and a *mehmankhana* (east) in the corners. The mausoleum and the main gateway are on the main axis, while the terminals of the transverse axes are marked by a pavilion on each side. The structures on the terminal points of the axes of the garden result in a cruciform shape which is similar to the plan of the cruciform (*chahartaq*) tombs and mosques of Iran, such as the *Musalla* of Gauhar Shad, Herat (1417–38) and the Jami' Masjid Turbat-i Shaikh Jam (1440–43). This shift of emphasis from the centre to the terminus is, however, first seen in the Tomb of I'timad-ud Daulah where, although the mausoleum was retained in the centre, a riverside decorated pavilion was added.[8] A forecourt (*jilau khana*) with a series of cloistered cells was also added to the *chaharbaghs* in the Tomb of Jahangir and in the Taj Mahal.

The *chaharbagh* was first introduced in India by Babur who constructed a number of them at Agra and nearby places. One of the earliest gardens on the *chaharbagh* pattern to be laid out by Babur was the *Bagh-i Fath* situated between the lake and the ridge at Fathpur Sikri. Rectangular in plan, it comprises intersecting water channels and *khiyabans*. In the centre is constructed an Iranian-inspired pavilion (*baradari*). Aligned on an east–west axis, it is surrounded on all sides by a cloistered *riwaq* (verandah) pierced by an entrance in the north. The water channels, which are provided with *mahi-pusht abshars* (fish-scaled chutes), are connected with a stepwell (*baoli*) in the west and a well (*chah*) in the east.[9] A more elaborate *chaharbagh* of Babur, the *Bagh-i Nilufar* (Lotus Garden), survives at Dholpur (Rajasthan). Two other gardens of his which have been identified are the so-called *Rambagh* (*Aram Bagh* or *Bagh-i Gul Afshan*, later renovated by Nurjahan and thus renamed *Bagh-i Nur Afshan*), and the *Bagh-i Hasht Bihisht*, which are located on the left bank of the Yamuna at Agra.[10]

The *chaharbagh* introduced by Babur not only became a major element of urban landscape under the Mughals, but also inspired the lay-out of the Mughal cities themselves. The centripetal symmetry of the *chaharbagh* was invoked in the planning of the Mughal city. The organizing instruments of the garden, such as the axes, joints defined by pavilions, platforms and walkways, were transformed and enlarged architecturally into roads, caravanserais, monumental structures and quarters.[11] Examples of such town planning on the *chaharbagh* pattern are provided by the towns of Fathpur Sikri and Shahjahanabad (Delhi). The cross-shaped or quadripartite symmetry encountered at Shahjahanabad and, to an extent, at Fathpur Sikri, reminds us of Isfahan of the Safavid period with its *maidan* (promenade) and *chaharbaghs.* The use of the *chaharbagh* as an instrument of urban landscaping and town planning involves the Iranian imagery of paradise which is central to the Parthian genus of architecture.

Idiomatically, apart from the *chaharbagh,* there appear to be a number of other Iranian features which are encountered in Mughal architecture. Some of them, like the double dome (which developed in Iran during the fourteenth century) and the squinches on which the domes are raised (Sassanid) had been introduced into India during the period of the Delhi Sultanate and are generally found in Tughluq monuments. The Iranian four-centred (as well as two-centred) pointed arch, as we have seen, was also known in India; but subsequently it came to be identified as the typical Mughal arch during the reign of Akbar. It was ultimately replaced during Shahjahan's period by the cusped (multi-foliated) arch which was ultimately derived from the Gandharan lobed arch. The bulbous double dome, on the other hand, is first encountered in a hesitant form in Humayun's Tomb and is subsequently perfected during the reign of Shahjahan when we find it in the Tomb of Taj Mahal.

India, however, showed less inclination to imbibe the distinctly 'Muslim' idiomatic forms of adornment, calligraphy, arabesque and *muqarnas* (stalactites). The use of the typical mosaic tile was confined to a handful of monuments under the Mughals. For example, it appears on the Tomb of Afzal Khan (*Chini ka Rauza*) at Agra in its most profuse form. At other places the use of coloured glazed tiles—so popular in Iran—remained confined to the outer facing of the domes (for example, *Nili Gumbad* and *Sabz Burj* near Humayun's Tomb, Delhi, constructed some time during the early sixteenth century). Brick-tile decoration is also found in the Lahore Fort. Calligraphic bands, so preferred in Iranian architecture, make their appearance under the Mughals but are generally confined to the rectangular panels encircling the arched openings of the gateways. Under the Mughals, the calligraphic decoration is accomplished with black-stone lettering inscribed on white marble bands (for example, *Buland Darwaza,* Fathpur Sikri; the gateway to Akbar's Tomb, Sikandara, Agra; and the entrance gate of the Taj Mahal). The most representative example of calligraphic decoration under the Mughals comes from the facades of the Taj Mahal.

The *muqarnas* pattern with its distinct Iranian and Timurid antecedents also appears in Mughal architecture, though it seems that it was not the preferred style. The *muqarnas* lozenges which were developed in ninth-century Iran have their best Mughal example in the tombs at *Khusrau Bagh*, Allahabad, built during the reign of Jahangir. The Mughals, however, employed the indigenous idioms of sculptural form of chiaroscuro effect which were based on offsets and recesses, layers of horizontal mouldings, columns and brackets, curved motifs like the pot, lotus flower and myrobalan (*amalaka*). Yet the typical Jahangiri *Chini khana* motifs based on stunted arch filled with embossed flower designs and wine goblets and *surahis* evoke the Iranian symbolism of paradise (see, for example, the Tomb of I'timad-ud Daulah, Tomb of Firuz Khan, gatehouse of *Surajbhan ka Bagh*, etc., at Agra.)

Aesthetically, the tile and faience mosaic of the Iranian style was replaced in Mughal India by the red and white bichromy or marble monochromy which is so typical of Akbari structures and monuments (for example, Humayun's Tomb; *Badshahi Darwaza*, Jami' Masjid, Fathpur Sikri; *Jahangiri Mahal*, Agra Fort). The *Buland Darwaza* at Fathpur Sikri, however, depicts a red–yellow bichromy.

Two further Iranian idiomatic innovations, the 'arch-and-panel' articulation[12] and the stellate vaults (the *chahartaq*) based on cruciform domed chambers, found wide acceptance under the Mughals. Iranian architects of the thirteenth and fourteenth centuries had imposed order on architectonic and decorative forms by a consistent system of articulation which had a five-fold relationship between arch and panel, and arch and arch. In this system the theme was primarily curved and arcuate (arch), and only secondarily rectangular or trabeate-based (panel). By repeating the identical arcuate patterns, the 'arch-and-panel' idiom aesthetically and idiomatically unified the surfaces and voids of a structure, while controlling the decoration covering its walls. The five features of its relationship—alignment (when the arch symmetrically alternates with a panel or an arch vertically or horizontally), empanelling (arch contained within a panel), multiplication (progressive increase upwards of arches, etc.), enframing (arch framed by arch) and intersecting (arch crossing arch)—initially found their way into Sultanate architecture (for example, the

Alai Darwaza at the *Quwwatul Islam*), but gained much greater prominence under the Mughals. The most prominent presence of this system is found on the facade and the side bays of the *Buland Darwaza* at Fathpur Sikri, the exterior facade of *Jahangiri Mahal* at Agra Fort and the exterior surface of the Taj Mausoleum. However, in these Mughal structures, the typical Iranian arch-and-panel system was modified by the traditional articulation of wedge-shaped fluted or octagonal shafts technically known as 'quoins', which are shaped like columns. These quoin shafts divided the whole area horizontally and acted as pivots for knitting together the planes of the facade.

The arch-and-panel system without the modifying pivotal quoin system is represented in the *baradari* structure of Muqarrab Khan at Kairana (district Muzaffarnagar); the Tomb of Sultan Nisar Begum at *Khusrau Bagh*, Allahabad; the *Naulakha* Pavilion and *Shah Burj* at Lahore Fort; the upper portions of the interior walls of the *Diwan-i Khas*, Agra Fort; and the *Bhadon* Pavilion at the Delhi Fort.

As far as the *chahartaq* is concerned, it was formed in Iran through intersecting arches. Generally, a square vaulted chamber spanned by four large intersecting arches, resting on massive wide piers, form a cruciform with an open square in the centre. This square is then turned into a polygon or circle with the help of smaller arches, supplemented by decorative ribs rising from the main arches. In this *chahartaq* plan, the Iranian architects improvized a new type of vaulting system, now generally known as the Khurasanian vault. The Khurasanian (multi-partite) vault was invoked by the Timurid architects by reviving the Ilkhanid and Seljuq stelliform vault on the system of intersecting arches. This type of vault consists of four large intersecting ribs which create a central vaulted area, four lozenge-shaped squinches and four rectangular fields. In this plan, the centre of each side of the square contains an arched recess, the width of which is equivalent to the diameter of the dome, supported by the four arches which in turn spring from the forward edge of the recess arches, each adjacent pair intersecting to form the square. The secondary ribs springing from the haunches of the arches converts the square into an octagon by a series of lozenge-shaped squinches. At the second stage of the phase of transition, sixteen fan-shaped pendentives complete the transition to the circular dome. With this system the vaulting techniques reach perfection. The need of supporting walls is eliminated and the dome now sits directly on the four arches. The first building based on this pattern was the twelfth-century Jami' Masjid of Isfahan. Under the Timurids, this type of vault was employed in the Bibi Khanum Mosque at Samarqand (1398–1405), the *Musalla* of Gauhar Shad at Herat (1417–38), the Mosque of Turbat-i Shaikh Jam (1440–43) and the *Madrasa* at Khargird (1442). In the Mughal empire, we find its occurrence in the imperial *hammam* (the so-called Hakim's Baths), the private *hammam* in the *daulatkhana*, the *hammam* attached to the *Haramsara* ('Jodhbai Palace'), all at Fathpur Sikri, as well as at Akbar's *Khilwatgah* in Allahabad Fort, the Barber's tomb in the garden of Humayun's Tomb and the Govind Dev Temple at Vrindavan near Mathura (1590s).

The *Kabuli Bagh* Mosque of Babur at Panipat and the Kachhpura Mosque of Humayun at Agra, on the other hand, depict the arch-netted transition zones in pseudo-structural plaster relief work applied to the pendentives of the small domes of the lateral side bays. These are also later found in the central dome of Humayun's Tomb and at the Tomb of Tambolan Begum at *Khusrau Bagh*, Allahabad. This 'arch-net' or 'squinch-net' in the form of fake arches in plaster was also inspired by Timurid architecture. The corbelled pendentive concealed by elaborate plaster ribs is first found at the *Khanqah* (hospice) of Mulla Kalan, Ziyaratgah (1472–1501). Arch-netting similar to that on Tambolan Begum's tomb occurs at the *Khanqah* of Khwaja Zainuddin at Bukhara (sixteenth century).

The *chahartaq* plan was extensively employed by the Mughals in their mosque and tomb architecture. The naves of the western *liwans* of the Jami' Masjids of Fathpur Sikri and Shahjahanabad (Delhi), and the Badshahi Masjid of Lahore, are all constructed on the *chahartaq* pattern. The earliest Mughal example is the *Kabuli Bagh* Mosque (*c.* 1527) of Babur at Panipat, where the *chahartaq* is employed on its central nave. The nave and aisles of the central rooms of Muqarrab Khan's *baradari* at Kairana (district Muzaffarnagar) are also constructed on the *chahartaq* pattern. The square Mughal tombs, such as the *Khusrau Bagh* Tombs at Allahabad, are also *chahartaq* structures.

Axiomorphic borrowings from the Persian style are also quite prominent in Mughal architecture. They are in the form of gatehouses, portals (*peshtaq*), pillared halls (*aiwans*) and plans of tombs and mosques.

In Iran and Central Asia (Trans-Oxiana), masonry buildings were constructed with 'post-and-beam' (timber) porches. Two prominent examples are Ali Qapu in the *Maidan-i Shah*, Isfahan and the Balyand Mosque in Bukhara. Porched pillared halls raised on slender wooden pillars were known as *talar* in Iran and *aiwan* in Trans-Oxiana. In Iran, the term *aiwan* was used for an open-fronted room with a barrel vault. The use of the term *aiwan* to designate pillared constructions was adopted by the Mughals. Most such pillared constructions in India took place during the reign of Akbar. The *Badgir* (*'Hawa Mahal'*) of the Jodhbai Palace, the *Chahar suffa* (*'Panch Mahal'*), the *Aiwankhana ('Diwan-i Khas'* or 'Jewel Treasury'), the entrance to the *Naqqarkhana* near Hathipol, the *'Rang Mahal'*, all at Fathpur Sikri, and the inner quadrangle of the *Jahangiri Mahal* at Agra Fort, are examples of quadrangular *aiwans* inspired by Iranian prototypes. This building form was also sometimes adapted to an octagonal plan. The *'Qush-khana'* near the *Ajmeri Darwaza* at Fathpur Sikri, the *Chihilsutun* in Allahabad Fort and the *Shah Burj* at Agra Fort are all octagonal *aiwans*.

Iranian architecture also initiated the expression of the aesthetics of the facade in its portal (*peshtaq*), an endeavour that was brought to fruition in Turkey and Mughal India. The construction of high *peshtaqs* and *aiwans* had long been established in the Iranian tradition.[13] The high *peshtaq* of the sanctuary chamber was also an important feature of the Sharqi architecture of Jaunpur.[14] It has generally been argued that the high *peshtaq* of the Mughals, especially under Babur, was a result of the influence of Sharqi architecture. Parallels have been drawn between the facade of the Atala Masjid and Jami' Masjid, Jaunpur, and the facade of the Baburi mosques, the *Kabuli Bagh* Mosque of Panipat, the recently destroyed Mir Baqi's Mosque at Ayodhya and the Mir Hindu Beg Mosque at Sambhal.

A closer look of our sources and a comparison of the plans of these mosques with Iranian–Timurid structures however unfold a different story. Before coming to India, Babur had briefly occupied Samarqand (*c.* 1501), and re-occupied it later (1507) and campaigned in Bukhara up till 1511. The Sambhal Mosque was constructed by one of his nobles in 1526. Soon after his victory at Panipat in 1526 Babur had ordered the construction of the *Kabuli Bagh* Mosque. In 1528–29, Mir Baqi had the Ayodhya Mosque constructed. In 1530, during the reign of Humayun (and with four years of Mughal conquest) the Kachhpura Mosque was constructed. It was too short a time for the Mughals to familiarize themselves with the regional architectural traditions of India. Further, as we have noted earlier, Babur had been accompanied to India by two master masons who were well-versed in the Timurid traditions of architecture.

If we compare the plan of the *Kabuli Bagh* Mosque and the Kachhpura Mosque with the *Namazgah* Mosque at Qarshi, a town southwest of Samarqand, we enounter a striking similarity of style and planning. In all the Baburi and Humayuni mosques, as in the Qarshi mosque, we find the high *peshtaq*, *chahartaq* nave and lower lateral wings with four domed bays. It is also interesting to note that in his memoirs, Babur mentions the town of Qarshi near Samarqand.[15] Coupled with the existence of the typical Timurid feature of arch-netted transition zones in pseudo-structural plaster relief covering the pendentives, we can safely assume that these mosques took shape under the Iranian–Timurid influence.

The high *peshtaqs* subsequently emerged as the hallmark of Mughal architecture, not only in mosque but also in tomb construction. The earliest Mughal tombs with elongated *peshtaqs* are the *Sabz Burj* and *Nila Gumbad* near Humayun's Tomb.[16]

As far as the ground-plan is concerned, the Mughal mosque closely followed the Iranian axiomorphic prototypes. By the fourteenth century, the Iranian architects had perfected the two- and four-*aiwan* (open-fronted construction with a barrel vault). The form of the two-*aiwan* mosque was achieved by having the sanctuary chamber with a high *peshtaq* preceded by an enclosed open quadrangle. The entrance portal (*aiwan* of the Iranian architecture) was constructed on the same axis as the *peshtaq*. The centrally located courtyard, which was also an indigenous idiom, was surrounded by double-storeyed cloisters (*riwaq*). Under the Mughals, this Iranian–Timurid prototype was used in conjunction with Delhi Sultanate elements to produce a new form. Thus, in the Khairul Manazil Mosque at Delhi we find that the tall *peshtaq* of the western *liwan* and the double-storeyed *riwaq* are typically Timurid. The single-aisled western *liwan* was itself built on Delhi Sultanate traditions. As in the Iranian examples, this single-aisled, five-bayed mosque has a single dome. In the Akbari Masjid near the Ajmer Dargah, the western *liwan* with multiple aisles and a dominant dome over the nave is Timurid, while the low single-aisle cloisters are typical of Delhi Sultanate architecture. The Jami' Masjid of Fathpur Sikri is again a two-*aiwan* mosque, which acquired its third portal (*Buland Darwaza*) at a later stage.

By the twelfth century the four-*aiwan* congregational mosque with domed chamber and cloisters had been perfected in Iran. In fact, it was the Jami' Masjid at Varamin (1322–26) which established the general plan for the subsequent Jami' Masjids of Iran.[17] In this type of mosque a harmonious synthesis of such traditional elements as the *aiwan*, the four-*aiwan* court and *aiwan*-dome combination was effected. The courtyard was framed by cloisters (usually double-storeyed) of equal height, on three sides, while the prayer chamber (western *liwan*) was given a heightened importance through its crowning dome and a higher *peshtaq*. In the middle of each of the other three arched faces of the interior court, an *aiwan* (in the form of an arched and vaulted niche) is introduced. As in the overall plan, these four *aiwans* can be seen as the arms of a cross. This type of mosque plan has been termed a cruciform plan.

The cruciform or four-*aiwan* mosque made its appearance in India during the Sultanate period (*supra*). Under the Mughals it is first encountered during the reign of Jahangir, but it became popular during the reign of Shahjahan. The first cruciform mosque constructed under the Mughals appears to be the Begum Shahi Mosque at Lahore (1611–14). The second mosque on the same plan is the Wazir Khan Mosque (1634–35), again at Lahore. Later, the Jami' Masjids of Agra and Shahjahanabad were also constructed on the same pattern.

Contrary to the Iranian four-*aiwan* mosques, these Mughal mosques emphasized the importance of the sanctuary by tending to isolate it from the cloisters of the courtyard and by diminishing the size and width of the latter. The Wazir Khan Mosque has two other changes. As at the Taj Mahal, this mosque has an additional court in front of the entrance (*jilaukhana*) which acted as a *bazar*. Secondly, the transverse *aiwans* of this mosque are no longer open-fronted in the Iranian manner, but are gate-houses with doors.[18]

Iranian architects and builders of the fourteenth century had also developed a technique for providing domed roofing to long rectangular structures. This was the technique of applying transverse arches and groin vaults.[19] In such construction the rectangular space to be covered was divided into square units by crossing it transversely from one longitudinal wall to the other. Short arches were applied to bridge the transverse arches, and provide the base for the domical vaults erected on the top. The in-filled spaces between the transverse arches were pierced with windows to let in light. This technique made its appearance in Eastern Iran where it was adopted in *Masjid-Kirmani* near the Tomb of Turbat-i Shaikh.[20] It is then found in such religious structures as the oratory near the Jami‘ Masjid at Yazd and the Tomb of Shaikh Ahmad Yasavi in Turkestan. In India we find one example of this kind of elongated vaulted structure from the reign of Shahjahan. But here it is in the form of a Safavid-inspired *bazar*, the *bazar-i musaqqaf*. This unique structure is the covered *bazar* adjoining the *Lahori Darwaza* of the Delhi Fort.

One of the most important axiomorphic impresses of Iranian tradition on Mughal architecture was in the form of a plan which has been labelled *hasht bihisht* or noni-partite plan.[21] In this plan the lay-out, which is preferably an irregular octagon (a chamferred square—*musamman-i baghdadi*), is divided by four intersecting constructional lines into nine parts, comprising a domed octagonal chamber in the centre, rectangular open halls (in the form of either *peshtaq* or flat-roofed *aiwans* supported by pillars) and double-storeyed octagonal vaulted chambers in the corners. This plan provided the buildings a radial symmetry which hitherto was missing. The radial symmetry was further emphasized by the axial and radial passages which linked the nine chambers with each other. Typical Timurid examples of this were the Tomb of Abu Nasr Parsa at Balkh (*c.* 1460), the *Ishratkhana* at Samarqand (1464) and the Tomb of Sharif Abdullah at Herat (1487). A direct influence of the Tomb of Abu Nasr Parsa is found during the Mughal period in at least four tombs, three of which are in Delhi. The *Sabz Burj* and *Nili Gumbad* Tombs (*c.* 1530–40) near Humayun’s Mausoleum, the ‘Afsarwala Tomb (1560s), again at Delhi, and the Tomb of Shamsher Khan at Batala (1588–89) have a noni-partite plan with angular units as semi-octagonal niches. As at the Abu Nasr Tomb, their central chamber is on a square plan.

The most famous Mughal monumental funerary structures constructed on this Timurid plan are the Humayun’s Tomb at Delhi and the Taj Mahal at Agra. The plan of Humayun’s Tomb also appears to have been inspired from a ‘boat-house’ which, according to Humayun’s court historian, was contrived on the orders of the emperor himself. Khwand Amir writes:

> Of all the wonderful innovations (*ikhtara‘at*) prepared in that time on the Imperial orders, which owing to their novelty (*gharaib*) and beauty (*nazahat*) have spread to all parts of the world was the one

> which on royal directions, the royal carpenters constructed with the help of four boats in the river Jamuna (*Jayhun*). On each of these (boats) were constructed platforms (*saffa*) which are double-storeyed *chahartaqs* of elegent style. These four boats were joined with each other in such a way that these *chahartaq* (platforms) face each other. And in between each two of the four boats, another apartment (*taq*) was produced. Consequently an octagonal tank (*hauz*) resulted in the middle. And these *chahartaqs* were decorated with fine cloths and other valuable objects, due to which the mind of the intelligent (*aql-i darrak*) would be amazed by its beauty and magnificance.[22]

If we compare the plan of Humayun's Tomb, which was designed by Mirza Ghiyas, the master architect who had accompanied Babur to India, the tomb appears to be a copy of Humayun's boat-house. The *chahartaqs* of the boat pavilions were transformed into stone double-storeyed vaulted octagonal corner chambers. The four 'apartments' connecting the boats were transformed into rectangular side chambers, and the central octagonal tank was now transformed into the octagonal domed sepulchural chamber. The Taj Mahal, on the other hand, is a single *baghdadi octagon* (chamferred square) laid out in the typical noni-partite plan. The Iranian axiomorphics are brilliantly coupled with indigenous idiomatics and aesthetics.

Another example of a noni-partite tomb is the Tomb of Anarkali at Lahore, which, again, is one of the most ingeniously planned of Mughal structures.

The noni-partite plan was also applied by the Mughals to tombs which were regular octagons. The Tomb of Shah Quli Khan at Narnaul, the Tomb of Haji Muhammad at Sirhind and the Tomb of Qutbuddin Muhammad Khan at Vadodara are some of the funerary structures of Akbar's reign which were regular octagons with noni-partite plans.

This plan was applied to palace buildings like Akbar's Pavilion at the Ajmer Fort and the *Buland Darwaza* at Fathpur Sikri, and *Rani ka Mahal* at Allahabad Fort. Pleasure pavilions and water palaces like the *Hada Mahal* at Fathpur Sikri, Shah Quli's Water Palace at Narnaul and I'timad Khan's Water Palace (popularly known as *Burhia ka Tal*) at Etmadpur (Agra) were also constructed on this pattern.

The noni-partite plan was also applied to square structures.

Akbar's Ajmer Pavilion and Shah Quli's Water Palace were square structures. The best example of this type is, however, the Tomb of I'timadud Daulah at Agra. These square noni-partite structures were probably constructed in the style of the *Khanqah* of Qasim Shaikh at Kermin, Bukhara and the Tomb of Ulugh Beg and Abdur Razzaq in the vicinity of Ghazni.

This plan was applied to a large number of Mughal *hammams*, for example, the *hammam* of Abdur Rahim Khan-i Khanan at Burhanpur and the imperial *hammams* at Fathpur Sikri.

From the above description it thus appears that the medieval Indian architects and planners, especially those of the Mughal period, heavily borrowed their idiomatic, axiomorphic and aesthetic traditions from Iran. The beauty and uniqueness of the medieval Indian and Mughal architecture, however, was owing to these inspirations being intelligently synthesized with older indigenous elements. This synthetic tendency is seen at its best in the Taj Mahal, making it one of the best architectural achievements of world civilization.

Notes

1 See, for example, Ebba Koch, *Mughal Architecture: An Outline of its History and Development (1526–1858)*, Prestel-Verlag, Munich, 1991; and Catherine B. Asher, *Architecture of Mughal India*, being Vol. I, pt. 4 of *The New Cambridge History of India*, Oxford University Press, 1995. See also Lisa Golombek, 'From Tamerlane to the Taj Mahal', in *Essays in Islamic Art and Architecture in Honor of Katherina Otto-Dorn*, (ed.) Abbas Daneshwari, Malibu, 1981 (reprinted in Monica Juneja, *Architecture in Medieval India*, New Delhi, 2001, pp. 315–27).

2 See Jose Pereira, *Islamic Sacred Architecture: A Stylistic History*, New Delhi, 1994, pp. 4–5.

3 Ebba Koch, on the other hand, differentiates between the Iranian and Timurid styles of architecture; see Koch, *Mughal Architecture*, p. 14.

4 Tokifusa Tsukinowa, 'The Influence of Seljuq Architecture on the Earliest Mosques of the Delhi Sultanate Period', *Acta Asiatica*, No.43, 1982, pp. 54–60.

5 *Baburnama*, (tr.) A.S. Beveridge, New Delhi, 1970, pp. 343, 642.

6 Lisa Golombek, 'From Tamerlane to the Taj Mahal', pp. 43–50.

7 For a study and survey of Mughal gardens, see S. Ali Nadeem Rezavi, 'Exploring the Mughal Gardens at Fathpur Sikri', *Proceedings of the Indian History Congress*, Indian History Congress, Bangalore session, 1997.

8 For further such examples from the reigns of Jahangir and Shahjahan, one might refer to the *Buland Bagh, Bagh-i Nur Afshan* and *Bagh-i Jahanara*, all situated on the left bank of the Yamuna at Agra. For the *Bagh-i Jahanara*

(Zahra Bagh) see Ebba Koch, 'The Zahara Bagh (Bagh-i Jahanara) at Agra', *Environmental Design*, n.d., pp. 30–37 (special issue on 'The City as a Garden'.

9 For the identification of this garden, its plan and its site, see S. Ali Nadeem Rezavi, 'Exploring the Mughal Gardens at Fathpur Sikri'.

10 See, for example, Ebba Koch, *Mughal Architecture*, pp. 32–33; Catherine Asher, *Architecture of Mughal India*, pp. 22–24. See also Catherine Asher, 'Babur and the Timurid Char Bagh: Use and Meaning', *Environmental Design*, no. 11, pp. 56–73.

11 Attilio Petruccioli, 'The Process Evolved by the Control Systems of Urban Design in the Mogul Epoch in India: The Case of Fathpur Sikri', in *Environmental Design*, (ed.) A. Petruccioli, Roma, Italy, 1984, pp. 18–27; S. Ali Nadeem Rezavi, 'Town Planning under the Mughals', paper presented at the seminar on Urbanization in Medieval India, sponsored by Regional Institute of Archaeological Studies and Training, Government of West Bengal and Asiatic Society, Calcutta, 1997.

12 For a discussion of 'Arch-and-Panel System', see Jose Pereira, *Islamic Sacred Architecture*, pp. 249–50, also pp. 92, 100.

13 See, for example, Pinder-Wilson, 'Timurid Architecture', in *Cambridge History of Iran: The Timurid and Safavid Period*, Vol. VI, (eds) Peter Jackson and L. Lockhart, Cambridge University Press, 1986, pp. 729, 731; D. Wilber, *The Architecture of Islamic Iran, the Ilkhanid Period*, Princeton, 1955, p. 158.

14 A. Fuhrer, *The Sharqi Architecture of Jaunpur*, ASI, new series, Vol. XI, Calcutta, 1889; Percy Brown, *Indian Architecture, Islamic Period*, Bombay, 1958.

15 *Baburnama*, p. 84.

16 For details on these tombs, see Ebba Koch, *Mughal Architecture*, pp. 36–37.

17 D. Wilber, *The Architecture of Islamic Iran*, p. 731.

18 For the non-Iranian influences on the Mughal congregational mosques, see Jose Pereira, *Islamic Sacred Architecture*, pp. 231–32.

19 Pinder-Wilson, 'Timurid Architecture', p. 732; Lisa Golombek, 'Discourses of an Imaginary Arts Council in Fifteenth-Century Iran', in *Timurid Art and Culture: Iran and Central Asia in the Fifteenth Century*, (eds) Lisa Golombek and Maria Subtelny (being Vol. VI of *Studies in Islamic Art and Architecture: Supplements to Muqarnas*), E.J. Brill, Leiden, 1992, p. 5.

20 Pinder-Wilson, 'Timurid Architecture', p. 732.

21 See Ebba Koch, *Mughal Architecture*, pp. 44–45; Jose Pereira, *Islamic Sacred Architecture*, pp. 236–37.

22 Khwand Mir, *Qanun-i Humayuni*, (ed.) Hidayat Husain, Royal Asiatic Society of Bengal, Calcutta, 1940, p. 52.

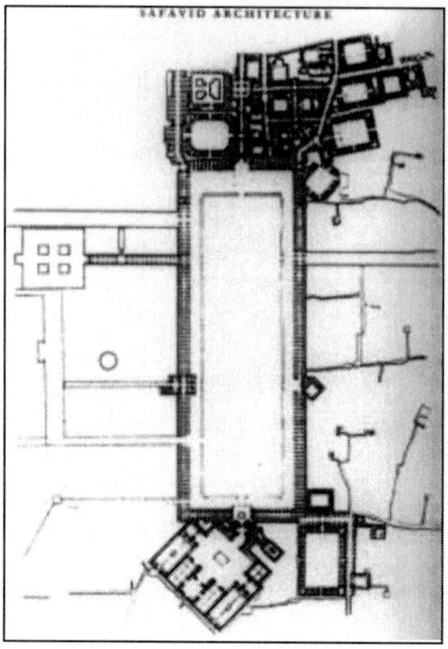

Town planning: Plan of *Maidan-i Shah*, Shiraz

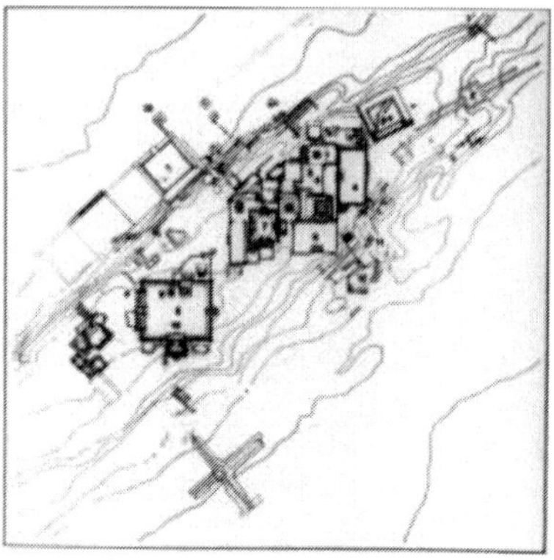

Town planning: Plan of Fathpur Sikri

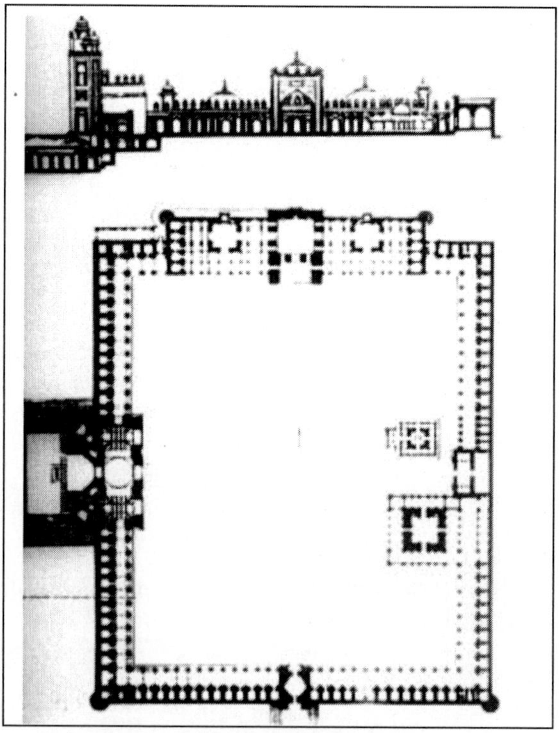

Mughal *peshtaq*: Jami' Masjid, Fathpur Sikri (Note the two-*aiwan* plan)

Iranian *aiwans*: Mashhad and Isfahan

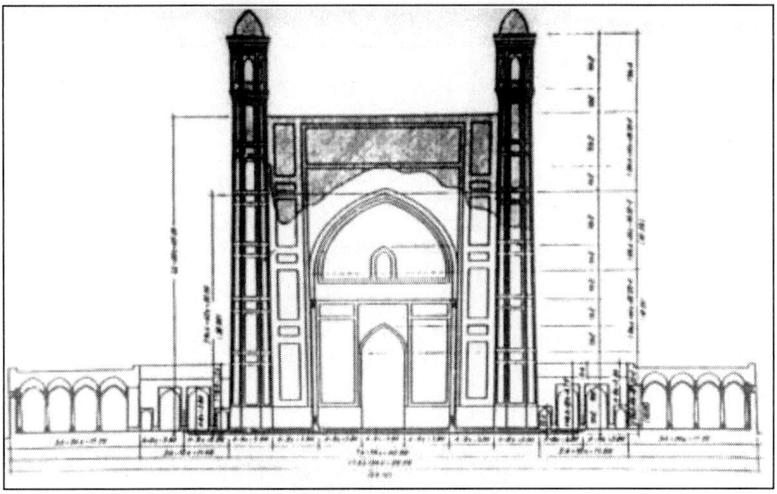

Iranian *aiwans*: Bibi Khanum, Samarqand

Mughal *aiwans*: Kachhpura Mosque, Agra

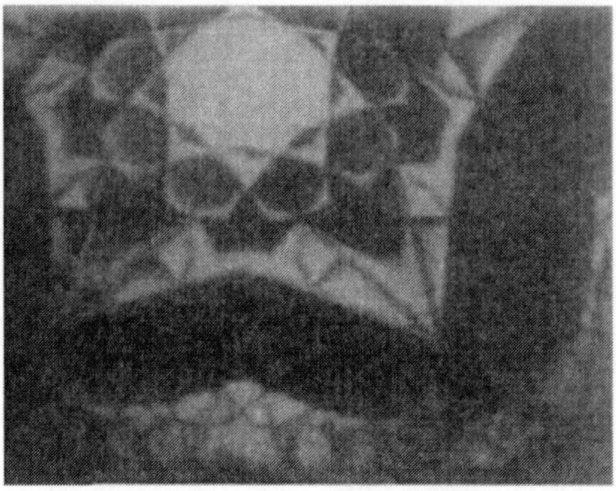

Khurasanian vault: Imperial *hammam*, Fathpur Sikri

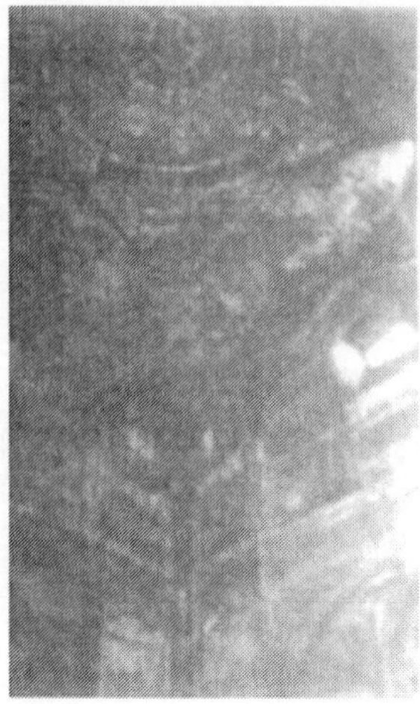

Khurasanian vault: Barber's tomb, Delhi

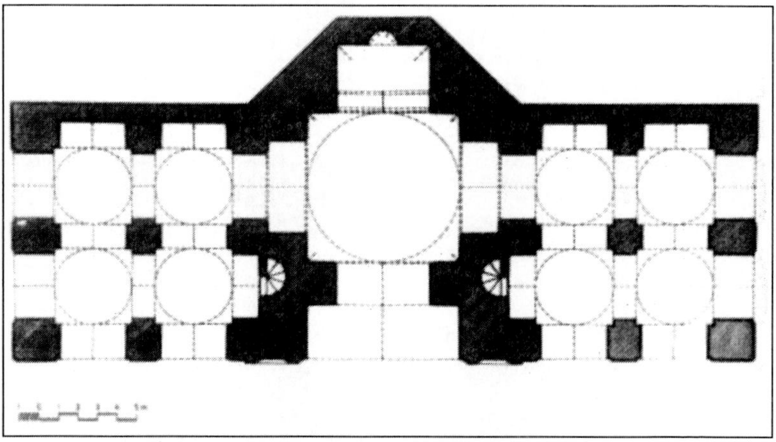

Chahartaq mosques: Plan of *Namazgah* Mosque, Qarshi

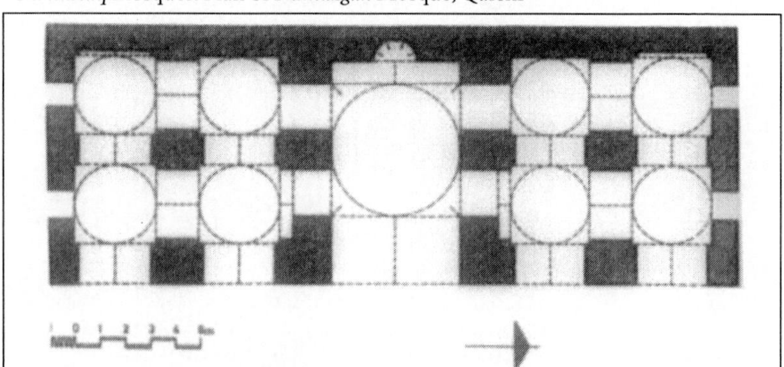

Chahartaq mosques: Plan of Kachhpura Mosque, Agra

Chahartaq mosques: Kachhpura Mosque, Agra

Chahartaq mosques: *Kabuli Bagh* Mosque, Panipat

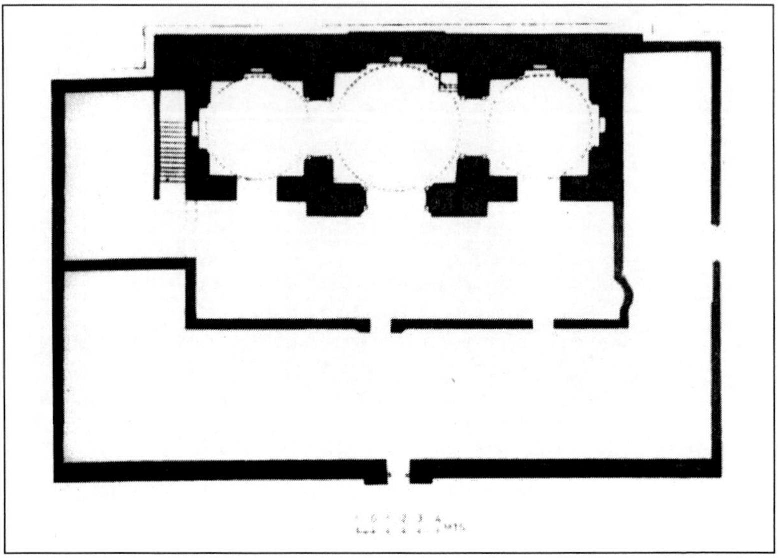

Chahartaq mosques: Plan of Baburi Masjid, Ayodhya

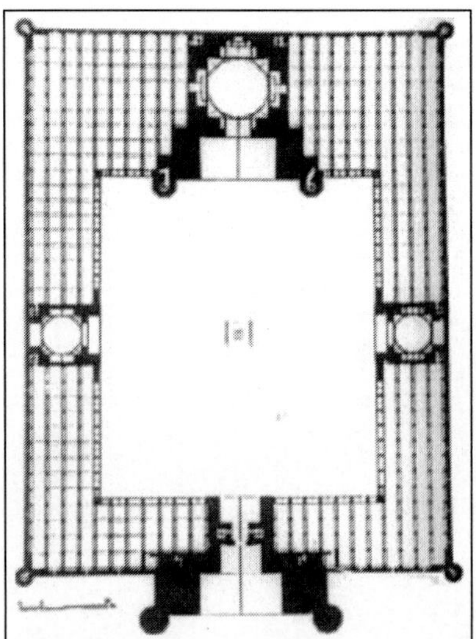

Timurid four-*aiwan* mosque: Plan of Bibi Khanum Mosque, Samarqand

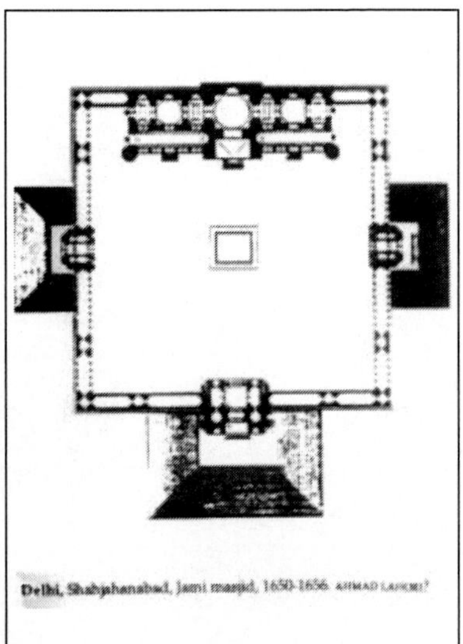

Mughal four-*aiwan* mosque: Jami' Masjid, Shahjahanabad

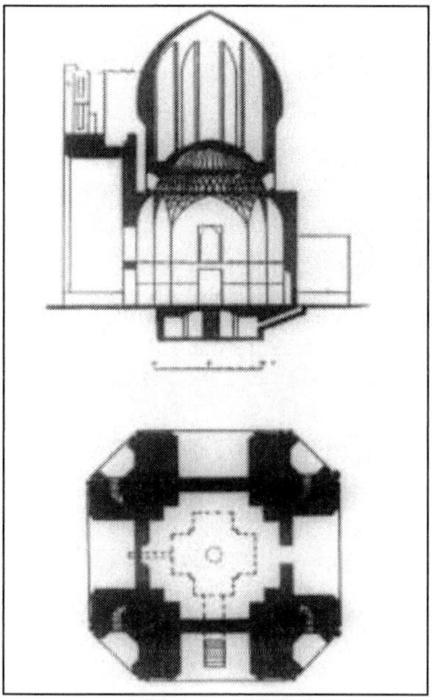

Noni-partite plan: Tomb of Abu Nasr Parsa, Balkh

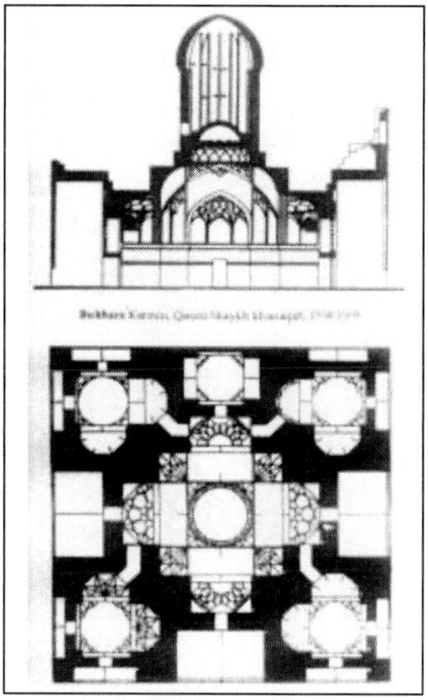

Noni-partite plan: *Khanqah* of Qasim Shaikh, Bukhara, Kermin

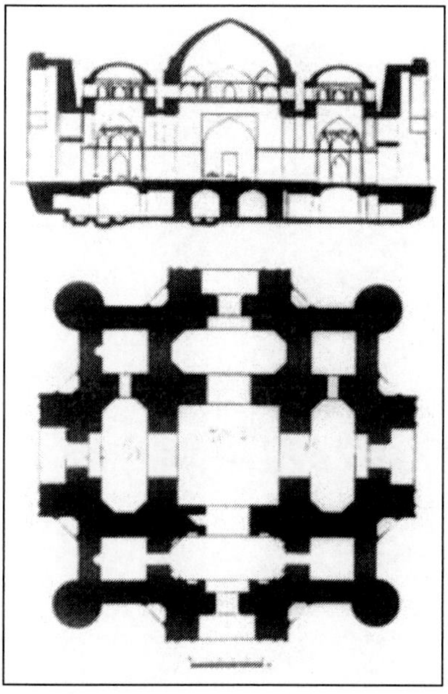

Noni-partite plan: Tomb of Ulugh Beg and Abdur Razzaq, Ghazni

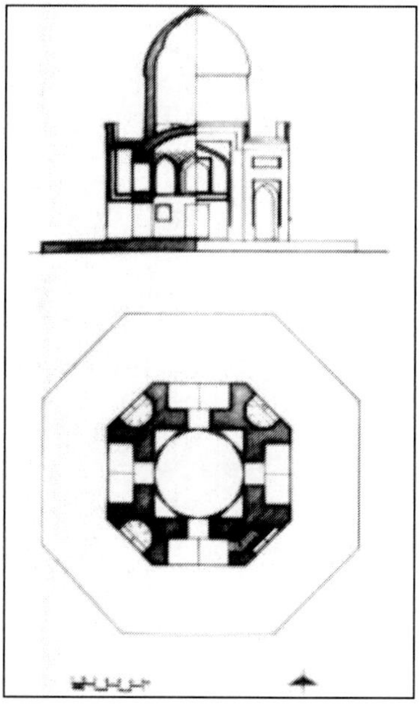

Noni-partite plan: *Sabz Burj*, Delhi

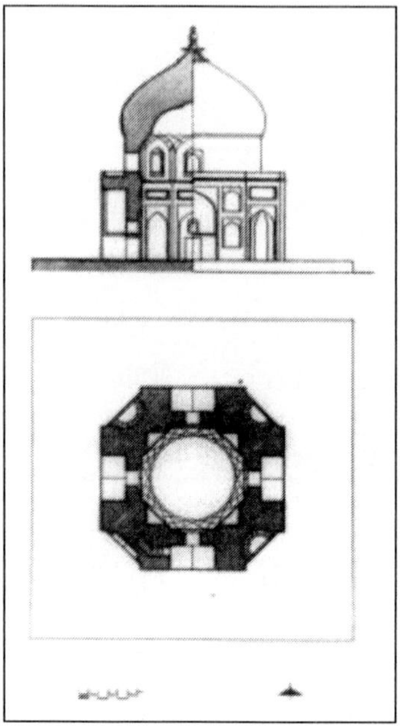

Noni-partite plan: *Nili Gumbad*, Delhi

Noni-partite plan: Tomb of I'timadud Daulah, Agra

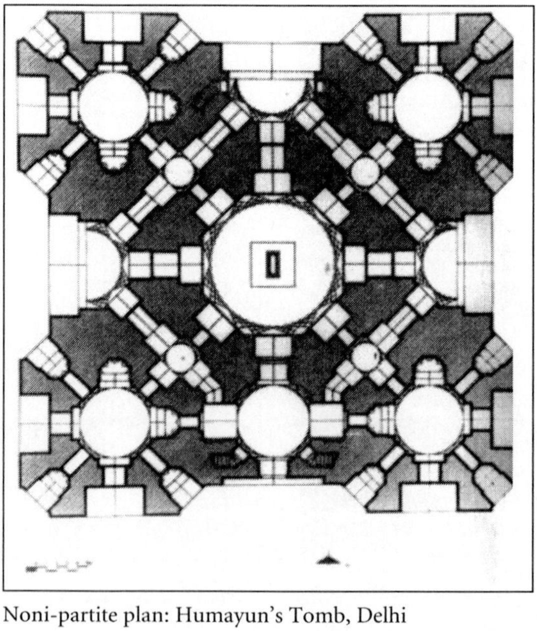

Noni-partite plan: Humayun's Tomb, Delhi

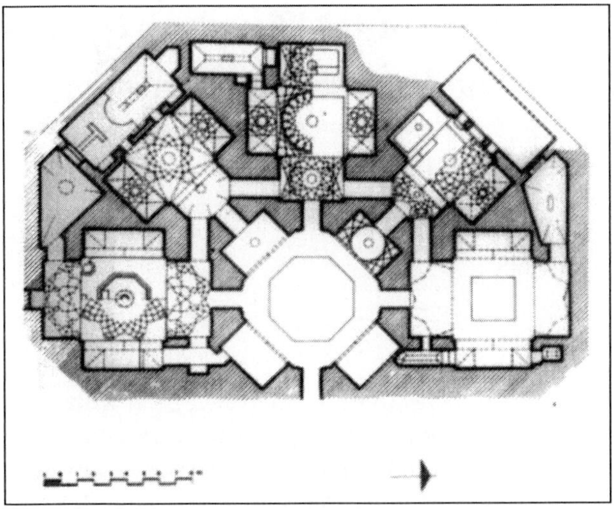

Noni-partite plan: *Hammam* of Khan-i Khanan, Burhanpur

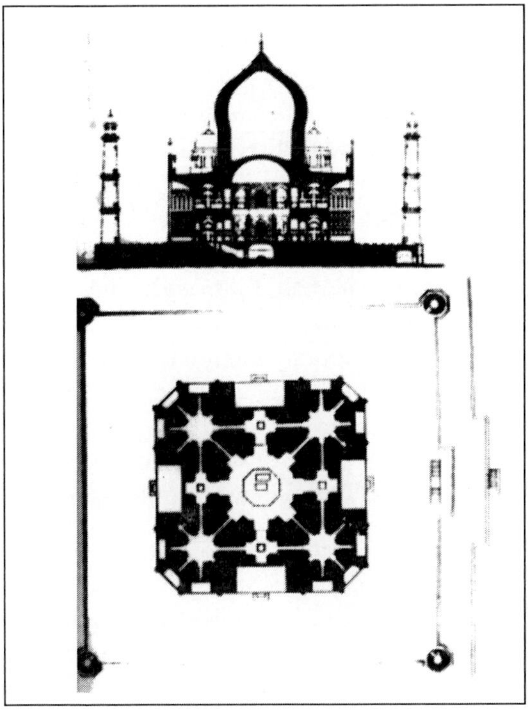

Noni-partite plan: Taj Mahal, Agra

Persian and Mughal Painting
The Fundamental Relationship

Som Prakash Verma

The Mughal emperors are known to have been great patrons of art. Their master artists initially hailed from centres of Persian art that flourished in Central and Western Asia, or worked under the influence of these schools. Babur (1526–1530), says of the famous Persian master painter Bihzad that 'His work was very dainty but he did not draw beardless faces well; he used greatly to lengthen the double chin (*ghab ghab*); bearded faces he drew admirably.'[1] Of another famous Persian painter, Shah Muzaffar, he writes that 'he painted dainty portraits, representing the hair very daintily'.[2] The *Zafarnama* MS (mentioned below), previously in Babur's collection, contained Bihzad's paintings.[3] Adle has noticed two artists (gilder-ornamentalists): Maulana Muhammad Muzahhab and Arayish Khan who were active at Babur's court.[4]

Humayun, while a fugitive, came into direct contact of the Persian painters active at Shah Tahmasp's court in 1544. A Persian wall-painting 'Shah Tahmasp entertaining Humayun' in the Chehel Sutun is a unique contemporary pictorial record of this event (Fig.1).[5] Humayun utilized his forced sojourn at the Safavid court to gather notable Iranian painters around him.[6]

Qazi Ahmad in his treatise on painters and calligraphers of Iran writes of Mir Musawwir and his son Mir Sayyid Ali:

> Mir Musauwir was a native of Badakhshan. He was a portraitist, working neatly, and made very pleasant and pretty images. When Humayun Padshah came to Iraq, he said to [Shah Tahmasp]: 'If that Sultan of the Universe gives me Mir Musauwir, I shall send him from Hindustan one thousand tumans as a present.[7]

Humayun himself, in his letter to the Khan of Kashghar,

Fig. 1. Shah Tahmasp entertaining the Emperor Humayun (*c.*1544–55). Safavid school. A wall painting in the Chehel Sutun. (After P.M. Sykes)

describes the skill of Dost Musawwir who was in his service in AH 959/ 1551–52:

> And also being sent is one paper leaf containing a picture drawn in black ink by the learned *Nadiru'l Asr* ('Unique of the Age') Maulana Dost Musawwir who has long been in our service, and in painting is the Mani of the age. In gilding he is unique in these times and in setting [margin] lines (*khat bari*) and writing has without doubt no equal.[8]

Earlier for some time, Dost Muhammad had left Humayun to join the service of Humayun's brother, Mirza Kamran at Kabul. Bayazid Bayat writes: 'At that time Mulla Dost was the leading painter [at the court] but he could not stay [in service] because His Majesty had given up wine. Without getting permission he had taken service with Mirza Kamran.'[9] The Persian painters who served Emperor Humayun, namely, Dost Musawwir, Maulana Yusuf, Maulana Dervish Muhammad, Mir Musawwir (or Mir Mansur), Mir Saiyid 'Ali and Khwaja 'Abdu's Samad, greatly contributed to the evolution of the Persianized school of Indian art which matured as the Mughal school.[10] We need hardly say that the great masters Mir Saiyid 'Ali (Safavid school) and Khwaja 'Abdu's Samad (Shiraz school), who are credited with supervising the earliest project at the Mughal atelier, the illustration of the *Hamzanama* (in twelve volumes, each containing a hundred large pictures executed on cloth), left their impress on the early Mughal school, and to a great extent formulated the narrative modes of the art of book-illustration in Mughal style. In this project fifty painters are said to have been employed under Mir Saiyid 'Ali, and later Khwaja 'Abdu's Samad.[11] The *Hamzanama* paintings vary considerably in style, several being purely Persian in drawing and colour. However, in general, non-Persian elements are quite pervasive, yet none of the *Hamzanama* illustrators can be described as being unfamiliar with Persian painting. Persian art became more prevalent at the Mughal atelier as several indigenous artists worked under the tutelage of Persian master painters. Khwaja 'Abdu's Samad was the foremost amongst them, becoming the teacher of many notable Indian artists. Daswant was one who received highest recognition rivalling his colleague, Basawan.[12] Abu'l Fazl writes in his *A'in-i Akbari*: 'From the instructions they received, the Khwaja's pupils became masters'.[13] He further writes, 'One day the eye of His Majesty fell on him [Daswant]; his talent was discovered, and he himself handed him over to the Khwaja. In a short time he surpassed all painters, and became the first master of the Age'.[14] Aqa Riza of Herat, at Jahangir's court,[15] was another painter from Iran, who like 'Abdu's Samad gave instruction in painting. According to an inscription on a miniature 'A saint reading a book' in the *Muraqqa'-i Gulshan* (Gulistan Palace Museum, Tehran), the woman painter Nadira Bano is described as the pupil of Aqa Riza.[16] Besides, painters from Bukhara, Kabul and Samarqand and other parts of Central Asia were active at the imperial Mughal studio: the most distinguished amongst them are Farrukh Beg Musawwir of Kabul, Muhammad Nadir of Samarqand and Farrukh Qalmaq (of Mongol origin).[17] Their style and technique set the trend in the Mughal atelier; it not only shaped the Mughal *qalam*, but also inspired the artistic expression in general for at least two centuries. Persian elements became an integral part of the Mughal painting: and no Mughal painting can be explained without a knowledge of the Persian schools of art. Even so, the Mughal school should not be considered a mere offshoot of the traditions of Persian painting; in fact it is always possible to distinguish a Mughal from a Persian painting.

The development of the Mughal school is credited to Akbar who showed great interest in manuscript painting under the impact of Persian book-illustration. Under Akbar, copies of Persian classics were made and manuscripts acquired from Persia were decorated with pictures and border paintings. Akbar is said to have received instruction in painting from Khwaja 'Abdu's Samad while he was a prince.[18] While 'Abdu's Samad's instruction might have made Akbar familiar with the technique of the Persian painter, it was probably also the mystical feeling which pervaded Persian art which synchronized with Akbar's own increasingly mystical temperament. He was quoted as saying:

> There are many that hate painting; but such men I dislike. It appears to me as if a painter had quite peculiar means of recognizing God; for a painter in sketching anything that has life, and in devising its limbs, one after the other, must come to feel that he cannot bestow individuality upon his work, and is thus forced to think of God, the giver of life, and will thus increase in knowledge.[19]

Subsequently, a good number of Persian classics, in prose and verse, as also historical works, became the objects of Mughal narrative art, Abu'l Fazl says,

> Persian books, both prose and poetry, were ornamented with pictures, and a very large number of paintings was thus collected. The *Story of Hamzah* was represented in twelve volumes, and clever painters made the most astonishing illustrations for no less than one thousand and four hundred passages of the story. The *Chingiznama*, the *Zafarnama*, this book [*Akbarnama*], the *Razmnama*, the *Ramayan*, the *Nal Daman*, the *Kalilah Damnah*, the *'Ayar-i Danish*, etc., were all illustrated.[20]

The surviving illustrated manuscripts of Akbar's court exceed the short list given by Abu'l Fazl.[21] Major Persian literary works, the *Diwans* of Hafiz, Amir Nizamuddin Hasan, Anwari and Amir Khusrau; the *Gulistan* and *Bostan* of Sa'di, the *Baharistan* of Jami and the *Nafhat'ul-Uns*, were repeatedly illustrated at Mughal atelier, the trend continuing until the end of Shah Jahan's reign (1626–56), though with less energy. During the seventeenth century the art of book-illustration became of secondary importance, giving place to album pictures, especially portraits.

In the depiction of Persian subjects, most Mughal painters followed Persian models, and mystical feelings accordingly find expression. But the Mughal artists interpreted the Persian themes in their own way. It is true that the Persian painters who sought employment at the Mughal atelier probably never consciously made a serious attempt to make their work conform to the style of the Mughal school.[22] However, the fact remains that though there was no such conscious effort to shift from one tradition to another; the Persian masters' work did not remain uninfluenced by the native traits of Indian art. Their encounter with the latter obviously marked the beginning of an integration of the two great oriental art traditions, Persian and classical Indian, at the Mughal studio.

Signs of this significant phenomenon in the art of India is visible even in some of the works executed during Humayun's time. Brand and Lowry emphasize the naturalism and interaction of figures in the miniature, 'Princes of the House of Timur' (*c.* 1555), and in several other miniatures of the *Khamsa* of Nizami (*c.* 1555) in the Lalbhai Collection, Ahmedabad.[23] These miniatures clearly differ from the more stylized composition of the Safavid school. In their opinion with this shift there evolved a coherent and dynamic mode of expression. Even the art of an orthodox Persian master-painter such as Khwaja 'Abdu's Samad bears evidence of a shift from strict Persian conventions during his stay at the Mughal atelier. The earliest miniatures ascribed to him show a strong affliation with the fifteenth–sixteenth century Tabriz school, where the crowded composition is filled with surface decoration. In his early works, we see a profuse use of decoration with geometrical motifs in the architectural columns; angels on doorways (spandrels); wall-paintings depicting lovers and hunting scenes; the sky painted flat in gold pigment occasionally embellished with flame-shaped clouds; dense craggy hills spread all over the landscape and trees (the chinar and cypress pre-eminently), all in the Persian tradition.[24] A change from this exclusive Persian tradition in 'Abdu's Samad's art, was first noticed by Ettinghausen. With reference to the miniature, 'Akbar presenting a miniature to his father Humayun' (datable before 1580), he says, 'the hustle and bustle of the subject, the realistic approach of the painter, and the way of showing attendants and servants outside the wall with the main scene behind, that is higher up in the painting, betray an Indian style' (Fig.2).[25] Ettinghausen's observation on another miniature of the same painter, 'Khusrau hunting with dogs and cheetah' (*c.* 1595–96) is equally relevant. He finds that 'the conception and the perspective of the rocky landscape, the spirited composition, and the costumes are in Akbari style, with

Fig. 2. Akbar presenting a miniature to his father Humayun (*c.*1580). By 'Abdu's Samad. Mughal school. *Muraqqa'-i Gulshan*, Gulistan Palace Library, Tehran.

Fig. 3.Khusrau hunting (1596–97). By 'Abdu's Samad. Mughal school. *Khamsa* of Nizami, British Museum and Library, London (Or. 12208), folio 82.

none of the pure Persian mannerism' (Fig.3).[26] This change in a Persian master's work would not have happened without a liberal attitude towards an integration of diverse trends of art at the royal atelier. Scerrato, indeed, sees the influence of the Indian traditions, particularly the vigorous realism of the Rajput school, on Mir Sayyid Ali's style whose work belonged to 'the classic' tradition of the Tabriz school. He writes: 'His figures acquired greater strength, at the same time retaining their characteristic and refined grace.'[27]

Of the Persian classics, the *Khamsa* of Nizami, the *Khamsa* of Amir Khusrau, the *Diwan* of Hafiz, the *Gulistan* and the *Bostan* of Sa'di the *Diwan* of Mir Sher 'Ali Nawa'i, the *Kalilah va Damnah*, the *Anwar-i Suhaili* (a Persian abridgement of the Sanskrit classic *Panchatantra*) and the *'Aja'ib al-Makhluqat* were illustrated both in the Persian and Mughal styles, but some of the Persian favourites that were repeatedly illustrated in Central Asia and Western Asia find little place in the imperial Mughal atelier. A case in point is the *Shahnama* of Firdausi, of which no illustrated manuscript from the Imperial Mughal school is known. An illustrated copy of the *Shahnama*, containing ninety miniatures, preserved in the British Museum, (Or. 5600) belonging to the late sixteenth-century Mughal school is, however, is supposed to have been prepared at the library of the Mughal noble 'Abdu'r Rahim Khan-i Khanan.[28] It may be noted here that the royal library of the Mughal Emperors had a famous illustrated copy of the *Shahnama* (Timurid school, *c.*1440) in its possession;[29] and in 1582, Akbar also had an illustrated Mughal copy of the *Shahnama*,[30] but, no such version seems to have survived.[31] As against this, classics, like the *Dastan-i Amir Hamza* (Tales of the Adventures of Amir Hamza), and the *Darabnama* illustrated at the Mughal atelier, are not known to have been illustrated in Persian painting. However, much before Akbar, copies of the *Dastan-i Amir Hamza* were illustrated in India in the period of the Sultanate.[32]

Of the historical chronicles, the *Zafarnama* and the *Jami'u't Tawarikh* (or *Chingiz nama*) were also illustrated at the imperial Mughal studio, where there was relatively a greater emphasis on the visual narration of historical literature. The *Tarikh-i Alfi*, compiled at the instance of Akbar in 1580,[33] was later illustrated with pictures in 1594.[34] Likewise, several illustrated copies of the *Baburnama*, translated into Persian in 1590 from the original Turki text, were prepared.[35] Undoubtedly, the illustrations of the greatest historical importance are those of the two official histories respectively of Akbar and Shah Jahan the *Akbarnama*[36] and the *Padshahnama*.[37]

The Mughals had Arabic and Persian books in the imperial library. The illustrated manuscripts not only had a decisive influence on the formation and development of the Mughal school, but also greatly influenced the themes and subjects of Mughal painting. Mention may be made of the famous manuscripts of the Timurid school, the *Shahnama* mentioned earlier and the *Zafarnama* (dated 1467–68), now preserved at Johns Hopkins University, Baltimore.[38] These remained in royal collections for a long period. A copy of Jami's *Yusuf va Zulaikha* (*c.* 1500) inscribed with the name of Mirza Kamran, a brother of the Emperor Humayun, has also survived.[39] It contains illustrations in the Bukhara style. Two other illustrated works of the Bukhara school, the *Bostan* of *Sa'di* (Fogg Art Museum, Harvard University, Boston), dated 1531–32[40] and the *Tuhfat al-Ahrar* (Chester Beatty Library, Dublin),[41] datable to 1544–45, which belonged to Prince Murad, were placed by Jahangir in the imperial library in 1605.

Paintings of the Bukhara style can also be seen in the Mughal manuscripts, *Duval Rani Khizr Khani* (dated 1567),[42] *Anwar-i Suhaili* (dated 1570),[43] and *Gulistan* (dated 1567–68).[44] These bear testimony to the close association of Mughal painting with the art of Transoxania and the interaction between the painters of these two art traditions.

The Mughal school whose distinct style emerged by 1580, even so bears identifiable marks of the impact of the Shiraz, Safavid, Timurid and Bukhara art traditions, especially in the case of manuscript painting. In the manuscripts of the *Anwar-i Suhaili* (dated 1570, School of Oriental and African Studies, London), the *Tutinama* (*c.* 1565–70, Cleveland Museum of Art, Cleveland) and the *Hamza-nama* (*c.* 1565–80) we find all the hallmarks of Persian painting: 'single-scene' representation, symmetrical composition, breaking up of a visual field into two or more units, figures extending beyond the picture frame, multiple views comprising a 'bird's-eye view', high horizon lines, objects shown only in part on the extreme outer margin of a visual field, patterning of architecture and tent hangings, and restricted movement. The very conception of illustration on pages of books in the codex form is clearly Persian.

In portraits the picturisation of faces in 'three-quarters view'—a characteristic trait of Persian art—dominated the Mughal portraiture at least still the end of the sixteenth century. Again, the technique described as *siyahi qalam* or *nim qalam* was brought to India by the painters from Transoxania. In this context, the role of Muhammad Nadir of Samarqand (active at the studio of Jahangir and Shah Jahan) is important. His works comprise a good number of portraits, executed especially in *siyahi qalam.*[45] This particular technique practised at centres such as Herat and Bukhara becomes noticeable in the Mughal school during the last phase of Akbar's region. In this technique, the whole drawing is finished with thinly-shaded black lines with minimal of modelling and very limited use of colours. The two miniatures ascribed to Shankar and Hiranand in the MS *Akbarnama* of c.1604 (British Museum, Or. 12208, folios 136a and 139a, respectively) offer the best examples.[46] At Akbar's atelier, the pictures finished in this technique are still rare, but it seems to have become popular during Jahangir's reign, especially in portrait painting. Anupchhatra, Chitarman and Hashim are amongst other seventeenth-century Mughal school who showed great fascination for the technique of *siyahi qalam.*[47] Numerous portraits ascribed to them were executed in this technique.

It is important to note that the Mughal margin-decoration in gold, which almost became an integral part of margin painting under Jahangir and Shah Jahan, bears traces of earlier Timurid traditions. Border painting in gold was introduced in the Timurid period and then extended from Bukhara to various Persian centres, and, thence to Mughal India.[48] It is characterized by fantastic rocky landscape with trees, bushes and plants often interspersed with fighting and hunting scenes and mythical birds and animals executed in 'gold', frequently with an application of undertone of green, red and yellow.

The linear art form, the use of limited brilliant colours and profuse embellishment of architectural columns in a jewel-like manner seen in the Mughal miniatures also reflect the Persian technique of line-drawing and the colour palette of Persian painters. Similar is the case of the abundant use of gold pigment and a propensity for ultramarine blue in Mughal painters' work. The latter inivites special attention since ultamarine is obtained by grinding calcined lapis lazuli (*lajward*), a costly semi-precious material imported from either Persia or Badakhshan. Its use in Persian and Mughal paintings further shows a relationship between these two traditions.[49] Significantly, in Mughal India, this stone was considered an article of royal gift. Bernier observes that the ambassadors from Khans of Balkh and Samarqand presented some boxes of lapis lazuli to Aurangzeb after his accession.[50] Tavernier mentions Badakhshan as the source of lapis lazuli.[51]

The use of ultamarine blue in Indian painting goes back, however, to ancient times, for example, in the frescoes at Ajanta and in the palm-leaf manuscript painting of eastern and western Indian schools.[52] It would not be out of place to notice here a bacchanalian scene from cave no.1 at Ajanta (*c.* 600) which shows foreigners (in all probability Persians as can be judged from their features and costumes) enjoying wine (Fig.4).[53] This points to the direct interaction of the Indian painters at such an early date with the Persian examples, not known, which would have served as a source of this scene. In another instance, the illuminated margins of the manuscripts *Kalpasutra* and *Kalkacharya-katha* (*c.* 1475) from the western Indian school show abundant borrowings in terms of form and subject from Persian painting.[54] These include floral meanders; scrolls and cartouches comprising figures of female dancers, warriors, angels, birds and animals, composite and

Fig. 4. A bacchanalian scene from Cave No. 1 at Ajanta (*c.* 600). Notice a distinguished looking foreigner (most likely a Persian) enjoying his drink.

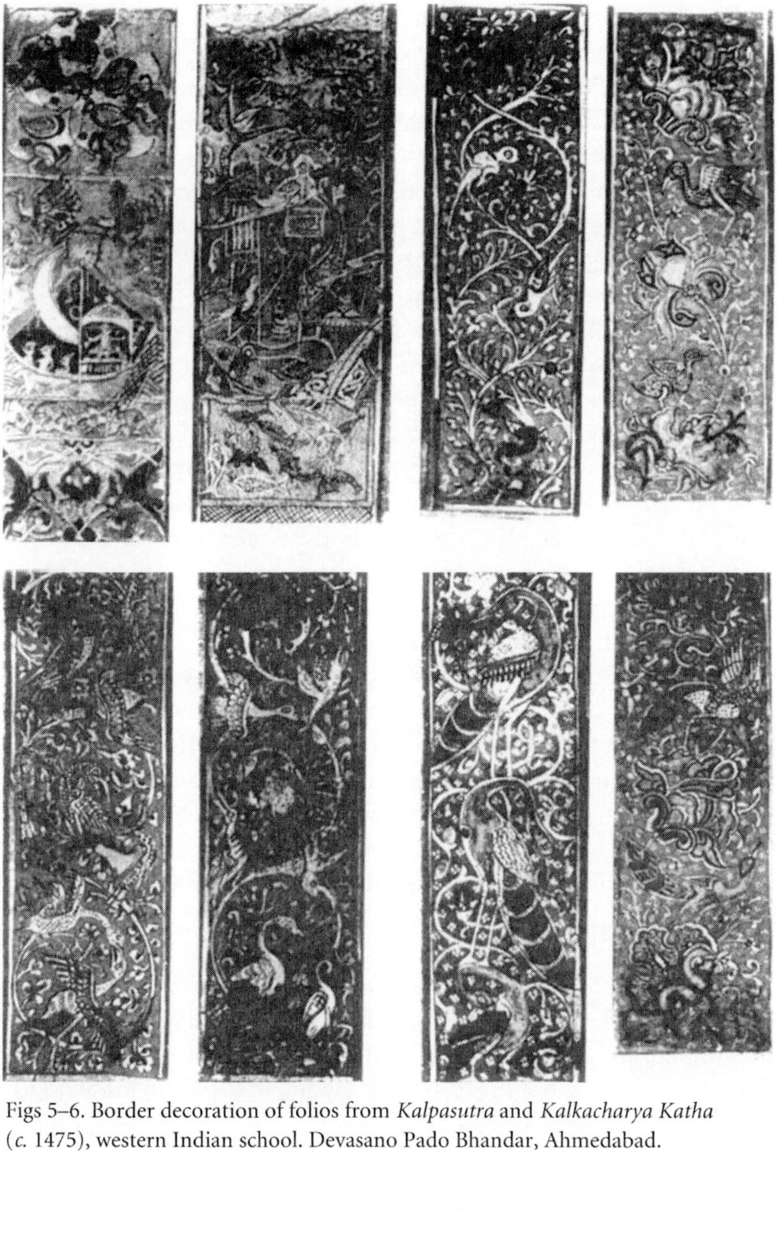

Figs 5–6. Border decoration of folios from *Kalpasutra* and *Kalkacharya Katha* (*c.* 1475), western Indian school. Devasano Pado Bhandar, Ahmedabad.

mythical forms of birds and animals, a variety of trees, and arabesques (Figs 5 and 6). The use of bright colours, lavish use of gold and luxuriance of detail in the illustrations were the main traits of Persian art acquired by the Indian artists of this school during the fifteenth century (after 1450).

We thus deal with a relationship which did not simply begin with Mughal painting, but had ancient and medieval antecedants. Mention may also be made of the illustrations of the *Nimatnama* and *Miftah ul Fuzula* (Mandu school, *c.* 1500–30)—representative of the Turkman school, that have been considered by some scholars as the source of some of Persian features absorbed in the Mughal painting.[55]

Further, a variety of geometrical motifs comprising an octagon or hexagon with a star, curvilinear forms and interlacing patterns seen in the Mughal paintings, too, bear testimony to their affinity with Persian painting.[56] The aureole, figure of the dragon, lion with flame-like lines emanating from its body, water monsters, and the mythical animals like phoenix, unicorn, etc., were also adopted in the Mughal paintings from Persian miniatures.

As with European pictures, copies of Persian miniatures were also often ordered by the Mughal Emperors. On a few known Mughal versions of Persian paintings, we can see ascriptions containing the name of the the Mughal artists who copied them. It seems that the works of the great Persian master, Bihzad, were of great attraction for the Mughal patrons. Nanha, a court painter of Akbar and Jahangir, is known to have copied at least two works of Bihzad: 'Masons at work' and 'Camel-fight' (Figs 7 and 8). The latter also contains Jahangir's autograph which shows that it was executed by Nanha in 1608–09 at his command.[57] Daulat copied the portrait of Maulana Abdur Rahman Jami (a poet) from an original by Bihzad.[58]

The works of Bihzad and other Persian artists were preserved in Mughal albums: Nasiruddin Album and *Muraqqa'-i Gulshan* (Gulistan Palace Museum, Tehran,[59] Jahangir Album (National Library, Berlin)[60] and Dara Shukoh Album (India Office Library, London).[61] It is also notable that the paintings of Persian origin were also put into Mughal manuscripts. The best example of this is the MS *Anwar-i Suhaili* (dated 1596–97) now preserved at the Bharat Kala Bhawan, Varanasi. At its beginning, it contains two full-page Persian miniatures of the sixteenth-century Safavid school.[62]

Jahangir in his account of the year 1619 gives a graphic

Fig. 7. Camel fight. By Bihzad, 'painted in his seventieth year'. *Muraqqa'-i Gulshan*, Gulistan Palace Library, Tehran.

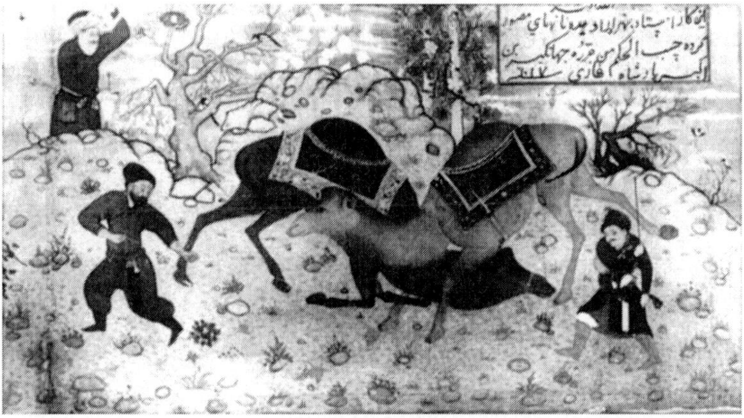

Fig. 8. Copy of Bihzad's Camel fight (above) by Nanha (1608–09). Mughal school. *Muraqqa'-i Gulshan*, Gulistan Palace Library, Tehran.

description of a Persian miniature ascribed to Khalil Mirza Shahrukhi brought from Isfahan by Khan 'Alam — a Mughal ambassador sent to Persia:

> Among them was the picture of the fight of Sahib Qiran (Timur) and Tuqtamish Khan, and the likenesses of him and his glorious children and the great Amirs who had the good fortune to be with him in that fight, and near each figure was written whose portrait it

> was. In this picture there were 240 figures. The painter had written his name as Khalil Mirza Shahrukhi. The work was very complete and grand, and resembled greatly the paint-brush of Ustad Bihzad. If the name of the painter had not been written, the work would have been believed to be his. As it was executed before Bihzad's date, it is probable that the latter was one of Khalil Mirza's pupils, and had adopted his style. This precious relic had been obtained from the illustrious library of Shah Ismail I, or had come to my brother Shah Abbas from Shah Tahmasp. A person of the name of Sadiqi, a librarian of his, had stolen it, and sold it to someone. By chance (the painting) fell into the hands of Khan 'Alam at Isfahan. The Shah heard that he had found such a rare prize, and asked it of him on the pretence of looking at it. Khan 'Alam tried to evade this by artful stratagems, but when he repeatedly insisted on it, he sent it to him. The Shah recognized it immediately he saw it. He kept it by him for a day, but at last, as he knew how great was our liking for such rarities, he – God be praised – made no request whatever for it, but told the facts of the case (about its being stolen) to Khan 'Alam, and made the picture over to him.[63]

Jahangir, who loved to have an authentic portrait of Shah Abbas (1587–1629), sent Bishandas, a master portrait-painter of his atelier, along with his ambassador Khan 'Alam to Persia. He writes:

> At the time when I sent Khan 'Alam to Persia, I had sent with him a painter of the name Bishan Das, who was unequalled in his age for taking likenesses, to take the portraits of the Shah and the chief men of his State, and bring them. He had drawn the likenesses of most of them, and especially had taken that of my brother, the Shah exceedingly well, so that when I showed it to any of his servants, they said it was exceedingly well drawn.'[64]

He further writes, 'Bishan Das, the painter, was honoured with the gift of an elephant'.[65]

A few such portraits have survived, which certainly bear witness to Bishandas's success as a portrait-painter (Fig. 9).[66] However, it is intriguing that this historic event remains unnoticed in the chronicles of Persia despite the fact that the Persian painters gave some importance to Khan Alam's embassy. At least two Persian versions of Bishandas's work 'Khan Alam with Shah Abbas I and courtiers in a

Fig. 9. Khan Alam, Ambassador of Jahangir, with Shah Abbas I and courtiers in a landscape. By Bishandas. Mughal school. Museum of Fine Arts, Boston.

landscape' painted by Muin Musawwir and Kheriat Khan are known.[67] Other two pictures on this theme belong to the Isfahan school, and are ascribed to Riza-i Abbasi. The first miniature is a signed work of this painter executed in 1632 at the command of Hakim Shamsa Muhammad (Fig. 10).[68] The second, of ground 1650, shows the figures of Khan Alam and Shah Abbas which are almost identical with Bishandas's work, and bears a doubtful ascription giving the artist's name, with signature (Fig. 11).[69]

In other portraits of Shah 'Abbas from the Mughal school Shah Abbas is shown with Jahangir: (i) 'Jahangir embracing Shah Abbas' and (ii) 'Jahangir entertains Shah Abbas' (here Asaf Khan (left) and Khan Alam are also shown standing in the foreground), were executed after 1619, i.e., after the return of Bishandas from Persia (Figs 12 and 13).[70] Jahangir invariably addressed Shah Abbas as his brother. The inscription in the second miniature above the figure of Shah Abbas also reads: *Shabih-i biradaram Shah Abbas* ('Likeness of my brother Shah Abbas'). The inscriptions given at top and bottom of the miniature further testify to the high esteem in which Shah Abbas was held at the Mughal court (Fig. 13):

> (Translation) Shah Jahangir and Shah Abbas, two brave young kings, representatives of God — they seized with joy the cup of Jam [i.e., the world]. Hearing the call to world dominion, both heroes and world conquerors are united in the purpose of bringing together all people as friends and brothers in peace. May God give them victory.[71]

The gifts exchanged between Jahangir and Shah Abbas often included the rare species of birds and animals. A falcon sent by Shah Abbas in 1619 is described thus by Jahangir:

> The Shahi falcon, too, got mauled by a cat owing to the carelessness of the Mir Shikar [of Shah 'Abbas]. Though it was brought to the Court, it did not live more than a week. What can I write of the beauty and colour of this falcon? There were many beautiful black markings on each wing, and back, and sides. As it was something out of the common, I ordered *ustad* Mansur, who has the title of *Nadir-ul Asr* ('Wonder of the Age') to paint and preserve its likeness. I gave the Mir Shikar Rs.2,000 and dismissed him.[72]

Fig.10. Shah Abbas and Khan 'Alam (*c.* 1632). Isphahan school. Signed: Riza Abbasi. St Pittsburg Collection.

Fig.11. Shah Abbas and Khan ʿAlam (*c.* 1650). Isphahan school.
Signed: Riza Abbasi(?) John Rylands Library, Manchester.

Fig. 12. Jahangir and Shah Abbas I shown united (*c.* 1620). By Abu'l Hasan. Mughal school. Freer Gallery of Art, Washington, D.C.

Fig. 13. Jahangir and Shah Abbas I seated on a throne (*c.* 1620). Mughal school. Freer Gallery of Art, Washington, D.C.

Fig. 14. Falcon (1619). Likeness of the bird – a gift from Shah Abbas I to Jahangir in 1619. By *Ustad* Mansur. Mughal school. Museum of Fine Arts, Boston.

A likeness of this bird executed by *Ustad* Mansur is preserved in the Museum of Fine Arts, Boston (Fig. 14).[73]

Jahangir never failed in acknowledging Shah Abbas's appreciation for rarities and in 1621 Jahangir included a zebra among the royal gifts sent to Iran.[74] Of his own curiosity aroused from seeing this animal Jahangir records in detail in his memoirs.[75] A picture of this animal executed by *Ustad* Mansur bearing Jahangir's autograph, dated 1621, has survived and, is lodged in the Victoria and Albert Museum, London.[76]

To sum up, the relationship of Persian and Mughal painting was profound as it emanated from common cultural traits, which went beyond sectarian affinities. Indian art did not remain uninfluenced by Persian painting which encompassed Central and Western Asia. The Mughal miniatures themselves thereafter travelled far and wide, and the most celebrated painter of Europe, Rembrandt (1606–69) not only had Mughal miniatures in his collection, but also tried his hand at working in the Mughal style.[77] Contemporary Persian painters too were influenced by Mughal painting, especially such as had been to India.[78] On the Indian side the assimilation and adaption of the Persian traits at the Mughal atelier was so quick that Robert Skelton feels amazed at the skill of the indigenous painters unfamiliar as they were with the refined Persian style, adopting so soon the tenets of that school.[79] Yet their effort was one of creative adoption not slavish imitation. They infused into their enterprise not only certain interests and techniques of the Indian tradition, but also a concern for realism and a sense of humanism, which surely derived in part at least from that figure of unequalled greatness, Jaluddin Muhammad Akbar. With an infusion, again, from Renaissance painting, what was brought into being now was a style of painting that has its own place in the history of world art. It is not to be forgotten, however, that the achievement was, still in essence, one of the many products of the cultural collaboration between India and Iran that has subsisted in the past.

Notes and References

[1] *Baburnama*, tr. A.S. Beveridge, New Delhi (rpt) 1979, p. 291.

[2] Ibid.

[3] T.W. Arnold, *Bihzad and His Paintings in the Zafar Namah MS.*, London, 1930; M. Brand and G.D. Lowry, *Akbar's India: Art from the Mughal City of Victory*, New York, 1985, pp. 91, 150, pl. on p. 89. It contains six double-page illustrations by Bihzad. See also S.P. Verma, 'Illustrations of Persian Classics in Persian and Imperial Mughal Painting' in *The Making of Indo-Persian Culture, Indian and French Studies* (ed.) Muzaffar Alam and Francoise 'Nalini' Delvoye, New Delhi, 2000, pp. 226–27.

[4] Chahryar Adle, 'New Data on the Dawn of Mughal Painting and Calligraphy', in Alam and Delvoye, *The Making of Indo-Persian Culture*, pp. 190–91.

[5] Published: P.M. Sykes, *History of Persia*, London, 1915, pl. facing, p. 248.

[6] Sukumar Ray, *Humayun in Persia*, Calcutta, 1948, the most comprehensive study of Humayun's journey to Persia, seems to overlook this aspect altogether, except for two casual references (pp. 42, 67n.).

[7] T. Minorsky, *Calligraphers and Painters: A Treatise of Qazi Ahmad son of Mir Munshi circa A.H. 1015/AD 1606)*, Washington, 1959, p. 185. See also Verma, *Mughal Painters and Their Work, A Biographical Survey and Comprehensive Catalogue*, New Delhi, 1994, pp. 276–77, pl. XLII.

[8] Bayazid Bayat, *Tadhkira-i Humayun wa Akbar* (1585) (ed.) M. Hidayat Hosain, Calcutta, 1941, p. 69.

[9] Ibid., p. 66.

[10] Ibid., pp. 67–69, 117; see also V. Minorsky, tr., *Calligraphers and Painters: A Treatise by Qadi Ahmad, Son of Mir Munshi (circa AH 1015/AD 1606)*, Washington, 1959, p. 180.

[11] Mulla 'Ala ud-Daula Qazwini, *Nafa'is al-Ma'asir*, MS. no. 920/45, dated 1573, Maulana Azad Library, Aligarh Muslim University, f52a.

[12] Abu'l Fazl, *A'in-i Akbari*, Vol. I, English translation H. Blochmann, Calcutta, 1868 revd edn, 1927; rpt, 1989, Vol. I, p. 114.

[13] Ibid.

[14] Ibid.

[15] Jahangir, *Tuzuk-i Jahangiri or Memoirs of Jahangir*, English translation, A. Rogers (ed.) H. Beveridge, London, 1909–14, (rpt), 2 Vols in 1, Delhi, 1989, Vol. II, p. 20.

[16] S.P. Verma, *Mughal Painters and Their Work &c.*, p. 309.

[17] Ibid., pp. 147–52 and 297–9.

[18] M.A. Muqtadir, *Catalogue of the Arabic and Persian Manuscripts in the Oriental Public Library at Bankipore*, Vol. VII, Patna, 1921, p. 18.

[19] *A'in-i Akbari*, p. 115.

[20] Ibid.

[21] Verma, *Mughal Painters and Their Work, &c.*, pp. 32–33.

[22] R. Skelton, 'Indian Painting of the Mughal Period', in B.W. Robinson, *et al.*, (eds), *Islamic Painting and the Art of the Book*, London, 1976, p. 234.

[23] Brand and Lowry, *Akbar's India*, pp. 24–27.

[24] Verma, 'A court-painter of sixteenth century: Khwaja Abdu-s Samad', *Roopa-Lekha*, Vol. LIX, New Delhi, 1987, p. 53.

[25] R. Ettinghausen, 'Abdu-s Samad', *Encyclopedia of World Art*, Vol. I, Mc Graw Hill, London, 1958, p. 19, pl. 16.

[26] Ibid., p. 20, pl. 17.

[27] U. Scerrato, 'Mir Sayyid Ali', *Encyclopedia of World Art*, Vol. X, Mc Graw Hill, London, 1968, p. 190.

[28] A.K. Das, *Mughal Painting During Jahangir's Time*, Calcutta, 1978, pp. 78, 95.

[29] M. Brand and G.D. Lowry, *Akbar's India*, pp. 82–92, fig.10.

[30] 'Abdul Qadir al-Bada'uni, *Muntakhabut-t Tawarikh*, Vol. II, English translation, W.H. Lowe, Calcutta, 1924; rpt, Delhi, 1978, Vol. II, p. 329.

[31] See Skelton, 'Indian Painting', pp. 237–38, plate 31.

[32] J.P. Losty, *The Art of the Book in India*, London, 1982, p. 46, plate 33, and p. 63.

[33] *A'in-i Akbari*, pp. 113, 498.

[34] Verma, 'A Court Painter of Sixteenth Century', p. 32. See M.M. Haq, 'Discovery of a portion of the original manuscript of *Tarikh-i Alfi*, written for the Emperor Akbar', *Islamic Culture*, Vol. V, No. 3, Hyderabad, October 1931, pp. 621–30.

[35] Abu'l Fazl, *Akbarnama*, Vol. III, English translation, H. Beveridge, Calcutta, 1897–1939, rpt, Delhi, 1989, p. 862. For illustrated copies of the *Baburnama*, see Verma, 'A Court Painter of Sixteenth Century', p. 32.

[36] Verma, 'A Court Painter of Sixteenth Century', p. 32; also his 'Aspects of Paintings in the British Museum Manuscript of the *Akbarnama*', *Lalit Kala*, No. 27, 1993, pp. 20–29; Geeti Sen, *Paintings from the Akbarnama*, New Delhi, 1984.

[37] Verma, 'Seventeenth Century Illustrated Manuscript of the *Padshahnama*', *Roopa-Lekha*, Vol. LVIII, 1986, pp. 56–62.

[38] T.W. Arnold, *Bihzad and His Paintings in the Zafar-Namah* MS., London, 1930; Brand and Lowry, *Akbar's India*, pp. 91, 150, Plate on p. 89. It contains six double illustrations by Bihzad.

[39] Losty, *The Art of the Book*, p. 74. It contains six miniatures in the Bukhara style.

[40] S.C. Welch, *The Art of Mughal India: Painting and Precious Objects*, New York, 1963, p. 70.

[41] L. Binyon, J.V.S. Wilkinson and B. Gray, *Persian Miniature Painting*, London, 1933, plate LXXXI (B); Brand and Lowry, *Akbar's India*, p. 94.

[42] Losty, *The Art of the Book*, p. 86 ('In composition these miniatures owe something to Bukhara prototypes').

[43] J. Seyller, 'The School of Oriental and African Studies *Anvar-i Suhayli:* the Illustration of a *de Luxe* Mughal Manuscript', *Ars Orientalis*, Vol. XVI, 1986, p. 120, fig.5; Verma, 'Origins of the Mughal Painting', in A.J. Qaisar and S.P. Verma, (eds), *Art and Culture: Felicitation Volume in Honour of Professor S. Nurul Hasan*, Jaipur, 1993, pp. 58–59.

[44] Losty, *The Art of the Book*, p. 86.

[45] Verma, *Mughal Painters and Their Work & c.*, p. 297 (miniatures nos. 4, 7, 9 and 11).

[46] Verma, 'Aspects of Paintings in the British Museum Manuscript of the *Akbarnama*', p. 25.

[47] Verma, *Mughal Painters and Their Work & c.*, pp. 61–62, 121–22, 170–75.

[48] Kuhnel, E. and Goetz. H., *Indian Book Painting*, London, 1926, p. 45.

[49] Moti Chandra, *The Technique of Mughal Painting*, Lucknow, 1946, pp. 25–7. P. Brown, *Indian Painting under the Mughals*, AD *1550 to* AD. *1750*, Oxford, 1924, p. 189.

[50] Bernier, *Travels in Mughal Empire*, (ed.), A. Constable, London, 1891, p. 118.

[51] Travernier, *Travels in India*, tr. V. Ball, Vol. II, London, 1889, p. 156.

[52] V.A. Smith, *A History of Fine Art in India and Ceylon*, Bombay (n.d.), p. 90; A. Ghosh (ed.), *Ajanta Murals*, New Delhi, 1967, p. 54; Karl Khandalavala and Moti Chandra, *New Documents of Indian Painting—a reappraisal*, Bombay, 1969, pp. 34–35.

[53] Smith, *A History of Fine Art*, pl.86(B); Ghosh, *Ajanta Murals*, pl. XLI.

[54] Khandalavala and Chandra, *New Documents*, pp. 32–37, pls. 6–7, figs. 59–96.

[55] Ibid., p. 62. See also, Verma, 'Origins of the Mughal School of Painting', pp. 62, 70.

[56] Verma, *Art and Material Culture in the Paintings of Akbar's Court*, New Delhi, 1978, p. 39, pl. XXVII 'In the illustrations, the designs appear in different settings and forms, e.g., the geometrical and ornamental patterns and the stylized version of natural objects—a legacy of the Persian *qalam*. The motifs, five-petalled flowers with two stems on each end, a lotus with elongated petals, interlaced with curvilinear leaves in onion-shaped units are quite common. Geometrical designing is based on the repetition of such units as a triangle, a square a rectangle, lines and semi-circles. The hexagon, however, is the most commonly used'.

[57] See Asok Kumar Das, *Mughal Painting During Jahangir's Time*, Calcutta, 1978, p. 127, pls 30–31; Verma, *Mughal Painters and Their Work & c.*, p. 517, no. 36.

[58] Das, *Mughal Painting*, p. 185, also see p. 127. See Verma, *Mughal Painters and Their Work & c.*, p. 128, no. 11.

[59] Godard, Y.A., 'Un album de portrait des princes Timurides de l' Inde', *'Athar-e Iran, Haarlem*, Vol. II, 1937, figs. 67, 94.

[60] Kuhnel and Goetz, *Indian Book Painting*, pp. 51–52; Das, *Mughal Painting*, pp. 127–29.

[61] Falk, Toby and Archer, Mildred, *Indian Miniaturese in the India Office Library*, London, 1981, p. 78, pls. on p. 390.

[62] Verma, '*Anwar-i Suhayli*—an illustrated manuscript of Akbar's Court', *Roopa-Lekha*, Vol. XLIV, New Delhi, 1977, pp. 18–19.

[63] *Tuzuk-i Jahangiri*, tr. A. Rogers and ed. H. Beveridge, Delhi, second (rpt), 1994, Vol. II, p. 116.

[64] Ibid., pp. 116–17.

[65] Ibid.

[66] Verma, *Mughal Painters and Their Work & c.*, pp. 111–13 (miniatures nos. 11–14).

[67] A.K. Das, 'Bishandas', *Chhavi* (ed.) Anand Krishna, Banaras, 1971, p. 189, n. 41.

[68] F.R. Martin, *The Miniature Painting and Painters of Persia, India and Turkey*, London, 1912, Vol. II, pl. 160.

[69] B.W. Robinson, *Persian Paintings in the John Rylands Library*, London, 1980, p. 342 (no. 1581), pl. XV. For the reproduction of Bishandas's painting, see Verma, *Mughal Painters and Their Work & c.*, pl. 10.

[70] For their reproductions, see Milo C. Beach, *The Imperial Image, Paintings for the Mughal Court*, Washington, D.C., 1981, pls on pp. 74, 78.

[71] Ibid., p. 170.

[72] *Tuzuk-i Jahangiri*, p. 108.

[73] Verma, *Mughal Painter of Flora and Fauna, Ustad Mansur*, New Delhi, 1999, pp. 114, 47, pl. VIII.

[74] *Tuzuk-i Jahangiri*, p. 201.

[75] Ibid.

[76] Verma, *Mughal Painter of Flora and Fauna & c.*, pp. 51, 120–1, pl. XV.

[77] T.W. Arnold and L. Binyon, *The Court Painters of the Grand Moghuls*, Oxford, 1921, pp. 35–36; Ettinghausen, *Paintings of Sultans and Emperors of India in American Collections*, Delhi, 1961, pp. 3–4.

[78] See O. Akimushkin in: C. Adle and I. Habib (eds), *History of Civilizations of Central Asia*, V, Paris, pp. 578–79.

[79] Skelton, *Indian Painting*, p. 233.

Sharing the 'Asiatic Mode'?
India and Iran

Shireen Moosvi

When the French physician Francois Bernier visited India in 1659–67, he sent letters home in which he elaborated an idea that later germinated a succession of larger concepts of 'oriental history' and influenced broader notions of historical processes in general. Bernier began with the then widely held view that the ruler was the owner of the soil in countries like India, Iran and Turkey. He regarded this (and not religion or race or other factors) as the basic cause of the economic and cultural retardation of these countries. He argued that these countries had no institution of private property and so no incentives for progress. Instead of private property, there was only state property, which gave rise to another disastrous phenomenon: the periodic transfers of territorial charges, which impelled the governors, to excessively exploit the peasants and artisans, leading to the ruin of agriculture and crafts.[1]

The apparent rationality behind Bernier's thesis made it (along with Chardin's account of Iran)[2] a very persuasive reading for eighteenth century Encyclopaedists in France and for Marx in the nineteenth century. It seemed to European readers of his letters that countries like India and Iran must have shared certain essential institutions between them, which made them part of a zone of backwardness, the Orient. Karl Marx could even speculate on whether there was an Asiatic Mode of Production, with its twin pillars of Village Community and Oriental Despotism.[3] Today one may sense an excessive simplification in the broad generalization, though the theory itself does not for this reason fall.

This paper addresses itself to only a part of the question. How far did Mughal India and Safavid Iran have common features in the spheres of agrarian, economic and political structures? Undoubtedly, the two countries were culturally closely connected. Persian was the administrative language in both empires; and Mughal India seemingly produced more books in Persian than Iran itself. The Iranian 'diaspora' in the sixteenth and seventeenth centuries was especially directed to India, so that it looks, as if the Mughal and Safavid empires belonged in many respects to the same cultural world.

In both Mughal India and Safavid Iran the economy was mainly based on agriculture and other economic activities were of rather secondary importance. But such general features could be shared with even many European countries at the time. We, therefore, need to look at the structure of rural society in both countries to establish the degree of similarities. In India in spite of the presence of village community, an institution that has been subjected to theoretical analyses from Hegel to Maine, agriculture was undertaken on the basis of individual peasant cultivation. The village community did not imply a communal ownership of land or the cooperative cultivation. As Baden Powell suggested, the community was mainly concerned with the collection of land-revenue. Throughout the Mughal period, the village remained the basic unit of revenue assessment and collection and, in spite of repeated protestations by the imperial administration, the distribution of revenue burden was left to the village headmen or the dominant village strata (the *muqaddams*, the *panch*) who utilized the privilege for their own benefit to the detriment of the lower peasantry (*reza-riaya*).[4] The village community was thus considered by Irfan Habib 'a framework for sub-exploitation'.[5] The village maintained a common pool out of which the land-revenue was paid and the perquisites of village officials such as the *patwari* (village-accountant), and other common expenses of the village were met. The caste system, with its hereditary division of labour and hierarchical system of caste-dominance, also played a part in shaping the village organization. Village craftsmen and 'servants', to whom customary payments were made by individual peasants, often also held small tax-free lands, in lieu of which they were obliged to serve the village and its inhabitants. The villagers themselves were divided into two major classes, the caste peasantry and the 'menial' strata, who mainly worked as labourers on the fields of the caste-peasants.[6]

Individual peasant cultivation prevailed in Iran as well. There too the unit of tax assessment and collection was the village, with the apportionment (*bunicheh bandi*) of the collective assessment of the village (*bunicheh*)[7] left to the village headmen (*kadkhuda*) and elders (*rish-i safed*). The *kadkhuda* was also responsible for the collection of tax and local administration. He was the link between the villagers and the officials of the state or the assignee.[8] Whether this rural *elite* was hereditary or formed out of assertive individuals is difficult to determine. The peasantry was stratified, just as in India, and the presence of an 'underclass of landless' labourers, perhaps quite large in number has also been detected.[9] There are references of deductions made from the harvest for the payments to village craftsmen and others.[10] Where rural Iran saw an area of collective activity, not found in India, was in the realm of irrigation. In India, with the ordinary well providing access to ground water in most areas, the irrigation was normally based on the resources of individual peasants. In Iran, the making of underground water channels (*qanat, kariz*), a necessity for agriculture in all arid areas, was an enterprise far beyond the means of individual peasants. It is often difficult to establish how the *qanats* were originally dug, but in areas outside great landowners' estates, the distribution of water from these channels was certainly based on village custom.[11] While watermills appear to have been a common phenomenon, these were often set up by individuals, though in some cases instructions were issued for their maintenance and repairs to officials.[12] On the whole, villages in Iran seem to have existed as distinct social units even more than in India. As Lambton notes: villages in Iran 'appear to have enjoyed a considerable degree of autonomy and to have been organized as self-contained and virtually self-governing communities.'[13] The autonomy of the village communities, seems however, to have been circumscribed under the Safavids by the *tuyuldars* or assignees, who increasingly interfered in its administration.[14]

Another feature more specific to Iran was its extensive pastoral sector, which called for an organization more analogous to the tribe than to the community. The tribes (especially the 'Qizilbash' tribes of Diyarbakr) remained politically important till Abbas I (1588–1629) shifted the reliance for military support from tribal forces to newly recruited non-tribal regiments of 'slaves'. Still, pastoral Turkmen from Khorasan continued to be important in Iranian forces (Nadir Shah came from such a Turkmen tribe). The tribal system, being used not only for protecting the tribes' pastoral grounds, but also for providing military levies, had an hierarchical organization[15] that had hardly any parallel in India. While the pasture-lands were held collectively, the herds were owned by individual (extended) families. On the top were tribal chiefs appropriating the major part of the surplus produced by the pastoralists, while only a smaller (an uncertain proportion) was claimed by the state in the form of a tax on animals. At the lowest rungs was an underclass of tribesmen who owned either flocks too small for their subsistance or none at all and thus worked as shepherds under the more prosperous tribesmen.[16] It was the tribal chiefs or their subordinates who carried out cattle trade on a large scale and earned considerable profits. There was a tendency among such leaders to settle in the towns, but not to the extent of breaking ties with their kinsmen.[17]

Looking at the village community as it existed in both countries, we can thus see two essential differences: the absence of the hereditary castes in Iran; and the much larger presence there of pastoral tribalism. For the rest, however, the relationship between the village and the state seems to have been remarkably similar in India and Iran.

In India the organization of craft production too was considerably influenced by the caste system. Essentially, the caste system reserved particular occupations to particular persons on a hereditary basis, and thus served the same purpose as guilds were so often designed to serve in Western Europe. Max Weber had thus held that the caste system by preventing inter-occupational mobility was a great obstacle to economic growth. This has been contested in an important essay by M.D. Morris,[18] and the point that there were sufficient elements of flexibility within the system has been underlined by Irfan Habib.[19] There was also possibility of common action undertaken on the basis of caste: each caste had a headman (*chaudhuri*) in the towns, and there are reports of a caste council (*mahajan*), who decided on occasions on such collective action as closing the shops (*hat-tal*)—although such information comes generally from material about commercial castes.[20] In Iran a corresponding place seems to have been occupied by the very highly organized craft guilds, most of which had their own bazars. These guilds worked under the control of some kind of guild court consisting of the elders (*rish-i safed*) and presided over by the head of the guild known as the *kadkhuda, rais* or *bashi* who was chosen normally by the members but by custom tended to become hereditary.[21] Besides presiding over the guild court to decide the disputes among the members of his guilds,[22] the *kadkhuda* was responsible along with the elders (*rish-i safed*) for *bunicheh bandi*, that is, apportionment of the tax that an official (*naqib*) fixed in the first quarter of every year.[23] Different guilds were given tax exemptions from time to time as inscriptions put mainly on the mosques indicate.[24] Under the Safavids, guilds of carpenters and masons received exemption from tax but in return were obliged to render services to the king by which, in Tavernier's opinion, they fully compensated the state.[25] The heads of the guilds that were exempted from taxes, though normally chosen by the members, were formally appointed by the king and so carried more authority.[26]

Neither the caste in India, nor the guild in Iran, substantially affected the nature of craft production. The craftsmen's household remained the unit of production and thus women's labour was equally utilized in India and Iran. In India women worked even at building sites. They here engaged in breaking stone, pounding bricks into rubble, preparing bitumen-cement and staining and mixing lime and carrying the mortar up to the masons. To judge from their dresses as shown in paintings, both Hindu and Muslim women were engaged in such work.[27] In Kashmir 100,000 women are said to have been engaged in shawl-making in *c.* 1820.[28] In Iran, Budaq Qazvini offers an eye witness account (1527–77) of how in the houses of Shiraz 'the wife is a copyist (*katib*), the husband a miniaturist (*musawwir*), the daughter an illuminator (*muzahhib*) and the son a binder (*mujjalid*)'.[29] Thus, though women had no share in caste or guild decision-making, their labour was fully used both in the households and outside in non-agricultural work.

Marx gave a central position to the State in the economy of the Asiatic Mode, generalizing from both Bernier and the known fact of tax-rent equivalence that the English East India Company had inherited from the Mughals.[30]

There is little doubt that whether in India or Iran, wherever the state obtained the necessary power, the fiscal right of the state approached the full surplus (or economic rent), even in fertile lands, often exceeding the permissible level of *kharaj* (land tax) in Muslim law, namely, half the produce. Abu'l Fazl (*c.* 1595) makes this statement especially in respect of 'Iran and Turan', that is, the Safavid empire and the Uzbek khanates.[31] Yet an almost similar assertion is made about the Mughal land-tax in India early in the eighteenth century by a theological writer out to prove that this tax was not *kharaj*, but *ujra* or rent.[32]

The concentration of such enormous fiscal resources in the hands of the state, which gave rise, as we have seen, to the sovereign being seen as the universal land-owner, naturally raises the question whether we are in the presence here of 'Oriental Despotism'.[33] This is not the place to enter into a debate on the nature of Oriental Despotism, or its place in Marx's concept of the Asiatic Mode of Production, first mentioned by him in 1859.[34] It is not very clear how matters would be different if one applies the term 'Tributary Mode of Production' to an economy containing such a rent-receiving state.[35] The real question is whether a rent-extracting state would throttle trade and urban development or by generating 'induced' trade (for transfer of agrarian surplus to towns) help maintain a money economy and promote urban growth. It can be shown that Marx's different statements can lead to both conclusions.[36] While Marx's own contradictory views are important in indicating the futility of reconstructing unreal frameworks on the basis of a selection of his statements, as in the case of Wittfogel,[37] what is surely crucial is not simply to pursue theoretical deductions, but to see what our historical evidence tells us in respect to both the nature of the pre-colonial state and its economic environment in India and Iran.

We need, perhaps, to ask, first, how far the fiscal collections actually went into the hands of the state and to what purposes these were used. In different forms both the Mughal and the Safavid empires had systems of apanages, by which the sovereign alienated his fiscal and often administrative rights to members of the nobility temporarily or for all time. The most rigorous system appears to have been followed in the Mughal empire, where the *jagirs* (fiscal territorial assignments) were temporary and constantly subject to transfer, and did not involve any rights of civil or judicial administration.[38] In Iran under the Safavids, the *tuyul* was a land assignment either in lieu of salary or conditional upon maintaining a military contingent, while the *suyurghal* was an outright grant for all time with practically no conditions attached. It seems that in Iran the *suyurghal* grants were far more extensive than in the Mughal empire,[39] while the *tuyuls* tended to become hereditary and so continuously reduced the royal domain, the *khalisa*.[40]

Such assignments compel us to consider the social situations of those who held them. If the assignees had rural seats, and they and their retainers lived off the land, the room for induced trade could have been quite limited. Much work has been done on the composition of the Mughal nobility in India. The results as summed up in the most authoritative study are that immigrants from Iran and Turan (the Uzbek territories) accounted for 51.5 per cent. of the high nobility (*mansabdars* of '1,000' and above) in 1656–57 and 51.6 per cent during the period 1658–76.[41] Such immigrants were least likely to spread out among villages. The *jagirdars* who came from within the limits of the Empire, such as Afghans, Rajputs, local Indian Muslims, and others, too were hardly ever posted even temporarily in their ancestral localities (unless they were hereditary chiefs as well, the total area under the chiefs being fairly limited);[42] and, when transferred, they tended to move with their entire establishment (*sarkar*) to the new location.[43] In such circumstances any fixed rural associations were out of the question. Farming of revenues, a practice which grew in the eighteenth century, did not alter the situation very greatly, since the *jagirdars* and their retinue then lived away from the *jagir* and depended on remittance of the tax collections in money form. In either circumstance, induced trade must have been the consequence. By a statistical study from the detailed fiscal and administrative data available for the Mughal empire in *c.* 1595, I found that over 50 per cent of the revenues flowed to the urban sector;[44] and this would well accord with the structure of the *jagir* system, and the induced trade it might be expected to generate.

When we turn to Safavid Iran, we discover that in the beginning a very important and influential part of the nobility consisted of the Qizilbash Turkmans who came from the eastern parts of Asia Minor, a territory largely lost to the Ottomans after Chaldiran (1514). Their language being different from the Persian, it is unlikely that the Qizilbash commanders and soldiery could have spread out in the Iranian villages: perforce they had to be town- or camp-based.[45] In time as the Qizilbash dominance declined, or was forcibly restricted under Shah 'Abbas I (1587–1629), it was partly replaced by the royal *ghulams* or slaves, recruited mainly from the Christian lands of the Caucasus, and so were largely in the same position of aliens in Iran proper.[46] The nobility began to be persianized, but this does not mean that it was necessarily ruralised, since the Persian nobility came largely from the bureaucracy (*mirzas*) rather than the rural land-owners. The Shi'ite religious establishment, which received large grants of land, was also mainly Persian (overlooking the immigrants from the Jabal 'Amil in Lebanon).[47] The institutionalization of religious instruction in Iran and the emphasis on Shi'ite shrines, tended to give an urban orientation to Shi'ite clergy; and it is, therefore, likely that the taxes in large *auqaf* estates created for its benefit were not collected in a way different from those in the apanages of town-based potentates.[48]

The structure of the state in both India and Iran was closely connected with the growth of towns. Bernier's account of India in the seventeenth century had been widely understood to mean that in India and other eastern countries, the towns were mere nomadic encampments, though it can be legitimately argued that this was not really what the French traveller had intended to say.[49] One, however, wonders how the large archaeological remains of Mughal cities and several eighteenth- and nineteenth century descriptions of these could have been ignored by writers who continue to speak of Mughal Indian towns as camp cities. To go by the reported populations of certain towns, Agra in 1630s had a population of 660,000; and Lahore had around 250,000 inhabitants in 1581.[50] Urban populations in Iran were similarly considerable, though in the early 1820s in Iran the population of Meshed was estimated at only 32,000, and Shiraz at 40,000.[51] But by then the economic decline of Iran had long set in.

Towns ever since they came into existence have depended on the rural surplus for their existence, and in this the state had a crucial role to play. The rulers' dependants and retainers and craftsmen, labourers and servants, who met their consumption and service requirements, had to be fed and clothed from resources obtained from the countryside through tax-generated trade. There was also the long-distance trade by which goods of high value were conveyed. This brings us to the character of the mercantile classes in the two countries.

The mercantile classes were miscellaneously composed. There were semi-nomadic communities like Banjaras in India, transporting goods of bulk on pack oxen,[52] and Afghan tribesman who combined horse-breeding with extensive horse-trading.[53] But trade in finer goods was conducted by other communities, who combined the commerce with banking and other credit operations. From their headquarters at Julfa in Iran, the operations of the Armenians almost spanned the whole of Eurasia.[54] The Banyas and Khatris, often called Multanis, not only controlled much of long distance commerce and banking in India, but also in Iran.[55] The mercantile practices in the two countries were so similar that the Banyas in Iran conducted their business as bankers and brokers almost the same way as in India.[56]

The relationship between the rulers and merchants was not necessarily antagonistic, either in India or Iran. For Mughal India there has been much debate over the treatment of merchants by the rulers; Moreland's description of the oppressions from which the merchants suffered, has been widely contested.[57] With regard to merchants in Iran, Malcolm had this to say early in the nineteenth century:

> The merchants of Persia are a numerous and wealthy class; and there is no part of the community that has enjoyed, through all the distractions with which this kingdom has been afflicted, and, under the worst princes, more security, both in their persons, and property. The reason is obvious: their traffic is essential to the revenue . . .[58]

If, then, there was a system of despotic states in India and Iran different from other state-forms, then such despotism was not necessarily inimical either to towns or to trade, despite many violent upheavals and individual acts of oppression.

What we find in both countries then, is a strong state with claims on the land-tax limited only by the ability to collect; a large amount of induced trade to sustain an impressive degree of urbanization; and a generally 'free market' economy with only few restrictions imposed by caste or guild. This could be an 'Asiatic Mode', but only if we have a definition of it that is fundamentally different from what has been presented, following Marx, by writers like Karl Wittfogel.[59]

Notes

1 Francois Bernier, *Travels in the Mogul Empire 1656–68*, tr. Irving Brock and A. Constable, revised by V.A. Smith, London, 1916.

2 Sir John [Jean] Chardin, *The Travels of Sir John Chardin into Persia and the East Indies*, 2 Vols, London, 1686; *Sir John Chardin's Travels in Persia*, 2 [further] vols, London, 1720 (rpt), 1927. These English versions comprise Vols I–IV of the 10-volume edition of Chardin's entire original work, pub. M.A. Langles, Paris, 1811.

3 Cf. Daniel Thorner, 'Marx on India and the Asiatic Mode of Production', *Contributions to Indian Sociology*, IX (December 1966) for a survey of the development of Marx's views on the Asiatic Mode. See also further on, below.

4 See Akbar's minister, Todar Mal's memorandum of 1582 (Abul Fazl, *Akbarnama*, B.L. MS. Add. 27,247, 332bf.) and Aurangzeb's *farman* to Rasikdas, Art. IV, tr. S. Moosvi in: *Medieval India*, I (ed.) Irfan Habib, Delhi, 1992, pp. 197–208.

5 *Cambridge Economic History of India*, Vol. I (ed.), Tapan Ray Chaudhuri and Irfan Habib, Cambridge, 1982, p. 249.

6 For a detailed discussion of village community, see Irfan Habib, *Agrarian System of Mughal India*, Delhi, 1999 (revised edn), pp. 123–68.

7 Ann K.S. Lambton, *Landlords and Peasants in Persia*, Oxford, 1953, p. 425.

8 Ibid., 122, Amin Banani, 'Reflections on the Social and Economic Structure of Safavid Persia at its Zenith' *Iranian Studies*, IX, Massachusetts, 1978, p. 97

9 John Foran, 'The Modes of Production Approach to Seventeenth Century Iran', *International Journal of Middle East Studies*, 20, USA, 1988, p. 353.

10 Ann K.S. Lambton, *Islamic Society in Persia*, Oxford, 1954, p. 829.

11 Lambton, *Landlords and Peasants*, p. 117.

12 Ibid., p. 101.

13 Lambton, *Islamic Society in Persia*, p. 8.

14 Ibid., p. 9.

15 Bert Franger, 'Social and Internal Economic affairs', in: *Cambridge History of Iran*, Vol. 6 (ed.), P. Jackson and L. Lockhart, Cambridge, 1986, p. 497.

16 Foran, 'The Mode of Production Approach', p. 352.

17 *Cambridge History of Iran*, Vol. 6, p. 497.

18 M.D. Morris, 'Values as an Obstacle to Economic Growth in South Asia', *Journal of Economic History*, XXVII (December 1967), pp. 588–607.

19 Irfan Habib, *Essays in Indian History: Towards a Marxist Perspective*, New Delhi, 1995, pp. 216–18.

20 Cf. ibid., pp. 256–57 and notes.

21 Jean Chardin, *Voyages* (ed.), L. Langles, Paris, 1811, VI, pp. 119–20. Tavernier (*Voyages en Perse*, pp. 224–25) reports that the leader of the carpenters' guild (*najjarbashi*) of Isfahan was an Armenian who retained his position in spite of being a non-Muslim against the normal practice of having only Muslims as heads of the guilds. He did not change his religion though the king asked him to do so, 'he still only suffered in his office by the excellency of his genius and protection of the king' Lambton, *Islamic Society*, pp. 22–23.

22 Chardin, VI, p. 119, thus called the *kadkhudas* police judges of the trades in small affairs, see Lambton *Islamic Society*, p. 21, from which I take this.

23 Anonymous, *Tazkirat al-Muluk* (ed. and translated), V. Minorsky, London, 1943, p. 82.

24 Lambton, *Islamic Society*, p. 25.

25 Tavernier, *Voyages en Perse*, p. 239, Quoted from Lambton, *Islamic Society*, p. 25.

26 Chardin, VI, p. 119, (Lambton *Islamic Society*, p. 22).

27 Geeti Sen, *Paintings from the Akbarnama*, Calcutta, 1984, Plates 31 and 61, showing women at work at the buildings of Agra and Fatehpur Sikri under Akbar (1556–1605).

28 W. Moorcroft and G. Trebeck, *Travels in the Himalayan Provinces, &c.* (ed.), H.H. Wilson, London, 1837, Vol. II, p. 174.

29 Cf. O. Ahimushkin and A. Ivanov, 'The Art of Illumination', *The Art* of

Book Illumination, 1979, p. 50. I owe this reference to Professor Chahryar Adle, Paris.

30 Cf. Karl Marx, letter of 2 June 1853, in: Marx and Engels, *Selected Correspondence 1846–1895* (ed.), Dona Torr, Calcutta, 1945, p. 58; also *Grundrisse*, tr. with foreword by Martin Nicolson, London, 1973, pp. 472–73.

31 Abu'l Fazl, *Ain-i Akbari* (ed.), Blochmann, Calcutta, 1867–77, I, p. 293: 'In Iran and Turan, since olden times one-tenth [of the produce] has been taken [as tax], but often it happens that it exceeds one half, and out of the habit of cruel-mindedness it does not seem disreputable.'

32 See Irfan Habib, *Agrarian System of Mughal India*, pp. 123–4, for a discussion of the views of Qazi Muhammad A'la.

33 Marx, *Capital*, III, English translation, Moscow, 1959, pp. 771–72: 'Should the direct producers not be confronted by a private landowner, but rather, as in Asia, under direct subordination to a state which stands over them as their landlord and simultaneously as sovereign, then rent and taxes coincide, or rather, there is no tax which differs from this ground-rent.' Marx does not use the word 'Oriental Despotism' here.

34 Marx, *Preface to A Contribution to the Critique of Political Economy* in Karl Marx and Frederic Engles, *Selected Works*, I, Moscow, 1950, p. 329.

35 I take Chris Wickham 'The Uniqueness of the East' in T.J. Byres and Harbans Mukhia (ed.), *Feudalism and Non-European Societies*, London (1985), as an uncompromising spokesman for the applicability of this concept, originally proposed by Samir Amin.

36 Cf. Irfan Habib, *Essays in Indian History: Towards a Marxist Perspective*, 1995, pp. 22–29, for quotations from several passages from Marx, of dual (and contradictory) import mentioned here.

37 Karl A. Wittfogel, *Oriental Despotism—a Comparative Study in Total Power*, New Haven, 1957.

38 See Irfan Habib, *Agrarian System*, 1999, pp. 298–341, and Athar Ali, *The Mughal Nobility Under Aurangzeb*, (second edn) Delhi, 1997, pp. 74–94, for excellent studies of the system.

39 In the Mughal empire moreover the grantees were largely a town-based class (Moosvi, *The Economiy of the Mughal Empire, c. 1595: A Statistical Study*, Delhi, 1987, pp. 164–68).

40 Lambton, *Landlords and Peasants*, 1953, pp. 107–19.

41 Athar Ali, *The Mughal Nobility* 1997, pp. xvi–xvii. The results are worked out from Athar Ali, *The Apparatus of Empire: Awards of Ranks, Office and Titles to the Mughal Nobility*, Delhi, 1985, a uniquely detailed work.

42 On the area under chiefs see Habib, *Agrarian System*, 1999, pp. 222–29.

43 Ibid., p. 330.

44 Shireen Moosvi, *Economy of the Mughal Empire*, 1987, pp. 272–95.

45 On the tension between the Qizilbash and the Persian elements, see Banani, *Iranian Studies*, 1978, pp. 89–91.

46 Minorsky, *Tazkiratul Muluk*, pp. 14–19; M.G. Hodgson, *The Venture of*

Islam, Vol. III: *The Gunpowder Empires and Modern Times*, Chicago, 1974, pp. 32–33.

47 Cf. Lambton, *Landlords and Peasants*, 1953, pp. 126–27, for large grants of land to the religious classes. On the scholars (*'ulama*) from Jabal 'Amil, see Abisaab, 1994. The 'Amili immigrants 'shared no fundamental or ethnic ties with any of the military and aristocratic elites of Safavid society' (ibid., pp. 121–22).

48 On the growing emphasis on shrines, see S. Arjomand, *The Shadow of God and the Hidden Imam*, Chicago, 1984, pp. 169–70.

49 Bernier, *Travels in Mughal Empire*, 1916, pp. 219–20, 251–52, 281–90. For the understanding obtained from Bernier of Indian cities being just military camps, see Marx, *Selected Correspondence of Marx and Engels, 1846-1895* (ed.), Dona Torr, Calcutta, 1945, pp. 57–58.

50 Cf. Irfan Habib, *Agrarian System*, 1999, pp. 83–84.

51 James B. Fraser, *Narrative of a Journey into Khorasan in the Years 1821–1822*, London,1984, pp. 169, 463–64.

52 Irfan Habib, Merchant Communities in Precolonial India', in James D. Tracy (ed.), *The Rise of Merchant Empires*, Cambridge, 1990, pp. 372–79.

53 Irfan Habib, 'Evaluation of the Afghan Tribal System', in *Papers from the Aligarh Historians Society*, Aligarh, 2001, p. 33.

54 F. Mauro, 'Merchant Communities, 1350–1750', in: James D. Tracy, *The Rise of Merchant Empires*, Cambridge, 1990, pp. 270–74, for a summary account.

55 For the Banyas and Khatris see I. Habib, 'Merchant Communities', pp.379-88. For the Banyas in Iran see J. Chardin, *The Travels of Sir John Chardin into Persia and the East Indies*, London, 1686, pp. 98–101, etc.

56 On this there is much information in Chardin. From a document of 1684, included in a collection of Persian documents in Biblioteca Apostolica Vaticana, Vat. Persiano 33, 37af., it transpires that a Hindu (*muti' al-Islami*) Baddu was acting as the shroff (*sarraf*) or banker to the Dutch Company at Isfahan, and two Banyas (whose signatures appear in Nagari characters) acted as brokers for two Muslim merchants of Shiraz.

57 W.H. Moreland, *India at the Death of Akbar*, London, 1920, pp. 50–52, 264–65. For a contrary view, see especially Habib, *Essays in Indian History*, pp. 223–29.

58 John Malcolm, *The History of Persia from the Most Early Period to the Present Time*, London, 1815, II, p. 430.

59 Karl A. Wittfogel, *Oriental Despotism*. Cf. Foran, 'The Modes of Production Approach', pp. 348–50.

Global Networks of Exchange, the India Trade and the Mercantile Economy of Safavid Iran

Najaf Haider

This paper attempts to analyze the structure and dynamics of the mercantile economy of Iran within the framework of global trade networks, movements of merchandise, money and commercial groups. The information I wish to present is organised around three axes which, between themselves, comprehend major aspects of Iranian mercantile economy as it shaped within the territorial nexus of Eurasia in the sixteenth and seventeenth centuries.

Trade routes and Entrepôts

The first axis is geography, which determined the pattern of trade routes and Iran's place within the global network of exchange. Iran occupied an intermediate position between two highly commercialized zones of the medieval world: the Levant in the west and India in the east. Iran's strategic location provided it with an opportunity to stretch its arms in opposite directions while acting as a big market as well as a transit point for long distance trade between Europe and the East. Raphael Du Mans, a seventeenth-century French Jesuit and resident of Isfahan, graphically summarized Iran's unique geographical locale by calling it a carava-*sarai* with two doors, one opening to the west and the other to the east.[1]

Iran's location was buttressed by a complex network of primary and subsidiary trade routes, which criss-crossed its vast plateau and linked a string of cities serving as entrepôts for regional and international trade between the Mediterranean and the Indian Ocean. From Tabriz, Baghdad or Isfahan as the centre, four sets of routes ran in four different directions. The western route went to Syria and Anatolia, notably to the cities of Aleppo, Bursa and Izmir; the northern (Transcaucasian) route, to Russia via the western Caspian coast, and to Poland and the Baltic; the eastern road, to Central Asia via Mashhad and to the plains of northern India via Qandahar; and the southern route, for the port cities of the Persian Gulf—Basra, Hurmuz and Bandar Abbas. Jean Baptiste Tavernier, the peripatetic French jeweller, offers the best description of all the four routes which he took, at one time or another, between 1631 and 1665; and other European travellers and merchants have documented the individual route which they traversed in order to reach India from Iran.[2]

Time and Transaction Costs

The choice of a route by a merchant was dictated essentially by three considerations: the length of travelling time, safety of the self and of goods and money in possession, and transaction costs. Time was an important element, insofar as any round trip could claim the best part of the year and goods had to be purchased and kept ready for shipment in the right season. However, time had to be weighed against security and costs. The shortest land route between Isfahan and Agra, via Bhakkar and Ajmer, which took two months on horseback including compulsory halting days, was least frequented by caravans due to the difficult passage through Thar desert, whereas the most preferred was the much longer route via Qandahar, Kabul and Lahore, which took double the time.[3] Similarly, of the two routes between Aleppo and Isfahan the most popular was the one via Mosul and Hamadan (two months) because it was less burdened with transit dues in comparison with the shorter route via Baghdad (over one month). On the latter route, merchants had to make payments to the local Amir of Ana as well as Ottoman state officials.[4]

Political Unification and Protection: The Rise of the Sindbad Route

If we take a long-term view of the routes which gave the Mediterranean world its access to the Orient, it would appear that the Persian Gulf route to India had begun to decline from thirteenth century onwards due to the Mongol invasion and destruction of Baghdad (1258) as well as the devastation by the Mamluks of the port towns on the Syrian coast, in possession of the Crusaders (1291). The Papal prohibition, after the fall of Acre in the same year, also influenced the choice of trade routes by European merchants. Crushed between Mamluks and Mongols the celebrated Sindbad passage gave way to its

Red Sea rival (running via Tor, Aydhab and Aden) which was to dominate the east-west trade for many centuries to come. The numismatic evidence of a large coin hoard discovered at Broach (Gujarat) suggests that while Iran's trade with India continued in some measure, the Levantine link with the Red Sea definitely deepened in terms of the volume of money and merchandise exchanged with India.[5]

The Persian Gulf route began to regain importance in the sixteenth century, and a number of factors were responsible for the revival of its fortune. The first was the political unification of trade routes from Aleppo to Basra. Between 1516 and 1538 AD, the Ottomans made major territorial gains in Syria, Iraq, Yemen and Iran. The protection provided *en route* to merchants by the Ottoman state was an important factor behind the transformation of Aleppo into the biggest Levantine entrepôt, and an increase in the biannual caravan traffic to Basra and Hurmuz.[6] We have the testimony of a Portuguese observer, of the 1540s, that the Ottoman authorities instructed caravans (*qafilas*) of 'spice merchants' starting from Basra to take the Baghdad route to Aleppo (rather than the shorter Damascus road) not only because they were concerned for the safety of the merchants but also because they wanted to tax the passing merchandise.[7] Descriptions of the functioning of the Aleppo-Basra route in the second half of the sixteenth century as provided in Turkish and European sources present a picture of the port city as a very busy place on the eve of the departure of these caravans. In the months of April and September, an assembly of five to six thousand merchants, swelled by a host of service providers, gathered in time to unload Indian goods arriving from Hurmuz and to make preparations for a long overland journey. Each time, a caravan of at least 4,000 camels left Basra for Aleppo, headed by a *karvanbashi* and accompanied by a big posse of Ottoman soldiers and their commanders.[8] One such caravan had 120 merchants, mostly Iranians from Basra and Baghdad, ten Indians and a few Venetians.[9]

At Aleppo, a settlement of Indian merchants was soon established, and when the Venetians shifted their factories from Damascus to Aleppo in the middle of the sixteenth century, the idea was to get a closer to the principal route to obtain Indian merchandise as well as to get a ready access to the silk mart of Tabriz.[10]

On the southern terminus of the Levantine-Persian Gulf axis, these developments were complemented by a different set of circumstances triggered by a shift in the Portuguese policy of controlling the movement of ships in the Indian Ocean. The policy initially advocated by Lisbon to monopolise the spice trade required military intervention in the commercial circuits of the Indian Ocean. Such an option imposed serious constraints on the resources of the *Estado da India.* The pressure of Ottoman presence in the Red Sea and the interests of the Luso-Indian officials in sharing revenues raised from an open trade gradually revealed the practical limitations of the priority set by Lisbon.[11] Consequently, the thrust of the Portuguese policy now shifted towards the development of Hurmuz as a competing entrepôt to Ottoman controlled Aden and Jiddah. This was reflected in the incorporation of the Hurmuz customs into the revenues of the Portuguese state (AD 1543), the continuation of the official blockade of the Red Sea and the imposition of an additional tax (*curujo*; Ar. *kharaj*) on all merchandise leaving for Ottoman Basra.[12]

While the effect of this new policy on the Red Sea trade was marginal, the protection provided by the Portuguese to the merchant convoys (for which an additional tax of one per cent was levied) helped Hurmuz to develop into the biggest emporium of eastern products in the second half of the sixteenth century. The rise and fall in its fortune offered a fair indication of the mercantile activities in the Persian Gulf as well as along the north-bound land routes.[13]

The Hurmuz trade, as reflected in customs records, exhibits a steady upward trend from 1524 to 1543, a fall between 1544 and 1548 during the Portuguese siege of the Diu, a rise in 1549–51, and a substantial rise from 1574 (of the order of 50 per cent).[14] It appears that the Portuguese policy of opening up the sea and extending protection was bearing fruit.

The Decline of Hurmuz and the Rise of Bandar Abbas

After a sustained increase spanning six decades, the Hurmuz trade began to show signs of decline from 1610 onwards, and an annual loss of revenue suffered by the Portuguese (60,000 *pardaos*) began to be reported from 1611.[15] The Safavid campaign to regain Hurmuz and the mounting pressure of the English and Dutch attacks on Portuguese shipping may account for the loss of trade on this route.[16] As a result, the currents of trade turned away from Hurmuz to the caravan route linking Tabriz and Isfahan with Lahore and Agra through Qandahar. The annual traffic on this parallel route, eclipsed earlier by the sea passage to Hurmuz from Sind and Gujarat, had reportedly grown four times by 1615 from the previous level. In his letter from Isfahan, Richard Steel (1615) mentioned the passing of 12,000 to 14,000 camel loads of merchandise from Lahore to Isfahan every year while, according to him, not more than 3,000 camels travelled on this route in times of peace.[17] A reduction in maritime traffic and a corresponding increase in caravan trade was noted by Portuguese observers as well who suggested measures to rectify the perceived imbalance by bringing the merchants back to the sea.[18]

Regular movement of ships in the Persian Gulf appears to have resumed in the 1630s, and continued, with brief interruptions, throughout the seventeenth century. The settlement of the conflict over Hurmuz and the rise of Bandar Abbas contributed to the successful renewal of this branch of Indian Ocean commerce.[19] Unlike the island of Hurmuz, the port of Bandar Abbas had convenient connections with the Iranian hinterland, and it seems that the decision to fortify its customs house was part of a comprehensive plan by the Safavids to harness its potentials in developing their overseas trade.[20] Figures for customs revenue derived from Bandar Abbas bear this out. The customs revenue of Hurmuz in 1610 was 3.6 metric tons of silver, but the corresponding figure for Bandar Abbas in 1643 was 5.5 metric tons, 6 metric tons in 1654 and 7 metric tons in 1657.[21]

There was a third development, now on the Indian side, which contributed favourably to the expansion of the Persian Gulf trade, viz. the consolidation of Mughal polity and economy. India was the biggest trading partner of Iran in this period, and the figures worked out from a detailed inventory of Indian exports to Iran in the 1630s suggest that the total value of the merchandise was over 32 metric tons of silver.[22] Compared to the estimated silver value of merchandise brought to Hurmuz at the turn of the seventeenth century (36 metric tons), the share of India appears to be quite overwhelming (89 per cent). Out of the total value exported from India in the 1630s, over 55 percent came from the Mughal empire (17.76 metric tons of silver). The integration of Gujarat into the Mughal empire and the unification of trade routes between the western coast and inland regions provided the institutional and material basis for the rise of Surat as the biggest emporium of the east from the second quarter of the seventeenth century.[23] The territorial expansion of the empire linked the entrepôts and hinterlands in a single network of commodity exchange, fiscal remittances, and currency circulation. While the fiscal and monetary policies of the

Mughal state increased the volume of transactions, abolition of transit dues, reduction in customs and mint charges, and absence of legal restrictions on capital accumulation, business methods (including usury), and the movement of artisans and professionals created a favourable commercial climate for merchants and manufacturers to operate in a competitive market.[24] An expansion in the scale of commodity production and exchange in the Mughal empire had important implications for the long distance trade of the participating regions.

Movement of Merchandise and Money

Merchandise movement in Safavid Iran was of two types: one in which goods produced in Iran were exported to Ottoman Turkey and Europe in the west and to India in the east. The other type represented goods in transit, those moving in the long distance network from India to the Levant for which Iran worked essentially as a redistributive centre.

The biggest item of export to the west was silk. Different varieties of silk were cultivated in the Caspian provinces of Gilan, Shirvan, Mazandaran and Georgia, and other minor centers of production such as Khurasan. Although figures for annual silk production vary around an average quantity of 8,000 bales (1 bale = c. 98 kgs) estimated for the seventeenth century, one thing is quite certain, almost half or three quarters of the produce was exported, while the rest was consumed domestically in the manufacture of silk and gold thread cloth and velvet.[25] Bulk of the silk produced in north-western Iran, particularly the two great varieties of Gilan (*sha'rbaf* and *kadkhuda pasand*) was exported to Turkey from Tabriz either through Armenia (Julfa, Yerevan, Erzerum), where Georgian silk also joined in, or through Aleppo. A smaller quantity was sent northwards to Moscow via Astarkhan. Central Asia and India were recipients of raw silk mainly from Khurasan. Indian merchants often bought this variety at Lahore on their return journey from Iran in order to invest part of their cash into commodities, although there are indications that by the middle of the seventeenth century they were finding it less and less profitable.[26] The silk brought to the Persian Gulf ports from Shirvan (called *ardas* by the Europeans) and from Lahijan (called *kharwar*) via Isfahan was increasingly bought by the Dutch and the English merchants in the first half of the seventeenth century. Later it had to compete, rather unsuccessfully, with the Bengal and Chinese silk in the markets of Amsterdam and London.[27]

The European participation in silk trade was limited and geared to their plan of raising extra cash from regional markets for purchases made in India and South-east Asia. It is true that spice and textile markets were open to them, but money markets in London and Amsterdam were not big enough to meet the constant mercantile yearning for liquid capital. Therefore, even when the Safavid state tried to encourage the alternative sea-borne silk route to Europe to end its dependence on a hostile neighbour, the Levant still remained the most popular destination due to the presence of a well-organized Armenian and Turkish mercantile network in this region.

The Iranian silk was a highly marketable product and therefore could be obtained mainly for cash. The silk trade was reckoned by the dealers as a monetised business, and the European merchants always reminded their financiers at home that only a regular supply of money could sustain seasonal purchases of silk in the local market. It is therefore not surprising to find the penetration of merchant capital right to the primary level of production. Silk was cultivated in a tripartite arrangement between peasants, landowners and merchants who advanced interest-free loans to finance sericulture and obtain supplies.[28] This kind of forward trading, known as *pish-furush*, is reminiscent of the Indian system of *dadani* where money was advanced to cultivators and manufacturers, particularly in textile and indigo sectors, to secure supplies in time and at pre-fixed prices.[29]

Iran exported to the Levant and India other items as well though these were much less important in comparison with silk. There were three star items of export to India: the dye-root, madder (*runas*), cultivated around Ardebil and Astarabad and used as a red and crimson dye for Indian cotton; bitter almonds (*badam*), which circulated as small change in western India; and cavalry horses employed in the armies of the Vijayanagara and Mughal empires and the Deccan kingdoms.[30] Wine from Shiraz, despite prohibitions, was quite popular both at home and abroad. While one quarter of it was consumed in courtly circles, the rest was sent to Europe and India in glass bottles manufactured in the factories of Shiraz and neatly arranged in cases after being wrapped in straw. It appears that mostly Jewish, Armenian and Zoroastrian merchants were engaged in the wine trade, while

Indian and Iranian merchants dabbled in the sale of rose water, jam and marmalade, and fruits preserved in vinegar.[31]

Goods imported by Iran largely consisted of those destined for the Levantine and European markets, a portion of which was retained for domestic consumption. In addition, Iran obtained supplies of two types of textiles from England: broad-cloth, a thick densely woven tweed preferred in bright colours, and kersies, a narrow, coarse and light coloured woolen cloth. In the seventeenth century, factors of the English East India Company (EIC) tried hard to push the two products into Iran to boost their purchasing power, but they had to compete fiercely with the Armenians who imported similar varieties from the Levant. Other items included camlets and mohairs from Turkey, hides from Russia, and non-precious metals, and clocks, mirrors, paintings, maps and dogs from Europe for elite consumption.[32]

Of goods in transit, the share of India was the largest. We have already noticed that in the 1630s, the estimated silver value of total imports from India, by land and sea, was 32.23 metric tons or 2.83 million rupees (1 rupee = 175.3 grains of fine silver) of which the contribution of the Mughal empire was 17.76 metric tons or 1.56 million rupees.[33] Textiles, indigo (*nil*), sugar and spices formed four major groups of merchandise regularly exported to Iran from India. There was a great variety in cotton fabrics brought from India (*guldar*, *rupak*, *atlas*, *dhoti*, *nirma*, etc.) manufactured mostly in villages and towns of Gujarat, Sind, Agra, Allahabad (*mandil* and *alacha* of Mau and Banaras) and Bihar (*amriti* and *alacha* of Lakhawar and Baikunthpur).[34] This was indicative of the gradual integration of rural commodity production with the growing sphere of monetised exchange and long-distance trade. The best variety of Indian indigo was exported from Bayana (*suba* Agra) mainly by the land route (hence the term Lahori used for it) except during the days when Shah Jahan (1628–59) instituted a monopoly and the resultant high price cost the product its competitive edge in the markets of Isfahan. The variety produced at Sarkhej, Sehwan and western Deccan, regions lying closer to the coast, took the sea route.[35]

The Long Journey of American Silver

The most enduring feature of global commerce in medieval times was the movement of money from the West to the East. Europe and the regions of the Ottoman empire had very little to offer to their eastern trading partners in merchandise, and the balance of payment, leaning heavily in favour of Iran and India was settled with silver and gold coins and bullion. The transmission of precious metals into Iran broadly followed the pattern of commodity exports along the major trade routes outlined above: Iranian silk and Indian goods moved westwards, and European money travelled eastwards. It is therefore not surprising that merchant caravans and ships were more vulnerable to attacks from highway robbers and pirates on their outward journey when they carried treasure.[36]

Devoid of domestic sources of precious metal supply, the export surplus which Iran earned in the form of money from silk trade or by handling goods in transit, became an important source of monetization of its economy. This aspect of the Iranian mercantile economy was of critical importance for the working of the Safavid fiscal system. In the 1560s, an English merchant noted with despair that Shah Tahmasp (1524–76) never agreed to barter his silk for European cloths and preferred to sell it to any merchant who paid him in money.[37] Describing the export of Shirvan silk to Turkey, the same merchant also observed that Turkish merchants brought 'great store of silver… Dollars [and] Hungarie Ducket. . . . And having monie in readiness at the time of the yeere, they buy silke the better cheape, when the country men bring it first to be solde.'[38] We do not know how much of this money Iran was able to retain since it ran an adverse balance of trade with India and had to part with an unknown portion of its domestic stock in order to pay for the imports.

In another, less circuitous, stream, money touched or crossed the frontiers of Iran on its way to the Indian Ocean to match the reverse remittance of merchandise. Du Mans has documented (AD 1660) both the long and the short haul of monetary movements across the three continents in his characteristic style:

> Persia is like a big caravansarai which has only two doors, the one on the side of Turkey by which silver from the West enters; [in the form of] piastres which come from the New World to Spain, from there to France . . . [and] leaving France by Marseilles they enter into Turkey, from where they arrive here [Iran], where one recasts them into abbasis. . . . Some carry their piastres to the Indies. The other door of exit is Bandar Abbas or Gombroon in the Persian Gulf for going to the Indies, to Surat, where all the silver of the world unloads,

and from there as [if] fallen in an abyss, it does not re-emerge.[39]

This general description of the exodus of New World silver, in the shape of Mexican and Spanish dollars or *reales of eight* (also called *piastres* from the image of pillars inscribed on the obverse), is corroborated by quantifiable contemporary estimates. In the 1590s, the export of bullion from Hurmuz was estimated at two million *crusados* or 42 metric tons of silver per annum.[40] In 1645, the director of the Dutch East India Company (VOC) at Surat reported that the amount of silver and gold annually imported from Iran by the maritime merchants of that city was to the tune of 22.7 metric tons of silver or 2 million rupees.[41]

Our authorities for these statistics rarely offer a clear break up of gold and silver components of bullion consignments. However, there can be little doubt that from *c.*1550 to *c.*1660, it was silver which dominated the flow of treasure in different forms, notably *reales of eight*, Dutch and German dollars (*rijks* and *lion*), Ottoman *ghurush* (often counter-struck reales and dollars) and, of course, *laris*, *shahis* and *abbasis*. The European companies also delivered bar silver of standard fineness which fetched a higher price than the specie particularly in Iran and the Mughal empire. Coined money, as legal tender, always circulated at a premium, i.e. at a value higher than its weight in fine bullion, on account of brassage and seigniorage. This premium was lost when foreign coins were melted and restruck in Safavid and Mughal mints. This factor of loss undermines recent explanations of international bullion flow premised on the argument of arbitrage (metals gravitating towards high price markets). As we shall see, mono-metallic arbitrage (silver carrying a higher value in eastern markets due to the direction of its flow) became operational only when foreign coins were accepted as legal tenders in local markets. Similarly, the hypothesis of bi-metallic arbitrage (silver flowing to the east and gold, in exchange for it, to the west) is also problematic since there is no empirical basis for the suggestion that gold was flowing in the opposite direction.

Mint Policy, Debasement and Bullion Flows

All major entrepôts and emporia of the Levant and Iran, centres of export of Iranian and Indian goods, were also recipient of foreign currencies and bullion. Some of them were important mint towns, such as Tiflis, Yerevan, Tabriz, Qazvin, Isfahan, Basra and Hurmuz, where monetary metals could be converted into coins.[42] These mints were tightly controlled by monetary authorities and often ran on the basis of fiscal rather than monetary considerations. The Safavid state, like all medieval regimes, believed that money was wealth and the possession of gold and silver brought prosperity to the kingdom. The bullionist policy it pursued, imbued indeed with the economic reasoning of expanding the extent of monetization, was articulated in the compulsory reminting of all foreign coins, and prohibitions imposed on the outflow of precious metals to India, as well as to the Ottoman empire.[43] Shah Abbas I's much publicized pilgrimage to the tomb of Imam Reza at Mashhad, and his vision of the spiritual founder of Iranian Shiism, were greeted with suspicion by a few foreign observers who saw them as an attempt to pull the Iranian devotees away from the usual holy cites in Hejaz and Iraq, which were parts of the Ottoman empire, because large amounts of money in gold was spent there by Iranian pilgrims in charity and other expenses.[44]

While pious pilgrims remained undeterred,[45] clever merchants too devised their own ways to circumvent prohibitions and avoid the expenses and inconvenience of a double exchange: foreign coins into Iranian money, and the latter into currencies of India. Tavernier reveals the ways in which they concealed money, particularly gold coins, in vests and shirts, and avoided rigorous checkpoints en-route. However, once discovered, the merchant was obliged to pay double the customs or suffer confiscation of his money.[46]

Merchants' efforts to carry their money to the point where it could fetch the highest price (in terms of merchandise) were intensified precisely at a time when the Safavid state decided to control and enlarge monetary circulation in Iran. This was a curious paradox. In the last quarter of the seventeenth century, when a fiscal and monetary crisis engulfed Iran, the state resorted to the strictest scrutiny of incoming bullion, and also debased its silver currency in order to stretch the existing money supply and enlarge its fiscal earnings. Ironically, the Iranian monetary policy to overcome the contraction of the circulating medium served to worsen the situation and further contributed to the drainage of specie from the country. Foreign coins were now greatly undervalued at the official rate of exchange and it became practically impossible for the merchants to obtain the true value of their bullion in Iran, compelling them to export it directly to

India.[47] Merchants defying the Safavid ban avoided the tightly controlled port of Bandar Abbas and chose Basra for shipments bound for India.[48] The cargo of a Dutch ship which sailed from Basra at about this time and was intercepted by Iranian port officials when it drifted towards Bandar Abbas, comprised over 24 metric tons of silver in Spanish *reales* owned by the Armenian merchants of Iran.[49]

Laris and Reales: Mono-metallic Arbitrage and Silver Influx

For one reason or another, a large portion of precious metals imported by Iran, made its way to India and further east. Du Mans, graphic once again, likened the riches of Iran to the 'humidity of water (*humidite de l'eau*) which attaches itself to canals while it drains into the basin.'[50] The two important channels of money flow, one direct the other circuitous, were represented by two prominent coins, the *reales of eight* and *laris*. Along with the *reales*, the export of *laris*, a unique silver coin crafted as a double twist of silver purl in the mints of Lar and Basra, assumed a very high proportion in the second half of the sixteenth century.[51] The reason for this increase was two-fold. The first was the policy of the Lar administration to earn profit from seigniorage rather than money-changing by offering higher mint price for the conversion of *reales* into *laris*.[52] The second reason was the market which had developed for the sale and purchase of *laris* as a commercial currency of the Indian Ocean. The market for *laris* in the Indian Ocean trade, limited by the predominance of the Hurmuz *ashrafi* of gold in the first half of the sixteenth century, expanded enormously as a result of the influx of American silver into Spain after 1531 and its dispersion by Genoese and Venetian merchants into the Levantine circuit soon after.[53] By the end of the silver century, both *reales* and *laris* had acquired a high reputation in the markets of Indian Ocean littorals and China due to their intrinsic fineness (92 and 98 percent respectively) and uniformity of weight standard ensured at the mints of Seville and Lar. In an interesting passage (quoted below), Van Linschoten (*c*.1584–89) provides a first-person account of the mechanism of silver circulation in these regions and the artifice of money-changing:

> There are others [at Goa] that use exchanging of moneyes, and to buy money [when it cometh], as tyme serveth to sell it againe, for they buy the Rials of eight, when the shippes come from Portingale,

> whereof some buy at the least 10 or 12 hundreth,[54] and keepe them till the Moneth of April, which is the time when the shippes sayle to China, for then are the Rials of eight sought for to carry thether, and are commonly worth 25 or 30 in the hundreth [profite], and then they receive for them a certaine money, which at the same time is brought from Ormus, called Larriins, that come out of Persia, which they buy for 8 or 10 in the hundreth [profite], and keep them till the Portingales on the moneth of September come thether, and so deliver them againe for 20 or 25 in the hundreth [profite], in exchange for rials of eight, as I said before, for they must have these Larriins [with them] to Cochin, to buy pepper and other wares, for that is the best and most profitable money. There are yet other sorts of money called Pagodes, Venetianers, and Santhones, which are gold, al which they doe likewise buy and sel . . .[55]

Interesting aspects of preferred means of exchange and mono-metallic arbitrage (buying one set of coins in lean seasons and selling them when the demand hiked their exchange rates in money markets), can be gleaned from this description. As a result of regular trade with Hurmuz, the *lari* had already become an established medium of payment on the coasts of Gujarat and the western Deccan.[56] Even though exports from the Persian Gulf were mostly in gold in the beginning, silver too made its appearance in merchants' ships sailing for India. According to Barbosa (1518), *ashrafis* and *tangas* (*laris*) of Hurmuz were obtained by the Indian merchants, after they had sold their goods and bought horses, since these coins circulated in India and had a better value.[57] *Laris* of Hurmuz (100,000 in number) were the cargo of a Cambay-bound ship plundered by the Portuguese in 1521.[58] *Laris* were also exported to Bengal and Malacca in some quantity in the early sixteenth century.[59] By the second half of the sixteenth century, *laris* had gained currency in the spice exporting areas of the south-western coast as well which were predominantly gold based.[60] Whenever spices were paid for in silver at Malabar and the western Deccan, it was *laris*, and not *reales*, which were accepted.[61] Therefore, the Portuguese merchants bringing *reales* from Lisbon, in September, had to exchange them for *laris* in order to obtain spices, and such was the demand for this specie that a profit of at least 12 per cent (20 per cent!) could be earned by the money-changers on a single transaction. The *reales* obtained by the money-changers were then sold to the China merchants, against *laris*, on the eve of the ships' departure in April, and a profit was again earned on this transaction (25 to 30 per cent). The circuit which Linschoten described was completed when the money-changers exchanged *laris* once again for *reales* towards the end of the year.

In another testimony, Gomes Solis, who was a big merchant in Indo-Portuguese trade at the turn of the seventeenth century, described how *reales* were converted into Turkish and Iranian coins and then taken to India in large quantities.[62] Much of this silver, as we observed earlier, was brought not only to the western coasts of India but into the heartland of the Mughal empire as well. Abul Fazl, the historian of Akbar's empire, has indeed mentioned, as one of the features of Gujarat, the import of silver from the Ottoman Empire and Iran (*walayat i Rum wa Iraq*).[63] Although he does not explicitly mention Iran as the point of origin of foreign specie, his inventory of coins delivered to the inland mints of the Mughal empire for recoinage includes names such as *lari* and *shahi* along with Turkish and Portuguese *reales* (*narjil i rumi wa firangi*).[64]

Merchant Communities and Mercantile Practices

Trade routes, entrepôts, marchandise and money laid the material foundation of the global network of exchange. Merchants and men of affairs fashioned its human environment. Mercantile economy became active and organized due to the presence of diverse merchant communities working with numerous artifices of trade. Here, one can identify two ubiquitous merchant groups operating in Iran, viz. Armenians and Indians. Both were in a sense, foreigners to Iran even though they were permanent residents of the country, and both participated extensively in commodity and bullion trade. Both communities were known for their well-knit kinship and ethnic ties, family firms, frugality and perseverance, and commercial techniques. They deployed all their skills in handling the long distance commerce of Iran and contributed significantly, in varying degrees, to the development of its mercantile economy.

The Armenian merchants had their main seat at Julfa, a small town near the Ottoman-Safavid border, which rapidly rose into prominence in the late sixteenth century for at least three reasons: its strategic location on the river Aras, a crossing point on major trade routes linking Transcaucasia and Iran with Anatolia, Syria and the

Mediterranean; the access which Julfa had to the silk producing regions of north-western Iran; and, with an overwhelming Christian population, its somewhat neutral position in the Ottoman-Safavid conflict usually expressed in Shii-Sunni rhetoric.[65] When Shah Abbas I relocated the Armenians at New Julfa, in the suburbs of Isfahan, they began to enjoy very close relations with the political elites of the Safavid empire. For protection and privileges, they bankrolled state ventures and aided the state in its mercantilist phase. They were compared with the Genoese bankers of the Spanish kings, and members of the Shafraz family of New Julfa indeed became the bankers of the Safavid Shah.[66]

The Armenians were most active in the export of silk to the west and the import of foreign bullion. Almost all European accounts testify to their extensive presence in the market where silk was exchanged for silver. Tavernier, for instance, singles them out while making a general point about the bullion trade:

> From the reign of Shah Abbas I to that of Shah Abbas II there has been plenty of silver in Persia than is to be seen now; and the Armenian merchants used to transport it from Europe into Persia and then got them converted into local money (*le reduisoit en monnoye du pays*). But in these past years they bring nothing but ducats and sequins since these are more portable. They have also invented new ways of hiding the money in their vests and shirts to safeguard against robberies which take place on caravans travelling from Turkey, and also to avoid payments of customs and other dues at places which are not rigorous in searching for what the merchants are carrying.[67]

Such identifications of a merchant group with money also made it an easy target for attack in times of distress. It was reported to Shah Sulayman, when he was galvanizing supplies of silver to his mints, that the Armenians were now bringing no more foreign bullion into the country than they were exporting to India. This, in the opinion of the officials, was causing a crisis of money in the empire.[68] It is interesting to note that popular prejudice against members of an Indian mercantile group or *baniyas* for being usurers and bullion exporters was also expressed during similar monetary crises:

> These Indians, like true leeches extract all the gold and silver and send them to their own country so that in the year 1677 when I

departed from Persia, one could not see there any more gold or silver. These usurers had made it disappear entirely.[69]

Indian merchants too had a powerful presence in Iran although not of the same order as the Armenians. There were two types of Indian merchants trading in Iran: those who were itinerant, notably the Khatris (concentrated mainly in southern Iranian ports and commercial centres), who were cloth merchants, and those who lived in Iran, notably the *baniyas* from Gujarat and Multan.[70] There were at least ten to twelve thousand *baniyas* living in Isfahan alone, described as money-changers, bullion merchants and bankers (*banquiers*) by Tavernier, Chardin and Du Mans. They lent money on interest against security, accepted interest-bearing deposits from the notables of the town, issued and discounted bills of exchange, and changed money. Their business allowed them tremendous access to capital, both local and international, and they too, like the Armenians were derided for bleeding the country.

It is important to remember that mercantile credit was a critical factor in the exchange of goods and bullion in the global network. Through a system of deposit banking and money-lending, capital was made available to finance commodity trade by mercantile groups. It often happened that when Indian ships called, there was more merchandise than money at Bandar Abbas and word was quickly sent to those who held cash reserves (*l' argent contant*) at Lar, Shiraz and Isfahan to finance purchases. Loans were then advanced to the merchants buying goods for inland towns to be repaid after the goods reached their destination. Similarly, money taken up by merchants at Baghdad was paid at Aleppo or the debts owed at Erzerum were settled at Bursa, Smyrna and Leghorn. In this process, which, according to Tavernier, linked the entrepôts of the two continents, the remittance of commercial papers was matched by a reverse remittance of cash which was eventually transferred physically from Bandar Abbas to India.[71]

Foreign merchants' position can be compared with that of the Iranians. It appears that in the beginning they traded with both Europe and India, but from the second half of the sixteenth century, the western sector was wrested from them by the Armenians. Subsequently, the Iranian merchants concentrated more on India trade and were active on both sea and land route.

Mehdi Keyvani has argued that Shah Abbas I's shortsighted policy of encouraging foreign merchants for personal gain inhibited the transformation of Iranian merchants into a proper bourgeoisie by not allowing them to share the benefits of long-distance trade. At the same time he attributes the success of Indian merchants in Iran to a growing imbalance in the trade with India which necessitated payments in gold and silver.[72] Keyvani does not pay adequate attention to the strengths of the social and commercial organization of Armenian and Indian merchant communities. It was here that they had a real competitive edge over their Iranian counterpart. As well-knit and highly skilled groups dabbling in the business of money, credit and merchandise they took full advantage of Iran's position as a conduit of European bullion as well as the structural imbalance in bilateral trade with the east. It is also not true that Indian and Armenian merchants were operating in an ideal commercial climate. Usury was prohibited in Iran and merchants had to devise methods (*hiyal*) to circumvent the law. As a result, money-lenders were not able to get institutional support for the full recovery of debts or settlements of dispute, and had to employ their own ways, not always civil, to pursue their business intersts. Also, money-changing, money-lending, banking and sale and purchase of bullion were multiple portfolios of the same branch of commerce and a person dealing in one needed to have expertise in others as well. In this the *baniyas* were the major specialists, and the absence of Iranian merchants here, even Indian Muslim merchants, appears quite natural.

Notes and References

1 Raphael Du Mans, *Estat de la Perse en 1660,* (ed.) C. Schefer (Paris, 1890), p. 192.

2 J.B. Tavernier, *Les Six Voyages de Jean Baptiste Tavernier, en Turquie, en Perse, et Aux Indes*, 2 vols. (Paris, 1679), I, pp. 157–69.

3 Ibid., pp. 69–80; *Travels in India*, 2 vols., tr. V. Ball, 2nd edn. rev. W. Crooke (London, 1925), I, p. 73.

4 Tavernier, *Les Six Voyages*, I, pp. 192–206, 306.

5 Out of 448 gold coins recovered from the Broach hoard, 367 are *ashrafis* of the Mamluks while only 4 are of Ilkhanid origin. The remainder are Genoese and Venetian ducats. For an analysis of the Broach hoard see Najaf Haider, 'International Trade in Precious Metals and Monetary Systems of Medieval India: 1000–1500', *Proceedings of the Indian History Congress*, 59th Session (Patiala, 1998), pp. 238–40.

6 For the rise of Aleppo see Bruce Masters, *The Origin of Western Economic*

Dominance in the Middle East Mercantilism and the Islamic Economy in Aleppo, 1600–1750 (New York, 1988), pp. 12–14 and Neils Steensgaard, *Carracks, Caravans and Companies: The structural crisis in the European-Asian trade in the early 17th century* (Copenhagen, 1972), p. 62.

7 [The Book of India and Japan Affairs] cited by Sanjay Subrahmanyam, *The Portuguese Empire in Asia, 1500–1700: A Political and Economic History* (London, 1993), p. 76.

8 See Van Linschoten, *The Voyage of John Huyghen van Linschoten to the East Indies*, 2 vols., (ed.) Arthur Coke Burnell (London, 1885), I, pp. 47–50 for a detailed description of this route and the protection provided by Ottoman troops.

9 Halil Inalcik, 'India Trade', *An Economic and Social History of the Ottoman Empire, 1300–1914*, (eds) Halil Inalcik and Donald Quataert (Cambridge, 1994), pp. 339–40, 349–50.

10 Frederic C. Lane, 'The Mediterranean Spice Trade: Further Evidence of its Revival in the Sixteenth Century', *Crisis and Change in the Venetian Economy in the Sixteenth and Seventeenth Centuries*, (ed.) Brian Pullan (London, 1968), pp. 47–54

11 Vitorino Magalhaes-Godinho, *L' Economie de l' Empire Portugais aux XVe et XVIe Siecles* (Paris, 1969), pp. 757–8, 773–4.

12 Vitorino Magalhaes-Godinho, *Les Finances de l'Etat Portugais des Indes Orientales (1517–1635)* (Paris, 1982), p. 46; *L' Economie de l' Empire Portugais*, p. 771.

13 Observing these developments from the Iranian mainland, an English merchant wrote that 'the citie and Island of Ormus, lying in the gulfe of Persia, is the most famous mart towne in all East India, whither all the merchandises of India are brought, . . .' Arthur Edwards, 'Notes Concerning this fourth voyage into Persia, begun in the monthe of Julie 1568, etc', *Early Voyages and Travels to Russia and Persia by Anthony Jenkinson and Other Englishmen*, (eds) E.D. Morgan and C.H. Coote (Hakluyt Society, 1886), II, p. 419. Also see Caesar Fredericke, 'The Voyage and travell of M. Caesar Fredericke, Merchant of Venice, into the East India etc.', *The Principal Navigations Voyages Traffiques and Discoveries of the English Nation*, (ed.) Richard Hakluyt (Hakluyt Society, 1904), V, p. 372.

14 Magalhaes-Godinho, *Les Finances de l'Etat Portugais*, pp. 45–9.

15 Ibid., p. 50.

16 The Dutch factor Pelsaert offered a vivid description of the decline in the western Indian Ocean trade and pointed out that the 'Portuguese, Moslems and Hindus all concur in putting the blame for this state of things entirely on us and the English . . .' Francisco Pelsaert, *Remonstrantie*, tr. W.H. Moreland and P. Geyl, *Jahangir's India* (Cambridge, 1925), pp. 39–40. Also see C.R. Boxer, 'Anglo-Portuguese Rivalry in the Persian Gulf, 1615–1635', *Chapters in Anglo-Portuguese Relations*, (ed.) Edgar Prestage (Watford, 1935), pp. 46–87; Steensgaard, *Carracks, Caravans and Companies*, p. 206.

17 Richard Steel and John Crowther, 'A Journall of the Journey of Richard Steel and John Crowther, from Azmere in India, the place of the Great

Mogols Residence to Spahan the Royall Seat of the King of Persia, in the affaires of the East India Society. Ann 1615–16', in *Hakluyts Posthumous or Purchas His Pilgrimes, Contayning a History of the World in Sea Voyages and Lande Travells by the Englishmen and Others*, (ed.) Samuel Purchas (James Maclehose ed., 1905), IV, pp. 268–9. Robert Coverte (1610), who travelled with a caravan from Agra to Isfahan, reported that '7 or 8 thousand camels' carried merchandise from Qandahar alone. Robert Coverte, *A True and Almost Incredible Report of an Englishman that (being cast away in the good ship called the Assention in Cambaya the farthest part of the East Indies) Travelled by Land through many Unknowne Kingdoms and great Cities* (Amsterdam, 1931), p. 74.

18 Steensgaard, *Carracks, Caravans and Companies*, p. 207.

19 *English Factories in India* (1618–1669), 13 vols. (each volume titled by the years it covers), (ed.) William Foster (Oxford, 1906–27), *1618–21*, p. 46; Steensgaard, *Carracks, Caravans and Companies*, pp. 398–462.

20 See Tavernier, *Les Six Voyages*, I, pp. 755–62.

21 For Hurmuz see Magalhaes-Godinho, *Les Finances de l'Etat Portugais*, pp. 45–9. For Bandar Abbas see *Generale Missiven van Gouverneure-Generaal en Raden aan Heren xvii der Verenigde Oostindische Compagnie*, 7 vols, (ed.) W. Ph. Coolhaas ('s-Gravenhage, 1960–79), II, p. 207; III, p. 107; *English Factories, 1655–60*, p. 28. All figures are originally given in *toman* (= 50 *abbasis* of 107 grains of fine silver).

22 *Bronnen tot de Geschiedenis der Oostindische Compagnie in Perzie, 1611–38*, (ed.) H. Dunlop ('s-Gravenhage, 1930), I, pp. 482–494.

23 Najaf Haider, 'The Quantity Theory and Mughal Monetary History', *Medieval History Journal*, 2,2, 1999, pp. ----; Haider, 'Mughals and Mahmudis. The Incorporation of Gujarat into the Imperial Monetary System', Parthasarthi Gupta Memorial Volume (Forthcoming).

24 Najaf Haider, 'Structure and Movement of Wages In the Mughal Empire', Paper Presented to the Seminar on *Wages and Currency: Global and Historical Comparisons*, May 2002, International Institute of Social History, Amsterdam (unpublished).

25 Rudolph P Mathee, *The Politics of Trade in Safavid Iran. Silk for Silver, 1600–1730* (Cambridge, 1999), pp. 33–42.

26 R.W. Ferrier, 'An English View of Persian Trade in 1618', *Journal of Economic and Social History of the Orient*, XIX (1976), p. 203.

27 Om Prakash, *The Dutch East India Company and the Economy of Bengal: 1630–1720* (Delhi, 1988), pp. 210–11.

28 Mathee, *Politics of Trade*, p. 43.

29 Najaf Haider, 'The Monetary Basis of Credit and Banking Instruments in the Mughal Empire', *History of Finance and Banking in India*, (ed.) Amiya Bagchi, 2002 (forthcoming).

30 Jean Chardin, *Travels in Persia* (1927), p. 117; Ferrier, 'An English View', pp. 198–203.

31 R.W. Ferrier, 'Trade From the Mid-Fourteenth Century to the End of the Safavid Period', *The Cambridge History of Iran: The Timurid and Safavid*

Periods, VI, (eds) Peter Jackson and Laurence Lockhart (Cambridge, 1986), pp. 481–2.

32 Ibid., pp. 482–3; Ferrier, 'An English View', pp. 210–14.

33 For early seventeenth century Mughal empire, a higher estimate of 2.5 to 3 million rupees has been offered by Shireen Moosvi. See *The Economy of the Mughal Empire c. 1595 A Statistical Study* (Delhi, 1987), p. 382.

34 *Bronnen tot de Geschiedenis der Oostindische Compagnie in Perzie*, pp. 482–92.

35 For the sale of 'Lahore' indigo at Aleppo, see ibid., p. 133. Also see Pelsaert, *Remonstrantie*, p. 18.

36 *Factory Records, Surat*, Oriental and India Office Collection (OIOC), series G/36, Vol. 94, ff. 69a–b.

37 Edwards, 'Notes Concerning this fourth voyage into Persia', p. 411.

38 Ibid., p. 401.

39 *Estat de la Perse en 1660* , p. 192.

40 Steensgaard, *Carracks, Caravans and Companies*, p. 198; Magalhaes-Godinho, *L' Economie de l' Empire Portugais*, p. 772.

41 H.W. Van Santen, *De Verenigde Oost Indische Compagnie in Gujarat en Hindustan, 1620–1660* (Leiden, 1982), p. 75.

42 Tavernier, *Les Six Voyages*, I, pp. 134, 361, 418.

43 Ibid. Also see *Pacifique de Provins* cited by Minorsky in his introduction to [Samia, Mirza], *Tadhkirat ul Muluk, A Manual of Safavid Administration (circa 1137/1725)*, facsimile reproduction of B.L., MS Or. 9496 and tr. V. Minorsky (London, 1943), pp. 26–7.

44 Pere Sanson, *Voyages ou relation de l'etat present du royaume de Perse* (Paris, 1694), p. 171–2; Tavernier, *Les Six Voyages*, I, pp. 588–9; Najaf Haider, 'Precious Metal Flows and Currency Circulation in the Mughal Empire', *JESHO*, xxxix (1996), p. 303; Rudi Mathee, 'Between Venice and Surat: The Trade in Gold in Safavid Iran', *Modern Asian Studies*, 34, I (2000), pp. 242–3.

45 Mohammad Mufid, *Jami i Mufidi*, OIOC, Or. Ms. 210, f. 9a; Mathee, 'Between Venice and Surat', pp. 243, 251.

46 Ibid., pp. 134, 136, 418.

47 Sanson, *Voyages ou relation*, pp. 160–1. For the report of an English factor (1684 AD) on debasement see Ferrier, 'Trade', *Cambridge History of Iran*, VI, p. 485.

48 Sanson, *Voyages ou relation*, p. 14. Also see John Fryer, *A New Account of East India and Persia being Nine Years' Travels 1672–81*, 3 vols., (ed.) W. Crooke (Hakluyt Society, 1909–15), I, pp. 282–3.

49 Sanson, *Voyages ou relation*, pp. 13–14.

50 *Estat de la Perse en 1660* , pp. 192–3.

51 The *lari* weighed over 74 troy grains in which 98 per cent was pure silver. H.L. Rabino, *Coins, Medals and Seals of the Shah of Iran, 1500–1941* (Hertford, 1945), p. 16. On numerous occasions the *lari* was described by foreign travellers and observers, who took care to note its size and shape and testified to its high degree of fineness. See Van Linschoten, *Voyage*, I, p. 18;

Francois Pyrard, *The Voyage of Francois Pyrard of Laval to the East Indies, the Maldives, Moluccas and Brazil,* 2 vols., 3 pts., tr. Albert Gray and H. C.P. Bell (Hakluyt Society, 1887–9), II, pt. ii, p. 239.

52 M. Will Barrett, 'The money and measures of Babylon, Balsara, and the Indies, with the customes, & c. written from Aleppo in Syraia, An. 1584', *The Principal Navigations Voyages Traffiques and Discoveries of the English Nation,* VI, (ed.) Richard Hakluyt (Hakluyt Society, 1904), pp. 11, 15; Tavernier, *Les Six Voyages,* I, pp. 589–90.

53 Earl J. Hamilton, *American Treasure and the Price Revolution in Spain, 1501–1650* (Cambridge, Mass., 1934), p. 40 (Table 2); Fernand Braudel, *Civilization and Capitalism,* Vol. III, *The Perspective of the World,* tr. Sian Reynolds (London, 1985), pp. 138–68; Brandel, *The Mediterranean and the Mediterranean World in the Age of Philip II,* tr. Sian Reynolds, 2 vols. (London, 1975), I, pp. 487–505.

54 The Dutch version reads: 'and they get as much as 12 per cent (*12. ten hondert*)'. See editor's note in Van Linschoten, *Voyage,* I, p. 186.

55 Ibid., pp. 186–7.

56 Barrett, 'The money and measures of Babylon', p. 17. In the seasons for making purchases in the markets of Cambay, Diu, western Deccan and Bengal, the *lari* enjoyed a premium of over 20 per cent. Magalhaes-Godinho, *L' Economie de l' Empire Portugais,* p. 513.

57 Duarte Borbosa (*c.* 1518), *The Book of Duarte Barbosa. An Account of the Countries Bordering on the Indian Ocean and their inhabitants,* 2 vols., tr. Longworth Dames, (1918–21; repr. New Delhi, 1989), II, pp. 100–1. It seems that merchants, especially Portuguese, who went to Hurmuz to buy horses carried with them gold rather than merchandise. Gold was also brought to Aden from the western coast of India to pay for the Arabian horses. Tome Pires (*c.* 1515), *The Suma Oriental of Tome Pires. An Account of the East from the Red Sea to Japan, written in Malacca and India in 1512–15 and the Book of Francisco Rodrigues,* 2 vols., tr. Armando Cortesao, (Liechtenstein, 1967), I, pp. 17, 21. Pires speaks of the export of silver coins (*tangas*)to India from Hurmuz (p. 20). The general flow of gold and silver to India, particularly Gujarat, from Cairo, Aden and Hurmuz is also described by Pires (pp. 13, 43, 44).

58 Magalhaes-Godinho, *L' Economie de l' Empire Portugais,* p. 512.

59 Ibid.

60 Barrett, 'The money and measures of Babylon', p. 19. It is worth remembering that gold coins were very much in use to settle the purchase of spices, and the demand for *laris* here had grown out of the rising silver influx and the currency they had acquired on the western coast to settle regional trade balances.

61 In 1582, an Italian merchant reportedly invested 20,000 *ducats* (here money of account) in *laris* at Cannanore to buy pepper. Magalhaes-Godinho, *L' Economie de l' Empire Portugais,* p. 332.

62 Magalhaes-Godinho, *L' Economie de l' Empire Portugais,* p. 513.

63 Abu'l Fazl, *Ain i Akbari,* 2 vols. (ed.) H. Blochmann (Bib. Indica, 1872–77),

I, p. 19. The reader may be reminded that in Persian texts of the time 'Iraq was the name employed for Persia or Iran. Rum meant originally Byzantium and now its successor, the Ottoman Empire.

64 Ibid., p. 486.

65 Edmund Herzig, 'The Rise of the Julfa Merchants in the Late Sixteenth Century', *Safavid Persia,* (ed.) Charles Melville (London, 1996, pp. 307–17.

66 Herzig, 'The Family firm in the Commercial Organisation of the Julfa Armenia', *Etudes Safavides,* (ed.) Jean Calmard (Paris-Tehran, 1993), p. 295.

67 Tavernier, *Les Six Voyages,* I, p. 418.

68 Sanson, *Voyages ou relation,* pp. 12–3.

69 John Chardin, *Voyages du Chevalier Chardin, en Perse, et autres lieux de l' Orient,* 10 vols., (ed.) L. Langles (Paris, 1811), VI, p. 164. For similar remarks see Tavernier, *Les Six Voyages,* I, pp. 586–8.

70 Tavernier, *Travels in India,* I, p. 74.

71 *Les Six Voyages,* I., pp. 767–8.

72 Mehdi Keyvani, *Artisans and Guild Life in the Later Safavid Period. Contributions to the socio-economic history of Persia* (Berlin, 1982), pp. 215–16, 228.

The Message of Iqbal in Persian and Urdu Poetry

V.N. Datta

چون چراغ لاله سوزم در خیابانِ شما
ای جوانانِ عجم، جانِ من و جانِ شما
می رسد مردے که زنجیر غلامان بشکند
دیده ام از روزنِ دیوارِ زندانِ شما

Like a tulip-red lamp. I burn in your flower-garden
My own life and yours, O youth of Iran.
A man is coming who will break the slaves' chains
I have seen him through the window in your prison walls.

—Iqbal

Today, Iqbal is officially recognized in Pakistan as one of its founding fathers though he died nearly ten years before Pakistan came into being. In India patriots have sung *Sare jahan se achchha Hindustan hamara*, the anthem of the Indian National Army. Everywhere he is held to have revolutionized Urdu poetry. Iqbal's own heritage was, indeed, composite. It was in the first instance, India's own ancient civilization, of which he sang with such fervour in his early youth. Important too for him were the sources of inspiration that lay embedded in Persian poetry. When he was to make his great turn towards Islam, he rejected a large part of both these inheritances, as we shall see. Yet the vehicle he adopted for this rejection was mainly Persian. In this essay I examine how this happened, and what the poet strove to do through a poetry which deservedly occupies a high literary status in the languages of both Iran and India.

Sir Muhammad Iqbal (1877–1938) was undoubtedly the

greatest Urdu and Persian poet of his time. Being a self-conscious poet and preacher, his poetry was essentially didactic and rhetorical. As a poet he ignored the formal distinction between poetry and rhetoric. He did not follow Aristotle's prescription of 'Art for Art's sake'. His poetry is overweighted with allusions to religious and philosophic doctrines and to contemporary scenes. He dominated his times from so great an altitude that he could not be merged into it and rose in sudden flights from the material to spiritual heights. Like Dante, Iqbal combined poetry with doctrine. Just as John Milton was inspired by Christian ardour, so Iqbal's poetical works in parts are a fruit of prolonged meditations on the Quran. But Shakespeare had no philosophy or ideology to disseminate. Matthew Arnold in his poem addressing Shakespeare wrote, 'Others abide thy question. Thou are free'.[2] T.S. Eliot regarded poetry as no substitute to philosophy or religion. Ghalib had retained his freedom as a poet and never let poetry serve the interests of society. There was no question of his showing a predisposition to one theory of life. His theory of life was that of a pagan.[3]

Ghalib's poetry cannot be reduced to any logical paraphrase, and his experience is purely aesthetic. On the other hand, Iqbal's poems are philosophical statements constructed around moral homilies and lessons. While Mir Taqi Mir and Ghalib's poems are to be enjoyed for their internal aesthetics, Iqbal's poems have bold and daring themes focussing on issues of social and political importance. W.W. Yeats had articulated Irish nationalism; Iqbal too expressed the dynamic force of nationalism in his poetical utterances. It is difficult for a poet to be self-consistent and more so in the case of Iqbal because what he said and wrote can be contradicted by other things he said and wrote. Iqbal composed much of his poetry with an overwhelming purpose of awakening the Muslim community which he thought had sunk into inertia and slumber.

For Iqbal poetry was not an image-making activity or a brief enchantment but a mission of resolving human problems. He wanted to give men what they needed because poetry was able to console, soothe and inspire them. About his function as a poet, Iqbal like Shelley firmly believed that poets are the unacknowledged legislators of mankind. Iqbal presented poetry as a kind of regent which needed a code, and a law of morality. Iqbal wrote:

شاعر اندر سینۂ ملّت چو دِل
ملّتے بے شاعرے انبار است

The poet is like the heart in the breast of a nation
A nation without a poet is like a sack of corn.[4]

Again:

شاعرا مقصود اگر آدم گری است
شاعری ہم وارثِ پیغمبری است

If poetry aims at producing an ideal man
It may rightly be said to be the heir to Prophecy.[5]

Iqbal, though not a prophet, performed the functions of a poet as a prophet, by virtue of being a poet:

شاعری جزوے پیغمبری است

Poetry is a part of prophecy.

Like Milton, Iqbal was one of the most learned of poets. He relished speaking in his mother tongue Punjabi, but he composed his poetry in Urdu and Persian. His Urdu poetry established him as an outstanding poet in the country. Yet he wrote two-thirds of his poetry in Persian, knowing full well that the Persian-knowing reading public in the country was small. Could it be that he wanted to address a larger audience outside the country? Persian was certainly the language of the elite in Muslim countries, particularly Persia and Afghanistan, and this would be a good enough reason.

Iqbal gave his own explanation for writing in Persian at the Iqbal Literary Association, London on 6 November 1931. He had gone to London, to attend the first Round Table conference as a delegate:

> Some people have been expressing the view that I adopted Persian language for the reason that my thoughts might be accessible to wider circles. But my purpose was contrary to that: I had written my *masnavi Asrar-i Khudi* (1915) originally for the Indians only, and in doing so my object was that my ideas should be disseminated among a limited circle of intelligentsia. At that time I did not know that the *masnavi* would become popular beyond the confines of India and

> would reach Europe. It is no doubt true that thereafter I was attracted to writing in that language.[6]

S.M.H. Burney suggests that Iqbal adopted the Persian medium of poetry because the genre of *masnavi*, the poetic form, lends itself easily to the exposition of philosophical ideas which Iqbal wanted to express.[7]

It is difficult to identify the influences that worked on Iqbal in his development as a Persian poet. At an early age like many educated Muslims of the sub-continent he read the *masnavi* of Jalalud Din Rumi (1207–1273). Rumi was to Iqbal a divine model. Except in Iqbal's *Zabur-i Ajam* (1903), we meet Rumi in all his poetical works including *Metaphysics of Persia* and *The Reconstruction of Religious Thought in Islam*. Rumi's verses haunted Iqbal like a passion, and moved him to tears.[8]

Iqbal looked on Rumi as his spiritual guide who appears time and again in his poetical works. Iqbal adopted Rumi's metre in the *masnavi*. He regarded Rumi's *masnavi* as the second most important book after the Quran. He was also instrumental in persuading Abdul Majid Daryabadi to publish his *Fihe and Fih*.[9] As a student Iqbal's close association with Sir Thomas Arnold Walker of Government College, Lahore, and R.A. Nicholson, lecturer in Persian at the Cambridge University deepened his interest in Rumi. Nicholson was a leading authority on Islam, and later translated Rumi's *masnavi* in eight volumes.

Iqbal wrote in *Javidnama*:

پیر رومی را رفیق راه ساز
تا خدا بخشد ترا سوز و گداز

> Make the *pir* Rumi your companion on the road
> So that God may give you sorrow and suffering (to bear).[10]

In his introduction to *Asrar-e-Khudi* he acknowledged his debt to Rumi.

پیر رومی خاک را اکسیر کرد
از غبارم جلوه ها تعمیر کرد

> The *pir* Rumi has turned earth into elixir.
> What splendour he has created out of the dust I have raised.[11]

Again:

اس کشمکش میں گزریں مری زندگی کی راتیں
کبھی سوز و سازِ رومی، کبھی پیچ و تابِ رازی

In this struggle, I have passed my nights
With the pathos and sorrow of Rumi
And Rhazes' turns and twists.[12]

Iqbal thought that by writing poetry in Persian, he would strike his individuality and enhance his own reputation like Omar Khayyam (1809–1883) whose *Rubaiyat* had gained world-wide reputation as one of the most frequently quoted of lyrical poems. Iqbal's own great predecessor, Ghalib had said:

فارسی بین تا بہ بینی نقشہائے رنگ رنگ
بگذر از مجموعۂ اردو کہ بے رنگ من است

Study my Persian poetry so that thou mayst
find many—coloured pictures
Pass over my collection of Urdu verses because
it is without my colour.[13]

Nobody perhaps had such a profound and lasting influence on Iqbal's poetic talents as Thomas Arnold Walker (called 'Arnold' by Iqbal), Principal, Government College, Lahore, with whom he studied the M.A. course in Philosophy in 1898–99. Walker brought Iqbal closely in touch with western philosophy and imparted to him 'something of his own taste and methods in scholarly study'.[14] He was also instrumental in securing for Iqbal the teaching assignments in Government and Oriental Colleges without the qualifications required for the job. It was finally due to to his influence that Iqbal went up to Cambridge for philosophical studies in tripos and for Ph.D. to Munich for his thesis, on 'The Development of Metaphysics in Persia'. At a critical moment when Iqbal thought of giving up writing poetry due to criticism of his poetical compositions, Walker dissuaded him from doing so. He brought Iqbal and Shibli Nomani (1857–1916) closer to each other, a contact that was to influence his poetic and prose writings.[15]

When Walker left Lahore for England, Iqbal wrote a poem of deep and steadfast affection 'Nala-i Firaq' (Cry of Separation), expressing how he felt abandoned at a critical turn in his career.

ذرّہ میرے دل کا خورشید آشنا ہونے کو تھا
آئینہ ٹوٹا ہوا عالم نُما ہونے کو تھا
نخل میری آرزوؤں کا ہرا ہونے کو تھا
آہ! کیا جانے کوئی میں کیا سے کیا ہونے کو تھا

The atom of my heart was about to become bright as the Sun.
My broken mirror was about to display the entire universe.
The plant of my aspirations was about to become green.
Alas! No one will know what I was about
to become from naught.[16]

Iqbal's training as a researcher at Munich gave him a firm grasp of Persian literature. In his Prelude to *Asrar-i Khudi*, he wrote:

شاعری زین مثنوی مقصود نیست
بُت پرستی، بُت گری مقصود نیست
ہندی ام از پارسی بیگانہ ام
ماہِ نو باشم تہی پیمانہ ام
حُسن اندازِ بیان از من مجو
خوانسار و اصفہان از من مجو
گرچہ ہندی در عذوبت شکّر است
طرزِ گفتارِ دری شیریں تر است
فکرِ من از جلوہ اش مسحور گشت
خامۂ من شاخِ نخلِ طور گشت
پارسی از رفعتِ اندیشہ ام
درخورد با فطرتِ اندیشہ ام
خُردہ بر مینا مگیر، اے ہوش مند
دِل بذوقِ خردہ ی مینا بہ بند

Poetizing is not the aim of this *mathnavi*:
Beauty-worshipping and love-making is
Not its aim.
I am an Indian. Persian is not my native tongue.
I am like the crescent moon and my cup is empty.
Do not seek from me charm of style in expression,
Do not seek from me a table-decker and (the idiom of) Isfahan.
Although the language of Hindi is like sugar in sweetness,
Yet sweeter is the fashion of Persian speech.
My mind was enchanted by its loveliness;
My pen became a twig of the burning bush.
Because of the loftiness of my thoughts,
Persian alone is suitable to them.
Do not, O wise reader, judge the wine by the wine-cup,
But turn your heart towards the wine in the cup.[17]

Iqbal's own Urdu poetry became increasingly Persianized and consequently lost its earlier classical simplicity and the vivacity of the spoken language. Iqbal was essentially an intellectual. His reading was various and extensive, his mind was fertile and vigorous, and his poetry attains at times a heightened sublime style reflecting both fortitude and audacity of spirit. He was endowed with an original sense of the language and a gift of clear-sighted vision. He crossed even at times national frontiers with greater ease than any one of his contemporaries. In *Bal-i Jibril*, he wrote:

خاکی ہے، مگر اس کے انداز ہیں آفاقی
رومی ہے، شامی ہے، کاشی ہے، نہ سمرقندی

He is earthy but his manners are those of the Universe.
He is neither Turk, nor Syrian nor of Kash, nor of Samarkand.[18]

Like Francis Bacon, Iqbal took all knowledge to be his province. A scholar of comparative religions he had grasped the fundamentals of Islamic religious thought and culture, western philosophy, and Buddhist and ancient Hindu thought. He gave to philosophy a human face. A severe critic of traditional scholasticism, he ridiculed dry-as-dust scholarship that relied on rote and blind adherence to traditional authorities. He wanted young people to do their learning and thinking for themselves without expecting short-cuts and relying on other men. Addressing the students, he said:

خدا تجھے کسی طوفان سے آشنا کر دے
کہ ترے بحر کی موجوں میں اضطراب نہیں
تجھے کتاب سے ممکن نہیں فراغ کہ تو
کتاب خواں ہے مگر صاحب کتاب نہیں

May God acquaint you with the stormy life,
For there is no commotion in the waves of your ocean.
You cannot get fulfilment through books,
For you read books, but can master non.[19]

Again:

دین مجو اندر کتاب اے بے خبر
علم و حکمت از کتب، دین از نظر

Do not seek for faith from books, O ignorant one!
Knowledge and wisdom come from books, but faith from perception.[20]

Again:

فقط نگاہ سے ہوتا ہے فیصلہ دِل کا
نہ ہو نِگاہ میں شوخی تو دِلبری کیا ہے

Only a seeing eye can decide for the heart.
If there is no boldness in the eye, then how can one charm the heart?[21]

In the early part of his life until he went to Cambridge in 1905, Iqbal's poetry was imbued with a burning passion of patriotism for India. In this period, his poems expressed his catholicity of outlook, his broad human sympathy, his reverence for Hindu and Sikh religious leaders and his profound feelings for the rivers, hills and landscape of the country. His 'Tarana-e-Hindi' (national anthem) in *Bang-e Dara* (1924) sang the praise of Hindustan.

سارے جہاں سے اچھا، ہندوستاں ہمارا
ہم بلبلیں ہیں اُس کی یہ گلستاں ہمارا
مذہب نہیں سکھاتا آپس میں بیر رکھنا
ہندی ہیں ہم، وطن ہے ہندوستاں ہمارا
یونان و مصر و روما سب مٹ گئے جہاں سے
اب تک مگر ہے باقی نام و نشاں ہمارا
کچھ بات ہے کہ ہستی مٹتی نہیں ہماری
صدیوں رہا ہے دشمن دورِ زماں ہمارا

Our India is better than the whole world.
We are her nightingales, and she is our garden.
Religion doesn't peach mutual strife.
We are Indians, and our country is India.
Greece, Egypt and Rome disappeared from the world,
But our name and identity survives still:
Something within us makes our existence continue,
Though Fate has been our enemy for centuries.[22]

Again in *Bang-e Dara* Iqbal spoke in high terms of Lord Rama describing him as Imam-e-Hind (the spiritual leader of India) in the following verse:

ہے رام کے وجود پہ ہندوستاں کو ناز
اہلِ نظر سمجھتے ہیں اُس کو امامِ ہند

India is proud of Rama,
The wise revere him as the spiritual leader of India.[23]

He called Guru Nanak '*Mard-e-Kamil*' (the perfect man):

ہند کو اک مردِ کامل نے جگایا خواب سے

A Perfect man woke up India from slumber.

About his own ancestry, Iqbal took pride in being a scion of a Brahmin family and wrote:

مرا بنگر کہ در ہندوستانِ دیگر نمی بینی
برہمن زادہ آشنائے روم و تبریز است

Look at me, you will never come across any one else in India (like me):
The son of a Brahman, acquainted with (the *pir* of) Rum and (Shams of) Tabrez.[24]

In his poem 'Naya Shivala' (New Temple) emphasizing a harmonious blend of *shakti* (power) and *bhakti* (worship) he summed up the teachings of the *Bhagavad-Gita.*

شکتی بھی، شانتی بھی، بھگتوں کے گیت میں ہے
دھرتی کے باسیوں کی مکتی پریت میں ہے

Power and peace both are found in the songs of the *bhagats*
In Love lies the salvation of the people of the land.[25]

In the same poem he declared:

خاکِ وطن کا مجھ کو ہر ذرّہ دیوتا ہے

For me every particle of my country is a deity.[26]

For his poem 'Aftab', a loose rendering of the Gayatri mantra, a Muslim cleric even prepared a *fatwa* (a religious edict) against him.[27]

On his return from Europe in 1908, however, a striking change occurred in his world-view. According to Professor Muhammed Mujeeb, Iqbal came to regard himself after 1908 as Islam's messenger to the Muslims or *Sha'ir-i Islam,* the Poet of Islam.[28]

As a principle of social action for integration of humankind, Islam became for Iqbal a poetic or contemplative image. He expressed the finest values of Islam in his powerful poetic rhetoric, exhorting Muslims to foster among themselves a strong spirit of consolidation. He did not emulate the humanistic intimations of Ghalib or the supreme beauty and lyricism of Mir, but followed Altaf Husain Hali's call to Muslims to return to Islam and Akbar Allahabadi's plea for self-cultivation.

By his powerful rhetoric Iqbal anatomized the piteous spectacle of the Muslim community, its moral degeneration, its false idols, and hypocrisy. In anguish, he cried, in his smoothly flowing poem 'Saqi-nama'.

بجھی عشق کی آگ اندھیر ہے
مسلمان نہیں، راکھ کا ڈھیر ہے۔

The fire of love is quenched, it is all dark.
There is no Muslim left, only a heap of ashes.[29]

In his poem 'Shikwa' he expostulated with God on His ignoring the Muslims and bestowing His favours on non-Muslims.

رحمتیں ہیں تیری اغیار کے کاشانوں پر
برق گرتی ہے تو بیچارے مسلمانوں پر

Favours are showered on the houses of strangers (not Muslims);
If lighting falls, however, it falls on Muslims.[30]

In his 'Tarana-e Milli', Iqbal gets all aggressive and starts extolling the glory of Muslim domination.

چین و عرب ہمارا، ہندوستاں ہمارا
مسلم ہیں ہم، وطن ہے سارا جہاں ہمارا
تیغوں کے سائے میں ہم پل کر جوان ہوئے ہیں
خنجر ہلال کا ہے، قومی نشاں ہمارا
مغرب کی وادیوں میں گونجی اذاں ہماری
تھمتا نہ تھا کسی سے سیلِ رواں ہمارا

China and Arabia are ours, Hindustan is ours
We are Muslims; the whole world is our native land.
We have been reared to manhood under the shadow of the sword:
The dagger-like Crescent is our national symbol.
The valleys of the West resonated with our call to prayer,
Nobody could stem the swelling tide of our marching flood.[31]

Again another sample of Iqbal's aggressive tone:

میں تجھ کو بتاتا ہوں تقدیرِ اُمم کیا ہے
شمشیر و سناں اوّل، طاؤس و رباب آخر

Let me tell you what makes the destiny of nations:
The sword and dagger take precedence
over singing and dancing.[32]

Not on the Indian soil, was Iqbal prepared to die; his choice was the area around Mecca and Medina.

میں موت ڈھونڈتا ہوں زمینِ حجاز میں

I seek death in the land of Hejaz.[33]

In his later poems in *Bang-e Dara* and in his *masnavis Israr-i Bekhudi* and *Ramuz-i Bekhudi* (1918), Iqbal was passionately Muslim.[34] In fact, he became a powerful spokesman for the Islamic world. In his poem 'Masjid-e Qurtaba' (Cardova Mosque) in *Bal-i Jabril* (1916) which equals in its grandeur Milton's 'Paradise Lost', he waxes lyrical over the divine message of Islam and Muslim conquests.[35] He was convinced that the only way to inspire the muslim community was by the propagation of Islam. According to him, the Quran embodies the source of what is greatest and best in human thought and values, and evolved a concept of *Khudi* (self-cultivation) for the advancement of Muslim society. When Maulana Husan Ahmad Madni, Sheika-ul-Muhaddas, President of Jamiatul Ulama-i Hind, addressing the Hindu and Muslims at Bara Hindu Rao, Delhi, on 9 January 1928, exhorted them to sink their differences and join together in their fight against British imperialism, and emphasized that nations are formed on the basis of countries, Iqbal contested his views sarcastically, and retorted that religion alone is the foundation of nationality. In a satirical vein he wrote:

عجم ہنوز نداند رموزِ دیں ورنہ
ز دیوبند حسین احمد این چہ بوالعجبی است
سرود بر سرِ منبر کہ ملّت از وطن است
چہ بے خبر ز مقامِ محمدِ عربی است

Non-Arabian countries do not know what true faith is
A strange interpretation of true faith comes from
[Husain] Ahmed of Deoband.
He declares from the rostrum that one's 'nation' is one's native country.
How ignorant is he (of the message) of Muhammad the Arab![36]

Thus, according to Iqbal, a separation of Islam from politics is un-Islamic. As Muslims already constitute a nation, so another conception of nationhood is unwarranted. Iqbal thus rejected the western idea of territorial nationalism, and developed a notion of Muslim nationalism and Islamic universalism for the consolidation of Muslims.

From the above discussion, I wish to emphasize that Iqbal's passionate commitment to Islam, his advocacy of Muslim universalism, his notion of separate Muslim identity and citizenship, and his complete disregard of territorial nationalism which he regarded as a by-product of a perverse idea of Western Democracy provide sound and valuable clues to the understanding of his political conduct. It is, therefore, within an Islamic framework that his politics is to be understood.

Iqbal regarded Time and Space a question of life and death and he projected it eloquently in his poetical compositions. He examined the notion of Time in the light of Sufism, Islam and modern philosophical and scientific systems of thought. He wrote, 'Space and time are interpretations which thought puts upon the creative activity of the ultimate ego'.[37] Iqbal made a clear distinction between serial and pure time, the latter he called pure doctrine, as *elan vital* in Bergson's expression, which T.S. Eliot described as 'an intense living existence of self-illumination'. For Iqbal time is God's attribute, not a thing apart but an integral part of human activity.[38]

Iqbal emphasizes that the creative activity of Time is never repeated, implying thereby that for leading a full creative life maximum use ought to be made of time by the rigour of human efforts. In his poem 'Alwaqt Saif' in *Asrar-e- Khudi*, he wrote:

وقتِ ما کو اوّل و آخر ندید
از خیابانِ ضمیرِ ما دمید
زنده از عرفانِ اصلش زنده تر
هستی او از سحر تابنده تر
زندگی از دهر و دهر از زندگی است
"لا تسبوا الدهر" فرمانِ نبی است

Our time which has neither beginning nor end
Blows from the flowerbed of our mind.
The one living who knows its essence, gets more alive.
His being is more splendid than the dawn.
Life is of Time and Time is of Life:
'Do not abuse Time' was the command of the Prophet.[39]

Lord Rama whom Iqbal called 'Imam-e-Hind' spoke on Time, 'For in the whole world of life, time is a most potent activity'.[40] In 'Khizr-e Rah' (The Guide) in '*Bang-e Dara*', Iqbal describes the concept of Time as a ceaseless quest for introspection. According to Iqbal, Time is a creative force, a continuous process of change. Time, being an independent, restless struggling activity tends to influence humankind in negative and positive terms. Iqbal wrote, 'History is not the unfolding of reason, absolute and infinite, but a ceaseless activity of the ego'. Iqbal regarded Time as a weapon to be used for elevating the mind and soul, widening intellectual horizons, strengthening moral fibre and attaining supreme bliss by the force of *Ishq* (Love), which serves as the key to open the mystery and wonder of the universe.

Iqbal's conception of God differed from the pantheistic Sufism (*Wahdut ul Wajud*) and *Advaita Vedanta* (non-duality). He rejected the Marxist notion of Determinism; He exhorted man to play a free and independent role unrestrained by the compulsive necessity or conditioning circumstances.[41] According to Iqbal, God had created the universe so that man could play his creative role with passionate zeal for the noble ideals of truth, justice and exploration of spiritual awareness. Iqbal expected man to reach such perfection and pristine heights of will power that he might stand up and claim, 'I have Time with God'.

It is not intended to expound Iqbal's concept of *Khudi* (self-cultivation or life-force) on which a spate of literature has appeared nor need we trace the genesis of the idea, whether Iqbal derived it from the Quran, Nietzshe, Fichte or Bergson. There is however, one important aspect of *Khudi* which has been paid insufficient attention, if not overlooked, on which it is necessary to comment.

Iqbal had indicted the incurious, lazy-minded, sleeping and intoxicating Persian Sufism and Arab paganism. In the first edition of *Asrar-e Khudi*, Iqbal had criticized in thirty verses the bombastic mysticism of Hafiz's poetry, which he thought deviates from the original pious faith of Islam due to the Hellenic influence and was producing harmful effects on the moral life of the people. He challenged the philosophical content of Hafiz's poetry, and wrote scornfully:

بے نیاز از محفل حافظ گزر
الحذر از گوسفندان الحذر

Pass by the company of Hafiz without seeking anything.
Keep away from the sheep, keep away![42]

According to Iqbal, knowledge of God is dependent on *Khudi* (Self) which means a ceaseless quest for self-illumination, self-affirmation and self-realization. Iqbal has called *Khudi* as *elan vital* and 'belief in the Self'. He wrote:

حکم دشوار است، تاویلی مجو
جز بقلب خویش قندیلے مجو

What God commands is difficult to do. Do not seek (convenient) interpretation.
Except your heart, do not look for light anywhere.[43]

In his poem on Shakespeare, Matthew Arnold had lauded the same values as 'self-schooled, self-scanned, self-honoured, self-secure'.[44]

Iqbal has given a dynamic view of life full of fire, passion and vitality of wherein one has to charter one's own course and make one's destiny. Great things are done when 'men and mountain meet' and not by frittering away energies on idle pursuits. In this context, like Shakespeare's 'Ripness is all', we have Iqbal's eternal line:

تو نہ شناسی ہنوز، شوق بمیرد ز وصل
چیست حیات دوام، سوختنِ ناتمام؟

You do not yet realize that union kills passion.
What is eternal life but the unending burning (of the soul).[45]

Again:

یقیں محکم، عمل پیہم، محبت فاتح عالم
جہادِ زندگانی میں ہیں، یہ مردوں کی شمشیریں

Firm faith, determined action, all-conquering love
These are the swords of men of action in the battle of life.[46]

The same Faustian view is projected in the following verse:

اگر خواہی حیات، اندر خطر زی

If you want to live, live amidst danger.[47]

As distinct from a passive, unwordly and ascetic attitude of mind, Iqbal presents a dynamic approach of wrestling boldly with philosophic detachment and fortitude the manifold problems of human life. As a positive thinker, he is opposed to asceticism and unworldliness. He insists that men must face bravely the grim and sordid realities of life. Such a view is similar to what Krishna tells Arjuna, his disciple and a warrior-prince, in the *Bhagavad-Gita*, a great philosophical poem to be placed next to Dante's *Divine Comedy*. Krishna gave his message of divine peace, action and human endurance to Arjuna at a critical moment when he was swerwing from his moral duty on the eve of the Mahabharata war. In his original introduction to *Asrar-e Khudi*, Iqbal expressly commended Krishna's philosophy of action.[48]

Krishna had exhorted Arjuna to realize that it is only by discovering one's self and living according to its truth that the reality of life can be apprehended and understood. Iqbal's admiration for Krishna is understandable, because like Krishna, he too preaches the Doctrine of Action. Philosophically, there is much similarity of views on the problems of human existence in the poetry of Iqbal and Krishna' message in the *Bhagavad-Gita*. As in the *Bhagvad-Gita*, Iqbal's idea of free-will is a necessary preliminary presumption for spiritual existence and perfectability of man. A harmonious blend of faith in God combined with *Bhakti* (devotion) and *Shakti* (power) bears a close similarity to Iqbal's *Khudi*, and imparts it a universal and transparent significance irrespective of caste, creed and religion.[49]

But Iqbal is quite conscious of the frailties to which flesh is heir to. He wrote at the end of *Bang-e-Dara*:

اقبال بڑا اپدیشک ہے، من باتوں میں موہ لیتا ہے
گفتار کا یہ غازی تو بنا، کردار کا غازی بن نہ سکا

> Iqbal is a preacher who wins the heart by his talk;
> He has become a warrior in words, but has not been able to be a warrior in deeds.[50]

This is like T.S. Eliot's verses in 'The Hollow Men':

> Between the idea
> And the reality
> Between the motion
> And the act
> Falls the shadow
>
> Between the conception
> And the Creation
> Between the emotion
> And the response
> Falls the shadow.[51]

Iqbal had thus formed a coherent framework of ideas, a philosophy of his own, a code of conduct which he expounded and preached with lofty and sublime thoughts expressed with passion. Iqbal's poetry assumed a human will to power on the basis of an all-embracing development of mind and soul. He emphasized in his poetry that only that life is worth living which develops the strength and integrity to withstand unresolved sufferings and misfortunes rather than flying into an imaginary world of illusion. To Iqbal, will is of more vital importance than industry, and character is more decisive than richness of mind. For Iqbal *Khudi* is the luminous centre of love, wisdom and action. His *Shahin* (falcon) is a symbol of bold idealism and lofty purpose. There persists in his poetry an aggressive belief in spirituality and doctrine of love as the touchstone of men and the foundation of their values.

Philosophically, Iqbal was a positive thinker and his poetry glowing with a fiery passion consists of dispersed meditations rather than sustained lines of development. There is usually a moral preoccupation in his attitude. He made his poetry thunder and echo like a drum that never ceases. Such energies generated by the power of his message were unmatched in Persian and Urdu poetry. He gives free rein to his imagination, soars through time and space and selects from history such personalities as attract him on the strength of their exceptional deeds. As a poet, by force of his individual genius, Iqbal stands alone without an equal, and his poetic message left a profound stamp on the character of his times, and constitutes an imperishable bequest to the coming ages.

Notes and References

[1] For a revised version of this paper originally presented at Indian History Congress, Bhopal, I thank S.M.H. Burney, Irfan Habib, P.N. Dhar, S.A. Ali, M. Zubari, Gopichand Narang, R.K. Kaul and Monica Datta for their valuable suggestions.

[2] *Selections from the Poems of Matthew Arnold*, London, The Grasham Publishing Company, p. 122.

[3] M. Mujeeb, *The Indian Muslims*, London, 1967, p. 260.

[4] Iqbal, *Javidnama*, Delhi, 1984, p. 46.

[5] Ibid., p. 45.

[6] Quoted in S.M.H. Burney, *Iqbal's contribution to Indo-Persian literature*, Calcutta, 1987, p. 9.

[7] Ibid., p. 10.

[8] Franklin, D. Lewis, *Rumi: Past and Present, East and West, The Life, Teachings, Poetry of Jalal ud Din, Rumi*, Oxford, 2000, pp. 481–83.

[9] Ibid., p. 483.

[10] Iqbal, *Javidnama*, p. 244.

[11] Iqbal, *Asrar-e-Khudi* (ed.), Professor Salim Chishti, Delhi, 1988, p. 158.

[12] Iqbal, *Bal-e-Jibril*, Lahore, 1999, p. 12. Muhammad Abu Zakarya Al Razi, *Latin* Rhazes (865–923/934), a celebrated alchemist and Muslim philosopher. He is considered to be the greatest physician of the Islamic world.

[13] See Jagannath Azad, 'Iqbal ki Shairi' in *Nigar, Salnama, Iqbal Number*, January 1962, Lucknow, p. 16.

[14] Katherine Watt, 'Thomas, Arnold Walker and Islam (1864–1930)', in *Modern Asian Studies*, Vol. 36, Part I, February 2002, Cambridge, p. 66.

[15] Ibid., p. 68.

[16] Ibid., p. 69.

[17] *Asrar-e-Khudi*, p. 228.

[18] *Bal-e-Jibril*, p. 55.

[19] *Zarb-e-Kalim*, (ed.), Yusuf Salim Chishti, Delhi, 1998.

[20] Ibid., p. 349.

[21] *Bal-e-Jabril*, p. 37.

[22] *Bang-e-Dara*, Aligarh, 1975, p. 83.

[23] Ibid., p. 77.

[24] *Nigar*, p. 16.

[25] *Bang-e-Dara*, p. 166.

[26] Ibid.

[27] Ibid.

[28] M. Mujeeb, *Indian Muslims*, p. 41.

[29] *Bal-e-Jibril*, p. 102.

[30] *Bang-e-Dara*, p. 166.

[31] Ibid., p. 159.

[32] *Bal-e-Jabril*, p. 40.

[33] *Bang-e-Dera*, p. 198.

[34] M. Mujeeb, *Indian Muslims*, p. 486.

[35] *Bal-e-Jabril*, pp. 71–74.

[36] *Armaghan-e-Hijaz*, (ed.), Yusuf Salim Chisti, 1982, p. 272.

[37] Sir Muhammad Iqbal, *The Reconstruction of Religious Thought in Islam*, Delhi, 1974, p. 66, see also pp. 88–99.

[38] For a discussion on Time and Space, see, Wahid Akhtar 'Iqbal's conception of Time', in *Iqbal: Essays and Studies*, (ed.), Asloob Ahmed Ansari, New Delhi, 1978, pp. 66–99 and Dr Hamid Nasim Rafiduadi, *Khutbat-e-Iqbal ka Tanqidi Matalia*, Srinagar, 2002, pp. 103–58.

[39] *Asrar-e-Khudi*, pp. 482–83.

[40] Swami Sudahasatwananda, *Thus spoke Sri Ram*, Madras, 1972, pp. 56–57.

[41] V.N. Datta, 'Iqbal and Religious thought in 'The Tribune', Chandigarh, 5 May 2002.

[42] *Asrar-e-Khudi*, p. 29.

[43] *Javidnama*, p. 339.

[44] *Selection of the poems of Matthew Arnold.*

[45] *Piyam-e-Mashriq*, (ed.), Yusuf Salim Chishti, Delhi, 1993, p. 268.

[46] *Bang-e-Dara*, p. 272.

[47] *Piyam-e-Mashriq*, p. 143.

[48] M. Rafique, *Sri Aurobindo and Iqbal*, Aligarh, 1974, p. 137. This passage relating to Krishna was deleted by Iqbal in the subsequent editions.

[49] For details on the similarity of verses in Iqbal and Krishna's discourses on the Doctrine of Action, see Ibid., M. Rafique, *Sri Aurobindo and Iqbal*, Chapters IV and Conclusion.

[50] *Bang-e-Dara*, p. 291.

[51] T.S. Eliot, *Collected Poems*, 1909–1962, London, XXVI, pp. 91–92.

Reflections on Cultural Encounters
India and Iran

Mushirul Hasan

> I used to dream of a Persia where bulbuls made love to the roses, where in dreamland gardens poets sat around their wine cups and invoked visions of ineffable meaning. But now that I have come to your country my dream has been formed into a concrete image and finds its permanent place in the inner chamber of my experience... I have visited Saadi's tomb; I have sat beside the resting place of Hafiz and intimately felt his touch in the glimmering green of your woodlands, in blossoming roses. The past age of Persia lent the old world perfume of its own sunny hours of spring to the morning of that day and the silent voice of your ancient poet filled the silence in the heart of the poet of Modern India.
>
> Rabindranath Tagore, 9 May 1932

Contacts between different civilizations have often in the past proved to be landmarks in human progress. Greece learnt from Egypt, Rome from Greece, the Arabs from the Roman Empire, medieval Europe from the Arabs, and Renaissance Europe from the Byzantine. Persia, or Iran, after being no more than a mere name in the west, became in the eighteenth century progressively better known as contact became closer and more frequent. The conceptions of Persia formed by the Europeans differed widely, some regarding her merely as a country to trade with, others as a land to evangelize, while others again looked upon her as an ally against the Turks. No wonder, two small volumes entitled *Persia* were added, in the year 1835, to 'Uncle Oliver's Travels' in the Library for the Young Series published by Messrs Charles Knight of Ludgate Street.

Again, as in the India of Warren Hastings and his successors, European soldiers, diplomats, politicians, archaeologists, and missionaries visited Persia and wrote documented accounts of flora and fauna, of religious practices, of the system of taxation and education, or the method of tying horses by the leg in the stables. As time went on, it came to be realized in Europe that Persia—a land in which civilization has flourished for nearly 5,000 years of recorded history—meant something more than all this, that she had a real culture and literature of her own, and that her people, having long since appreciated the virtue of being *jahan-dida* (one who has seen the world), had a fine taste for poetry and a keen zest for mysticism and for philosophical speculation. The Persians themselves, like the elites of Bengal and Maharashtra in nineteenth-century India, retained great pride in their glorious past long after they were conquered, and guarded the traditions of the past, so that they would not, and could not, give up such traditions by deliberately wiping out their glorious memories. 'There is as much sense in Hafiz as in Horace, and as much knowledge in the world.' So Sherlock Holmes took leave of *A Case of Identity* and the sad romance of Mary Sutherland.

Maxime Rodinson identifies three tendencies at work in the nineteenth century: a utilitarian and imperialistic sense of western superiority, full of contempt for other civilizations; a romantic eroticism, with its delight in a magical east whose increasing poverty spiced its charm; and a specialized scholarship whose main concern lay with past ages. These three tendencies were more complementary than opposed. The unconscious eighteenth-century view, guided by the universalist ideology of the age, respected non-European peoples and cultures. This was replaced by the conscious, theoretical European self-centredness of the nineteenth century ('The Western Image and Western Studies of Islam', in Joseph Schacht and C.E. Bosworth (eds), *The Legacy of Islam*, Oxford, 1979, p. 43).

India was colonized but Persia was not; yet the two countries were equally affected, especially because they were coming into conflict with the expanding and aggressive imperialism of Europe. In the subcontinent, the widely different concerns and pursuits of, say William Jones, founder of the Royal Asiatic Society of Bengal, and Macaulay, author of the Minute on Education (1835), exemplified the changing language and vocabulary of colonialism and its construction of images and perceptions. Indeed European self-centredness and racial arrogance, detailed by scholars like Bernard S. Cohn and Thomas Metcalf, became a marked feature particularly after the 1857 revolt in India.

Most British were convinced, as reflected in the writings of R. Kipling, that they possessed the virtues necessary to dominate the world, and history seemed to bear them out. Until the end of the Boer War their superior position was evident, and it is from this position of confident superiority that they looked at India.

What I am saying is that while textbooks dwell upon the sensuous imagery of the great Persian poets—Omar Khayyam and the mid-fourteenth-century poet Hafiz—their authors take insufficient notice of the impact of colonialism or neo-colonialism on our respective societies. At a time when ideologies are gasping for breath in a unipolar world and globalization appears to have overwhelmed most countries, this tendency is much more pronounced in India than in Iran. Nonetheless, whether it is for the purpose of exploring our heritage or for the purpose of forging closer economic and cultural ties, we need to incorporate rather than discard the colonial factor in our discourses. The critique of Orientalism irritates some people, but it sensitizes us, both as an idea and as an explanation, to the unpleasant and unlovely aspects of cultural hegemony and political domination of the west. This is what Ranade, Dadabhai Naoroji and R.C. Dutt talked about in the last quarter of the nineteenth century. This is what 'economic nationalism' was all about. In Iran, too, freedom and independence from western economic dominance were at the heart of the Tobacco Protest of 1891–92 and the Constitutional Revolution of 1905–11. Much the same issues have provided energy to the unfinished Iranian Revolution.

Orientalism sensitises us to western misrepresentation, stereotyping, and the colonial construction of a hostile politico-ideological structure, a different civilization, and an alien economic region. Apart from everything else, these representations have lent depth and legitimacy, even after decades of Independence, to 'primordial' loyalties and identities in India and Iran. To resolve these problems, some of which are threatening to tear apart the fabric of our neighbours, notably Pakistan and Afghanistan, we need to question, whether it is the context of the nation or its fragments, the colonial assumptions about our societies and develop our own theories (indigenous, if you like) of state and society. One can draw comfort from Tagore's comment in 1932 that, 'my visit to Persia has given me faith in the power of the Eastern peoples to assert themselves and quickly find their way to a united manifestation of their undying heritage in spite of conflict and difficult economic circumstances'.

I realize that, under the influence of Ali Shariati (the most popular exponent of Shia modernism) and his *Husayanuiyyah-i Irshad* in Tehran, the tone and tenor of the intellectual discourses has changed in Iran after the Pahlavi dynasty came crashing down. However, our own scholars in South Asia, mostly trained and tutored in British and American Universities, continue to follow, often uncritically, western models, methodologies and frameworks.

I personally believe that the basis of a meaningful Indo-Iran dialogue rests on some degree of shared values and traditions, if not ideological affinity, a sensitive understanding of colonialism and its legacy, and the adoption of refined methods to explore and interpret our past. Furthermore, our engagement must rest not so much on Samuel Huntington's introduction of the concept of culture—albeit a dated and deeply flawed one—to the study of foreign policy and international relations, but on a nuanced understanding of our respective societies.

When Sir Hamilton Gibb published *Modern Trends in Islam* in 1947, he set aside the religious aspects of the modern Turkish and Persian revolutions. Fortunately, this theme has since been well explored. Yet one would like to reiterate, first and foremost, that religion and the state have been intertwined ever since the establishment of the Safavid dynasty, reaching the apex of its power under Abbas I (1588–1629), and to assert that it is impossible to delegitimize, as the Shah of Iran had discovered much to his dismay, the role of Islam or the *ulama* in popular mobilization. We will do well to remember that on two more recent occasions—the Tobacco Protest (1891–92) and the Constitutional Revolution (1905–11)—Islam and the Muslim divines played an important oppositional role in the emergence of modern Iranian nationalism. Today, Islam continues to be, despite the rumbling in certain quarters, a source of government legitimacy and national development in Iran. Governments, both in Tehran and some other Muslim capitals, appeal to Islam to enhance their authority, buttress nationalism, legitimate policies and programmes, and increase popular support.

In this context, one would like to underline the role of Shia Islam, with its powerful invocation of grief, sorrow and martyrdom (somewhat akin to Sikhism after Guru Gobind Singh). Shia emotionalism, which manifests itself most vividly in the annual mourning ceremonies for Imam Husain, grandson of the Prophet and the martyr of Karbala, took on special significance and provided the inspirational model for the Iranian Revolution. Husain's martyrdom symbolized the role of Islam as a protest movement against the forces overwhelming forces of evil (incidentally, the Abbasid rulers came to power on the back of Shiite protest). Self-sacrifice and even death in God's path were to be freely accepted, for to die in God's struggle was to become a martyr and win eternal reward (See John L. Esposito, *The Islamic Threat: Myth or Reality*, p. 110). Indeed, evocative Shia symbols, especially the *aza-khanas* or *imambaras* and the sites where the *Imams* and their family members are buried, contribute to the making and crystallization of Iranian self-consciousness and lend a special and distinct character to Iranian nationalism.

At the same time it is worth mentioning in passing that the tradition of the martyred emphasized the importance of legitimate political power rather than the theme of righteous suffering. Hence, the martyrdom of Stephen or the pathetic death of Teresa of Lisieux would strike Muslim consciousness, not as parables of adoration, but as almost disgraceful events (Bryan S. Turmer, *Weber and Islam*, p. 64).

Historically, Shia Islam exercises a far-reaching influence on Shia political culture than Sufi tendencies have in Sunni societies. Among other aspects, it has influenced the nature and character of Iranian nationalism. According to the late Oxford-based scholar Hamid Enayat, there is nothing in the theoretical principles of Shiism to make it more amenable to ethnic or racial particularism than Sunnism. If Arab nationalism is a quest for the unity of all Arabic-speaking peoples who lost their identity and independence after the Mongol invasion in 1258, by contrast, what is called Iranian nationalism has been concerned less with the problem of *nationhood* than with that of *freedom*. This is simply because Iran had been an independent state since 1502, and the unity and identity of her people had been an accomplished fact (*Modern Islamic Political Thought*, pp. 120–21). Besides, Iranian nationalists have often found themselves driven to understand the purely Iranian elements of their culture, mostly reminiscent of pre-Islamic times, or of the resistance to the Arab invasion during the first two centuries of Islam. In their eyes, the real renaissance of the national self-consciousness starts with the great epic poet Firdausi AD 1020), whose account of the Arab conquest remains to this day the most poignant epitaph on the destruction of the Sassanian state (ibid., p. 125).

Turning to the knitty-gritty of politics, it is worth pointing out that the symbolic component of politics in Iran, especially after the inglorious regime of the Shah, is especially significant because it could have been used as an instrument of persuasion as well as coercion. Yet bargaining models of politics, especially in recent years, suggest that persuasion rather than force, is increasingly considered to be the basis of politics in that country. This may appear to be oversimplification; perhaps it is. At any rate, what we need to be aware of is that politics in Iran, as indeed in other Muslim countries, is sufficiently complex. As a result, attempts to reduce it to a single formula leads to mystification; rather than being monolithic, Muslim politics, while aspiring to *umma*-wide universals, derives its force and significance from the specific contexts, times, and localities in which it takes place. 'Islam' cannot thus be a threat, any more than the 'West' can be for Muslims. Muslim politics have a transnational dimension, as is illustrated by the responses to Israel's unjust occupation of Palestine, but this does not imply that one Muslim cultural unit has coalesced or that a transnational Islamic space has acquired dominance. Even Muslims who denounce western values accept many western borrowings (Dale F. Eikelman and James Piscatori, *Muslim Politics*, p. 163).

Whether it is Shia emotionalism and the nationalistic sentiments it generates, we have to come to terms with an Iranian personality and an Iranian ethos that is different from Arab or Turkish nationalism. Both historically and contemporaneously, Iran has plotted its own trajectory even when it was vulnerable to the assault of the great Islamic empires or the western countries. This must serve as a reference point for a cultural dialogue between India and Iran.

Of course, long-standing contacts between India and Iran provide the obvious reference point. In his *Glimpses of World History*, Jawaharlal Nehru talked of Persia as 'the country whose soul is said to have come to India and found a worthy body in the Taj'. The zenith of Indo-Iranian cultural contact was reached in the Gupta period. From the third century AD the Sassanians extended their sway over much of northwestern India. Their motifs and techniques contributed much to the making of classic Indian art. Such influences were much more directly felt after soldiers, statesman and merchants started arriving by sea in Gujarat and in the Deccan: a famous example being Mahmud Gawan (d.1481), who served the Bahmani Sultanate in the Deccan, founded the famous *madarsa* in Bidar, modelled after Mirza Ulkugh Beg's *madarsa* in Samarqand, and thus facilitated the dissemination of Indo-Persian learning. In other words, an influx of administrative and intellectual talent from Iran and Central Asia kept the medieval state in the mainstream of Islamic culture.

The Deccani rulers, mostly Shias, were emotionally attached to Safavid Persia (1502–1722). Babur, a Timurid, had formed an alliance with Shah Ismail in 1510–12, and his successor Humayun (1530–40) was given refuge and help by Shah Tahmasp I. Turkish was the language spoken in the private chambers of the Mughal imperial family, but it was not Turkish but Persian that was the literary language of India. For generations past, schoolboys in Indian *makatib* and *madaris* had to learn by heart the *Gulistan* and *Bustan* of Shaikh Sadi of Shiraz. It remained the official language in India until 1835. It was in Persian that Ghalib's progress was most marked, and by the age of eleven, he was already writing Persian poetry. He held the view that Persian was *par excellence* the language of literature, and that Urdu, by contrast, was an inferior medium for peotry and no medium at all for prose. He asserted his own excellence in Persian. The twentieth-century Urdu poet, Mohammad Iqbal—who had written 'I am of India, Persian is not my tongue'—composed in Persian, outstanding *masnavis*—*Asrar-i Khudi* (1915), *Rumuz-i Bekhudi* (1918) and *Payam-i Mashriq* (1923)—along with several collections of poems, including, *Zabur-i Ajam* (1927), *Javidnama* (1932).

Persian poetry had flourished at the Mughal court, though Ghalib did not think much of its quality. In this period, a particular school of Indo-Persian poetry, the *sabk-i Hindi*, assumed its specific features, though its beginning can be traced to the Ghaznavid Punjab. It is said that more Persian literature was produced in India than in Central Asia and even in Iran during this period. It is this Persian culture, adapted to the Indian environment, which came to be known as Indo-Persian culture. Moreover, Persian influences are evident in history writing, in the world of the Sufis and the spread of numerous Sufi orders, in architecture, and in the field of what used to be called the 'minor' arts—the weaving of carpets and textiles, the making of pottery and metal work, and the writing, binding, illuminating, and illustrating of books.

The Sultans of Delhi were largely influenced by the political and cultural ideals of Persia. They turned to the ancient kings like Jamshed, Khusrau and Bahram for guidance in political affairs rather than Muslim law. Autrocracy, the keynote of Persia's political system, thus found its devotees in Delhi; the elective *imam* was forgotten and, in his place, the sultan ruled by a right that could not be questioned. Thus Balban's (1266–86) monarchical ideals were those of the ancient kings of Iran whose precepts and examples gave form and content to his autocracy; he could think of no illustrious names for his grandson but Kaikhusrau, Kaikaus, Kaiqabad and Kaiumars. For him, Persian was the only channel through which he could reach the intellectual world of Islam and thus buttress his claim to the championship of civilization against Mongol barbarism. For the eastern Muslims it was impossible to get away from Persian influence; in India it was to exercise a practical tyranny.

In some ways, the creative encounters between two civilizations are a fascinating story. Indeed, we can and should build on our knowledge to provide a solid foundation for greater Indo-Iran cultural exchanges. Yet we must be alerted to a painful reality and initiate immediate corrective measures. What I refer to is the dwindling number of scholars and generalists who are currently equipped to interpret the Indo-Persian culture and its rich and vibrant legacy. Sadly, our universities are depleted of medieval Indian historians for a variety of reasons. One of them is the absence of adequate facilities and the lack of motivation for learning Persian. In short, we have reached a stage in our intellectual journey when one may well be tempted to write the obituary of medieval Indian history in South Asia. But let us not do that as yet, and echo, in the words of Tagore, the sentiment:

> The night has ended.
> Put out the light of the lamp
> Of thine own narrow dark corner
> Smudged with smoke,
> the great Morning which is for all
> appears in the East.
> Let its light reveal us to each other
> who walk on the same path
> Of pilgrimage.

My plea is to contextualize Iran's history and contemporary

politics, turn to a serious examination of the Iranian revolution of the 1908–14 period, and, more generally, question the images, myths, and the existing categories invented by some scholars in the west. I wish to conclude this paper by urging my Iranian counterparts to understand our own society differently, and to come to terms with the strength and vitality of our democratic and secular experimentation. It is important, furthermore, to recognize the nature and character of Islam in India and delineate the loose and widely divergent tendencies amongst the Muslim communities (rather than community). Let me suggest a few tentative issues for discussion.

Many scholars working on South Asian Islam dwell on the so-called Muslim mind, detail the 'Muslim outlook', and construe a unified 'Muslim identity' around the symbols of Islam; in other words, they underline the analytic primacy of culture and ideology and assign a privileged place to Islam. Assuming that Islam is not only distinctive but also inherently incompatible with western ideals of democracy and secularism, they regard the religion to be essentially different from all the others in that the concepts of beliefs and political rule are fused through the unity of *din wa dawla*, the Prophet having both revealed a religion and founded a state. Predicated on this statement is an assumed resistance to secularism.

These theories need to be challenged. First, the mere fact of people being Islamic in some general sense should not be conflated with that of their adherence to beliefs and policies that are strictly described as 'Islamist' or 'fundamentalist'. Secondly, the commitment of some Muslim groups to specifically Islamic ideas and Islamic symbols does not indicate a unified structure of consciousness or community acting in unison. What should not be assumed is a monolithic conception of Islamic ideology and practice or teleology dictating the actions of the Muslims or a general acquiescence in the actions of few. We must bear in mind that the Muslim communities, like their counterparts in any other religious community, have multiple identities, with many acts to perform and many diverse roles to play. This explains why they, while remaining true to the faith, relate to the more immediate and pressing socio-economic needs in broadly secular terms and have greater affinity with members of their class or caste and not just with their co-religionists. The debate on the depth and nature of this interaction would go on, but one should not at any rate be guided by the contemporary experiences of Hindu–Muslim relations. Equally, one should guard against a discussion centred on the notion of an absolute Muslim/Islamic consciousness and steer clear of the reification of Islam in the realm of political ideas. We should, instead, consider what political/social ideas particular group of Muslims hold, and the relations between these and their social conditions and practice. The Syrian scholar, Aziz al-Azmeh, has pointed out:

> The very premises of Islamic studies are radically and thoroughly unsound; their very foundation, the identification and the construal of relevant facts, is based upon a political and cultural imagination. . . . Any proper writing of Islamic history has to rest on the dissolution of Islam as an orientalist category. . . . It has to liberate itself from Islam, and scrutinize Islamic histories, societies, economies, temporalities, cultures and sciences with the aid of history, of economics, of sociology, critical theory and anthropology. Only then will Islam be disassociated, and reconstituted as historical categories amenable to historical study.

Finally, identities in South Asian history and politics have seldom been unified; in colonial India they were increasingly fragmented and fractured. Indeed, they were not singular but multiple, and thus difficult to capture on a single axis. Constructed across different, intersecting and antagonistic discourses, and practices, they are subject to a radical historicization, and are constantly in the process of making and unmaking. (See Mushirul Hasan (ed.), *Islam, Communities and the Nation: Muslim Identities in South Asia and Beyond*, New Delhi, 1987).

Who, then, are *the* Muslims? What, if any, specific identity is associated with them? Is it divenely ordained or related to features that have always been characteristic of *Islamic* governments and societies? How important is the community's own self-image which is subtly moulded by a combination of 'internal' factors and external interventions? Is it the outcome of colonial images, of treating Muslims as an undifferentiated religious category? To what extent has the post-colonial state, too, viewed Muslims as a religious collectivity, who are also presumed to represent a separate political entity?

Interestingly enough, when the first all-India census was tabulated and analysed in 1881, the enumerators found that Muslims numbered only 19.7 per cent of the population. They uncovered a geographically dispersed aggregate of Muslims forming neither a collectivity nor a distinct society for any purpose, political, economic and social. Out of a total population of about 50 million (or one-fifth of the computed total population of 'British India'), the Muslims in Bengal spoke Bengali and those in Punjab used largely Punjabi as their language. Those living in Tamil Nadu spoke Tamil; those settled on the Malabar coast, mostly Mapillas, spoke Malayalam. They found Muslims whose religious rituals had a very strong tinge of Hinduism and who retained caste and observed Hindu festivals and ceremonies. Islam in these regions became a religion of accommodation rather than a religion of transformation, especially after the rise of Sufism which catered to the emotional and orgiastic needs of the masses. As the historian Peter Hardy pointed out:

> The entry of Muslims in South Asia by so many and separated doorways, their spread over the subcontinent by so many different routes, over a period of centuries, and the diffusion of Islam in different forms from one area to the another, ensured that this religion would present itself to the peoples of South Asia in many different epiphanies seen from different angles. Neither to its own adherents nor to non-Muslims in South Asia has Islam seemed monochromatic, monolithic or indeed mono-anything. It has indeed been said that Islam in South Asia has been united only by a few common rituals and by the aspirations of its scholars. (Peter Hardy, 'Islam and Muslims in South Asia', in R. Israeli, ed., *The Crescent in the East: Islam in Asia Major*, London: Humanities Press, 1982, pp. 39–40)

Islam came to the subcontinent not in a single time span, but in succession divided unevenly in different periods; consequently, its diffusion took place in a variety of forms from class to class and from one area to another. The difference in the phases in which people 'experienced' Islam brought with it variations in the nature of challenges facing its followers in different regions. As in Iran where Islam incorporated a variety of outlooks and orientations and has been capable of multiple levels of discourse and interpretation, in its local and regional specificity, the 'essential' core of Islam in India was not immune to changes by historical influences. Ordinary Muslims were not, as one is often led to believe, members of a monolithic community sitting sullenly apart, but were active participants in regional cultures whose perspectives they shared. They look upon their commitment to Islam not only as one among other values, but also as something which was itself differentiated internally into a number of detailed commitments.

Thus Islam in India, past and present, unfolds a bewildering diversity of Muslim communities. No statistical data is required to establish their location in multiple streams of thought and interactions with them. Their histories, along with social habits, cultural traits and occupational patterns, vary from class to class, from place to place, and from region to region. They speak numerous dialects and languages and observe wide-ranging regional customs and local rites despite the intervention of the Islamists. Caste exists as a basis of social relations, although it differs from the Hindu caste system in details. In several domains Muslims make up an integral part of the larger sociocultural complex dominated by values and ideologies of the Hindu caste tradition.

The noteworthy point is how, in the aftermath of Independence and Partition, the secular and democratic regime rather than the Islamic dimension provided the overarching framework to religio-political leadership of the Muslims to forge new alliances and electoral coalitions. Those holding the reins of leadership located problems and found answers to contemporary dilemmas within the democratic and secular paradigms and sought adjustments not as members of a larger collectivity. They accepted state laws without insisting on the application of the Islamic law, except in the case of marriage, divorce and inheritance. Although this simple truth is not widely accepted, it is none the less necessary for social scientists to spell out the nature and implications of these internal differentiation and the negotiated commitments flowing from them (See my *Legacy of a Divided Nation*, London, 1997). Beneath the so-called unity of the 'Muslim community', we need to identify a variety of religious and political outlooks and competing agendas. This will enable us to unravel the 'mysteriously known essence' (Edward Said, *Orientalism*, p. 305) of Islam in India and Iran, and challenge the widely held perception of a monolithic 'Islamic threat'.

Contributors

M.K. Dhavalikar. Former Director, Deccan College Post Graduate College, Pune.

R.S. Sharma. Former Professor of History, Delhi University, Delhi.

K.M. Shrimali. Professor of History, Delhi University, Delhi.

U.P. Arora. Professor of History, Rohilkhand University, Bareilly.

Ishrat Alam. Senior Lecturer, Aligarh Muslim University, Aligarh.

Iqtidar Alam Khan. Former Professor of History, Aligarh Muslim University.

Najaf Haider. Lecturer of History, Delhi University, Delhi.

Shireen Moosvi. Professor of History, Aligarh Muslim University, Aligarh.

Syed Ali Nadeem Rezavi. Reader in History, Aligarh Muslim University, Aligarh.

Som Prakash Verma. Professor of History, Aligarh Muslim University, Aligarh.

Iqbal Husain. Formerly Professor of History, Aligarh Muslim University, Aligarh.

V.N. Dutta. Professor Emeritus, Kurukshetra University, Kurukshetra

Mushirul Hasan. Professor of History, Jamia Millia, New Delhi.

Index